"Every American must put the achievement of financial independence on the front burner. Bill's book will show you how to do it quicker, faster, and easier than any other investment strategy ever known."
   —Brian Tracy, author of the best-selling *Maximum Achievement*

"Bill Staton is an inspired investment guide who makes the process more fun than you ever guessed. But the real fun comes in seeing your results from Bill's straightforward instructions."
   —Eugene Dickson, President, Leslie Advertising

"Bill takes textbook material and makes it as entertaining as a novel."
   —Ty Boyd, CSP, CPAE

"*The America's Finest Companies Investment Plan* is one of the finest treatments of investing with the divinity of simplicity."
   —Cavett Roberts, CSP, CPAE

"[Bill Staton makes] a Tremendously confusing subject Tremendously simple."
   —Charles E. "Tremendous" Jones, author of the best-selling *Life Is Tremendous*

"The most logical, common-sense, effective approach I've ever heard."
　—Zig Ziglar

"[Bill Staton's] book really opened my mind and got me started on the path to stock investing. I couldn't put it down."
　—Thomas Winninger, CSP, CPAE,
　　CEO, The Winninger Companies USA

"Bill provides a simple plan anyone can use to begin building an estate and at the same time build their own self-confidence right along with it. Buy a copy for yourself and some others to pass along to people you care about."
　—Jim Cathcart, author of *The Acorn People* and *Relationship Selling*

"As [Bill Staton] promised on the program, getting started was incredibly simple and required minimal time."
　—Bill Michaels, 97X Radio, Davenport, Iowa

"I can see where financial advisors would want to have [Bill Staton] shot at dawn because [he has] taken concepts that they try to complicate and made them easy to understand."
　—Al Walker, CSP, CPAE

THE
AMERICA'S
FINEST
COMPANIES
INVESTMENT
PLAN
1997 EDITION

THE AMERICA'S FINEST COMPANIES INVESTMENT PLAN

1997 EDITION

Double Your Money
Every Five Years

Bill Staton

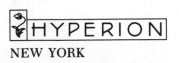

NEW YORK

The author gratefully acknowledges permission for use of the following:
The quotation from H. Bradlee Perry appears courtesy of H. Bradlee
Perry: The Babson Staff Letter, published by David L. Babson and
Company, Inc.
"The Equity Premium: Stock and Bond Returns Since 1802." by Jeremy J. Siegel. Adapted, with permission, from *Financial Analysts
Journal*, January/February 1992. Copyright © 1992, Association for
Investment Management and Research, Charlottesville, Virginia. All
rights reserved.
"A Conversation with Benjamin Graham." Adapted, with permission,
from *Financial Analysts Journal*, September/October 1976. Copyright 1976, The Institute of Chartered Financial Analysts, Charlottesville, Virginia. All rights reserved.
SRC Century-Plus Chart of Investment and Economic History® courtesy of Securities Research Company, a Division of Babson-United
Investment Advisors, Inc., 101 Prescott Street, Wellesley Hills,
Massachusetts 02181.
"Where America Was a Century Ago: History as a Guide to the Future" by John Center. Reproduced, with permission, from *The Futurist*, published by the World Future Society, 7901 Woodmont Avenue, Suite 450, Bethesda, Maryland 20814.
Dividend Reinvestment Plan statement courtesy of Public Service
Company of North Carolina, Inc.
Earnings and dividend ratings for common stocks used by permission
of Standard & Poor's, a division of McGraw-Hill, Inc.
Excerpt from *The Intelligent Investor*, Fourth Revised Edition by Benjamin Graham. Copyright © 1973 by Harper & Row, Publishers,
Inc. Reprinted by permission of HarperCollins Publishers, Inc.
Excerpt from *Where Are the Customers' Yachts?* by Fred Schwed, Jr.
Copyright © 1940 by Fred Schwed, Jr. Copyright renewed © 1967
by Harriet Wolf Schwed. Reprinted by permission of Simon &
Schuster, Inc.
Excerpt from "A Closer Look at Mutual Funds" from *Fortune*, October
7, 1991, appears courtesy of *Fortune*, © 1991 Time, Inc. All rights
reserved.

To me there is no greater wealth than being blessed with a wonderful family. I dedicate this book to my lifelong partner, Mary, and our four incredible children, Gracie, Tate, Whitney, and Will. You have my heartfelt gratitude for enriching my life so often and in so many ways.

CONTENTS

THE AMERICA'S FINEST COMPANIES INVESTMENT PLAN

1997 EDITION

CHAPTER ONE

Why You Should Invest in America's Finest Companies

In the big book of things people more often do wrong than right, investing must certainly top the list, followed closely by wallpapering and eating artichokes.

—*THE MONEY BOOK OF MONEY*, 1987

Millions of Americans—you may be one of them—have all their hard-earned dollars locked away in banks because they think their money is "safe." But after taxes and inflation are taken out, they're behind the eight ball.

If most or all of your money is in savings accounts, certificates of deposit, and money-market funds, it's a scary time because interest rates are so low. You'd like an alternative way to put your money to work, but you're concerned about high fees and bum advice. You may have heard stocks are the way to go, but you know little if anything about them. You may have been burned by a broker who cared more about his commission than your money.

That's why I've developed an investment program you can use without relying on stockbrokers or other financial advisors. Making your money work for you ought to be fun and easy, safe and sure. You don't have to be a professional or spend every waking moment to build funds for your future. You don't have to take a lot of time from your own career and personal life. And you don't have to hand your money over to one of the more than 8,000 mutual funds.

Investing isn't voodoo or hocus-pocus. The word *invest* comes from the Latin *investire*—to commit for a long period with the thought of future benefit. To invest means to put money to work today so that it will earn more money for the future. You invest your money in something to reap a profit.

Investing (as opposed to speculating and taking unnecessary risks) is a process. A process is a series of actions leading to an end. By definition, then, investing is something you should start now, or should have already started, and plan to continue indefinitely. Stocks are the best—and the easiest—asset to invest in.

During my twenty-five years as a money coach, I've learned that individuals can get the most from their money just by following a few simple guidelines. My investment program is built around America's Finest Companies, and will show you how to be your own money manager. There is no Wall Street jargon, there are no complicated rules, no complex formulas, nothing to buy. Everything you need is within these pages.

I'll explain in plain English how the stock market works—why certain principles apply and a lot of others don't. I'll show you that stocks have provided a higher return than any other investment, including real estate, for more than a hundred years. You'll learn what it takes for a company to be in America's Finest Companies and why these companies have far outdistanced the stock market. You'll also learn the simple process of investing for maximum profits with least risk.

America's Finest Companies is compiled once each year and is eagerly awaited by my newsletter subscribers and the financial media. That's because these companies are the elite of corporate America—the top 3 percent of all public companies—with at least ten straight years of higher earnings or dividends per share.

You wouldn't go to the racetrack and bet on the nags, would you? That would be a sure way to lose money. Doesn't it make sense, then, that your hard-earned dollars, the dollars you're accumulating for your children's college education, a larger home, another car, retirement, or whatever, should be invested in shares of the finest companies you can buy? If you wouldn't bet your money on nags at the racetrack, you shouldn't bet your money on companies that aren't proven winners.

Building and managing your own "mini-mutual fund" picked from America's Finest Companies will take very little time—one or two hours per year—and allow you to outperform 75 percent of the pros 100 percent of the time. This is the best way I know to reach your financial goals. It's even better than investing in mutual funds. Why? Because America's Finest Companies deliver spectacular returns.

Since World War II, a diversified portfolio (group) of stocks has grown at 12 percent compounded annually, a higher return than from any other investment. Just by earning 12 percent each year, you'll regularly outperform 75 percent or more of all professional money managers. But you should be able to earn more than that—13–15 percent annually—with a diverse portfolio chosen from America's Finest Companies. That doesn't sound much better than 12 percent, but, assuming you invest as little as $2,000 per year for thirty years, the 1–3 percent difference will be worth an additional $120,000 to $460,000.

This is an easy-to-read-and-understand guide to making money with the cream of American companies. I believe anyone can dramatically improve his or her financial health with my time-proven, powerful method, which is deceptively simple to implement. There are no gimmicks or tricks. A young person can begin to invest with as little as $500 and easily become a millionaire (even a multimillionaire) by retirement.

One cardinal principle holds true: By buying only the shares of high-quality companies, you'll become a successful investor. You'll be part owner of companies that are in sound financial condition, that won't go out of business, and whose earnings and dividends will continue to grow.

A company must earn money to remain in business. Otherwise it will eventually go bankrupt. Part of those earnings are paid to investors in the form of cash dividends. The rest is plowed back for research and development; to bring new products or services to market; to buy new, more productive equipment; to hire more employees. All earnings put back into the company enhance the value of the business. As the value of the business rises, so does the price of the company's stock. It has to.

One excellent example of a company that's done a superior job enhancing the value of its business—and its share price—is Wal-Mart Stores, one of the brightest lights in America's Finest Companies. Wal-Mart is among a handful of companies with more than thirty consecutive years of higher earnings per share. Through the end of 1995, Wal-Mart had thirty-four straight years of rising earnings and twelve of higher cash dividends paid out to owners of its stock. Since 1985 revenue skyrocketed from about $8.5 billion to more than $100 billion in 1996. The share price exploded eightfold, from $3 to $25.

Wal-Mart and its founder, the late Sam Walton, are practically household words, as are a lot of America's Finest Companies—Coca-Cola, Clorox, DuPont, Exxon, Johnson & Johnson, Merck, and Sara Lee, to name a few. But there are just as many that are totally unfamiliar to most people, whether they are investors or not. For example, there's The Washington Real Estate Investment Trust. Ever heard of it? I hadn't either until five years ago.

Washington REIT—you guessed it—invests in real estate. It prides itself on being maverick, unorthodox, and conservative. The company mails some of the most interesting annual and quarterly reports to shareholders. These reports tell how the company is doing. A 1993 quarterly noted the company moved out of its old headquarters (after selling it for a tenfold profit) into the basement of its new WRIT Building. I've never before seen a company press release about abandoning offices with windows for offices without. But Washington REIT isn't your typical enterprise. In early 1993 the company burned its last outstanding mortgage in the company stove and toasted a few marshmallows in the process. To be on the safe side, they asked the building fire marshal to stand by with a fire extinguisher, and they also mailed a press release about this extraordinary event.

Washington REIT does more than mail witty notices to the press and its shareholders. It earns lots of money. By the end of 1995, the company had put together a total of fifty-five years of higher earnings and dividends per share, a record just twenty-two other public companies (out of more than sixteen thousand) can match. For the past twenty years, the stock returned 16 percent annually, triple the rate of inflation, compared to about 12 percent for stocks on the whole. One thousand dollars invested at the end of 1972 is worth more than $20,000 today. Over the past fifteen years the stock grew at 18 percent, and at 19 percent in the last ten-, five-, and one-year periods. Again, that's a record few other companies or professional money managers can match.

If you want to begin your own investment program, you can quickly name ten or twelve financially sound companies whose earnings or dividends will continue to grow well into the future. How do I know that? Because everywhere I have led a workshop on investing, I've asked the audience to choose a portfolio of five to eight companies. In every instance to date, they've picked high-quality companies in a variety of industries. The majority of the companies they pick are in America's Finest Companies.

That is, they have at least ten years in a row of increasing earnings or dividends per share, establishing them as the top 3 percent of all public companies.

Of course, you may be thinking, "Why should I be in stocks at all? They're too risky. Look how far they fell during the Crash of 1987—23 percent in one day. That was worse than in the Great Depression. I wouldn't own any stocks. I couldn't sleep at night if I did."

If you're thinking that, you're not alone. The most frequent comments I hear about stocks and the stock market are negative. (I use the term *market, stock market,* and *market indexes* interchangeably. They mean the same thing in the investment world.) Here are a few I've heard in my seminars:

"High risk/high reward." (the emphasis is always on high risk).
"Frothy." (picture a rabid dog foaming at the mouth).
"A bottomless pit."
"Extremely volatile."
"Too complicated."
"A loser's game."
"Only an expert should try it."
"Like walking down a dark alley in a crime-infested neighborhood."
"I'd rather visit the dentist."

I do hear positives, too, but they're normally about as few as friends in a cobra pit. It's been like this for the twenty-five years I've been in the investment field.

Let's suppose you'd been in my office in December 1979 asking me what you should do with your money in the eighties and nineties. I would have said, "You should invest all the money you can in stocks, but first there are a few things you ought to know.

"An actor will become President of the United States and will preside over the biggest budget deficits in the nation's history. The deepest recession since the 1930s will occur in 1981–82. Nearly 20 percent of the workforce will be unemployed at some point during that period. There'll be another recession in 1990–91, in which that high percentage will again be without jobs.

"The biggest crash in stock-market history will occur in fall 1987, followed by a 'crashette' of huge proportions two years later. And oh, by the way, there'll be war in the Middle East with the United States leading the charge. A new plague—AIDS—will crop up around the world, plus there'll be record droughts and floods and some record-shattering hurricanes, too. There will also be a collapse of the dollar, scattered depressions in various states, a record number of personal, bank, and S&L bankruptcies, alongside numerous criminal convictions on Wall Street.

"Crime will appear virtually out of control in many major cities, and a riot in Los Angeles will turn out to be the most expensive in history. Some of the largest corporations in America will lay off employees ten thousand at a time.

"Now, do you still want to buy some stocks?" Your answer, most likely, would have been a resounding "No." Yet that would have been a bad answer. Between 1980 and today, stocks outperformed bonds, stamps, Treasury bills (roughly the equivalent of a savings account), diamonds, oil, gold, housing, the cost of living, Chinese ceramics, farmland, foreign currency, and silver. Stocks as a class were by far the number-one investment. Shares of America's Finest Companies were even better. There was no close second.

If you picture investing in stocks as buying pieces of paper that go up and down in value every day like yo-yos, I understand why you might be hesitant about owning shares of any companies. But you don't have to look at them that way. A better viewpoint is that you become part owner of one or more of the finest businesses in this country.

My guess is that if you had enough money, you wouldn't mind owning all of Coca-Cola or Wal-Mart or Exxon or Tootsie Roll Industries or Colgate-Palmolive or Procter & Gamble or McDonald's. You know they're well-established corporations with superior credentials. You also know that year after year their earnings and dividends will continue to grow, and you have no reason to suspect they won't remain viable for as long as you live and even for decades after that.

At this point, you might respond, "But what about companies like General Motors and IBM? They used to be among the best companies in America, but then had so much difficulty in recent years. Their stocks collapsed. I don't want to go through the agony of seeing one of my stocks fall from 176 to a low of 41 the way IBM did."

My answer is "I'll show you a foolproof technique in Chapter 7 that will allow you to make substantial profits in any environment—including the Great Depression—as long as you invest in companies that don't go out of business. Both GM and IBM, even though their share prices gave up a lot of ground, are still in business, so you could eventually make money if you own them. But America's

Finest Companies doesn't include either because they don't meet my strict requirement of subsequently higher annual earnings or dividends."

Even though you don't have the billions of dollars it would take to buy a Wal-Mart or PepsiCo and make it your own, you do have enough money to buy a few shares of one, if not both, of these companies. Those shares or pieces of the business represent your proportionate ownership of Coca-Cola, McDonald's, or whatever else you buy. They're great businesses to own parts of, and they're bound to increase in value over the long term—the next five, ten, fifteen, twenty years, or more—because the values of their businesses are growing every year. That hasn't been the case with GM and IBM.

By assembling a portfolio of at least five companies in America's Finest Companies, each in a different industry, and adding to the portfolio on a regular basis (preferably annually), you should regularly double your money every five to six years. That's far faster than from any other investment.

By investing only in corporate thoroughbreds, you can take a lot of worry from your shoulders. You can quit worrying about inflation, interest rates, government legislation, recessions, etc., and how they will affect your investments. Since you're only going to invest in the best American industry has to offer, you can let the companies do the worrying for you.

Think of yourself barreling down a river of white water like the Gauley in West Virginia, which has the fiercest rapids east of the Mississippi. I've rafted the entire length of this beautiful river three times. You have to cross the world's largest earthen dam to get to the foot of the

Gauley. It's extremely intimidating to look well over a hundred feet down at the treacherous water gushing through the chutes at the bottom of the dam. The roar of the water pushing through is so loud it's hard to hear anyone talk.

I was mildly terrified (all right, I was scared to death) the first time we put our raft into the water, despite the fact I knew we had a reliable guide to get us safely through the roughest parts. Contrary to what I thought, the most dangerous part of white-water rafting isn't shuttling through the turbulent rapids. It's other people clowning around with the paddles and hitting one another in the face. The next most dangerous thing is trying to stand up in the fast-moving shallow water and getting a foot caught under a rock. That's an easy way to drown.

The Gauley River isn't menacing when you know what you're doing. Buying shares of companies in America's Finest Companies isn't menacing either because these companies know what they're doing and have proven it over the past ten years or longer. They know how to circumnavigate problems in business and the economy and take maximum advantage of the opportunities. Placing your money on a portfolio of them is as sure a bet as you can make. Nearly two hundred years of American investment history proves that.

As "America's Money Coach," I don't tell Americans what they should do with their money, nor do I do it for them. By definition, I am a trainer, an instructor, an investment guide. I am not a drill sergeant. I coach people to manage their money themselves, to take charge of their financial affairs and to achieve financial security. I learned what I know the hard way.

Having graduated from an Ivy League school with an MBA in 1971, I toured Europe for twelve weeks with my roommate and then settled down as a freshman analyst with Interstate Securities (now Interstate/Johnson Lane) in Charlotte, North Carolina. Interstate had a small equity (stock) research department with a CPA, a nice fellow, as its director. One of the early lessons I learned at Interstate was never to make a CPA head of your research department. They may know their numbers, but they're usually not the greatest stock pickers.

Since I knew virtually nothing about stocks, the stock market, investing, or the economy, I was immediately assigned to review customer portfolios and make suggestions about what to buy and to sell. I'm glad our customers didn't know how little I knew. At the time, even I didn't realize how little I knew, but somehow I muddled through.

Three years into my career, the stock market entered a protracted bear market (bear markets fall, bull markets rise) that wouldn't finish killing investors until December 1974, two years after it began. This bear market was the most savage since the 1930s. It was my first but certainly not my last. The closing Dow Jones industrial average (the principal market index), which Dan Rather now reports every night on CBS, peaked in early 1973 at 1052 and finally troughed about twenty-four months later at 578, a 45 percent plunge.

Most of the stocks I and my department of analysts were recommending did far worse. Some fell 80 percent or more, and that was not particularly atypical. Brokerage houses across America were enduring similar fates. Besides all my recommendations being pounded beneath the floor, I lost about 75 percent of my personal portfolio in the carnage. After it was all over but while I was still thinking the world might end any day, I decided it was time to take a different tack. By then I had been put in charge of the research efforts. Toward the end of 1975 I was officially named research director and an officer of the firm.

By this point, three important lessons were engraved in my cranium:

1. Don't let a CPA run your research department.
2. Make sure an analyst knows what he's doing before you turn him loose on your customers.
3. Bear markets hurt.

Armed with these invaluable bits of wisdom, I set out on a quest to discover (1) how to keep from losing money, and (2) how to make substantial profits investing in companies. I had just entered a three-year program to become a chartered financial analyst (CFA), which is the security-analyst equivalent of a CPA in accounting. The most important thing I learned in the CFA program was discovering a book called *Security Analysis* by Benjamin Graham and David Dodd. Though this book was no longer used in the program, I found out it was a book I needed to own, so I purchased it and began the slow slog through its six-hundred-plus pages.

I uncovered one concept Graham developed—margin of safety—and took it to heart. There's more about this in Chapter 3, Valuable Lessons from Benjamin Graham. Warren Buffett, Graham's best and wealthiest student (he's worth more than $16 billion) at Columbia, likened margin of safety to building a bridge to accommodate forty tons, but nothing heavier than ten tons ever crosses it.

As Interstate's research director, I urged all the analysts to become students of Benjamin Graham and to adhere strictly to the margin-of-safety concept. In late 1974, contrary to the industry, we began keeping records of all our recommendations and how they stacked up against the market indexes. We also told our brokers and customers that when we thought it was time to sell a stock we'd say so in writing. Margin of safety worked. The research record, published annually, served as a check. When I left Interstate at the end of 1985, our research department had compiled an eleven-year performance record that was the envy of Wall Street.

Since I began my newsletter, *The Staton Institute*SM *Advisory,* in January 1986, I have published my record frequently. Every stock recommended to my clients (from the time I say buy to when I say sell) gained an average 30.8 percent annualized, compared with 12.4 percent for the Standard & Poor's 500 index. That's a record few other money experts can touch.

Now that I've shown you my track record, you're going to learn why stocks have always been, and will continue to be, the most profitable investment. The historical evidence is overwhelming, so I'll show you only a little of it. From there, you'll learn the value of a simple investment program. We'll examine what it takes for a company to become one of America's Finest, and you'll get an up-close look at 4 of the 406 that constitute the AFC universe.

Although it's tempting to pay a professional to take

charge of your money, in most cases I don't recommend it. You really can have superior results if you do it yourself. My daughter, who's eighteen now, started her own portfolio at age ten, and since then has beat two-thirds of the pros, doubling the return of the market indexes. Since May 1988 through June 30, 1996, the initial $4,300 investment has swelled to more than $17,000. If she can do it, why can't you?

Good old Uncle Sam and the state where you live will gladly help you make more money if you'd be interested in deferring taxes for years, if not decades, down the road. Most people don't know how to take advantage of Uncle's generosity, but I'll teach you how to make it work for you.

Being your own money manager sounds like a lot of hard work, but really it isn't. Is sixty minutes too much time to spend each year? That's the time most Americans use for lunch each day. I'm only asking for about one hour annually. That's all it takes, and you can become a millionaire if you'll stick with this easy-to-start-and-maintain investment program. If you don't need the annual cash dividends from your stocks for personal use, I'll show you how to make them make more money. I'll even show you how to buy shares direct and bypass the stockbroker. You can save thousands of dollars over a lifetime of investing.

You have to open your investment account somewhere. The mechanics aren't difficult. I'll show you how to get started the easiest way.

Do you want to embark your children on an investment program as I did with my daughter in 1988? The earlier they start, the more successful they'll be. What about giving money and securities to your children? We'll look at that option, too. Then we'll move into the companies themselves. There are 406 listed in the Appendix at the back of the book along with lots of helpful statistics. There's plenty of good merchandise from which to choose. There's something for everybody.

CHAPTER TWO

Stocks Are the Number-One Investment

It makes me nervous when I'm not nervous about the stock market.

—WILLIE WONDER

Millions of Americans are afraid to buy shares of companies. They get goose bumps just thinking about putting money into stocks, even of the top-rated companies, because they reason that one day prices might go over the cliff as they did between 1929 and 1932. Investing in stocks is as terrifying to them as skydiving would be to me. That's why I don't do it—skydiving that is.

Besides this large group that doesn't want to enter investment waters with stocks as the vehicle, there's a second large group—those who own shares of companies but are antsy during the day and don't sleep well at night either. They're like my fictitious friend Willie Wonder. They're always nervous about stocks. When stocks go down, they worry they'll fall further. When stocks go up, they worry they'll soon stop going up and then go down. Or if they don't know which way stock prices are headed, they worry that they don't know and that the direction might not be the way they want to go. These people are worrywarts and don't need to be. They're like the person George Burns described "who feels bad when he feels good for fear that he'll feel worse when he feels better."

If you fit into either of these categories, I want to convince you: Stocks are a great place to have your money, the safest, least risky place of all. Just for the moment, put aside any hesitation you may have and accept these words. You can always change your mind later. I believe that when you finish this chapter you'll know why stocks have always been, and will continue to be, the number-one investment. I don't want you to feel about investing in stocks as Gertrude Stein, the American writer, did about life in general, "There ain't any answer. There ain't going to be any answer. There never has been an answer. That's the answer."

Before we get into why stocks are right for almost everyone, I'll share a little history about how stocks came to be and why they *always* go up when given enough time.

By the time Columbus set sail for what he thought were the East Indies (he landed in the Caribbean instead), shares of various commodities and what were then called joint-stock companies were actively bought and sold in Antwerp, Belgium. The city of Antwerp claims that, of the world's 140-odd stock exchanges, its exchange is the oldest, having been founded in 1531. Amsterdam lays claim to the second with a start-up date of 1602.

Stock certificates of ownership were sold to investors in some European countries to finance powerhouse enterprises like the United East India Company, which came to life in 1602. This phenomenal company returned about 18 percent annually to investors for three decades ($1 grew to more than $143), an incredible performance, and remained in business until 1799.

Stock trading on a limited basis existed well before Jesus was born. The early Romans formed joint-stock companies and sold pieces of them to the public. The word *company* is from *cum* (with) and *panis* (bread) because business, even in those days, was often conducted over a meal, as it so frequently is today. Under the law, joint-stock companies of that time could do just two things— government contracting and tax collecting. What fantastic businesses to invest in! Capital (money) was raised by selling *partes* (shares) to willing investors.

Securities markets in the United States can be traced to the late 1700s. In 1789, Congress authorized and issued $80 million of government bonds to pay down war debts and to inject money into this fledgling country's economy, thereby creating the first "money market." According to *American Heritage* magazine, "The new United States was desperately short of money in any reliable or secured form. Accounts were still kept in pounds, shillings, and pence."

Brokers (they were first called stockjobbers) traded

securities literally in the street. The word *broker* was derived from wine merchants, who broached (tapped) their wine kegs. *Broacher* was later shortened to *broker*. Brokers bought and sold primarily government bonds as well as any stocks offered by the infant Bank of the United States. When the weather turned sour, they retreated to coffeehouses (presumably to warm up) and carried on their business.

The several dozen established brokers operated a highly risky "market." James Madison was so concerned he fired off a letter to Thomas Jefferson warning that "stock jobbing drowns every other subject. The coffeehouse is an eternal buzz with the gamblers." Since stock brokering, trading, or whatever you want to call it was so risky in the early days, the phrase "gambling in the stock market" still has deep meaning for most Americans.

In 1792, twenty-four brokers and merchants gathered at Corre's Hotel to sign the Buttonwood Agreement, which was written front and back on a sheet of paper:

> We, the Subscribers, Brokers for the Purchase and Sale of Public Stocks, do hereby solemnly pledge ourselves to each other that we will not buy or sell, from this day, for any person whatsoever, any kind of Public Stock at a less rate than one-quarter per cent Commission on the Special value, and that we will give preference to each other in our negotiations.

This unusual contract laid the foundation for the later-to-be-formed (in 1817) New York Stock & Exchange Board. The following winter the brokers built a home for themselves, the Tontine Coffee House, on the corner of

Water and Wall streets in New York, then the nation's capital.

The famous street named Wall, one of the best known in the world, is only four blocks long. It lies on the site of the original wall (stockade) built at the tip of Manhattan Island. In 1644, Dutch settlers laid a brushwood barrier to keep Indians out and cattle in. Nine years later Governor Peter Stuyvesant replaced it with a nine-foot-high palisade. Wall Street is named for this barrier, not for the high buildings on both sides of the street that currently create walls.

"Wall Street" is the common name for the American financial institutions, markets, and mechanisms that formalized and democratized the capital-formation (money-raising) process that helps companies thrive. Wall Street, with the New York Stock Exchange as its flagship, has allowed millions of Americans to participate in this country's unmatched growth through ownership of common stocks. *Life* magazine, in its spring 1992 issue, dedicated to the Big Board, observed, "For two centuries, men (and, much more recently, women) have met at the convergence of Wall and Broad streets in lower Manhattan to buy, sell and haggle, all in the name of capitalism. They have not always done so politely . . . or fairly. But as Americans traded, so the country was built. Canals, Railroads, Automobiles, Electronics. Ideas may spring from laboratories, but the money that turns them into reality is raised here."

With capitalism rapidly spreading across the globe, new stock exchanges have recently sprouted behind what used to be the Iron Curtain. Poland opened a stock market in early 1991 in the old Communist Party headquarters (ironic, isn't it?). The Polish market was funded by British money and modeled after France's Bourse, another name for stock exchange or place of meeting to conduct business. Initially, trading took place only once a week in five different companies, but the government expects lots more, since it plans to privatize more than 3,500 firms under its control. Communist Party headquarters must be luxurious because St. Petersburg opened its exchange (*The Wall Street Journal* calls a stock exchange the "icon of capitalism") on the third floor of its own party building.

What exactly is a common stock? It's a security (stock certificate) representing proportionate ownership (an investor's share) of a publicly traded company. There are more than sixteen thousand public companies in America. You can buy shares in most of them through any stockbroker. These shares are traded (bought and sold) on either the New York Stock Exchange (NYSE), the American Stock Exchange (ASE), or NASDAQ Over-the-Counter (OTC). They range in price from a penny to more than $38,000 for Berkshire-Hathaway on the NYSE.

Where did the word *stock* come from? Here's my theory. William Bradford, governor of the Plymouth Colony, reported that under an agreement with the Pilgrims' sponsors from England, "all profit" (crops, fish, and trade goods) would "remain still in the common stock." All Pilgrims were allowed to obtain their food and goods from the common stock (to share), just as all investors can make their profits by investing (sharing) in the "common stock" of public companies.

Stocks are priced in points instead of dollars. One point equals $1.00. One-half point equals $0.50, one-quarter point $0.25, one-eighth point $0.125. Stocks trade in eighths rather than tenths like money. Isn't that strange? There's a practical reason. When stock trading began in colonial days, coins were in short supply. To make coinage go further, Spanish silver dollars were sliced into halves, then halved and halved again. The result? The dollar could be divided into eight bits. Each bit was one-eighth of a dollar. Together, eight bits became a "piece of eight."

Here's how stocks work. In this example, MakeMoney Enterprises (MME), a fictitious company, has one million shares outstanding. Each share sells for 20 (note: stock prices are quoted without the dollar sign), so MME's total stock is worth $20 million. If you invest $4,000 in MME at its current price, you can purchase two hundred shares.

When you purchase your shares, you will own part of the company. Although it's a tiny part (1/5000th), it's all yours. Now that you are part owner of MME, what good is it? Let's use this example to find out.

MME earns $2 million after taxes in 1997. Dividing earnings by the number of shares (1 million), each share has $2.00. MME provides money out of earnings, a cash dividend, as incentive for you to buy and hold its shares. (Not all companies pay dividends, but the bulk of America's Finest Companies do.) Out of the $2.00 per share of earnings, MME pays you half, $1.00. The dollar is your immediate reward for owning a piece of the company. MME keeps (retains) the other half and plows it back into the business for reasons similar to humans eating daily to survive. Retained earnings go for research and product development, to build a new plant, to purchase new equipment, to hire more people—to grow.

By keeping the dollar not paid you, MME is now worth

	1997	2002	2007
MME share price	20	??	??
MME earnings per share	$2.00	$3.00	$5.00
MME dividend per share	$1.00	$1.50	$2.50
MME keeps (retains)	$1.00	$1.50	$2.50

$1.00 more per share for each share outstanding than before. The company's total asset value increases $1 million (1 million shares times $1.00 per share retained). MME's business prospers. Five years from now its earnings have risen 50 percent to $3.00 per share. And as further reward to you for holding the shares as opposed to selling them, the company boosts its dividend (as it has done every year since you bought your shares) to the newest annual rate of $1.50. Each year it keeps as much as it pays you, and that amount kept annually enhances MME's value.

Your annual income is increasing. By 2007, earnings per share are $5.00. Your dividend is now $2.50 per share, up 150 percent over 1997. The company keeps $2.50 per share that year, $2.5 million total, to further boost asset value by that amount.

QUESTION: If the share price is 20 in 1997 when you buy into MME, and the shares are not over-priced, do you think the price will be higher in 2002 than in 1997? Will it be even higher in 2007?

ANSWER: If the share price maintains the same relationship to its earnings and dividend, it will rise to 30 in 2002 and to 50 by 2007.

Your original investment of two hundred shares at 20 each will be worth $10,000 in 2007. Your cost: $4,000. Your profit: $6,000. Between 1997 and 2007, your annual income from MME will jump from $200 to $500. Your yield on original investment will rise to 12.5 percent ($500 divided by $4,000), a handsome return.

Over a period of years, the majority of publicly owned companies grow. (All the companies in the AFC universe are growing; otherwise they wouldn't be included.) Growing companies earn more money. They pay out more cash as dividends. They plow back a growing stream of earnings into their businesses, thus enhancing the value of those businesses. This explains why stock prices *always* go up in the long run. The Dow Jones industrial average, the most famous measure of stock prices, rose from 88 in 1912 to more than 5900 by the end of 1996. That's from price appreciation alone and excludes cash dividends.

Some time ago, H. Bradlee Perry, chairman of the David L. Babson investment counseling firm, neatly summed up investing in stocks this way: "In the long run the price of just about every individual stock and the market value of all stocks together are determined by the growth of earnings and dividends. This is so simple that many of the sophisticated people in our [investing] field seem to overlook it. That is too bad because it does provide the basis for a very sound and unworrisome investment approach.

"Over the span of many decades corporate profits and dividends have trended upward in all industrial nations because their economies have expanded, not without business cycle interruptions of course, but in an inexorable trend of long-term growth."

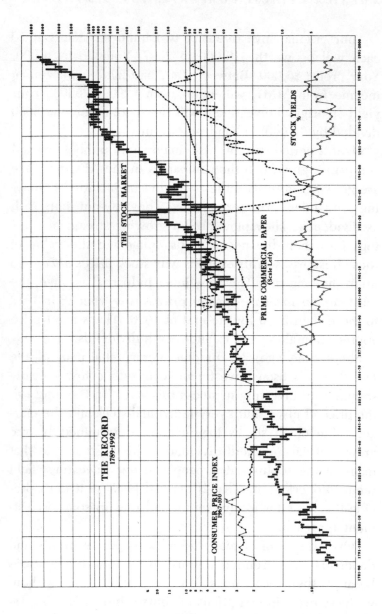

THE RECORD
1789-1992

THE STOCK MARKET

CONSUMER PRICE INDEX
1967=100

PRIME COMMERCIAL PAPER
(Scale Left)

STOCK YIELDS
%

You can participate in America's future growth by owning shares of common stock in a variety of businesses. But by investing in companies in America's Finest Companies, you're assured their businesses will continue to thrive and increase in value. As they do, so will the value of the stocks themselves and the cash dividends they pay. This is the reason you want to own your part of corporate America with America's Finest Companies. Stocks have outperformed all other investments for two hundred years.

The great patriot Patrick Henry addressed the Virginia Convention in 1775: "I know of no way of judging of the future but by the past." The past is important to investors because it gives us a picture of the future returns we can expect from various investments. The point I stress throughout this book is that stocks have always outperformed everything else, and America's Finest Companies have outperformed most other stocks. That being true, why would you want to invest your money in anything besides America's Finest Companies?

The scholarly *Financial Analysts Journal* published an article by Jeremy J. Siegel in its January-February 1992 issue. He's studied a lot of investment history as I have, and here's what he discovered. "Over the period from 1802 through 1992, equity [stocks] has provided returns superior to those on fixed-income investments, gold or commodities. Most strikingly, the real rate of return [with inflation taken out] on equity held remarkably constant over this period while the real return on fixed-income assets declined dramatically."

Going back to 1802, this is what $1.00 would have grown to by the end of 1992 without taking taxes into account.

Stocks	$3,050,000.00
Short-term government bonds	$2,934.00
Long-term government bonds	$6,620.00
Gold	$13.40
Inflation	$11.80

Over 190 years, stocks grew to be worth 1,040 times as much as short-term government bonds, 461 times as much as long-term government bonds, and astonishingly 227,612 times as much as gold. Stocks also came out 258,475 times ahead of inflation.

The obvious conclusion is—stocks knocked the socks off bonds and other fixed-income investments like savings accounts, money-market funds, and certificates of deposit. Since 1926 (the first year of Standard & Poor's stock-price index), the compound annual return of all stocks listed on the NYSE, after subtracting inflation, was 6.4 percent compared with only 0.5 percent for Treasury bills. To say it another way, money invested in T-bills or ordinary savings accounts would have taken 139 years to double compared to only 11 years in stocks. America's Finest Companies work even faster.

Speaking of inflation, over every thirty-year period from 1802 through 1995, there were only two when the annual total return from stocks wasn't at least 3.5 percentage points ahead of the consumer price index. They occurred in the Great Depression. Highest real (after inflation is deducted) returns were in the 1960s and outdistanced inflation by more than 10 percentage points.

At this point, I bet I know what you're thinking: Everybody knows how well real estate has done. That's where all the great fortunes are made. Wrong! I'm going to talk about real estate and pop one of the great investing bubbles. Despite what you think or have heard or read, real estate is not as good as stocks.

The Harris Bank of Chicago analyzed returns from seven assets over three periods of time covering nearly one hundred years. I converted their data into the table on page 31 and updated it through 1985. Stocks were the hands-down winner all three times.

Stocks, after inflation was removed, earned a 6.0 to 6.9 percent compound annual return, far ahead of any of the other investments including farmland and housing.

If you want to take a look at more recent investment history—twenty-, ten-, five-, and one-year periods, the table from *Forbes* on page 32 will do nicely.

Through all the ups and downs of these periods, stocks leaped well ahead of all other investment categories, including real estate. Eight different assets outpaced the Consumer Price Index for the last two decades. Stocks were solidly in first place, with bonds and collectible stamps a distant second and third.

For the past ten years, stocks were again in first place, although bonds gave them a run for the money. Chinese ceramics (how do you invest in those?) were third but provided only half the return of stocks. Silver came in last, as it also did in the twenty-year time frame.

For the last five years, stocks were also in first place (this is getting repetitive), again followed closely by bonds. Only three other assets beat inflation as measured by the CPI, Consumer Price Index—Chinese ceramics, three-month Treasury bills, and diamonds. Housing and farmland both lagged the CPI.

During the twelve months, bonds beat stocks by 3.2

percentage points. Of the four periods shown, this is the only one in which stocks failed to top the list. But coming in second just one of four times isn't bad.

Will stocks do as well in the future as they have in the past? Will they remain the number-one investment? History resoundingly says the answer is "yes." Every long-term study I've ever seen says that, given enough time, stocks will be the best investment.

Since stocks offer the best return on investment compared to anything else, why are certificates of deposit and money-market funds so popular today, especially in tax-deferred retirement plans? I think the answer must be because the principal is considered "safe." With a CD, people know exactly what their rate of return is going to be. A money-market fund doesn't earn a guaranteed rate, but it is easy to get into and out of, and the return can be closely estimated in three- and six-month periods. Unfortunately, the vast majority of people mistakenly perceive that returns from stocks are wildly uncertain. That is not true except over very short periods of time.

George F. Baker, founder of First National Bank of New York (the forerunner of Citicorp), said that patience is one of three prerequisites for making a fortune in stocks. He knew time is on the side of the investor. He also knew that the longer you invest the better your results will be. History proves it. The table on page 34 spans nearly seven decades.

By analyzing the one-year periods we find that 29 percent of the time stocks earned a negative return. Their total return, price appreciation plus dividends, was a minus figure between January 1 of one year and January 1 the next. This is the number the Doubting Thomases

REAL RETURNS ON INVESTMENT ASSETS
(ANNUAL RETURNS WITH INFLATION REMOVED)

	HOUSING	FARMLAND	GOLD	SILVER	COMMERCIAL PAPER	BONDS	STOCKS
1890–1985	4.8%	N.A.	(0.3)%	(1.9)%	1.8%	1.5%	6.2%
1912–1985	4.7	4.5%	(0.5)	0.1	1.1	1.0	6.0
1950–1985	4.6	6.5	2.2	1.9	1.7	(0.2)	6.9

INVESTMENT CLUES FROM THE PAST

ASSET	20 YEARS		10 YEARS		5 YEARS		1 YEAR	
	RETURN	RANK	RETURN	RANK	RETURN	RANK	RETURN	RANK
Stocks	12.2%	1	14.8%	1	15.1%	1	11.6%	2
Bonds	9.8	2	13.2	2	13.1	2	14.8	1
Stamps	9.6	3	(1.7)	11	0.5	11	8.8	4
3-month Treasury bills	8.8	4	7.3	4	6.6	4	3.3	8
Diamonds	8.5	5	5.9	5	4.3	5	1.5	11
Oil	7.5	6	(4.7)	12	1.7	9	(6.3)	12
Gold	6.9	7	(1.0)	9	(4.2)	12	9.6	3
Housing	6.7	8	4.4	7	3.7	7	1.8	10
CONSUMER PRICE INDEX	6.1	9	3.8	8	4.2	6	3.3	7
Chinese ceramics	5.8	10	7.6	3	9.8	3	(7.5)	13
U.S. farmland	5.4	11	(1.2)	10	2.1	8	2.3	9
Foreign exchange	3.4	12	5.6	6	1.7	10	6.2	6
Silver	2.7	13	(10.1)	13	(8.5)	13	8.4	5

Sources: Salomon Brothers Inc.; Diamonds, The Diamond Registry; Basket of U.S. stamps, Scott Inc.; Chinese ceramics, Sotheby's; Oil, American Petroleum Institute; Housing, National Association of Realtors; Farmland (excluding income), U.S. government statistics. Note: Old Masters were excluded because current data were unavailable.

cling to. They say, "Bill, in any given year the odds are about one in three that share prices will decline. I can't run the risk of having my portfolio fall in value."

This retort may be true if you're sixty-five or seventy-five, but what if you're twenty-five or thirty-five? You have some thirty to forty years before you retire. Since investing is all about saving for the future—putting something aside today for tomorrow—time is on your side. Even if stock prices fall one or two years in a row, as long as you keep adding to your portfolio, you're going to do extremely well. Share prices of America's Finest Companies always recover. And then they move on to new highs.

Now take a look at the five-year segments. You can see that 89 percent of the time stock prices earned positive returns. Seventy-nine percent of the time they beat inflation, too. Only 11 percent of the time were they negative.

Going into the ten-year segments, stocks were negative just 3 percent of the time. All the remainder they were positive, and 89 percent of the time they outdistanced inflation as well.

By extending the investment period to fifteen or twenty years, the investor is guaranteed a profit, assuming as I do that history will continue to repeat. There was not a single fifteen-year stretch since 1926 when an investor with a diversified portfolio of good-quality stocks lost money. Not one. That's even better than housing. Far too many people think real estate prices never fall. This is not true. The price of an average single-family home plunged 40 percent between the mid-1920s and the mid-1930s. Housing prices did not reach their 1925 peak until 1948, twenty-three years after. Yes, investing in stocks really can be risk free if you are patient.

BUY SHARES IN AMERICA'S FINEST COMPANIES AND HOLD THEM. THE LONGER, THE BETTER.
(1926–1995)

	1 YEAR	5 YEARS	10 YEARS	20 YEARS
Holding periods (years from 1926)	70	66	61	51
Times outpacing inflation	47 (67%)	52 (79%)	54 (89%)	51 (100%)
Times with positive returns	50 (71%)	59 (89%)	59 (97%)	51 (100%)
Times with negative returns	20 (29%)	7 (11%)	2 (3%)	0 (0%)

Copyright © 1995 The Staton Institute℠, Inc.

History is the only guide investors have for the future. History shows that CD and money-market investments barely keep ahead of inflation. Their future rate of return, after taking out inflation, will likely approximate the historic returns from commercial paper and bonds shown in the table on page 31, about 1.5 percent per year. At that rate it will take forty-seven years for money to double. But if an investor's money is in a balanced stock portfolio, it will grow at 6 to 7 percent per year (after inflation) and double in eleven to twelve years, four times as fast. In America's Finest Companies it will double even faster. I'll talk about how fast in Chapter 7.

Like commercial paper and bonds, gold and silver have been and should continue to be poor places for money. Housing and farmland ought to generate nice returns in the future as they have in the past but not nearly as great as the returns from common stocks.

No one knows what the future return from common stocks will be, or the inflation rate. If I were to guess, and I will, I'd say stocks—over the next thirty, forty, fifty, or sixty years—will grow at 10 to 12 percent annually, with inflation in the 3–4 percent range. Why is this important to know? Because if stocks and inflation continue to increase at their historic rates, you can project what a given amount of money today will be worth (with inflation taken out) in the future. You can also see what the miracle of compound interest does when you invest in companies in America's Finest Companies.

Compounding can be traced back to the Babylonians. They were the original mathematicians, scientists, engineers, and financiers. Babylon is perhaps most famous for its hanging gardens. It was protected by a huge wall completely surrounding the city. Thousands of Babylonian writings on clay tablets have been discovered. Tables of compound growth, a law as secure as gravity, were among them.

Einstein considered compound interest to be humanity's greatest invention, since it allows for the systematic, reliable increase of wealth. Baron de Rothschild, when asked to name the seven wonders of the world, remarked, "I cannot. But I know that the eighth wonder is compound interest."

Sidney Homer, formerly with the investment-banking firm of Salomon Brothers, described the awesome benefits of compound interest this way: "$1,000 left to earn interest at 8% a year will be worth $23 quadrillion [$23,000,000,000,000,000] in 400 years, but the first hundred years are the hardest."

CHAPTER THREE

Valuable Lessons from Benjamin Graham

To achieve satisfactory investment results is easier than most people realize.

The typical individual investor has a great advantage over the large institutions.

—BENJAMIN GRAHAM

As stock prices fell relentlessly, day after day, week after week (I was so depressed it often seemed second after second) in the savage bear market of 1973–74, I was beginning to think I'd entered the wrong profession. What good was it being a Wharton-trained securities analyst when all my stock recommendations were getting clobbered?

When the Great Bear finally went into hibernation in fall 1974, I'd been in the securities profession exactly three years and three months. By that time, I'd been named "coordinator" of my firm's research efforts. I thought "coordinator" was a strange title, but it was better than nothing and at least it meant I was in charge. Shortly after being appointed to that role, I was made an officer and research director.

Between January 1973 and December 1974, the Dow Jones industrial average, the most popular stock-price index, plunged 45 percent. Only two other drops since World War I had been worse. One was during the Great Depression. The Dow reached 381 in 1929. By the end of 1932 it had gotten as low as 41, an 89 percent fall, nearly twice as deep as 1973–74. The other was 1937–38, when the Dow declined 49 percent in a mini-depression.

The few stock recommendations I'd made up to that time had collapsed in value, along with everything else my fellow analysts had on the buy list. Looking back at the carnage was as painful to me as it must have been to all the South Floridians who saw what Hurricane Andrew did to where they used to live. My personal portfolio shed nearly 75 percent of its value, and I kept wondering how many millions, if not hundreds of millions, of dollars my company's customers had lost.

I tend to bounce back quickly, so rather than dwell on what had gone wrong, as research chief I began to search for a method, any method, that would prevent the devastating losses of 1973–74 from ever afflicting me or any of my clients in the future. I was working on my Chartered Financial Analyst certification, which would take other analysts three years to complete. Not me. I used four because I really enjoyed giving up a beautiful Saturday each June to endure a six-hour marathon exam.

I discovered that some years earlier the CFA program had used a different book from the one I'd been studying; it was *Security Analysis*, by Benjamin Graham and David Dodd. A third author, Sydney Cottle, was a later contributor. This bible of security analysts was originally published in 1934 shortly after the worst stock collapse in U.S. history ended.

The third edition, which I own, was essentially a rewriting rather than a revision of the original. When it came out in 1951, Benjamin Graham was president of the Graham-Newman Corporation, a money-management operation, and guest professor at Columbia University's graduate school of business. His collaborator and colleague, David L. Dodd, was a professor of finance there. What struck me about this particular edition was that it was dedicated to what the authors termed the "New Generation of Security Analysts." I'll never be able to ask either Graham or Dodd what they meant, but I suppose they were thinking World War II had escorted in a new era, both for the economy and for analyzing stocks and other securities. Their revised version was meant to educate a new breed of analysts and get them off on the proper footing.

Benjamin Graham is called the principal author of the five editions of *Security Analysis*. When he died in Aix-en-Provence in 1976 at age eighty-two, he was a millionaire. The dean of security analysts had sold more than

100,000 copies of his book before his passing. That's quite a large total for any book, especially a textbook.

Graham, born in 1894, grew up in New York, where he received his bachelor of science degree from Columbia in 1914. On graduating Phi Beta Kappa, Graham went to work on Wall Street. His first job was chalking up stock and bond prices on a board. From that lowly position he became a runner who delivered securities and checks, then on to assistant of a two-man bond department, where he wrote concise descriptions of the bonds in inventory to be sold. He also began writing a daily market letter.

Ben Graham was so proficient and got along so well with people he soon became a customers' man and personally visited customers as a bond salesman. A salesman he wasn't but a quick study he was. Young Graham soon realized how little his firm's customers really knew about the bonds they were buying and selling. He was later named a partner in the Wall Street firm of Newburger, Henderson & Loeb.

During the roaring bull market of the 1920s, Graham and Jerome Newman formed the Graham-Newman Corporation and an investment partnership, Newman & Graham. Even though they were pummeled in the 1929–32 stock freefall, their partnership churned out impressive returns before they dissolved it in the 1950s. Ten thousand dollars invested in Graham-Newman in 1936 threw off about $2,100 per year in income for the next twenty years (roughly $42,000), and the original principal was repaid when it liquidated.

I've often joked that *Security Analysis* isn't called the "bible of the trade" for nothing. It's thick, it's not easy or fun reading, and far too many of the professionals who have read it ignore many of its basic principles, just as have most readers of the Bible, the world's best-selling book. The edition I studied was the fourth, which had further refinements over the previous three, but the guts of it were still the same. I bought a copy and began to trudge through it on my own time. "Trudge" is the right word because, as in medical textbooks, there was much to learn on each page. I absorbed many lessons from Benjamin Graham, including his famous margin-of-safety concept: buy when stock prices overall are undervalued or pick out specific issues with promising prospects that sell well below their intrinsic worth.

When Graham started on Wall Street, a formal method for establishing the true value of stocks and bonds was all but nonexistent. There were various theories about how to speculate successfully in stocks, but not much attention was paid to investing. Speculating was a game of sorts. Graham knew investing to be the opposite, that it could and should be scientific. He believed basic principles could be uncovered that would enable students of the trade to learn how to buy $1.00 of assets at far less than their true worth. If this could be done, he reasoned, it was possible to earn handsome profits because few, if any, others were approaching securities analysis from such a solid quantitative base.

Since he was a teacher by nature and profession, Graham wanted to make his scientific investing principles available to others. That strong desire led him to write the epic on how to analyze securities. Unfortunately, *Security Analysis* is so unwieldy it has never reached the masses of individual investors as Graham so fervently desired, and it has managed to bypass more than its fair share of Wall

Street's best. Although the tools for investment success are within its pages, Graham's techniques are so cumbersome the vast majority of people whom he wanted to benefit, even if they were interested, didn't have the time to, and could never, put them to work.

Even so, Benjamin Graham's works and his various interviews and research papers were tremendously interesting to me. I was absorbed by everything I could learn from and about this investment master. I was especially fascinated to discover that Graham's primary reason for continually perfecting his craft was to show how to invest safely and with as little effort as possible.

This passion to share the gospel of investing with anyone who would listen led him to write *The Intelligent Investor* in 1949. In the introduction of a later edition of the book, Graham made certain the reader knew he wasn't writing for those who liked high risk or spending lots of time on their portfolios. Right away he had my attention.

Instead, *The Intelligent Investor* was dedicated to the defensive or passive investor who wanted to avoid large losses and the hassle of worrying about his investment strategy. Graham observed that the investor's worst enemy is himself or herself: "We have seen much more money made and *kept* by 'ordinary people' who were temperamentally well suited for the investment process than by those who lacked this quality, even though they had an extensive knowledge of finance, accounting, and stock-market lore." He made another astute observation: "Sound investment principles produced generally sound results."

By the time Graham was in his eighties, still as sharp as ever, financial institutions—brokerage firms, banks, insurance companies, and the like—were spending millions of dollars a year and grinding out thousands of pages of research on this or that security. This was the opposite of what was occurring when Ben Graham had stepped onto Wall Street some fifty years earlier. Little time or effort was then exerted on practical securities research. The kind of in-depth analysis Graham pioneered paid off handsomely, since there was virtually no competition.

As he grew older, Graham realized hordes of others were attempting to follow in his giant footsteps, so many in fact that they were bumping into one another while trying to pick undervalued securities—especially stocks— that would rise in value. He thought that since Wall Street was pouring such vast resources into stock research, the elaborate techniques he devised were rapidly losing their value. It seemed to be a case of what everybody else knows isn't worth knowing.

Graham communicated this view shortly before his death in 1976 in his final interview, which appeared in the September-October 1976 *Financial Analysts Journal*. Only one person in the United States is customarily introduced with no introduction—the President. Benjamin Graham was introduced almost as reverently as one "who needs no introduction to the readers of this magazine." Excerpts from that last interview appear here.

In the light of your sixty-odd years of experience in Wall Street, what is your overall view of common stocks?

Common stocks have one important investment characteristic and one important speculative characteristic. Their investment value and average market price tend to increase irregularly but persistently over the decades, as their net worth builds up through the reinvestment of undistributed earnings. However, most of the time common stocks are subject to irrational and excessive price fluctuations in both directions, as the consequence of the ingrained tendency of most people to speculate or gamble —i.e., to give way to hope, fear and greed.

What is your view of the financial community as a whole?

Most of the stockbrokers, financial analysts, investment advisers, etc., are above average in intelligence, business honesty and sincerity. But they lack adequate experience with all types of security markets and an overall understanding of common stocks—of what I call "the nature of the beast." They tend to take the market and themselves too seriously. They spend a large part of their time trying, valiantly and ineffectively, to do things they can't do well.

What sort of things, for example?

To forecast short- or long-term changes in the economy, and in the price level of common stocks, to select the most promising industry groups and individual issues—generally for the near-term future.

Can the average manager of institutional funds obtain better results than the Dow Jones Industrial Average or the Standard & Poor's Index over the years?

No. In effect, that would mean that the stock market experts as a whole could best themselves—a logical contradiction.

Turning now to individual investors, do you think that they are at a disadvantage compared with the institutions, because of the latter's huge resources, superior facilities for obtaining information, etc.?

On the contrary, the typical individual investor has a great advantage over the large institutions.

What general rules would you offer the individual investor for his investment policy over the years?

Let me suggest three such rules: (1) The individual investor should act consistently as an investor and not as a speculator. (2) The investor should have a definite selling policy for all his common stock commitments, corresponding to his buying techniques. (3) Finally, the investor should always have a minimum percentage of his total portfolio in common stocks and a minimum percentage in bond equivalents.

In selecting the common stock portfolio, do you advise careful study of and selectivity among individual issues?

In general, no. I am no longer an advocate of elaborate techniques of security analysis in order to find superior value opportunities. This was a rewarding activity, say, 40 years ago, when our textbook "Graham and Dodd" was first published; but the situation has changed a good deal since then. In the old days any well-trained security analyst could do a good professional job of selecting undervalued issues through detailed studies; but in the light of the enormous amount of research now being carried on, I doubt whether in most cases such extensive efforts will generate sufficiently superior selections to justify their cost.

In addressing the question about how individuals should create and manage their common-stock portfolios, Graham gave the two specific methods he preferred, both of which require a good deal of work on the part of the individual. He followed by saying that "to enjoy a reasonable chance for continued better-than-average results, the investor must follow policies which are (1) inherently sound and promising, and (2) are not popular in Wall Street," and "Investment is most intelligent when it is most businesslike."

In addition to margin-of-safety, the cornerstone of the Benjamin Graham philosophy of investing, these are the other valuable lessons I learned from him:

1. Stock prices rise "irregularly but persistently" over time because the value of the underlying businesses continues to increase as retained earnings are plowed back into those businesses.
2. Financial professionals, on the whole, are well educated, honest, and sincere but have a shallow understanding of common stocks.
3. Professionals spend far too much time trying to do what can't be done—predicting the future of the economy, the level of stock prices, and which industries and individual stocks will perform best.
4. The average professional money manager cannot beat the market as measured by the Dow Jones industrials, Standard & Poor's 500, or some other principal index. Professionals are the average, and it's a "logical contradiction" that they can "best themselves."
5. Individuals have tremendous advantages over the professionals.
6. In order to be most successful, individual investors (a) must invest rather than speculate, (b) have a rule of thumb for the appropriate time to sell, and (c) always have at least a minimum of their portfolios in stocks.

7. Complicated techniques of security analysis aren't necessary to unearth superior opportunities.
8. The stock-picking method an investor uses should be rational and easy to apply and have "an excellent supporting record." Investment that is most "businesslike" will generate the best returns, especially when it goes against the grain of Wall Street.

By investing in America's Finest Companies the way I'll detail, you'll be aligning yourself with the investment wisdom and success of Benjamin Graham, the father of security analysis and a multimillionaire when he died. I can't say for certain whether Ben Graham would endorse my techniques, but I strongly believe he would. They meet all the criteria outlined in his farewell interview. They are time-proven and they work. What else could an investor want?

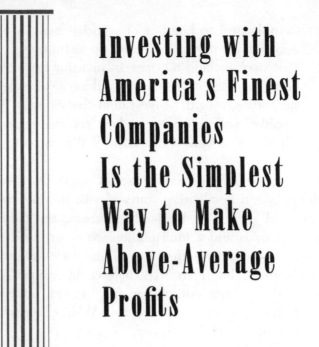

Investing with America's Finest Companies Is the Simplest Way to Make Above-Average Profits

The simpler your investment plan, the more likely it will work.

— *U.S. NEWS & WORLD REPORT*

A simple investment program—one that is uncomplicated, readily understood, and easily implemented—is best because it's efficient. Simple investing will work very well for you, as it does for me and other knowledgeable investors. Garfield Drew, a noted stock-market technician (one who charts market and individual stock patterns as a guide to the future) of the 1950s, stated, "Simplicity or singleness of approach is a greatly underestimated factor of market success."

When people think of investing, simplicity is the last thing they think of. Everyone knows that investing (setting aside money today for the future) is a complex chore and not any fun either, right? Fun is not mentioned in investment books, courses in securities analysis, or investment letters (except mine). It should be. Having fun while you invest is critical to success. My strong belief is that if investing in stocks isn't fun for you, it won't be nearly as profitable as it can be.

Even if investing is profitable but you're not having fun (you constantly worry about day-to-day fluctuations in stock prices, or what you heard on *Wall Street Week,* or what the Federal Reserve did with the money supply, or the direction of the economy, or which way inflation and interest rates will go, or that the fifteen newsletters you subscribe to render conflicting advice, or ABC News says we're on the brink of recession, or some of the above or all of the above), you should try a new strategy.

The one I'm unfurling here is a good one. It's simple. It's rational. It produces superior results. It's fun. And it will beat most professional money managers year in and year out. My method is too simple for Wall Street to adopt, so they ignore it.

Benjamin Graham was asked in 1976 whether he recommended "careful study of and selectivity among individual issues." He responded, "In general, no. I am no longer an advocate of elaborate techniques of security analysis in order to find superior value opportunities."

My own studies dating back to the early 1920s confirm exactly what Graham said. The more complicated your stock-market strategy, the more difficult it is to implement and to monitor. What's worse, it almost always leads to mediocre performance. Simple is far better. The pros make investing complicated, but it doesn't have to be.

If you think about it for fifteen seconds, you readily see why investment counselors, financial advisors, stockbrokers and money managers at banks, insurance companies, and mutual funds rarely beat the market indexes. Even those professionals who try to duplicate the market's results almost always fail. Here's why.

The Dow Jones industrials and Standard & Poor's 500 have no operating expenses. They go up and down without transaction costs. The money manager, trying to make his portfolio match one or the other market index, has to make frequent buys and sells to keep his portfolio in proportion with the stocks that make up the index he's working so hard to match. Stocks cost money to buy. They cost money to sell. The costs of trading, by themselves, make attempts to equal a market index virtually impossible.

If he's trying to beat the market instead of just equal it, the money manager has another dilemma. He usually cannot adopt a fun, businesslike, simple approach to investing like the one within these pages. Why? Because he (or she) wouldn't have to work a forty-hour week. He'd be taking so much time off, yet beating the indexes consistently, his boss would fire him. How could a company justify paying a money manager a full year's salary when he didn't have to work every day to profitably execute his investment plan?

The prudent money manager—one who wishes to remain employed—must create activities to fill his time. These include reading voluminous industry and company reports, dining with the managements of companies he owns or might like to own, attending numerous presentations to security analysts and portfolio managers, talking with friends in the business, sitting through an untold number of investment-committee meetings, scanning in-depth and ultra-thick computer runs, plus listening to the latest Wall Street gossip.

By doing all these things and more, the typical money manager's day is out of his control. He drowns in wasteful short-term activities, which history shows don't produce above-average results. Yet he generally cannot quit because he can't afford to lose his salary. If you were in his shoes, would you be any different?

Fortunately, you don't have to get sucked into the rut of the typical money manager. You can go your own profitable way. And you'll start by buying only the shares of highest-quality companies, America's Finest. You won't learn that in other investment books. They dwell on this method or that for picking the next Wal-Mart, Home Depot, or other company that is sure to make a million dollars for you from a small amount of money. The reason these books generally aren't worth much, besides being hard to understand, is they focus on the wrong things. Choosing the "right" stocks for your portfolio is less important than any other step for stock-market success.

Of course you do have to pick companies for your portfolio. There are two characteristics to look for when you invest in shares of companies:

1. The companies are in sound financial condition and won't go out of business.
2. Earnings and dividends will continue to grow.

Where are these companies? You can go out and uncover them on your own. That's the harder way, but it can be interesting to do the research. Or you can do it the easier way and pick from the alphabetical list in the appendix.

If you'll turn to the list for just a moment and skim quickly through it, you'll see there are a lot of companies that are household words. One is Coca-Cola, perhaps the most famous name in the world.

Eleven of the thirty Dow industrials are included in America's Finest Companies. Coca-Cola is one. Another is Procter & Gamble, one of the world's premier consumer-products companies. Merck is a major pharmaceutical firm, while McDonald's sells more hamburgers (and owns more commercial real estate) than any other company in America. The other seven are DuPont, Exxon, General Electric, Minnesota Mining & Manufacturing, J. P. Morgan, Philip Morris, and Walt Disney.

When you invest your money, you want it to be 100 percent safe. Will Rogers used to say, "Forget about a return ON my investment. What I want is a return OF my investment." When you buy shares of companies in America's Finest Companies, you are 99.9 percent guaranteed they'll remain in business. By investing in them exclusively, you know they will stay afloat in the worst economic storms.

Benjamin Graham believed in buying quality. In *The Intelligent Investor* he noted, "The risk of paying too high a price for good-quality stocks—while a real one—is not the chief hazard confronting the average buyer of securities. Observations over many years has taught us that the chief losses to investors come from the purchase of low-quality securities at times of favorable business conditions."

There are dozens and dozens of U.S. companies that have been around for well over a hundred years. Quite a few are among the corporations in America's Finest Companies. They've survived panics, financial crises, depressions, earthquakes, droughts, floods, political scandals, wars, and any other disaster you can name. Among these are "blue-chip" companies such as Colgate-Palmolive, J. P. Morgan, and American Brands. They've been through just about everything, yet are still healthy and growing.

"Blue chip" describes highly regarded enterprises that generally make up the Dow Jones industrial average and a large part of the S & P 500. Blue chips have long earnings and dividend histories and are assumed to be able to withstand the most adverse economic circumstances.

Not all the companies included in America's Finest Companies are blue chips by the widely accepted definition, but they are all highly regarded and have exceptional records—at least ten consecutive years of higher earnings and/or dividends per share. As a group, they are well above average in financial strength. They are the thoroughbreds of corporate America and should be on the shopping list for assembling your personal market-beating portfolio.

America's Finest Companies comprises the top 3 percent (406) of all U.S. public companies. How have they been able to string together at least ten years in a row of higher earnings or dividends per share when the other 97 percent of public companies have not? Have a lot of them gotten into industries that are so good it would be hard not to be superachievers, or have most of them just been lucky? Or are there other factors? Is it possible to find some common threads that tie this elite group of companies together?

In the next few pages, you'll learn about four of the companies in America's Finest Companies, each of which is in a different industry. You may be unfamiliar with all of them, or perhaps you've heard of at least one.

The first helps save lives in a variety of industries across the globe. The second and third companies are world leaders in their respective industries, while the fourth has an earnings-persistency record surpassed by very few corporations.

MINE SAFETY APPLIANCES

John T. Ryan, Jr. passed away in July 1995 after having developed Mine Safety Appliances (MSA) into an international company whose products and services assure that "men and women may work in safety and that they, their families, and their communities may live in health throughout the world."

As the company's leader for more than five decades, Ryan embodied the idea of making the world a safer place. He personally founded operations in Europe, Asia, and Latin America and helped get MSA a foothold in China and post-Communist Russia and Eastern Europe. Ryan left a company whose corporate vision is "to be the leading innovator and provider of quality safety and instrument products, services and specialty chemicals that protect and improve health, safety and the environment."

It is highly unusual for any company to issue a special report about its founder, but when I received the 1995 annual report of Mine Safety Appliances, there was also a four-color booklet about the colorful John Ryan. Since so much of what MSA is today stems from his beliefs and foresight, this profile will show you how excellent leadership can make a company a long-term winner.

Ryan is said to have given his company "an international vision" and "an impeccable ethical ideal" while giving his community "a tireless and generous benefactor." When he began his executive career in 1941, MSA was a smallish outfit serving a limited market. Worker safety for most companies was not a top priority the way it is today. Ryan shifted corporate emphasis from mine, the first word in the company's name, to the second word—safety. Once management and employees realized that focusing on employee safety opened up U.S. markets that the focus on mines never would, MSA began to look at possibilities in foreign countries.

Ryan and his team opened operations from Toronto to Tokyo, Sao Paulo to Sydney, Budapest to Buenos Aires. MSA began to see itself as a world-renowned leader in safety products and make money from it too. Ryan became internationally recognized as a powerful advocate for safety in the workplace, and this recognition helped the company to grow and to prosper.

MSA today manufactures more than 4,000 products to protect people's health, safety, and the environment in 143 countries. Industries served include firefighting, mining, chemical processing, construction, the nuclear industry, petroleum and environmental remediation. Long before others, Ryan and his management team began establishing a foundation in markets that are now termed "emerging." He believed that despite more than a few rough start-ups, being ahead of his competition would pay off handsomely in the long run. And that has proven true. MSA now has 29 principal operations in key geographic markets worldwide.

Taking the global approach enabled Mine Safety Appliances to become "international" in a big way long before many companies began to look outside North America to broaden their markets. MSA's diversity, in addition to boosting revenue and earning power, also somewhat reduced the company's cyclicality. Foreign revenue now accounts for nearly half the total.

While the company helps others do a better job protecting the environment, it has been doing a credible job on its own. MSA launched a Reduce At The Source Program in 1993 to pare waste and cut costs. The goals are to decrease scrap by 10% annually and slash utility demand and the use of certain chemicals. U.S. "RATS" teams are approaching a million dollars a year in savings with more on the way.

The company concludes its latest annual report by saying, "Diversification and initiative will propel MSA into the 21st century. While competitive influences concentrate on one or several product lines or markets, MSA today remains the only manufacturer dedicated to producing a full line of products that protect people's health, safety and the environment. In 1995, innovative strides were made to ensure MSA maintains its unequaled ability to serve industries on all continents. Through such leadership, MSA is well positioned to continue its mission of working for a safer world."

PALL CORP.

The word "pall" brings to mind the fabric used on a coffin, hearse, or tomb. Or you might associate pall with a dark, gloomy covering, such as a pall of smoke. But Pall, in the case of Pall Corp., means neither. It's simply the last name of the founder of the company, whose CEO is no longer a Pall.

Pall Corp. is the high-technology world leader in the mushrooming but little understood field of filtration and separations, a fast-growing $12-billion worldwide market. Company revenue is roughly 25% from each of these four sources: fluid processing, aeropower, patient protection and pharmaceuticals, diagnostics and nutrition.

Fluid processing, the oldest of the company's businesses, reaches out to a number of industries including oil, natural gas, electric, chemicals, semiconductors, photographic, and plastics. Pall's sophisticated products and services enhance fluid purity by removing microscopic-and-larger contaminants that devastate production equipment, product yields and quality. Lately this piece of Pall has been looking like a "youngster" as the manufacturers of semiconductor chips enjoy a renewed growth spurt. As that industry moves forward via the next technical leap to the 300mm wafer, the requirements for filtration and purity will be the most stringent ever. Electronics is just 10% of Pall's sales and places them #2 in the industry now. The corporate goal is to be #1 by the end of 1997.

In the Aeropower area, Pall's high-performance products remove particulates and water from hydraulic and lubrication fluids/systems, which extends their useful life and cuts down on waste while bolstering productivity. In Patient Protection, Pall filters protect patients in blood transfusions, intravenous feedings, inhalation therapies, anesthesia, and heart surgeries by removing particulates, bacteria, and various other contaminants.

In the fourth area, Pharmaceuticals, Diagnostics and Nutrition, Pall's customers rely not only on its filtration devices but also on its process-validation techniques, which insure purity to the minutest degrees. As a regular Red Cross donor of blood platelets, I appreciate Pall's improving the quality of what I am able to give to others.

As it approaches the $1-billion-revenue mark, Pall has broadened its corporate vision to the separations marketplace and according to CEO Eric Krasnoff has greatly expanded its "universe of opportunities" through an infrastructure to support future growth that may grow dramatically in importance.

In 1996 forward-thinking Pall unleashed a major productivity initiative, "Materials Management 2000," to fully exploit the company's unparalleled ability to design materials management systems. Management labels this a "potent competitive weapon" because everything that moves or is manufactured at some point requires separating or filtration. Enabling corporations to simultaneously monitor their progress, end up with purer products, and slash costs presents breakthrough opportunities for Pall.

Pall's attitude is summed up in the following statement:

"We can see the products and market potentials requisite for both near- and longer-term growth, and we have identified many ways to achieve that potential while continually striving to improve productivity."

PARKER HANNIFIN

Cleveland-based Parker Hannifin (a $3-billion+ enterprise) was founded in 1918 by inventor-engineer Arthur "Art" Parker. It has grown from a small company manufacturing automotive hydraulic-brake systems to become the world's leading maker of motion-control products. Parker's products include powerful hydraulic cylinders and hoses for large earthmovers (Caterpillar), light-control systems for jumbo jets (Boeing), shielding for electronic devices, and components for refrigeration and air-conditioning systems, to name but a few. The company has 31,000 employees around the world, 158 manufacturing plants, and 102 sales/administrative offices.

Its forerunner, Parker Appliance Company, started with one employee and began serving the aircraft industry in the 1920s because aviation demanded new, lighter controls, valves, and fittings. Throughout the twenties and thirties, Cleveland was known as the "Second Motor City" and a cradle of aviation. Parker's company worked closely with the fledgling airline industry, which was more than strong enough to survive the Great Depression, and some of its pioneers, Glenn Martin, Donald Douglas, and Robert Gross, founder of Lockheed. That helped Parker get through to the other side. When World War II broke out, Parker Appliance was the world's largest manufacturer of hydraulic connecting and flow-control devices. Its sole customer—Uncle Sam.

Following the war, industrial business dried up, and Parker came close to bankruptcy. Art Parker died in 1945, but his wife Helen refused to sell or shut down the company. She hired new management, which was gradually able to rebuild the industrial components business and keep the company afloat.

In what has been called the "single most important management decision" in Parker Hannifin's history, Parker Appliance decided to become "the GE of fluid power." That was followed in 1957 by the acquisition of Hannifin Manufacturing Company of Des Plaines, Illinois, the forerunner of numerous acquisitions which are still ongoing.

On December 11, 1972, astronaut Harrison Schmidt was guiding his lunar excursion module from the Challenger Apollo down onto the surface of the moon. The entire world was tuned in. As he landed, Schmidt was supposed to say, "Switch to the ascent engines" because all astronauts want to be able to escape in case of a bad landing or unstable conditions. Excitedly, Schmidt turned to his co-pilot and remarked, "Cycle that Parker valve," a phrase heard around the world. Parker Hannifin thus has the distinction of being the subject of the first radio or television commercial produced on and transmitted from another planet.

Parker Hannifin strives to maintain a balance between providing products for original equipment manufacturers and the maintenance, repair, and overhaul market. Its business is comprised of six product groups that operate on a decentralized, global basis. Two other groups—Latin American and Asia Pacific—market all product lines in developing regions.

Today Parker Hannifin is a member of the elite Fortune 500 with more than 1,000 product lines for hydraulic, pneumatic, and electromechanical applications serving some 1,200 industrial/aerospace markets.

WORTHINGTON INDUSTRIES

Using his 1952 Oldsmobile as collateral, John H. McConnell borrowed $600 to buy his first load of steel. Shortly thereafter, in 1955, the business was incorporated as The Worthington Steel Company. In its first year the company produced sales of $342,000 and earnings of $11,000 with one piece of equipment and five employees.

Six years later, in 1961, Worthington gained significant new processing capabilities by installing its first one-pass cold-rolling mill in Columbus, Ohio. This new process gave the company the ability to produce lighter-gauge specifications for customers, improve the quality of the product, and reduce costs to the customers. Before year's end, the company expanded into Louisville, Kentucky with a new steel processor.

In what was a novel plan in 1966, management implemented its current cash-profit-sharing plan to reward employees with a fixed percentage of earnings. All production employees were placed on salary. Today, salary payment for production employees and profit-sharing are a mainstay of the company's approach to making employees partners in Worthington's business.

The company went public in 1968, began producing its first consumer products in 1971, and changed its name to Worthington Industries. It acquired United Flat Rolled

Products in 1972 and Southeastern Steel Rolling Mills the next year.

Sales zipped through $100 million in 1976, twenty-one years after the company's founding, and Worthington made a series of fortuitous acquisitions over the next several years. In 1984 it was featured in the best-selling book, *The 100 Best Companies to Work for in America*. In 1995, following a record year, founder and chairman McConnell repeated a comment he'd made forty years earlier, "We've only scratched the surface."

In addition to its sterling balance sheet, Worthington has been lauded as a champion of "forward-looking employee practices." One example is that employees have the unique power to vote in their co-workers. That is not done by management. Employee councils put each employee's name up for a vote. To be hired, the employee must garner a majority vote. Also unique is the company's no-layoff policy in its mission statement: "We believe in the philosophy of continued employment for all Worthington people."

The first of Worthington's corporate goals is to earn money for its shareholders and increase the value of their investment. The company believes that the best measurement of that goal is consistent growth in earnings per share. For a company in a cyclical industry, Worthington has done an outstanding job. For the past forty years, earnings have reached a new high thirty-six times, one of the finest records among all companies in all industries.

In line with meeting this goal in the future, the company purchased Dietrich Industries of Pittsburgh in early 1996. Dietrich is the largest producer of metal-framing products in the United States, which gives Worthington a solid foothold in the building-products industry. Metal framing has many competitive advantages over wood and masonry construction, and Dietrich is the low-cost producer.

Worthington's growth has far surpassed its founder's ambition. When asked in 1981, "Did you ever dream you'd be this big?," John McConnell responded, "We have never worked to become the biggest, rather our aim has always been to be the best. We strive for quality; size will take care of itself. We take pride in the fact that our customers tell us we are the best at what we do."

Having studied and analyzed hundreds of the enterprises in America's Finest Companies, I believe they share the following traits:

1. The finest companies serve customers and employees with a passion.
2. Their managements are strong and decisive.
3. Each company knows where it wants to go.
4. They carve out their own paths for growth.
5. The companies are creative and innovative.
6. They carefully control expenses.
7. They respond to problems rather than react to them.

If you invest exclusively in the companies in America's Finest Companies, you'll be putting these traits to work for you in your portfolio. If the historic performance of their stocks continues, you'll do far better than most professional money managers.

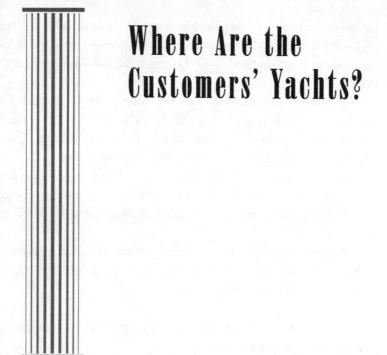

CHAPTER FIVE

Where Are the Customers' Yachts?

William R. Travers was a well-known nineteenth-century lawyer who regularly used to visit swank Newport, Rhode Island. J. P. Morgan, John D. Rockefeller, and other notable Wall Street financiers and millionaire industrialists built "cottages" (we call them mansions today) there for weekend and summer retreats. Yacht racing was the sport of that day, and Travers was present at all the best events. One Sunday he was in a small group at the finish line watching yacht after yacht glide across. As names of the owners were announced, Travers noticed each one was a wealthy stockbroker. While staring at the fancy flotilla, Travers, a stutterer, shouted out, "And w-w-where are the c-c-customers' yachts?"

Fred Schwed, Jr., wrote best-selling *Wacky, the Small Boy* in 1939. In the About the Author section, Schwed was said to have "attended Lawrenceville and Princeton and has spent the last ten years in Wall Street. As a result he knows everything there is to know about children." That doesn't say much about Schwed's forte in the financial arena, but it does give you a good idea of the terrific sense of humor he had. Schwed was an early skeptic of Wall Street and decided to write *Where Are the Customers' Yachts?* (or *A Good Hard Look at Wall Street*) to share his witty wisdom. He got Simon & Schuster to publish it in 1940. The book has been successful enough to have been reprinted several times since.

Schwed's opening reminds the reader that Wall Street has a river at one end and a graveyard at the other. Schwed said he viewed Wall Street's daily activities from a trading table with every conceivable form of communication except the heliograph. In such an enviable position, he was "constantly exchanging . . . quotations, orders, bluffs, fibs, lies and nonsense." Having observed all this for at least a decade, Schwed decided to dedicate his book to examining the nonsense, "a commodity which keeps sluicing in through the weeks and years with the irresistible constancy of the waters of the rolling Mississippi."

I particularly liked his discussion of investment trusts, which were the forerunners of modern-day mutual funds. They were formed under the assumption that

> the average individual is incapable of handling his own financial destiny. What is worse, he cannot, unless he is very rich, purchase the best financial advice. (We are assuming for the moment that there is such a thing as the best financial advice.)
>
> So a lot of us who clearly are not magicians pool our

money and hire a set of professional experts to do the guessing. They may not be quite magicians but they have everything that should be necessary—experience, reputation, trained staffs, inside information, and unlimited resources for research. Since the amount we pool together is often in the neighborhood of a hundred million dollars, we can afford to pay them fortunes for their ability. Paying them fortunes will be a great bargain for us, provided only that they come across with the ability.

One would think they could do this, or at least do it better than we could. If investment trusts would only function in actuality anything like as well as they do in theory, they would be a tremendous asset to the general welfare.

Schwed believed most investment professionals aren't dishonest. They're simply inept. He wrote, "This book has chiefly tried to paint a picture of thousands of erring humans, of varying degrees of good will, solemnly engaged in the business of predicting the unpredictable. To this effort most of them bring a certain cockeyed sincerity." I agree with Schwed.

Since I started my newsletter, *The Staton Institute*^{SM} *Advisory,* eleven years ago, I've amassed a thick file of evidence that proves that the large majority of professional money managers, the experts millions of people rely upon to help their money grow, consistently underperform the stock market. The file is more than two inches thick and growing. It's jam-packed with articles from all sorts of places, but for the most part they're straight from everyday business and financial journals, including *The Wall Street Journal, Forbes, Fortune, Business Week,* and *Financial World.* I haven't gone out of my way to obtain the evidence. It comes regularly and frequently in my mail.

Before I explain why most professionals cannot beat the market on a regular basis, I want to show you some recent evidence of the poor job they're doing:

1. One might expect that our investment judgments, given our training and experience, would prove sound and profitable for our clients. But this is, strikingly, not true.

   —ARNOLD S. WOOD, PRESIDENT
   MARTINGALE ASSET MANAGEMENT
   FINANCIAL ANALYSTS JOURNAL, MAY–JUNE 1989

2. In the 10-year period ending December 1988, SEI, a pension fund consulting firm, found only 40 percent of all pension funds were able to beat the S & P 500 at least half the time. Only one manager in 100 beat the market in each of 10 years, and only one manager in 50 beat the market in each of five years.

   —*THE FINANCIAL WEEKLY*, JANUARY 29, 1990

3. 75% of all professional money managers fail to beat the market in any given period, according to studies done by Ibbotson Associates of Chicago, an investment research firm.

   —*FINANCIAL WORLD*, MAY 1, 1990

4. Since 1969, the unmanaged S & P 500-stock index has handily outgained the average stock fund, rising 680% vs. 550%. $10,000 invested on Jan. 1, 1969, in a portfolio that matched the S & P would

have grown to $78,600 last Jan. 1. The same amount in the average stock fund: $65,800.

—*MONEY*, MAY 1991

5. Of the more than 1,000 equity mutual funds in existence, only a handful have beaten the market over the past 10 years.

—*THE MUTUAL FUND LETTER*, JULY 1991

6. Of the 41 domestic equity funds managed by Merrill Lynch, Shearson, Paine Webber, Dean Witter and Prudential Securities, only 2 have beaten the market since 1988. Over the period, not one of these five brokerage firm families outperformed the S & P 500.

—*FORBES*, SEPTEMBER 2, 1991

7. Many of the 400 or so investor newsletters aren't worth the price of a subscription, which can run $500 or more a year.

—*FORTUNE*, SEPTEMBER 23, 1991

8. Only four services [investment letters] outperformed the Wilshire 5000 over the $11\frac{1}{2}$-year period [6/30/80–12/31/91], which shows you how tough it is to beat the market.

—*THE CHARTIST*, FEBRUARY 6, 1992

9. "About a fifth of the investment letter universe appears to beat the market over the long term,"

says Hulbert, pointing out that less than 20% of all mutual funds outperform the market.

—INTERVIEW WITH MARK HULBERT, PUBLISHER OF *HULBERT'S FINANCIAL DIGEST* IN *FORBES*, SEPTEMBER 14, 1992

10. The average stock mutual fund climbed just 7.89% in the year [1992] through Dec. 23, slightly behind the Standard & Poor's 500-Stock Index.

—*THE WALL STREET JOURNAL*, JANUARY 4, 1993

11. According to Lipper Analytical, stock funds returned 13.5% a year over the 10 years through December [1992], compared with 16.2% for the Standard & Poor's 500-Stock Index.

—*THE WALL STREET JOURNAL*, MARCH 5, 1993

12. By and large, professional investors do a mediocre job of stock-picking. That, along with their expenses and fees, causes them to lag well behind the market.

—*BUSINESS WEEK*, MAY 31, 1993

13. Overall, money managers have done a dismal job.

—*FORTUNE*, OCTOBER 31, 1994

14. Over the last decade, according to Lipper Analytical Services, just 21% of mutual funds with a U.S. equity focus did better than an index fund.

—*FORBES*, SEPTEMBER 25, 1995

15. There is not a single academic study . . . that suggests that active manager performance is anything more than the expected distribution around the mean. And, since fund managers charge for their services, the mean will always be below the indices. The great majority of active funds fail to outperform the indices.

—*FEE ADVISOR*, NOVEMBER/DECEMBER 1995

16. Of the nearly 500 portfolios among 152 letters tracked by *Hulbert Financial Digest*, only 45 matched the 37.5% total return of Standard & Poor's 500-stock index in 1995.

—*KIPLINGER'S PERSONAL FINANCE MAGAZINE*, APRIL *1996*

Mutual funds have become the most popular way for individuals to invest. There are now in excess of 8,000 different mutual funds, with more than $3 trillion in assets at the end of 1995. About 3,000+ of them invest in stocks. With so much money on the line and pouring into the equity funds at a record clip, you'd think investors would be more careful about where they put their money. But they are often lured by the creative advertising of mutual funds, which seem to offer so much and in reality frequently produce so little. Thumb through any of dozens of investment publications, and you'll see ads for this fund or that. Note how they tout their "outstanding" records. One of my money-manager friends (who actually does beat the market) wryly noted, "Every money manager in the country says he's in the top 25 percent." But we know that's an impossibility.

If an investor is going to beat the market over the long term (I define long term as a minimum of ten years), he or she will have to invest strictly in funds that invest exclusively in stocks. The reason is that stocks have beaten all other investments, real estate included, for well over a century. I wanted to see how many equity mutual funds outpaced the market in the past decade, so I checked out the CDA/Wiesenberger Mutual Funds Update, which comes out monthly.

For the ten years through December 31, 1993, the Dow Jones industrial average provided a compound annual return of 15.7 percent, while the S & P 500 earned 14.9 percent. The Dow index is trackable well back into the nineteenth century, while the S & P 500, which got its start in 1926, measures the performance of five hundred different companies. These are the two benchmarks fund managers try to beat, but very few do.

CDA/Wiesenberger separates stock funds into various categories. Among funds for maximum capital gains, only five managed to beat the market for the ten years. Small company growth funds had six market beaters, while international equity funds had eight. Long-term growth, growth and current income, balanced, and equity income funds together had fewer than twenty that bested the two major market indexes during the past decade.

These seven fund categories produced less than forty (out of more than 1,000) stock funds that performed better than the market since the end of 1983. That's about 4 percent, a small handful of winners.

Since so few professionals, whether they be investment counselors, pension-fund managers, or mutual-fund managers, beat the market, investors need to understand why so they don't make the same mistakes the pros make. Financial institutions control about 80 percent of all trading volume on the New York Stock Exchange. On an average day some 200 to 300 million shares are bought and sold. Individuals account for 20 percent of that.

Vilfredo Pareto was an Italian sociologist and economist for whom the famous Pareto Principle is named. After observing thousands of workers in hundreds of businesses from the late nineteenth through the early twentieth century, he concluded that 80 percent of results comes from 20 percent of effort. To say it another way, 20 percent of an advertising budget results in 80 percent of the incremental revenue. Twenty percent of a day's work produces 80 percent of the benefits of that work. The top 20 percent of workers in any organization typically produce about 80 percent of sales and earnings. Although no results will divide exactly into 20/80, it's an excellent rule of thumb. And it's interesting to me that NYSE volume is now almost exactly 20 percent by individuals and 80 percent by financial institutions. As you've already seen, the 80 percent produces subpar results, which implies the 20 percent, individual investors, produces superior results.

I profiled Benjamin Graham, the father of modern-day securities analysis, in Chapter 3 and provided excerpts from the final interview he gave shortly before his death. In just ten sentences, Graham ripped apart the fantasy that the financial community can accurately predict short-term changes in the economy and stock prices. He also reasoned that the stock-market experts can't continuously beat the market because they are the market. You can't beat the average when you are the average.

On the other hand, "The typical individual investor," he said later in the interview, "has a great advantage over the large institutions." As I'll demonstrate, that advantage can lead you to above-average profits if you create and manage your own portfolio made up of America's Finest Companies.

I don't want you to think I'm bashing all professional money managers and advisors. For the record, I am not against professional advice or money management. I *am* against paying a so-called expert for subpar performance, something far too many individuals are doing. In fairness to the pros, though, their customers help create these inferior results. Here's how.

For whatever reasons—lack of time, no investment background, personal finance seeming too complicated— many people believe they can't manage their own money well. Since they have no confidence in their own ability, they turn to experts to take care of their money for them. An expert is defined as one "displaying special skill or knowledge derived from training and experience." Millions of people believe there are a large number of stock-market experts who earn superior investment returns, primarily through accurate forecasting and making savvy moves into and out of stocks. Even though this is a widely held belief, as you've already seen, it's false.

Investors must pay annual fees for services from trust departments, investment counselors, and mutual funds. If they use brokers, the brokers will charge a commission for each transaction. If they use financial planners, they'll pay fees and/or sales loads on the various financial products offered by the planners. Anywhere investors turn there's a charge for advice and management unless they choose to do it themselves. What pro in his right mind would manage money for free?

When investors pay to have their money managed, they expect the professionals they're paying to earn their keep by studying the economy and stock market, by buying and selling when the time is ripe, and by going into cash in case the market should go down. Isn't that right? Would you pay an expert to spend little of his time taking care of your money? Of course not. You want that expert to be working—and working hard—on your behalf. You want that expert to spend as much time with your money as he can, and because you want that, he does what you expect.

Professionals rely heavily on forecasts of expected performance of the economy, the stock market, and individual companies. That's not too surprising because forecasting, especially of the economy, has been in existence for centuries. People from all walks of life are attracted to it. Everyone wants that special peek ahead. When Marco Polo returned to his homeland from the Orient, he told of kites used as economic-forecasting devices. Before a merchant ship embarked on a trading voyage, a drunkard (you had to be drunk to do this) was tied to a kite and launched from the ship's deck. If, and it was a big if, the drunkard actually made it into the air, the voyage was expected to be successful. But if he crashed, the trip was postponed if not canceled.

Despite the awesome academic evidence that forecasts are usually wrong (because no one can see into the future), many money managers continue to defy logic and rationality. It's not really mysterious, though, when you consider that millions of people still smoke and chew tobacco, although they know that tobacco is harmful; or continue to gamble at the racetrack, in lotteries or Las Vegas, although the house wins 99 percent of the time; or abuse drugs; or drive without seat belts fastened. Each money manager believes he has found the forecast (or forecasts) that will allow him to gaze profitably into the future, even though his counterparts won't be successful.

Let me take you on a brief journey through history to show you some of the most widely heralded predictions about the economy and stock market made by acclaimed experts:

1. Stocks have reached what looks like a permanently high plateau.

   —IRVING FISHER, PROFESSOR OF ECONOMICS AT YALE, OCTOBER 17, 1929

   Seven days later, on October 24, panic struck Wall Street and stock values plummeted.

2. The end of the decline of the Stock Market . . . will probably not be long, only a few more days at most.

   —IRVING FISHER TRYING TO REGAIN SOME OF HIS LOST LUSTER, NOVEMBER 14, 1929

   Nice try, Irving.

3. Financial storm definitely passed.

   —CABLEGRAM TO WINSTON CHURCHILL FROM BERNARD BARUCH, NOVEMBER 15, 1929

   Security prices had just begun their freefall into 1932.

4. Gentlemen, you have come sixty days too late. The Depression is over.

    —HERBERT HOOVER RESPONDING TO A DELEGATION REQUESTING A PUBLIC-WORKS PROGRAM TO HELP SPEED THE RECOVERY, JUNE 1930

    What recovery? The economy hadn't come close to bottoming.

5. During the next four years . . . unless drastic steps are taken by Congress, the U.S. will have nearly 8,000,000 unemployed and will stand on the brink of a deep depression.

    —HENRY C. WALLACE, U.S. SECRETARY OF COMMERCE, NOVEMBER 1945

    Between 1945 and 1950, U.S. GNP rose nearly 50 percent.

6. Nineteen sixty promises to be the most prosperous [year] in our history.

    —ROBERT A. ANDERSON, U.S. SECRETARY OF THE TREASURY, APRIL 14, 1960

    Business conditions will stay good for some time to come. We are not about to enter any sharp recession.

    —HENRY C. ALEXANDER, CHAIRMAN OF THE MORGAN GUARANTY TRUST COMPANY, APRIL 22, 1960

    The recession of 1960 began that same month.

7. There ain't going to be no recession. I guarantee it.

    —PIERRE RINFRET, POPULAR ECONOMIST AND INVEST-MENT COUNSELOR, APRIL 1969

    The 1969–71 recession started the following summer.

8. There will be no recession in the United States of America.

    —RICHARD NIXON, PRESIDENT, STATE OF THE UNION ADDRESS, 1974

    The GNP dropped 5.8 percent the first quarter of 1974, and by July the economy was (you guessed it) in the deepest recession since the 1930s.

9. A drastic reduction in the deficit . . . will take place in the fiscal year '82.

    —RONALD REAGAN, PRESIDENT, MARCH 1981

    In fiscal 1982, the government had a record deficit up to that time—$110.7 billion.

10. A grim first quarter is projected for stocks.

    —*WALL STREET JOURNAL* HEADLINE, JANUARY 3, 1995

    Not only was the first quarter one of the strongest for stocks in history, so was the entire year 1995.

Will Rogers once said, "An economist's guess is liable to be as good as anyone else's." In spring 1990, the National Association of Business Economists (whose main function seems to be polling itself) "guessed" that the remainder of the year and the several beyond it would be good. Specifically, 80 percent of the members predicted no recession for 1990, while 67 percent said there wouldn't be one of these nasty little events for at least three more years. In response to their poll, supercolumnist Alan Abelson of *Barron's* wrote, "Near-unanimity in this case breeds contempt. Anyone with even a taint of contrarian blood can only pray that, please, Lord, just this once, let 68 economists be right." Despite Abelson's plea, the economists were dead wrong. The deep recession of 1990–91 began shortly after the NABE poll was released.

For the twelve years from the end of 1982 through 1994, the consensus prediction of economists polled by *The Wall Street Journal* missed the change of direction in interest rates 18 of 25 times, an error ratio of 72%. So-called "professional" stock analysts fared even worse. According to *Worth* magazine's "1996 Investing guide," analysts failed to see the earnings downturns heading into the 1981 recession, the slowdown of 1984–86, and the subsequent recession of 1990 too.

These are only a few examples of predictions that were way wide of the mark. I could provide hundreds of others, many of which in retrospect are quite humorous, but I think I've proved a point. David Dreman, author of *The New Contrarian Investment Strategy,* said, "Expert opinion—which investors naturally rely on—is very often wrong and not infrequently dramatically so." He devotes page after page to detailing the poor performance of the experts who try in vain to predict accurately.

If the evidence is so overwhelming that economic and

stock-market forecasting is a fool's game, why do people rely on it so heavily? Eric Hoffer believed society is addicted to pollsters and forecasters. "Even when the forecasts prove wrong, we still go on asking for them. We watch our experts read the entrails of statistical tables and graphs the way the ancients watched the soothsayers read the entrails of a chicken."

The final word on why forecasting is so often awry comes from *The Futurist* magazine (January-February 1990):

> Forecasts that a current trend will continue indefinitely are generally wrong, since most trends eventually reach a constraint.
>
> Forecasts that describe ominous doom are frequently wrong, since society usually addresses a problem once it has been identified as being critical.
>
> Forecasts that describe a traditional solution to a critical problem are usually wrong. Society seems to find creative and innovative solutions.

The Futurist wasn't completely negative on forecasting. They believe forecasting can be much improved if it's based on analogy. The forecaster looks at past developments and sees how a similar sequence of events might happen in the future. That's the technique I've successfully used for years as an economic historian and superior stock picker.

Professional money managers try to make a perfect science of forecasting and investing. If they put A into a computer, they expect B to come out. Although B always follows A in the alphabet, it doesn't always follow A out of a computer. Thinking and acting this way creates frequent mistakes. No one knows where the Dow or the S & P 500 will be a year from now. No one knows how much money any company will earn in 1995. No one knows how strong the economy will be. Yet much of the typical professional's time is involved in trying to find the answers, all for nought.

Bennett W. Goodspeed, who in his own words "overcame the handicaps of having an MBA and working for several prominent Wall Street firms," wrote *The Tao Jones Averages: A Guide to Whole-Brained Investing* in 1983. It's a fascinating little book (154 pages). Goodspeed said analysts and portfolio managers "create an overload of information in their frenzied activity." I call it Paralysis from Overanalysis. Overload is harmful. In the words of the Chinese philosopher Lao-tzu, "The more stuffed the mind is with knowledge, the less able one can see what's in front of him."

Even if their forecasts for the economy and direction of the stock market were always on the money, most professional money managers would still rarely beat the market. The reason is the market has no operating expenses, but the professional does. Expenses eat sharply into returns.

Even to duplicate the market (not try to outperform it), the money manager has to trade frequently. Because stocks change multiple times in value every day, at any given time each stock in the Dow, the S & P 500, the Wilshire 5000, or any other market index he's trying to copy changes in its proportional weighting to all the others in the index. The cost of buying and selling to keep stocks in correct proportion (although that's not the only reason) almost singly guarantees that attempts to mimic the market will fail.

There are other excellent reasons why most professionals can't match the market. One is cash. Mutual funds have to keep cash available for their customers who wish to redeem shares. That amount usually ranges between 5 percent when they're optimistic on stock prices and 10 to 15 percent when they're negative. On any given day they must have a reserve in case more of their customers want to redeem shares than buy them. The fund manager doesn't want to be forced to sell part of his portfolio to pay for these redeemed shares. He always opts to dip into the cash reserve. For the long term, stocks earn three to four times as much as cash. The higher the fund's cash reserve, the more its return is penalized. Every fund has such a reserve, and every fund is damaged by it. The individual doesn't need a cash kitty, so his results aren't impacted.

Still another problem for money managers, including mutual funds, is forced panic selling. During the Great Crash of 1987, mutual funds were bombarded with so many redemptions they had to sell even though they may not have wanted to. Fortunately their phone lines were jammed with panicked callers. Otherwise they would have had to sell even more of their portfolios. This unplanned selling occurred, you guessed it, at or near the bottom. Once the chaos subsided, they had to reinvest at higher prices.

On Black Monday, October 19, I mailed a one-page memo to all my clients urging them to stand pat because there was blood in the streets, and you never sell when the blood is running. This is one Wall Street maxim that's true. I also told them to wait a few days for orderly trading to resume and then add to their portfolios. Those who heeded my advice not only recovered all their paper losses but also added greatly to their coffers. Mutual funds were forced to react. Savvy individuals responded and took advantage of what looked like a horrible situation but was in reality one of the premier buying opportunities in history.

When a financial institution (I include mutual funds) buys or sells shares of a company, it normally does so at various prices. Their buying and selling power is so enormous it affects their own transactions. Let's say you and a money manager hear on *Wall Street Week* a great idea that sparks new interest in an underfollowed New York Stock Exchange (NYSE) company that doesn't trade in big volume. The following Monday you call your broker to buy 100 shares, and the price is 28 (remember: stock prices don't need the dollar sign). For $2,800 plus commission you own the stock. At the same time, the money manager calls his broker and wants to buy 10,000 shares. He gets the first 2,000 at 28, the next 3,000 at 29, 3,000 more at 29½, and the final 2,000 at 30.

Three years later the same analyst who recommended that stock is on *Wall Street Week* saying sell it. Coincidentally, you and the money manager are watching the show and both decide to sell on Monday. You call your broker and get out of your 100 shares at 42 less commission. The manager calls his broker and sells 3,000 at 42. Stock prices happen to be very weak that day, so the specialist handling the order on the NYSE takes the stock down a point on the next 3,000. Then he knocks it another 1½ points and clears the remaining 4,000 shares.

In both of these situations, which aren't unusual, the fund's average cost to buy is higher than the individual's.

The fund's proceeds from selling are lower. Financial institutions deal in thousands and tens of thousands of shares. Their buying and selling can drive stocks up or down before they complete their orders. It can take days if not weeks to accumulate or unload a position, whereas the individual can get in or out with one phone call with the price sometimes confirmed before he hangs up. This is another reason professionals have a tough time equaling or beating the market.

The Wall Street Journal asks, "How much does it really cost to have someone manage your money?

> Money managers and investment advisers all quote rates that seem straightforward enough. But the price that they give for their hand-holding usually doesn't include a variety of other charges investors typically end up paying. These include brokerage-firm trading costs to buy and sell stocks during the year and management and administration fees levied by mutual fund companies. There is also the cost of setting up a new portfolio in the first place.
>
> The differences in total costs can be huge. Depending on the adviser's investment style, total annual costs can range from a low of about 1% of assets under management to 4%, or more. Initial costs of setting up a portfolio can run from less than 1% of the portfolio to 10% or more.

For the rest of this chapter, I'll stick solely to the costs involved with mutual funds, since this book is about creating your own mini-mutual fund and outpacing most existing funds. The first cost I'll discuss is the load. That's the charge you may incur to buy or redeem a fund's shares. No-load mutual funds don't charge anything, and they make up about half the equity funds.

The other half is load funds. Their loads go up to 8.5 percent, although that's extreme. The industry average is 3–4 percent. Most loads are front-end. They're deducted before you invest in the fund. A few funds have back-end loads that are taken out only when you redeem your shares. The top twenty-five general equity funds, led by Fidelity Magellan, have more than $500 billion under management. Fifteen have loads.

The services rating mutual-fund total returns—capital appreciation with dividends reinvested—don't take loads into account. That makes comparing load funds to no-loads a more difficult chore, but there's one thing for certain. If a load fund and a no-load fund have exactly the same rates of return, the no-load will put more money into your pocket.

Taxes are another bugaboo. The performance-rating services usually don't consider them either. If your mutual funds are in a retirement account, taxes aren't a problem. But since the bulk of mutual funds is in taxable accounts, taxes are a sad reality. They can cripple returns, particularly if you're in a high tax bracket.

The Wall Street Journal wrote, "Beware Tax Consequences of Mutual Funds" in the February 22, 1992, edition. "Would you like to pay taxes on somebody else's gains? How about paying your taxes years earlier than you have to? Most people would answer both questions with a resounding 'No.' But mutual fund investors frequently subject themselves to such taxing situations, often without being aware of it." The *Journal* calculated how negatively taxes affected returns of the top ten mutual funds for the decade ending December 31, 1991.

Taxes took away one-quarter of the average total return

during the ten years. That's a huge bite, a bite that could be completely eliminated if you assemble your own mini-mutual fund. As your own money manager, you control when to realize a capital gain; therefore, you control when to pay taxes on a gain. If you're in a mutual fund, that's a choice you don't have.

The National Bureau of Economic Research released its study "Ranking Mutual Funds on an After-Tax Basis" by economics professors Joel M. Dickson and John B. Shoven of Stanford University. Their study covered sixty-two growth and growth-and-income mutual funds with thirty-year records from 1963 to 1992 on a pretax and aftertax basis. One dollar invested in the Standard & Poor's 500 index in 1963 grew to $22.13 by the end of 1992. The median result for the sixty-two funds was that one dollar grew to $21.89 over the same period. Thus, the typical fund underperformed the stock market over the three decades, and that was before taxes. After taxes, the results were much worse.

For the thirty years, one dollar invested by an individual in a low-tax bracket grew to $16.45. The same dollar invested by someone in a medium-tax bracket grew to $12.82, while someone in the highest-tax bracket saw his dollar grow to just $9.87. Taxes took away 24.9 percent of the low-tax investor's return; 41.4 percent of the medium-tax investor's return; and a whopping 55 percent of the high-tax investor's return.

If taxes and loads aren't enough heavy yokes on the investor's shoulders, there are also annual administrative expenses and the management fee to consider. Mutual-fund administrative expenses range from $\frac{1}{2}$ percent to $1\frac{1}{2}$ percent of assets. Yearly management fees are in the same range. Together they cost the investor between 1 and 3 percent of total assets under management.

And finally there are trading costs. According to *Forbes* (November 23, 1992), "Turnover is, like the annual expense ratio, one of those numbers that fund vendors are compelled to disclose [in prospectuses] but that fund buyers all too often ignore. Just how great are transaction costs? Higher than you might think. A round-trip trade (a sell and a buy) executed on one of the stock exchanges probably costs a fund at least 0.35% of the transaction amount; for small, illiquid Nasdaq stocks the cost is closer to 1%. That's an annual cost of 1% to 3% for a fund reporting a 300% turnover." Even the best of funds have high turnover rates. That is, they literally sell and rebuy the equivalent value of the entire portfolio one or more times every year. Each time they buy and sell, two commissions—no matter how small—are paid. And those commissions eat into the investor's return.

With so many different costs associated with mutual funds, it gets confusing trying to see how they impact on returns. So I've put together a simple example that shows the hypothetical returns from Jazzy Fund versus Standard & Poor's 500 index for the next five years in a taxable account. You've already seen that most equity mutual funds can't equal the market (and that's before loads and taxes are considered), but to make this really interesting I've given the fund the return advantage. I assume Jazzy Fund will grow at 14 percent annually with the S & P 500 growing at 11 percent, one percentage point under its historic average.

Jazzy is a low-yield fund, so its return will be 2 percent

from dividends and 12 percent from appreciation. S & P's total annual return will be 4 percent from dividends and 7 percent from appreciation, which is roughly the historic norm. One thousand dollars will be invested in the fund and the S & P index at the beginning of each of the five years. For ease of comparison, I assume no sales load to buy the fund nor any commissions to buy the S & P, and the investor in either is in the combined 35 percent tax bracket—28 percent federal and 7 percent state.

According to *Business Week* and a number of other reputable financial publications, mutual-fund returns in taxable accounts are 30–40 percent lower when both federal and state taxes are taken into account. Economists Shoven and Dickson said the take could be a lot more, so I'm being perhaps a little too biased in favor of mutual funds with this example.

At the beginning of year one, $1,000 goes into Jazzy. During the year, $20 (2 percent) is paid out in dividends. After taxes at 35 percent, $13 is left. The fund rises 12 percent in value to $1,120 and like so many funds turns the portfolio exactly one time. This means the $120 gain is taxed at 35 percent, leaving a net gain of $78 for a total of $1,078. The fund charges a 1 percent management fee and another 1 percent for expenses. Those come out of the $1,078 leaving $1,056 after all expenses and taxes. Adding back in the $13 in dividends, $1,069 is left. That's a 6.9 percent net return.

One thousand dollars also goes into the S & P 500 at the beginning of the year. During the year the S & P pays $40 (4 percent) in dividends. After taxes $26 is left. The fund rises 7 percent in value to $1,070. There is no turnover, hence no capital gain, so the entire $1,070 is left. Add back in the $26 in dividends and the amount is $1,096, a 9.6 percent net return.

At the beginning of each of the next four years, $1,000 is added to both accounts. And the scenario above repeats each time. Please see the table below.

Even though Jazzy Fund earns three percentage points more than the S & P every year, the S & P does better because there is no selling, hence no capital-gains taxes. If we continue the exercise, at the end of year ten the difference will be even more startling. Jazzy Fund will have grown to $14,701. The S & P will have swelled to $17,134.

Of course, you can argue this is an unfair comparison because the Jazzy Fund investor has already paid his taxes, and taxes are still owed by the investor who owns the "market." That's true to a degree but not as much as you may think. I have compared the S & P 500 index to a fund that outperforms it, a circumstance that doesn't happen too often.

You're going to learn how to build your own mini-mutual fund that will consistently outdistance the market indexes. That's one reason capital-gains taxes won't be a

	VALUE OF JAZZY FUND	VALUE OF S & P 500
End of Year 1	$1,069	$1,096
End of Year 2	2,212	2,297
End of Year 3	3,434	3,614
End of Year 4	4,740	5,056
End of Year 5	6,136	6,637

hindrance. The other is almost all the mutual funds you'll compare your results to won't beat the indexes as in the example above. They'll be behind.

Benjamin Graham was right when he said the individual has many advantages over the financial institutions. One major advantage is that you, the individual, can control your own financial destiny rather than be at the mercy of someone else. The other major advantage is that you can assemble your own equity mini-mutual fund, equal or beat the market year in and year out, and outperform 75 percent of the investment professionals. Then, it won't be just the stockbrokers and other investment pros who can afford to buy yachts. You'll be able to afford one, too.

CHAPTER SIX

Let Uncle Sam Help You Get Where You Want to Go

The reward of energy, enterprise and thrift—is taxes.

—WILLIAM FEATHER

For most families, the two most important financial goals are educating children and having enough money to live comfortably in retirement. I prefer to call it life after work because retiring has connotations of being old and inactive, when the opposite is usually true. If a man or woman reaches age sixty to sixty-five in good health, odds are very high he or she will live at least another twenty years.

One of the biggest problems older people in this country face is living a long, healthy life but not having enough money to travel and do whatever else they wish in their later years.

The typical married couple reaching age sixty-five has about $7,000 in liquid assets in addition to Social Security benefits and possible home ownership. At the rate you're spending money today, how long would $7,000 last? Two months? Three months? Four months? I doubt it would be beyond four months if that long.

Having enough money for life after work is easily achievable when you start early enough and invest your money on a regular basis. If you've already started, that's great. If not, it's still not too late, and you have lots of company. *Money* magazine conducted a survey a few years ago and discovered one of four people between ages forty-five and sixty-five has set aside nothing for life after work. Three out of four said they hadn't saved enough to live in the style they desired, and nearly one of two said their biggest fear was not having enough money to carry them through life after work. Those that were preparing for life after work said their preferred investment was a savings account, which historically has not kept up with inflation and taxes. Just 25 percent bought shares of stock, the best inflation hedge of all.

It's easy to see why so many people aren't prepared for life after work. If you're in your twenties or thirties, you're still some thirty to forty years away. Even if you're in your mid-forties as I am, it will still be about two decades before you reach sixty-five. Somehow twenty, thirty, or forty years seems so far away we imagine there's still plenty of time to get ready for life after work, so why worry about it now? That's the way all those who haven't begun planning think. If they don't think that way, then why haven't they started?

Another reason people don't get ready for life after work is they don't save any money. All their income is spent to pay the grocer, the mortgage company, the auto dealer, the department store, the phone company, the local utility, the doctor, the TV repairman, the movie theater, the video-rental store. The list goes on and on. These people spend every dollar they make. Sometimes they spend more than they make and borrow to make up the difference. They reason that one day they'll start to save some money as soon as they quit spending so much. But few really ever do it. It's a fantasy.

To be able to invest, you've got to be able to save. The first place you ought to invest your savings is in a retirement plan. The only way you'll be able to invest in a retirement plan is to budget for it using my formula.

As a teenager I read the wonderful story in Norman Vincent Peale's *Guideposts* magazine about Joseph Colgate, founder of the forerunner of Colgate-Palmolive and Colgate University. Mr. Colgate's business was so successful he quickly turned into a multimillionaire and decided he had far more money than he needed. So he started giving it away.

He first gave away 10% of each year's income, but after he started giving his income multiplied. He then upped the percentage to 15, and the same thing happened again. Next he gave away 20% of his income, but money poured into his coffers like water through a broken dam. After studying his "problem," Mr. Colgate finally turned his money over to a foundation and let others figure out what to do with it. Giving away his money created a giant hole which was then refilled with even more money than before.

In my business and personal lives, I operate under an amazingly simple formula:

> *100% of my income*
> less: some income for me
> less: some income for others
> spend: everything else

Americans who don't do well with their money use a different formula. When money comes in they spend it on everybody they can think of—the grocer, the utility company, the mortgage company, the car company, the clothier, the department store, the hardware, the water company—and if, and this is a big if, there's any money left they'll use it for their financial future. The dilemma is that there's never anything left because they don't plan for any to be.

If somebody says "I'll try to do it," what are the odds he'll do it as compared with if he says, "I will do it." You can't try to do anything. Either you do it or you don't. You can't try to save money for your future. Either you do it or you don't. There is no in between about saving money and because there isn't, people get trapped. Without actually paying themselves first, people rarely have any money left over to save and invest.

Any couple can easily save $600 a year by putting pocket change into a jar at the end of a day and taking it to the bank at the end of each month. Six hundred dollars a year put into a handful of companies, in America's Finest Companies (and reinvesting all dividends), can be as much as $1.5 million at the end of 40 years even though the total invested was just $24,000 scattered evenly over four decades.

Not only do I believe in paying myself first, I also believe in paying others first who need it. When I set aside pretax income for myself, I also set aside the same percentage for the charities, church, organizations, and causes I believe in. Joseph Colgate proved this works. Many others have proved it too.

I'm reminded of the story about a deep well with the purest, best-tasting water anyone for miles around had ever tasted. For generations the old well served all the descendants of a farming family and anyone else who wanted to partake of its goodness. Through drought after drought, the well always provided all the water the farmer, his family, and their animals ever needed. Not once did it ever run low.

During the Great Depression hard times hit, and the farmer had to sell his farm and move. The property stayed empty and the well unused for many years until finally a new family bought it. Even though they came from another county, they knew the reputation of the old well and its water.

When the family moved in and rushed to the well to sample its contents, they were shocked to find it completely dry. In great disbelief, they stared at each other and realized the terrible investment they'd made buying a farm with a dry well. What they hadn't realized was that a well needs to be used to keep the water flowing. The thousands of tiny rivulets that flow into the well's cavern will stop up just as blood will not circulate if veins and arteries become clogged.

And so it is with money. To do the most good, to help the most people, money must flow and must not be hoarded as Hetty Green hoarded it.

She could read the financial pages at age six. At age thirty she inherited her father's fortune and began trading on Wall Street with "bold audacity." It wasn't her looks but her fierce style that earned her the name, the Witch of Wall Street.

The Witch was so tightfisted she wore only a black dress (maybe because she had just one). To save soap, she seldom washed it. Working alone on the first floor of a bank from which she coerced free space (probably because she owned it), Green lived the life of a pauper. She bought *The Wall Street Journal*, read it, and then resold it each day.

Despite her brutal nature, she managed to marry and bear two children. Her son, Ned, hurt himself sledding, and Hetty took him to a charity ward where she was recognized as a multimillionaire who could easily afford a hospital. But she refused to pay, the wound became infected, and Ned's leg was amputated. She left her children $50 million each when she died of a stroke in 1916 after arguing over the price of milk.

Clint Murchison, Jr., the famous Texas wildcatter, had the right attitude about money. "Money is like manure. If you spread it around, it does a lot of good. But if you pile it up in one place, it stinks like hell."

James Redfield, author of *The Celestine Prophecy*, also has the right attitude. His book has sold more than three million copies despite the fact that the plot has been called "flaky" and all other sorts of unflattering names.

In a Fall 1994 interview, Redfield said that when you

view money as a scarce resource, you are locked into a scarcity mentality. "No matter how tight money is for you, if you don't open your hand and make it available, it'll be hard for you to get more. When you give, you create a void [like the old well] that is filled again. And [like Joseph Colgate] you always receive much more."

Redfield gave up his therapy practice, self-published 3,000 copies of his book, and traveled with his wife across the Southeast giving away copies. He sold 150,000 books that way before cutting a deal with Warner Books. Redfield has already made so much money he's set up a foundation to dispose of it.

I have a theory that good things—often unexpectedly great things—happen when people with a giving attitude "empty their glass." Only a completely empty glass can be totally replenished. One of Jesus' most famous parables is about the poor woman who gave her last two coins to help others. She trusted that even though she had no money, her needs would be met. And we must assume they were.

My mission is to reach everyone who will listen with the gospel (gospel means truth) of investing money to earn the highest return possible in the least time with least risk. I gladly give away my expertise to people who can't afford it without asking anything in return. The more I give the more I am rewarded, frequently in ways never anticipated. "What goes around comes around" is really true. We are all part of a giant circle, 5.6 billion of us, and each one has a part to play. Every person has a way to serve. Serving is what being human is all about. To serve is to give. The more you give, the more you get. The hand that gives gathers.

Before spending all your income, first allocate a certain percentage for investment, for your financial future. The amount can be 1 percent of pretax income, 2 percent, 5 percent, 10 percent, or more. It's up to you. You need to start with some percentage, regardless of how small, and then gradually increase it as fast as you can. Once you decide on a percentage to invest, allocate that same percentage for giving to others. Logically, the larger your income, the larger percentage you'll set aside to invest and to give.

Andrew Carnegie, the steel magnate who was once the richest man in the world, said, "You want to know if you will be rich? The answer is, 'Can you save money?' " I might add, "Rich in the broadest sense means having abundant supply. Money is only one part of that abundance, a tool to use and to use wisely. Giving, to me, is part of using money wisely by sharing our abundance with others."

Because I see so many adults failing to prepare for their financial futures, I have a strong sense of mission about teaching young people how to manage their money so they'll end up where they want to be financially. I know the earlier they start the easier it will be and the more likely they are to make it. Why? Because saving, investing, and giving are a habit, one of the best habits there is. Once a person adopts the saving-investing-giving habit, it's as hard to quit as smoking.

Each year I have the privilege of teaching Junior Achievement's superb applied economics course to juniors and seniors at my daughter's school. I always spend a lot of time on investing because that's the subject I know the most about. I've just completed my ninth year, and I think I learn more than the students do. These eager juniors and seniors tell me they "waste" between $10 and $15 per week. This is money that slips through their hands. They don't know where it goes. They just know it disappears.

The lesson I try to get across is that if they invest that "wasted" money in a retirement plan at 12 percent per year, the rate of return from stocks since World War II, they'll end up with $1 million or more. Even minors can have retirement plans, as I'll show later. And yes, it is possible to invest in a well-diversified portfolio of stocks with that small amount of money. I'll demonstrate how easy it is. You don't have to go the customary mutual-fund route and end up with inferior results.

By simply beginning to invest $50 per month at 12 percent in an individual retirement account (IRA)—and never increasing the amount—a 16-year-old will have $1,749,977 by the age of 65. If he waits until 18, the amount will be $1,377,071. By waiting two more years until age 20, he will have only $1,083,462. That's still more than a million dollars, but it's $666,515 less than the one who started at 16. The sixteen-year-old, who makes 48 more payments of $50 per month (a total of $2,400 extra) than the 20-year-old, will wind up with 62 percent more money at age 65. Clearly, the earlier you start investing, the more money you'll have when you need it.

A few years ago Theodore Johnson died in Delray Beach, Florida, at age ninety. Mr. Johnson never made more than $14,000 a year, working for United Parcel Service, but he invested a dollar or two in UPS stock every chance he got. When he retired in 1952 his stock was worth $700,000. When he died it had mushroomed to $70 million, and he left more than half of it to help disadvantaged young people get educations. If a man who never made more than $14,000 in a single year can become a multimillionaire, so can you.

Two young people aged nineteen graduate from high school. Both begin to work and have annual incomes. Investor Smart (a graduate of one of my Junior Achievement classes) opens an IRA through a stockbroker and begins to salt away the annual maximum of $2,000. He makes his contributions at the beginning of each year. Investor Not As Smart (who wasn't in my class) decides to wait a few years to open his IRA.

Investor Smart contributes $2,000 annually from age 19 through age 26 and quits. After contributing a total of $16,000, he decides (wrongly, in my opinion) to make no more contributions until he begins to withdraw funds from his IRA at age 65.

Investor Not As Smart, at age 27, wakes up to the realization he needs to begin preparing for retirement. He opens an IRA through his stockbroker and contributes $2,000 per year from age 27 through age 65, all the while earning 12 percent (the stock market's historic return) annually on his money as does Investor Smart.

For brevity, I've not shown every year, but Investor Not As Smart contributes $78,000 over the thirty-nine years he contributes to his plan. Thus, he puts nearly five times more into his IRA than Investor Smart. But when both are sixty-five, Investor Smart has $818,786 more than Investor Not As Smart. Even if Investor Not As Smart continues to invest $2,000 per year forever, he will never catch up with Investor Smart, who committed just $16,000. This is the best example I know to demonstrate the power of investing early for a new home, vacation, college education, life after work, or whatever.

Life after work will require a lot more money for some than for others. What will it take for you? When I launched my financial coaching career, the accepted rule of thumb was that if you were living comfortably on what you made when you were close to retiring, it would cost about 60 percent of that amount once you quit work. The theory sounded plausible. Your children were grown and gone. Since you were in your sixties, you weren't as active as when you worked. You didn't eat out as frequently, didn't travel as often, didn't buy as many "things" as before, etc. I guess the "experts" who came up with the 60 percent figure assumed everyone who retired sat around and played cards, or if they were really active played rousing games of shuffleboard in between naps.

Today we know the truth. More and more older people are very active and mentally alert. Milton Berle, Bob Hope, and my great aunts, Dot and Gladys, immediately come to mind.

I'm reminded of what Eubie Blake, the famous jazz pianist, said on his hundredth birthday: "If I'd known I was going to live this long, I'd have taken better care of myself." He died at 104. Dot and Gladys have taken excellent care of themselves. Gladys is the oldest of eleven children and is now 95. Baby sister Dot is only 93. They both spend much of their summers at Maple Grove, our 115-year-old family home in Hendersonville, North Carolina. Although they do require some help, especially Gladys, both these joyful ladies basically do for themselves. They didn't slow down a bit even at age 80. They zoomed through it like it wasn't there.

The most recent studies indicate people spend between 80 and 90 percent of their final working year's income in the first few years of life after work. The erroneous 60 percent figure of yesteryear wasn't in, or even close to, the ballpark. These same studies also show people emphatically do not want to reduce their lifestyles unless they're forced to.

If a young person begins his or her career around age 25, he or she will work for the next 35 to 40 years. During that period, money will have to be set aside for the 20 to 30 years of life beyond work. Social Security won't support more than a meager lifestyle at best. Fewer and fewer companies have pension plans employees don't have to contribute to. The chance of winning the lottery is one in many millions. Providing for the future is up to each individual, or else the future won't be provided for short of a substantial inheritance appearing out of the blue.

To calculate approximately how much you'll need in the future is easy. Just fill in the worksheet on page 105. You can use it over and over as your financial needs change.

For someone my age to be making $50,000 a year is not unreasonable, nor is it an outrageous amount of money. Fifty thousand dollars doesn't go nearly as far as it used to. I want to enter a comfortable life after work at age 65, which is only 17 years away. Inflation is a factor of life, and I want to take that into account. For this illustration, I assume it will increase at 4 percent per year in the future. That's higher than the rate for the last 70 years but about in line with the past 20. The higher the inflation number I plug in, the more conservative my estimate will be. Using the Rule of 72 (the inflation rate × the rate of

| AGE | Investor Smart | | Investor Not As Smart | |
---	IRA CONTRIBUTION	YEAR-END VALUE	IRA CONTRIBUTION	YEAR-END VALUE
19	$2,000	$ 2,240	0	0
20	2,000	4,748	0	0
21	2,000	7,559	0	0
22	2,000	10,706	0	0
23	2,000	14,230	0	0
24	2,000	18,178	0	0
25	2,000	22,599	0	0
26	2,000	27,551	0	0
27	0	30,857	$2,000	$ 2,240
28	0	34,560	2,000	4,748
29	0	38,707	2,000	7,559
30	0	43,352	2,000	10,706
35	0	76,401	2,000	33,097
40	0	134,645	2,000	72,559
45	0	237,290	2,000	142,105
50	0	418,186	2,000	264,668
55	0	736,987	2,000	480,665

60	0	1,298,823	2,000	861,327
65	0	2,288,969	2,000	1,532,183
Less Total Invested		(16,000)		(78,000)
Net Earnings		**$2,272,969**		**$1,454,183**
Money Grew (at 12%)		**143-fold**		**20-fold**

return = 72), I divide the inflation rate, 4, into 72 and arrive at 18. At a 4 percent inflation rate, the cost of living doubles roughly every eighteen years. If I use 3 percent, the number of years is 24; at 5 percent it's 14½.

If I'm doing well on $50,000 in 1997 and have seventeen years until life after work, my cost of living will increase 0.94 times. I multiply $50,000 times 1.94 and find that in 2014 what costs $50,000 today will cost almost twice as much—$97,000. My first year of life after work (when I'm sixty-five) I'll be spending at 90 percent of that rate, which is $87,300. Longevity runs in my genes, so I will probably live another eighteen years beyond that, at which time I'll be eighty-three. With inflation staying at 4 percent, my cost of living will double to $174,600, and since I fully expect to make it to three digits, I'll make it another eighteen years beyond that. My cost of living in the year 2050: $349,200. And don't forget, that's an annual, not a lump sum, number.

With a 4 percent inflation rate, the cost of living will slightly more than double every two decades. How many decades have you got to live? Once you make a stab at that figure, it's easy to zero in on how much the next twenty, thirty, forty, fifty, sixty, or more years will cost.

Life after work will take a lot more money than most people think, especially given they don't like to reduce their lifestyles and will probably live longer than expected. Wouldn't it be terrible to have plenty of good years left and a zest for life but no money for anything more than the bare necessities?

The simplest way to invest for life after work is to participate in your company's contributory 401(k) retirement plan or its equivalent, the 403(b), if you work for a govern-

HOW MUCH DOES LIFE AFTER WORK COST?

The pretax income I need in 1997 to live
comfortably is $50,000   (A)

My current age is   48   (B)

The number of years until I begin life
after work is   17   (C)

I think inflation will average __4__ % (D) each year
until I retire. My cost of living will double every
__18__ (E) years [E = 72 divided by D and rounded].

My cost of living will double __0.94__ (F) times
between 1997 and the year I retire. [F is
calculated by dividing E into C.]

My income the first year of life after
work will need to be
G = [1 + F] × A × 90%. $87,300   (G)

My income __18__ (E) years after I begin
life after work will need to be 2G.
[2G = H] $174,600 (H)

---

ment agency or nonprofit institution. Under the typical 401(k) arrangement, you can contribute up to 15 percent of your pretax income or $9,500 in 1996 (this amount is adjusted upward for inflation each year), whichever is lower, and invest your money in a variety of mutual funds. Few 401(k)s allow you to invest in individual stocks other than the stock of the company offering the plan.

Your choices usually range from three to about fifteen different mutual funds, plus one other—a GIC, guaranteed investment contract.

With a 401(k) or any other retirement plan to which you make annual contributions, the amount is excluded from your gross income for federal and state income tax purposes. Let's say you earn $50,000 pretax in 1997 and invest $4,000 in your company's 401(k). Your reported gross income will be reduced to $46,000. The taxes you would have paid on the $4,000 in your 401(k) are now invested for your future. This is how Uncle Sam becomes your partner when you invest in a retirement plan. He doesn't tax you on the dollars you put into it. Neither does the state where you live. Those unpaid tax dollars work for you tax-free until you begin withdrawals (which are then taxed many years down the road).

Uncle Sam will help you another way, too. He has made it expensive to voluntarily enter your retirement plan. Short of a loan, financial hardship, and a few other special considerations, once you invest money in any retirement plan you're not allowed to get it out before age 59½ without a 10 percent penalty on the amount removed. Plus you'll have to pay taxes, too. Yes, you can move your retirement funds from one plan to another. But you cannot spend the money unless you want to pay a high price. Because Uncle Sam doesn't want you to squander your retirement funds, he becomes an excellent financial friend.

Since you're probably not going to be able to structure your own portfolio in your 401(k), let me offer some advice to help you make the most of your investment dollars. First, put every single dollar you can into a 401(k).

Besides the initial tax deduction, your money grows free of taxes until you begin taking it out. This is reason enough to participate, but there's another goody that lots of 401(k) participants can enjoy—a matching contribution from their employer.

The average company chips in fifty to sixty cents for every dollar the employee sets aside, sometimes up to 6 percent of pay. In the example above, the employee earning $50,000 puts $4,000 into his 401(k) in 1997. That's 8 percent of pretax income. His employer puts in fifty cents for every dollar up to 6 percent of pretax income. Six percent is $3,000. The company adds $1,500, so the total contribution for 1995 is $5,500. Even before the employee's money is invested, he's already made a 37.5 percent return on his money ($1,500 divided by $4,000). Where else can anyone get such a phenomenal return on his money with absolutely no risk? The employer is actually paying employees to invest, and they're saving taxes to boot.

Assuming our theoretical employee is forty, sets aside $4,000 per year (with a $1,500 company match) through age sixty-five, and the money grows at 12 percent in stock funds, he'll be worth $821,337. Without the $1,500 match, his money will grow to $597,336. The employer match is worth an additional $224,000. The match adds firepower to a 401(k). It's the equivalent of adding a rocket engine to a race car.

It seems a no-brainer to invest in a 401(k) and it is, but about 40 percent of Americans who can participate don't invest anything. Sadly, they'll live to regret it. Of the 60 percent who do participate, most don't invest as much as they should and could. And most invest too conservatively. They opt for money-market funds, so-called low-risk bond funds, and GICs, which guarantee a fixed return. These alternatives barely keep ahead of inflation. Too few people have their money in stock funds, which are the only places to maximize their returns. A 1993 survey of more than two hundred California companies revealed two-thirds of 401(k) assets were in GICs and money-market funds. Stock funds were avoided because they are misperceived to be too risky.

According to a *Wall Street Journal* survey, only 8 percent of all U.S. companies with one hundred and fewer employees have retirement plans. This means more than 30 million Americans will not have retirement plans unless they set them up for themselves. If you're one of the 30 million, pay close attention. I'm going to give an overview of the most common retirement plans that are simple and inexpensive for you to set up. This isn't an exhaustive treatment of the subject. Too many other books have already done that. There are dozens at your local library with lengthy sections on the various retirement plans, and quite a few are dedicated exclusively to the subject. There's more available on retirement plans than you want to know or need to know.

The IRA—individual retirement account—has been available to just about everyone since 1982. Any individual, including a minor, with earned income from salary, commissions, or bonuses (interest and dividend income don't count) can set aside up to $2,000 each year in an IRA. The amount goes up to $2,250 for a married couple with one person working outside the home.

Until Congress passed tax "reform" legislation in 1986, any amount invested in an IRA was deductible from gross income. For example, if a twenty-one-year-old in college earned $3,500 from odd jobs, the student could put as much as $2,000 of that into an IRA. Only $1,500 would be taxable. Today, money going into an IRA may be totally tax deductible, partially tax deductible, or not deductible at all. If you aren't covered by a pension plan, you can deduct every dime that goes into your IRA.

If you're married and one of you is covered by a company retirement plan, the contribution is fully deductible only if annual adjusted gross income is $40,000 or less. Singles covered by a retirement plan at work may deduct the full IRA amount if they earn $25,000 or under. Couples earning between $40,000 and $50,000 and singles earning between $25,000 and $35,000 can deduct part of their IRA contributions. Above $50,000 and $35,000 gross income, respectively, there's no deduction. But gross income can be reduced. Here's how.

Let's suppose a super-saving young couple has an adjusted gross income of $50,000 annually before plan contributions. Each has a 401(k) and participates to the limit, and each can save an additional $2,000 to go into an IRA. As a couple, they set aside the maximum 15 percent—$7,500—into their 401(k)s. After the 401(k) contributions, their adjusted gross income is cut to $42,500. For each of the $2,000 IRA contributions, $1,500 is deductible. The other $500 isn't.

To avoid confusion, the man and woman set up two IRAs apiece—one for money that is tax deductible; the other for money that isn't. When money begins to be withdrawn from the IRAs, which can be as early as age $59\frac{1}{2}$ with no penalty imposed by the IRS, all the money from the tax-deductible IRA is taxed at the individual's rate in the year it's taken out. With a nondeductible IRA, taxes are paid on only part of the money withdrawn under an IRS formula.

If your situation doesn't allow you to deduct any of your IRA contributions but you can still afford to kick in $2,000 a year, I suggest doing it. The benefit to you is all the money grows with no taxes as long as the money remains in the account.

An IRA can be established at almost any financial institution—bank, savings and loan, credit union, stock brokerage. There may be a modest setup charge and what's called an annual maintenance fee in the $50–$100 range, although some firms waive all fees if the account is large enough. Since you're going to be buying shares of companies in America's Finest Companies in your IRA, you want what's called a self-directed account. This means you call the shots and decide what to buy and sell.

For the self-employed like me, there are two other retirement accounts to know about. In a sense, they are gigantic IRAs because they share many of the same features yet allow investors to sock away far more than $2,000 annually. The first is a SEP—simplified employee pension—which is almost identical to an IRA, with one huge difference. You can contribute 15 percent of your self-employment income up to a total of $30,000 per year.

As with an IRA, you can establish and contribute to a SEP for the present year as late as when you file taxes in the following year, including extensions. I don't recommend waiting that late. The earlier you make your annual contribution to a retirement plan, the harder the money will work for you. I'll show you what I mean. You have a SEP for twenty-five years and salt away $5,000 per year, which earns 13 percent in a portfolio of stocks picked from

America's Finest Companies. In the first instance, you invest the $5,000 on the first business day of the year. In the second, you invest the $5,000 the last business day of the year. By investing on the first day of the year instead of the last, you'll wind up with $879,250 rather than $778,098. That's a $101,152 increment on the same investment of $125,000 over two and a half decades. Quite a difference, isn't it?

SEPs can be opened at the same places as IRAs. So can another type of retirement plan, the Keogh. Like the SEP, a Keogh can be used if you're full-time or part-time self-employed. If you're eligible, you can contribute up to 20 percent of pretax income each year or $30,000, whichever is lower. Keoghs offer more flexibility than SEPs, and there's more paperwork involved, too. Another difference is a Keogh has to be set up by December 31 of the year in which you make the first contribution. As with a SEP, you can wait until tax-filing time to make the contribution.

Keoghs come in several types. One is the money-purchase Keogh, which allows up to 20 percent of annual self-employment income (with a $30,000 ceiling) to go into the plan. The hitch is that once you start you must put in the same percentage of income every year unless there's a loss. Skipping a contribution or falling short of the stated percentage may subject you to a huge tax penalty.

Another Keogh is the profit-sharing variety. The beauty of this plan is you can make or not make a contribution each year. You still have the $30,000 upper limit, but the percentage is lower—13 percent.

A defined-benefit Keogh allows you to salt away as much as 100 percent of your self-employment income to guarantee a certain minimum annual withdrawal once you retire. The nearer you are to life after work, the more income you can defer each year. A tax expert or actuary will need to help you if this is the route you choose to go. With the defined-benefit Keogh, you may be able to quickly "catch up" with where you need to be if you haven't planned for retirement and are in your late forties or fifties.

SEPs and Keoghs can be used for small businesses with more than one employee, and there are other retirement plans that might fit your particular needs. I won't get into them here, but I will reiterate the advantages of all contributory retirement plans. One, the money added each year reduces your gross income, hence your current tax liability. Two, your money grows with no tax consequences until it's taken out. Three, the federal government frowns on early withdrawals, so it pays you to stick with your plan. Four, you have the tremendous opportunity to create your own mini-mutual fund of stocks culled from America's Finest Companies within your retirement plan. By doing that, your money will grow steadily at an above-average rate.

CHAPTER SEVEN

Be Your Own Money Manager

Everyone has a scheme for getting rich that will not work.

—MURPHY, ORIGINATOR OF MURPHY'S LAW

One nice thing about being your own money manager and investing exclusively in companies in America's Finest Companies is you'll only have to spend an hour or two each year (the equivalent of a long lunch) on your investment portfolio or portfolios. Then you're finished for another 365 days. It will be that easy and take that little time. This is the message I spread wherever I give a keynote address or lead a workshop. I continually butt heads against the skeptics (mostly professionals who fail to match the market indexes) who say investing can't be that easy, otherwise everyone would be doing it. But it is.

If you'll follow the steps outlined in this chapter, you can ignore daily or weekly gyrations in stock prices. In fact, you can forget about what the Dow Jones industrials, the S & P 500, or other market indexes are doing. Wouldn't that be a big relief? You can also safely ignore all forecasts about the direction of the economy and interest rates. Which way they head won't matter to you.

For the moment picture yourself as the biblical character Noah. God told you the worst storm ever was going to occur in a few months, and you needed to build a boat to withstand the coming forty-day flood. How would you have prepared for such an unprecedented event?

Noah knew. He built the craft to strict proportions to withstand the most horrible storm in history. Replicas have been tested in laboratories under hurricane conditions. Even in storms of that magnitude, the ark remained upright at all times. It never came close to capsizing.

The same principles Noah used to construct his ark are the principles you can use to guide your portfolio through economic and stock-market storms of the future. Whatever happens, you will survive and prosper because you'll know what to do, and what not to do. Your success will not be tied to how much time and effort you spend keeping up with the economy, interest rates, and the anticipated direction of stock prices.

If you love reading about business and investing, you'll probably want to continue subscribing to the publications that deal with these subjects. I suspect, though, you're heavily involved—as a parent, in your business or profession, as a community volunteer. You have little time to track stocks actively or follow the economy, and you don't want to either.

What you'll learn in this chapter will allow you to feel good about everything you're not reading. If you spend a lot of money on newspapers, magazines, and newsletters you don't want to read, cancel them. You can save hundreds of dollars every year, and the savings can go into your portfolio.

Step No. 1. Be Patient

My philosophy of investing is anchored in patience. George F. Baker, founder of First National Bank of New York, the forerunner of Citicorp, said patience is one of three prerequisites for making a fortune in stocks. He knew time is on the side of the investor. He also knew that the longer anyone invests, the better his results will be. History proves it.

Since stock trading began in America in the late 1700s, the longer-term trend has been relentlessly upward. Even the Great Depression of the 1930s appears to be nothing but a blip on a two-hundred-year chart of stock prices. Naturally there are frequent, wide, day-to-day, month-to-month, and even year-to-year swings. But given enough time, stocks go only one way—UP!

Benjamin Franklin counseled, "He that can have patience can have what he will." This advice is certainly on the money for stock investors. It happens to be right for investors in every other field, too. If you'll be patient and give your stock investments time to work for you, you'll be uncommonly successful. Time (as opposed to timing) is on the side of the investor.

Perhaps the most patient investor in the world, and without question the most successful, is Warren Buffett, chairman of Berkshire-Hathaway on the New York Stock Exchange. Buffett was one of Benjamin Graham's students at Columbia University. He learned his lessons well. Berkshire-Hathaway is the most expensive stock in America and has traded for more than $38,000 per share. Buffett is one of America's wealthiest people with an estimated net worth in excess of $16 billion.

Warren Buffett is frequently quoted in the financial media because he has tremendous insight coupled with a quick wit. Many of his quotes are among my favorites, but perhaps the most useful for you is his response to the question "How long should you hold a stock?" Buffett has often said, "Our favorite holding period is forever." Talk about patient. What could be more patient than holding a stock forever?

I'm not asking you to hold any stock forever, but I am asking you to buy and hold for perhaps many years. I want you to be a long-term buyer and owner of companies in America's Finest Companies and sell only when necessary, which won't be that often. You may go for years at a time without selling shares of any company you own, but all the while you'll be buying. Think of a young child. Children are natural accumulators. They want to be surrounded with things—dolls, stuffed animals, toys, books, games—and they rarely want to get rid of any of them. When you invest, I want you to be like a child.

What I recommend is easy. Pick your portfolio of at least five companies, each in a different industry, from the listing in the appendix. Invest the same dollar amount in each. Once a year when the new-edition list comes out from the author, see if the stocks you bought the previous year are still included. If they are, buy more. If one happens to have been dropped, sell and replace it with another company from America's Finest Companies.

Step No. 2. Buy More of What You Already Own

When you buy more of what you already own each year, you'll be employing the time-proven way to buy shares at reasonable prices. This technique is one you'll seldom read about in investment books. It's the only way I know to make money in any stock environment, including the Great Depression. It demands 100 percent commitment to building a diversified portfolio of quality companies. What's the way? It's dollar-cost averaging—buying the same dollar amount of common stocks over time, i.e., quarterly, semiannually, or annually. I prefer once a year because that's easy to remember and requires less record keeping.

Under dollar-cost averaging, there is absolutely no need to predict the short-term direction of stock prices. We already know the long-term direction is up. If you continue buying stocks through good and bad years, dollar-cost averaging keeps the average cost of your purchases below their average market price, guaranteeing you a profit. Here's why.

If you buy a portfolio of stocks today and their prices fall every year for the next three years (as in the Great Depression), each time you buy additional shares you'll purchase them at a lower price than before. Each time you buy more, you'll lower the average cost per share until the stocks bottom and begin to go up again. Think of buying a $400 suit. It goes on sale three months later for $300, so you buy another one in a different color because the price is so attractive. Your average cost per suit drops from $400 to $350. If you buy a third suit for $200, you'll drive the average cost down again to $300. Each suit is still worth $400, but the average cost per suit is $100 less than that.

Assuming the companies you invest in are chosen from America's Finest Companies, their stock prices will stop falling at some point and then resume their long-term uptrends. Once those uptrends begin, you'll discover your average cost per share is under the market value. You'll have a profit. On the other hand, if your stock portfolio goes up immediately and continues up, you'll have a profit, too. Either way, you'll make money. That's the extraordinary attraction of dollar-cost averaging using companies in America's Finest Companies.

Under dollar-cost averaging, it's a mathematical certainty you'll always make money as long as the companies you buy don't go out of business. If you stick exclusively with companies in America's Finest Companies, you won't have to worry about that. A company headed for serious trouble will be delisted well before it gets there.

Assume you invest $1,000 at the beginning of 1995 in a stock that doesn't pay a dividend. The cost is 10 (note: stock prices are written without the dollar sign) per share. You purchase 100 shares. One quarter later the stock has fallen to 9, and you spend another $1,000. The price is 10 percent lower than when you began. Instead of purchasing 100 shares, you get to buy 111.1 shares. The next

A SIMPLE EXAMPLE OF DOLLAR-COST AVERAGING

STOCK PRICE	QUARTERLY INVESTMENT	SHARES PURCHASED	CUMULATIVE AVERAGE COST PER SHARE
10	$1,000	100.0	$10.00
9	1,000	111.1	9.47
8	1,000	125.0	8.93
7	1,000	142.9	8.35
6	1,000	166.7	7.74
5	1,000	200.0	7.09
6	1,000	166.7	6.91
7	1,000	142.9	6.92
8	1,000	125.0	7.03
9	1,000	111.1	7.19
10	1,000	100.0	7.38
Total	$11,000	1,491.4	

quarter the price falls to 8. Then to 7, 6, and 5 in subsequent quarters. Every three months you buy $1,000 of stock.

After six installments you've invested $6,000 of your hard-earned money. The stock has collapsed 50 percent in price. Even though you are very discouraged, you continue to add to your holdings because the company is sound. You believe the stock will eventually come back.

The stock finally turns around and slowly climbs to 7. At this point, the average cost of all shares purchased is $6.92. You have a small profit. From here the profits grow larger as the stock rebounds toward the original price at which you first purchased it.

Eventually the stock recovers to 10. By now you have invested $11,000 total. The stock, first purchased for 10 per share, is still only 10. It had zero appreciation. That's the bad news.

The good news is you paid an average $7.38 for each share purchased. Your profit is $2.62 per share (excluding dividends, which would boost profits if included). The shares are valued at $14,914, a handsome return of 35.6 percent in 2½ years. And the stock is no higher than when you started.

Dollar-cost averaging worked great for an investor even during the most hostile stock-market environment in American history—the Great Depression. Nineteen twenty-nine had to be the worst time ever to start an investment program. How did dollar-cost averaging leave you if you'd been unfortunate enough to begin investing, even in the soundest of companies, on the eve of the Great Depression?

Assume you invested $1,000 on December 31, 1929. Stock prices had already crashed and begun to come down. The worst was yet to come. Standard & Poor's 500 index was 21.4. With $1,000 you would have bought 46.6 "shares" of the index. These shares produced $46 in annual dividends, which were set aside until December 31 the following year. By then the S & P had fallen 28.5 percent to 15.3. You acquired 68.2 more shares for $1,046 (your $1,000 plus the $46 in dividends).

The next December you invested another $1,000, plus $94 in dividends, and bought 134.7 shares of the S & P 500. It plunged 47.1 percent in 1931 for a dreadful 62.2 percent cumulative loss since you started just two years earlier. Time really flies when you seem to be losing

YEAR END	REINVESTED DIVIDENDS	ANNUAL AMT. INVESTED	CUMULATIVE TOTAL INVESTED	S & P 500 12/31	TOTAL SHARES	MARKET VALUE	ANNUAL DIVIDENDS
1929	—	$1,000	$1,000	21.4	46.6	$1,000	$46
1930	$46	1,046	2,046	15.3	114.8	1,761	94
1931	94	1,094	3,140	8.1	249.5	2,026	125
1932	125	1,125	4,265	6.9	412.8	2,844	182
1933	182	1,182	5,446	10.1	529.8	5,351	238
1934	238	1,238	6,685	9.5	660.1	6,271	310
1935	310	1,310	7,995	13.4	757.7	10,176	546
1936	546	1,546	9,540	17.2	847.7	14,563	678

money as fast as hackers lose golf balls. At the end of 1932, the market was down a whopping 67.8 percent. You had shelled out $4,265. Your portfolio was worth $2,844, a dismal 33.3 percent loss, but only half the S & P's loss.

Because you knew dollar-cost averaging demanded total devotion (at this point it seemed more like total insanity), you continued to plunk down $1,000, plus dividends, at the end of each year. By December 31, 1935, you'd invested a total of $7,995. Your gain was 27.3 percent while the S & P index was down 37.4 percent from the end of 1929. One year later you'd made a 52.7 percent profit ($14,563 divided by $9,540) while the index was still almost 20 percent under water.

Dollar-cost averaging is mechanical and overcomes one of the investor's worst enemies, his emotions. Emotions encourage people to buy stocks at exorbitant highs and to dump them at ruinous lows. Dollar-cost averaging puts emotion on the back burner where it belongs and gives every investor the opportunity to amass the shares of highest-quality companies—America's Finest—at reasonable (and sometimes bargain) prices. Dollar-cost averaging unfailingly produces superior results even if you have the misfortune always to buy at market peaks.

T. Rowe Price, a large mutual-fund company, proved that the commitment to invest is far more important than timing the investment. Said another way, "time in" the market is much more valuable than "timing" the market. Their study calculated the growth of a $2,000 annual IRA contribution invested in "shares" of Standard & Poor's 500 index at its highest level each year from 1969 through

1988. On July 31, 1989, the account was worth $171,757, more than four times the total investment of $40,000 spread over two decades. The compound annual total return was 10.1 percent. At that rate, money doubles every seven years, quadruples in fourteen, and expands eightfold in twenty-one.

Another study came up with a similar conclusion. If a "hypothetical hapless" investor invested $10,000 of his savings each year at the market's high from 1979 through 1994, the $160,000 total investment would have grown to more than $540,000 by the end of June 1995. That's in excess of a 235% gain in just a little over 16 years. A portfolio of "safe" Treasury bills invested in similar fashion (at each year's market high) grew to less than $280,000.

Smart Money magazine's September 1995 issue pointed out that during the last 25 years "the worst possible day" to have purchased stocks was January 11, 1973, one day before stock-market indices began a 40% plunge over the ensuing two years. Investing in "the market" on that day, holding on for dear life, reinvesting all dividends and never adding another penny to your portfolio would have required you to wait until April 1978 just to get back to breakeven. Treasury bills and other cash equivalents would have looked much better in the short run, but in the long run they were a miserable comparison. Through mid-1995, stocks racked up a 1,022% gain compared to only 380% for cash.

Even if you wanted to, you couldn't invest at the highest point for stock prices every year for twenty straight years. You probably couldn't do it once. But even if you did, your results would still be excellent—and better than from any other investment. With America's Finest Companies, they'd be exceptional.

Step No. 3. Diversify Your Holdings

How many stocks do you need in your portfolio? You can start with one, but I recommend saving enough money until you can purchase five, each in a different industry. Then you can work your way toward seven, eight, or ten, perhaps even to twelve. More than that is excessive.

Warren Buffett's Berkshire-Hathaway has major stakes in relatively few companies. He believes, as do I, that owning several dozen or several hundred companies leads to mediocrity for investors. Buffett, the world's finest investor, has major stakes in several of the companies in America's Finest Companies including Coca-Cola, Walt Disney, Gillette, and McDonald's. GEICO, a major insurance company, was in America's Finest Companies

	NUMBER OF STOCKS	REDUCTION IN RISK AS % OF POTENTIAL
Underdiversified	2	46.3%
	4	72.0
Well-Diversified	6	81.0
	8	85.7
	10	88.5
Overdiversified	20	94.2
	50	97.7
	100	98.8

before Buffett acquired all of it in 1995. Other major holdings—The Washington Post Co. and Capital Cities/ABC (now owned by Walt Disney) once were in America's Finest Companies. Is it possible that Warren Buffett, like thousands of other investors each year, reads America's Finest Companies? I guess we'll never know for sure.

A number of studies show you can achieve about 90 percent of the benefits of diversification with as few as seven to eight companies, as long as each is in a different industry. The diversification table was adapted from Richard A. Brealey's excellent book *An Introduction to Risk and Return from Common Stocks* (Cambridge, Mass., and London: The M.I.T. Press, 1969). Others will be somewhat different, but all reach the same conclusion.

A ten-stock portfolio provides 88.5 percent of the possible advantages of diversification. Five stocks provide 77.4 percent, twenty stocks 94.2 percent. Once you own eight to ten stocks, each in a different industry, adding others reduces risk almost imperceptibly. It's hardly worth the time and effort to own lots of stocks. Warren Buffett has proved it.

Step No. 4. Buy Only Shares of Companies in America's Finest Companies

There's no special skill to making above-average profits in stocks if you (1) are patient and have an investment horizon of at least five to ten years, (2) add to your holdings regularly, (3) diversify properly, and (4) invest only in the shares of companies that will remain in business and have rising earnings and dividends. Virtually anyone, even a young person, can name at least twenty or thirty companies that fit this mold.

When my daughter was ten she picked a market-beating portfolio of eight stocks without my help. In the spring of 1988, about six months after the biggest stock crash in history, I wanted her to learn a little something about investing her own funds. She had slightly more than $4,000 cash in her college fund; the remainder was already invested.

I asked Gracie, as I fondly call her, to pick eight companies she'd like to own and purchase $500 of each through our stockbroker. It took her only a few minutes to come up with eight names. One was a private company that makes stuffed animals. Another was a yogurt chain, which neither of us knew much about. She scotched those two names and came up with two more. One was Pizza Hut, which is owned by PepsiCo. So she bought PepsiCo. She loves Coca-Cola, too, and bought $500 of that. She also loves Jeep, which is owned by Chrysler.

She was using the copier at my office, so Xerox was one stock to buy. Gracie reasoned electricity and phones will always be in vogue. She purchased Duke Power and Bell-South. She also added McDonald's and NCNB (now NationsBank, headquartered here in Charlotte).

That's a great portfolio, don't you agree? It's high quality and well diversified, even though Coca-Cola and Pep-siCo are in the same business. All eight companies are likely to survive the worst downturn in the economy any of us can imagine. How do I know that? Because all but one, McDonald's, survived the Great Depression. Even though America's Finest Companies wasn't in existence at the time, five of the eight are in it—Coca-Cola, Duke

Power, McDonald's, NationsBank, and PepsiCo. Even a ten-year-old knew that you should always buy the finest companies.

There are several ways to pick a portfolio. The technique you use is not nearly as important as that you invest in nothing but the companies in America's Finest Companies. Only 3 percent of all U.S. public companies make the cut. They have the most consistent growth records. That's why they're going to make money for you regardless of how you pick the portfolio. You can bank on it because the track record is so good. On page 128 is a list of the top performers for the past decade through July 31, 1996.

Most people will fill their portfolios with companies they've heard of. You probably will, too, and that's an excellent way to assemble your portfolio. Scan the alphabetical list of names in the appendix and circle or check the ones you like. If you need an eight-stock portfolio, you can probably find eight companies you like that are in different industries before you get into the Ds.

If you feel you need a certain amount of dividend income, your search may be limited to all the stocks yielding 4 percent and more. There are 105 of those. If you'd rather go for companies that pay little or nothing, you might choose from among the stocks yielding 1 percent or less. There are 40 of those. Maybe you like certain industries, such as banking, utilities, or consumer products. Instead of searching for companies by name, you'll scan the list in the appendix and pay close attention to the industry categories.

Another method to build your portfolio is to choose stocks randomly but not by throwing darts or drawing names. For example, you need eight stocks. Start any-

COMPANY	PRICE CHANGE
Microsoft Corp.	4430%
Home Depot	2228
Linear Technology	1238
Gillette	930
Medtronic	902
Federal National Mortgage	856
Coca-Cola Co.	777
Biomet	744
Superior Industries Intl.	686
Stryker Corp.	612
William Wrigley Jr.	603
Newell Co.	601
Albertson's	584
Crompton & Knowles	576
Franklin Resources	540
UST Inc.	522
Cooper Tire & Rubber	517
Great Lakes Chemical	499
Illinois Tool Works	496
Clayton Homes	475
PepsiCo	475
Circuit City Stores	467
Merck & Co.	457
Schering-Plough	455
Valspar Corp.	447

where on the list and pick every twentieth or thirtieth company until you have eight in various industries. Or pick one company from the As, Cs, Es, Gs, Is, Ks, Ms, and Os or any other group of eight letters you like. It really doesn't matter so much how you pick because you'll end up with a great portfolio in any case.

Step No. 5. Maintain the Same Dollar Amount in Each Stock

When you've chosen your portfolio of at least five companies, the next thing is to purchase approximately the same dollar amount of each. (We'll get into how to open an account and deal with a broker in Chapter 10.) The first place to establish your portfolio is a retirement plan, since money will grow without tax consequences until withdrawn. For now, assume your retirement account is already open. If you're buying five companies, put 20 percent of your money into each. With eight companies, $12\frac{1}{2}$ percent in each; with ten, 10 percent in each. Don't make the mistake so many professionals make when they try to apportion their money among the "best" companies and industries. That's speculation.

For example, a portfolio manager believes drug/health care stocks are undervalued, so he puts 25 percent of his funds into that sector. He also thinks utilities won't do nearly as well, so only 5 percent of his money goes there. When you allocate, you introduce guesswork into what otherwise is a simple process of spreading your money equally among all your holdings. Anyone can speculate about which groups and individual companies have the most promising outlooks, but that's about all they can say. They can't be sure they're going to be right until after the fact. You and I already know we can't peek into the future. I still don't understand why so many professionals believe they can.

Once you've purchased your portfolio, what's next? Nothing. You don't have to do anything until a year has passed. Let dividends accumulate in your account or automatically reinvest them (see Chapter 8). On the first anniversary date of your initial purchases, put more money into your account and buy more of what you already own.

Here's an example of what to do. With $5,000 cash in your IRA, you decide to buy $1,000 of each of five companies. You'll add a sixth later. To make this example easier, I won't take commissions into account in the initial purchases. To make it more convincing, I'm using five of America's Finest Companies, each in a different industry, and going back to the first business day of 1988, January 2, so I can use real results.

The five companies I chose would all have been in America's Finest Companies on that date. They are American Brands, a consumer-products company; Aon Corporation in insurance; Bristol-Myers Squibb, a major pharmaceutical firm; Emerson Electric, a capital-goods company; and SCANA, an electric utility.

I purposely chose five stocks that as a group appreciated far less than the market over the past five years. The odds anyone could pick five underperformers are about two out of a hundred. Odds are only one out of a hundred of choosing six. Even with this handicap, I'll demonstrate the awesome power of dollar-cost averaging and reinvesting your dividends.

It's important for you to know that I did not know in advance how this exercise was going to turn out, nor did I know what the results would be from year to year. I went through it as if I were in your shoes.

During the next twelve months, the market value of your portfolio rises 15.2 percent in value, from $5,000 to $5,760. Four stocks move higher in price, with American Brands the biggest gainer. Emerson Electric drops in price and becomes the most underweighted. At the end of 1988, here's the value of each stock ranked in descending order of value. Note each company raised its dividend during the year (a trait of stocks in America's Finest Companies), so total income is higher by 9.0 percent at year's end than at the beginning.

It's time to add another $2,000 annual contribution to your IRA. That, coupled with the $261.55 in dividends collected in the account in the first year, plus the $1 uninvested, is $2,262.55 ($2,263 rounded) for investment. Adding $2,263 to $5,760 ($8,023) and dividing by five means there should theoretically be $1,604 in each stock (again ignoring commissions). In theory, you'd buy $164 more American Brands, $400 more Aon, $479 more Bristol-Myers Squibb, $484 additional SCANA, and $734 Emerson Electric. That sounds fine on paper, but in reality it's impractical because there are commissions to consider. Most brokers charge a minimum $30 to $40 per transaction. At those rates, between $150 and $200 of the $2,263 new money to invest would be eaten up by commissions. That's too much, so I suggest a different tack.

With the $2,263, buy more of the two companies that are the most underweighted. If you used my full-service broker, you could buy thirty-five shares of SCANA for $1,120 plus roughly $40 commission ($1,160) and thirty-five Emerson Electric for $1,050 plus approximately $40 commission ($1,090). (All commissions are estimates.) There'd be $13 left in the account. The account would then look like this, with SCANA and Emerson Electric clearly overweighted, at least for now.

By the end of the second year, all five stocks have moved higher. Total value of the portfolio is $9,810, a 23.5 percent increase from the beginning of the year.

JANUARY 2, 1988

COMPANY/DIVIDEND	SHARE PRICE	NUMBER SHARES	COST	ANNUAL INCOME
American Brands/$1.16	22	45	$990	$52.20
Aon Corp./$1.26	23	43	989	54.18
Bristol-Myers Squibb/$1.68	41	25	1,025	42.00
Emerson Electric/$1.03	35	29	1,015	29.87
SCANA/$2.38	28	35	980	83.30
			$4,999	$261.55
		Money uninvested	$ 1	
		Total	$5,000	

DECEMBER 31, 1988

COMPANY/DIVIDEND	SHARE PRICE	NUMBER SHARES	VALUE	ANNUAL INCOME
American Brands/$1.26	32	45	$1,440	$56.70
Aon Corp./$1.37	28	43	1,204	58.91
Bristol-Myers Squibb/$2.00	45	25	1,125	50.00
SCANA/$2.45	32	35	1,120	85.75
Emerson Electric/$1.16	30	29	870	33.64
			$5,759	
Money uninvested			$ 1	
		Total	$5,760	$285.00

133

Here's where the portfolio stands, with highest value at the top.

Since it's the beginning of year three, it's time to kick another $2,000 into your IRA and redeploy that amount, plus the $411.35 in dividends and the $13 left over from the previous year. The total market value of your stocks is

JANUARY 2, 1989

COMPANY/DIVIDEND	SHARE PRICE	NUMBER SHARES	MARKET VALUE	ANNUAL INCOME
SCANA/$2.45	32	70	$2,240	$171.50
Emerson Electric/$1.16	30	64	1,920	74.24
American Brands/$1.26	32	45	1,440	56.70
Aon Corp./$1.37	28	43	1,204	58.91
Bristol-Myers Squibb/$2.00	45	25	1,125	50.00
			$7,929	
Money uninvested			$ 13	
Total			$7,942	$411.35

DECEMBER 31, 1989

COMPANY/DIVIDEND	SHARE PRICE	NUMBER SHARES	MARKET VALUE	ANNUAL INCOME
SCANA/$2.51	36	70	$2,520	$175.70
Emerson Electric/$1.28	39	64	2,496	81.92
Aon Corp./$1.49	42	43	1,806	64.07
American Brands/$1.41	35	45	1,575	63.45
Bristol-Myers Squibb/$2.12	56	25	1,400	53.00
			$9,797	
Money uninvested			$ 13	
Total			$9,810	$438.14

$9,797. That, together with the $2,424 to reinvest, adds up to $12,228, or $2,447 per stock. SCANA and Emerson Electric are a little above that. Leave them alone. The other three are less than their proportionate weighting, with Bristol-Myers Squibb most underrepresented, followed by American Brands.

What you want to do is take the $2,424 you're adding to your portfolio and buy more shares of American Brands and Bristol-Myers Squibb. Buy twenty-one more shares of Bristol-Myers Squibb for $1,176, plus $40 commission ($1,216), and thirty-three of American Brands for $1,155 and a $40 commission ($1,195). There's $13 left over. Now the portfolio looks like this:

JANUARY 2, 1990

COMPANY/DIVIDEND	SHARE PRICE	NUMBER SHARES	MARKET VALUE	ANNUAL INCOME
American Brands/$1.41	35	78	$ 2,730	$109.98
Bristol-Myers Squibb/$2.12	56	46	2,576	97.52
SCANA/$2.51	36	70	2,520	175.70
Emerson Electric/$1.28	39	64	2,496	81.92
Aon Corp./$1.49	42	43	1,806	64.07
			$12,128	
	Money uninvested		$ 13	
	Total		$12,141	$529.19

The portfolio has a modest gain in 1990 of 3.9 percent, but as in every year since the portfolio was begun, each of the five companies again raises its dividend. Your portfolio is now worth $12,610 with annual dividend income of $570.90, more than twice as much as when you started.

DECEMBER 31, 1990

COMPANY/DIVIDEND	SHARE PRICE	NUMBER SHARES	MARKET VALUE	ANNUAL INCOME
American Brands/$1.60	41	78	$ 3,198	$124.80
Bristol-Myers Squibb/$2.40	67	46	3,082	110.40
Emerson Electric/$1.34	38	64	2,432	85.76
SCANA/$2.60	34	70	2,380	182.00
Aon Corp./$1.58	35	43	1,505	67.94
			$12,597	
		Money uninvested	$ 13	
		Total	$12,610	$570.90

At the beginning of year four, you're going to invest another $2,000 along with the $529.19 in dividends collected during the previous year and the $13 of uninvested funds, a total of $2,542. That figure added to the portfolio's $12,610 brings the total to $15,152. This means that ideally $3,030 should be invested per stock.

A quick glance at the portfolio shows American Brands and Bristol-Myers Squibb to be slightly overweighted. Emerson Electric and SCANA aren't too far off the mark, while Aon is about half what it should be. Aon needs $1,525 more to bring it up to its ideal average. The portfolio is also big enough now to add a sixth company, which is what I would suggest.

Let's assume you pick Wallace Computer Services as your sixth company. You buy forty shares of Aon for $1,400 and $40 commission ($1,440). That leaves just $1,102 to go into Wallace. You buy fifty-three shares at

20, plus $40 commission. There's just $2 left. This is the portfolio at the beginning of the fourth year.

JANUARY 2, 1991

COMPANY/DIVIDEND	SHARE PRICE	NUMBER SHARES	MARKET VALUE	ANNUAL INCOME
American Brands/$1.60	41	78	$ 3,198	$124.80
Bristol-Myers Squibb/$2.40	67	46	3,082	110.40
Emerson Electric/$1.34	38	64	2,432	85.76
SCANA/$2.60	34	70	2,380	182.00
Aon Corp./$1.58	35	83	2,905	131.14
Wallace Computer/$0.51	20	53	1,060	27.03
			$15,057	
		Money uninvested	$ 2	
		Total	$15,059	$661.13

Your fourth year investing is very satisfying as your portfolio tacks on 24.0 percent more value. Again, as in every previous year, each of your companies raises the dividend. Now it's time to make another $2,000 contribution, alongside $661 of dividends and $2 of uninvested funds—$2,663. The portfolio is worth $18,669, so $3,555 should be apportioned to each of the six holdings ($21,330 divided by six). Bristol-Myers Squibb has the largest weighting. Emerson Electric is second and is just a few dollars off its ideal. Aon, SCANA, and American Brands aren't too wide of the mark either. Wallace Computer Services is $2,283 less than it should be.

Rather than make this complicated and to save commissions, too, I'd invest the whole $2,663 in Wallace. Buy 108 shares at 24. Assuming $60 in commissions, the total

DECEMBER 31, 1991

COMPANY/DIVIDEND	SHARE PRICE	NUMBER SHARES	MARKET VALUE	ANNUAL INCOME
Bristol-Myers Squibb/$2.76	88	46	$ 4,048	$126.96
Emerson Electric/$1.40	55	64	3,520	89.60
American Brands/$1.81	45	78	3,510	141.18
Aon Corp./$1.66	39	83	3,237	137.78
SCANA/$2.67	44	70	3,080	186.90
Wallace Computer/$0.55	24	53	1,272	29.15
			$18,667	
	Money uninvested		$ 2	
	Total		$18,669	$711.57

JANUARY 2, 1992

COMPANY/DIVIDEND	SHARE PRICE	NUMBER SHARES	MARKET VALUE	ANNUAL INCOME
Bristol-Myers Squibb/$2.76	88	46	$ 4,048	$126.96
Wallace Computer/$0.55	24	161	3,864	88.55
Emerson Electric/$1.40	55	64	3,520	89.60
American Brands/$1.81	45	78	3,510	141.18
Aon Corp./$1.66	39	83	3,237	137.78
SCANA/$2.67	44	70	3,080	186.90
			$21,259	
	Money uninvested		$ 11	
	Total		$21,270	$770.97

spent is $2,652 with $11 remaining. How will this work out? Let's go to the end of 1992 and see.

Nineteen ninety-two wasn't a great year, since your portfolio increased less than 1 percent. Nonetheless, it was up. Wallace Computer Services and Aon Corporation

DECEMBER 31, 1992

COMPANY/DIVIDEND	SHARE PRICE	NUMBER SHARES	MARKET VALUE	ANNUAL INCOME
Aon Corp./ $1.77	54	83	$ 4,482	$146.91
Wallace Computer/$0.60	27	161	4,347	96.60
Emerson Electric/$1.47	55	64	3,520	94.08
American Brands/$1.97	40	78	3,120	153.66
Bristol-Myers Squibb/$2.88	67	46	3,082	132.48
SCANA/$2.73	40	70	2,800	191.10
			$21,351	
	Money uninvested		$ 11	
	Total		$21,362	$814.83

scored nice gains. Emerson Electric was flat while Bristol-Myers Squibb lost 21 points, American Brands shed 5 points, and SCANA fell 4.

To date, you've shown the following results and a profit every year for five straight years:

1988 +15.2%
1989 +23.5
1990 + 3.9
1991 +24.0
1992 + 0.5

This is equivalent to a compound annual return of 13.0 percent, one percentage point better than the market's return since World War II. And remember, it was achieved with six stocks that all lagged the market, in some cases by a wide margin.

At this point you have a portfolio that's grown from

$5,000 at the beginning of year one (1988) to $21,362 at the end of five years (1992). You added $2,000 per year for four years, which combined with the original capital of $5,000 is a total of $13,000 invested. The $8,362 difference (64 percent more than you put in) is from appreciation and dividends reinvested. Annual dividend income is now more than three times what it was just five years ago.

The portfolio is out of balance because Aon and Wallace Computer Services are far larger than the other four positions. You're going to add another $2,000 at the start of 1993, and along with that $771 in dividends and the $11 uninvested. That adds up to $2,782 new dollars to invest. By adding $2,782 to the portfolio's value, $21,362, we get $24,144, which works out to $4,024 per stock. You could purchase thirty-five shares of SCANA for $1,390 and $40 commission ($1,430), and nineteen Bristol-Myers Squibb for $1,273 plus $40 commission ($1,313). There'd be $29 left over.

JANUARY 2, 1993

COMPANY/DIVIDEND	SHARE PRICE	NUMBER SHARES	MARKET VALUE	ANNUAL INCOME
Aon Corp./$1.77	54	83	$4,482	$146.91
Bristol-Myers Squibb/$2.88	67	65	4,355	187.20
Wallace Computer/$0.60	27	161	4,347	96.60
SCANA/$2.73	40	105	4,200	286.65
Emerson Electric/$1.47	55	64	3,520	94.08
American Brands/$1.97	40	78	3,120	153.66
			$24,024	
		Money uninvested	$ 29	
		Total	$24,053	$965.10

DECEMBER 31, 1993

COMPANY/DIVIDEND	SHARE PRICE	NUMBER SHARES	MARKET VALUE	ANNUAL INCOME
Wallace Computer/$0.64	34	161	$5,474	$103.04
SCANA/$2.74	50	105	5,250	287.70
Aon Corp./$1.80	48	83	3,984	149.40
Emerson Electric/$1.56	60	64	3,840	99.84
American Brands/$1.97	33	78	2,574	153.66
Bristol-Myers Squibb/$2.92	58	65	3,770	189.80
			$24,892	
	Money uninvested		$ 29	
	Total		$24,921	$983.80

At the beginning of 1994, you make the regular $2,000 contribution to your portfolio, which was up again for the sixth year in a row. That, coupled with $965 in dividends accumulated in 1993 and the $29 uninvested funds in your

JANUARY 2, 1994

COMPANY/DIVIDEND	SHARE PRICE	NUMBER SHARES	MARKET VALUE	ANNUAL INCOME
Wallace Computer/$0.64	34	161	$5,474	$103.04
SCANA/$2.82	50	105	5,250	296.10
Bristol-Myers Squibb/$2.92	58	85	4,930	248.20
American Brands/$1.97	33	130	4,290	256.10
Aon Corp./$1.80	48	83	3,984	149.40
Emerson Electric/$1.56	60	64	3,840	99.84
			$27,768	
	Money uninvested		$ 28	
	Total		$27,796	$1,152.68

account, adds up to $2,994. Add that figure to the $24,921 portfolio value and you have $27,915—$4,653 ideally invested in each of the six companies.

The two smallest positions are Bristol-Myers Squibb and American Brands. You can buy more of each: fifty-two shares of American Brands ($1,716 and $50 commission) and twenty Bristol-Myers Squibb ($1,160 and $40 commission), a total investment of $2,966. There's $28 uninvested.

The first edition of this book ended with the portfolio on page 141, but rather than show all the additional portfolios (which I track on my computer) since then in this newest edition, I'm going to describe the results to date. I'm certain that by now you understand how to keep adding to your portfolio and rebalance it, all the while keeping time and commissions to the bare minimum.

The portfolio dropped 3.1% in value in 1994 (following a meager rise of 3.6% in 1993), in line with the general market, from $27,796 to $26,945. During the year, Aon Corp. split its stock 3-for-2, which means that for every two shares an investor owned he received one additional share. At year's end the number of Aon shares had increased from 83 to 125.

Two thousand dollars was again invested in the portfolio on January 2, 1995, along with $1,168 in dividends collected during the previous year and a few dollars in uninvested cash. I decided to add a seventh stock in America's Finest Companies, McDonald's. I purchased 109 shares at 29 for a total cost of $3,161 plus commission. McDonald's had the lowest weighting of all seven stocks in the portfolio, but that was okay. Total value of the portfolio: $30,088.

In 1995 I had to make a sell for the first time. Wallace Computer Services was the subject of what I thought was a generous buyout offer from Moore Corp., so I sold all 161 shares on September 11 at 57¾ minus commission. (It was 29 at the start of the year.) I bought 200 shares of Loral Corp. (which was on the "Finest Buys" list in my monthly newsletter, *The Staton Institute*^{SM} *Advisory*) and added to McDonald's—103 more shares at 37. SCANA had a 2-for-1 stock split during the year, so the number of shares doubled from 105 to 210.

By the way, 1995 was one of the best years for stocks, but this portfolio outshone all but a handful of money managers. It rose from $30,088 at the beginning of the year to $48,479 at year's end, a whopping 61.1% gain. That was so spectacular even I had a hard time believing it, but it was true.

Through the end of 1995, the portfolio's annual returns look like this:

1988	+15.2%
1989	+23.5
1990	+ 3.9
1991	+24.0
1992	+ 0.5
1993	+ 3.6
1994	− 3.1
1995	+61.1

Excluding annual contributions, the compound annual return for the eight years to date is 14.6% per year, in line with the 13–15% historic performance of the companies in America's Finest Companies. Again, I'd like to reemphasize that I've stacked this IRA portfolio with companies (excluding McDonald's and Loral Corp.) that have been performing worse than stocks in general. The odds of doing that accidentally are less than one in one hundred.

As always, I added another $2,000 on January 2, 1996 to the IRA and used that, along with $1,169 in dividends and $22 uninvested cash, to purchase Emerson Electric, the most underweighted stock at the end of 1995. I bought 38 shares at 82, and that kicked the number of shares from 64 to 102. Here's what the portfolio looked like ranked in order of value.

JANUARY 2, 1996

COMPANY/DIVIDEND	SHARE PRICE	NUMBER SHARES	MARKET VALUE	ANNUAL INCOME
McDonald's Corp./$0.27	45	212	$ 9,540	$ 57.24
Emerson Electric/$1.96	82	102	8,364	199.92
Bristol-Myers Squibb/$2.96	86	85	7,310	251.60
Loral Corp./$0.32	35	200	7,000	64.00
Aon Corp./$1.36	50	125	6,250	170.00
SCANA/1.44	29	210	6,090	302.40
American Brands/$2.00	45	130	5,850	260.00
			$50,404	
		Money uninvested	$ 50	
		Total	$50,454	$1,305.16

Stocks came out of the starting gate with a bang in 1996 and by January 8 another company in the IRA was bid for. Lockheed Martin (in America's Finest Companies) said it wanted to acquire Loral Corp. I sold Loral at 44½ minus commission and bought 300 John H. Harland at 21 and 170 Washington REIT at 15, both plus commission. Both Harland and Washington were on my "Finest Buys" list on that date. Both had been relative underperformers for several years, but I thought the value was there. Certainly there appeared to be little, if any, downside risk because the dividend yields from both were so far above that of the typical stock.

At January 8, 1996, the portfolio looked like this:

JANUARY 8, 1996

COMPANY/DIVIDEND	SHARE PRICE	NUMBER SHARES	MARKET VALUE	ANNUAL INCOME
McDonald's Corp./$0.27	45	212	$ 9,540	$ 57.24
Emerson Electric/$1.96	81	102	8,262	199.92
Bristol-Myers Squibb/$2.96	84	85	7,140	251.60
Aon Corp./$1.36	51	125	6,375	170.00
John H. Harland/$1.02	21	300	6,300	306.00
SCANA/1.44	28	210	5,880	302.40
American Brands/$2.00	45	130	5,850	260.00
Washington REIT/$1.00	15	170	2,550	170.00
			$51,897	
		Money uninvested	$ 25	
		Total	$51,922	$1,717.16

Although there's no practical way to keep exactly one-eighth of your portfolio in each of the eight companies, you've done an excellent job so far by buying more shares each year of the one or two most underweighted companies in the portfolio. You're getting more than 85 percent of the benefits of diversification with just eight companies. With occasional juggling, you can keep the portfolio in good proportion while still adding the annual $2,000 maximum and reinvesting all dividends and uninvested cash. The balance doesn't have to be perfect, only as exact as you can make it.

STEP NO. 6. SELL RARELY

To recap: Start with a portfolio of at least five stocks in America's Finest Companies. Each year check the latest compilation of America's Finest Companies to see whether all the companies you own are still included. If they are, buy more as shown above. If one's been knocked out of the box, replace it with another. By using this simple approach, you'll sell infrequently while simultaneously continuing to accumulate shares of the finest companies on the market.

Stock-market and investing books are chock-full of all sorts of information, much of it half-baked, about how to time the market and sell at the right times. I'm not very good at selling because it's much more difficult to know when a stock is overpriced than it is to know when it's underpriced. Spotting a cheap stock and buying it is easy for me. Finding one that's not going any higher and may be headed for a fall is a lot tougher.

That's why I recommend only three reasons to sell. One is to bring a stock that's overweighted in your portfolio back into line. You sell part of it. Two is to get rid of a stock that's been dropped from America's Finest Companies. You sell all of it. Three is you need the money. You may sell part or all of your holdings depending on how much money is required. Other than these, I recommend buying and not selling.

I'm in the camp with Warren Buffett. Buffett says he loves buying, but selling is a different story. He compares the pace of his selling activity with a traveler stranded in Podunk's lone hotel. There was no TV in the room, so the stranger faced a long unfruitful evening. However, he soon discovered a book on his night table called *Things to Do in Podunk*. Excitedly opening it, the traveler found only a single line, "You're doing it."

You can be your own successful money manager by following these six steps:

1. Be patient.
2. Buy more of what you already own.
3. Diversify your holdings.
4. Buy only the shares of companies in America's Finest Companies.
5. Maintain the same dollar amount in each stock.
6. Sell rarely.

Of course you can make managing your money a lot more complicated than this. Most professionals and ordinary folk do. But it's not necessary. Why make money the hard way if there's an easier way? That's what I've always asked myself. By the time I was thirty-one, I had earned my first million from investing in stocks. I spent a lot of time analyzing and agonizing over my portfolios. Within five years, I was worth more than three million. Getting to that point was a lot easier because I was simplifying the process. Today my personal investment process is the same one I'm advocating for you. It's easy to understand, simple to put into practice, and most important, it works.

Opponents of my method will mention this or that mutual fund that has, according to some mutual-fund survey, beat the pants off the market in recent years. They'll wonder why you weren't investing in those funds. Good question. In Chapter 5 I proved most funds fail even to equal the market every year, let alone beat it. The percentage of stock funds that will beat the market over any ten-year period is remarkably small—less than 5 percent from 1983 to 1993. Will you be able to pick the market beaters from more than eight thousand funds? I'll give odds you won't, and I'll win more than enough bets to retire wealthy from the bets alone.

Stocks in America's Finest Companies, as a group, have consistently beaten the market by several percentage points, either from capital appreciation alone or with dividends reinvested. The eleven stocks from "The Super 50 Team" with dividend reinvestment plans returned 22.9 percent compounded annually versus 16.2 percent from the S & P 500. That's a 6.7 percent difference. Suppose five of those stocks were your portfolio over the past decade and commissions were a whopping 10 percent on each $2,000 investment as well as on the initial $5,000. The first $4,500 ($5,000 less $500 commission) investment would have grown to $35,377. The remaining nine $1,800 annual contributions ($2,000 less $200 commission) would have piled up to $52,135, a total of $87,512. That same money invested in the market, assuming no loads or annual fees, would have amounted to $63,503, or $24,009 less.

GETTING STARTED WITH A LITTLE OR A LOT

I've showed you how to start with $5,000 and add $2,000 a year, the maximum allowed by law, to an IRA. But you may have a lot less than that to begin with, or you may have a lot more.

Suppose you're eighteen and in college. You get a job as I did when I was in school and earn $2,500 each of the four years you're there. You need most of that money for living expenses but can invest $50 each month. Since you have earned income, you're allowed to contribute to an IRA.

You open an account with a discount brokerage firm (where commissions are cheaper) and mail them a $50 check monthly for twelve months; this is invested in a money-market fund earning 3 percent. At the end of the year you've saved $600 and earned about $9 interest. Pick one stock you like from the stocks in America's Finest Companies and buy it. Less $35 estimated commission (because you're using a discount broker) you'll put roughly $574 to work. Follow this same routine each of the next three years you're in school and buy a different stock each time. Make sure it's in a different industry.

When you graduate, you'll have invested $2,400 (less commissions) and will own a few shares of four different companies. Since you're armed with a college degree, you should soon start earning far more than $2,500 and be able to contribute the maximum $2,000 per year if your employer doesn't offer a 401(k) plan. If your employer does, you should invest in his plan first because you can put away far more than $2,000 a year. For this example, I'm assuming you're not covered at work.

You're now twenty-two and your little IRA has grown to $4,000. No doubt it's out of balance. When you make your first $2,000 annual contribution, you'll have enough money to add a fifth stock in a different industry. Follow the same technique outlined earlier to invest $2,000 annually and maintain balance. Sounds simple, and it is.

Now let's shift gears for a minute and pretend you're self-employed. No one else works with you. You realize you've got zero dollars set aside for life after work and need help, so you rush out and purchase a copy of this book. After completing Chapter 6 on retirement plans, you open a SEP or Keogh. Take your pick. You fund it with a $10,000 contribution at age 50 and bump up the contribution each year by 10 percent. By age 60, you're up to $25,937 annually, which is $4,063 less than the maximum $30,000 you're allowed to contribute under today's law. By the time you're 60 the limit is probably going to be significantly higher. Your money grows at 12 percent each year, the same rate as common stocks since World War II. Since you're investing exclusively in America's Finest Companies, it ought to grow at 13–15 percent, but I'm being conservative.

You see from this example that after eleven annual contributions (at the beginning of each year), you've put $185,310 into your SEP or Keogh. When you are age 65, it will have grown to $551,112 (nearly tripled) and five

A SEP/KEOGH GROWS RAPIDLY EVEN WHEN YOU START LATE

START AGE	ANNUAL $ CONTRIBUTION INCREASES 10% ANNUALLY/EARNS 12% TAX DEFERRED
50	10,000
51	11,000
52	12,100
53	13,310
54	14,641
55	16,105
56	17,716
57	19,487
58	21,436
59	23,579
60	25,937

Total Contributions:	$185,310
Worth at Age 65:	$551,112
Worth at Age 70:	$971,248
Worth at Age 75:	$1,711,671

years later will be approaching a million dollars (more than quintupled).

If you can start a portfolio with as much as $10,000 and add at a rate similar to this, you should spread the money equally among six companies rather than five. In the illustration you could stay with six stocks until age 55 and then add a seventh, which ought to be sufficient diversification. Again, you'll follow the same technique described earlier.

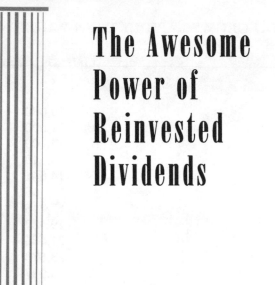

CHAPTER EIGHT

The Awesome Power of Reinvested Dividends

Whenever you see the compound annual returns from the Dow Jones industrial average and Standard & Poor's 500 composite index, they include quarterly reinvestment of all dividends. Without dividend reinvestment, annual returns from stocks would be about as exciting as watching a silent movie.

One dollar invested in the S & P 500 at the end of 1925, with dividends reinvested, mushroomed to $1,113.92 by the end of 1995. John Connallon, an investment strategist at Smith Barney, asked a number of the firm's research analysts to guess what percentage was from capital appreciation and what was from dividend reinvestment. The average guess came in at 60 percent capital gains, 40 percent dividend reinvestment. The answer is that about 95 percent was from reinvested dividends while 5 percent was from capital gains. Said another way, dividends reinvested generated nearly twenty times the return from capital appreciation.

Approximately one thousand companies allow you to automatically reinvest your dividends in shares of their stock through DRPs—dividend reinvestment plans. Two hundred ninety-three of America's Finest Companies (70 percent) have them; twenty-two offer a discount to market price in addition. The standard way to open a DRP is to buy a few shares of a company (like Hershey Foods) that offers it and have the shares registered in your name. The shares are then mailed directly to you, along with a simple DRP signup form. You fill in a few blanks and return it to the company. Each quarter, instead of mailing you a dividend check, Hershey and every company in whose DRP you participate will send you a form like the one shown on the following page.

All DRP statements are similar and easy to read. This one is the statement of my seven-year-old son, Will, who owns more than four hundred shares of this particular company. He also participates in four other DRPs. You probably already guessed the companies are among America's Finest Companies. Since he's a minor, an adult has to be custodian of the account. In this case Will's mother is his custodian.

The bottom left-hand corner of this statement shows that 412 shares are owned by Will and registered in his name outside the plan. Just to the right of that number, you see 25.7178. That's the number of shares Will had

DIVIDEND REINVESTMENT AND STOCK PURCHASE PLAN

Public Service Company
Of North Carolina Inc

FOR SHAREHOLDERS OF PUBLIC SERVICE COMPANY OF NORTH CAROLINA, INC.   XXX-XX-XXXX

ADDRESS ALL CORRESPONDENCE TO
FIRST UNION NATIONAL BANK, AGENT
DIVIDEND REINVESTMENT SERVICE
TWO FIRST UNION CENTER
CHARLOTTE, N.C. 28288-1154
(1-800-829-8432)

JOHN DOE
1111 MAIN STREET
CHARLOTTE NC 11111   AMOUNT ENCLOSED:

TO MAKE AN OPTIONAL CASH PAYMENT, PLEASE DETACH AND MAIL WITH YOUR CHECK

FOR SHAREHOLDERS OF PUBLIC SERVICE COMPANY OF NORTH CAROLINA, INC.

Shareholder Account Number:	Taxpayer Identification Number	Investment Date	Record Date	Dividend Payment Date	Quarterly Dividend Rate Per Share
XXXXX	XXX-XX-XXXX	10/01/93	09/10/93	10/01/93	S.19750

DATE OF TRANSACTION	TYPE OF TRANSACTION	AMOUNT OF TRANSACTION	SERVICE CHARGE	NET AMOUNT INVESTED	PRICE PER SHARE	SHARES ACQUIRED OR WITHDRAWN	TOTAL SHARES HELD IN PLAN
					PRIOR BALANCE ♦♦♦♦♦♦ ➤		10.1880
01/04/93	STOCK DIVIDEND	0.00	.00	0.00	0.0000	5.0940	15.2820
04/01/93	COMMON DIVIDEND	78.28	.00	78.28	16.2450	4.8187	20.1007
04/01/93	PLAN DIVIDEND	2.90	.00	2.90	16.2450	0.1785	20.2792
07/01/93	COMMON DIVIDEND	81.37	.00	81.37	15.6988	5.1832	25.4624
07/01/93	PLAN DIVIDEND	4.01	.00	4.01	15.6988	0.2554	25.7178
10/01/93	COMMON DIVIDEND	81.37	.00	81.37	17.5038	4.6487	30.3665
10/01/93	PLAN DIVIDEND	5.08	.00	5.08	17.5038	0.2902	30.6567

PLAN DATA FOR CURRENT PERIOD				
	PURCHASE PRICE			
FIVE-DAY AVERAGE CLOSING PRICE	WITH REINVESTED DIVIDENDS	WITH OPTIONAL CASH PAYMENTS	AVERAGE OR HIGH AND LOW PRICE ON	
			10/01/93	
18.425	17.5038	18.425	17.875	

Shares held on record date								
HELD BY YOU	HELD IN PLAN			TOTAL DIVIDENDS PAID	TAX WITHHELD IF ANY	NET DIVIDEND REINVESTED	SERVICE CHARGES	SHARES ACQUIRED WITH REINVESTED DIVIDENDS AND OPTIONAL CASH	TAXABLE DIVIDEND INCOME
FULL	FULL	Fraction							
412	25.7178		Current	86.45	0.00	86.45	0.00	4.9389	88.29
			Year to Date	333.37	0.00	333.37	0.00		349.14

(See the reverse side for additional information)
IMPORTANT: RETAIN THIS STATEMENT FOR YOUR INVESTMENT AND TAX RECORDS

FORM P903 (10.93)

in the plan before the most recent dividend was reinvested.

This is the last of four statements Will received in 1993. On October 1 a total of $86.45 in dividends was used to purchase more stock; $81.37 was from the 412 shares outside the plan, $5.08 from the shares inside the plan. There was no service charge to buy the new shares, so 100 percent of the dividend went to work for Will. The price per share was 17.5038, and 4.9407 shares were acquired (4.6987 plus 0.2902). After the dividends were reinvested, Will owned 30.6567 shares within the DRP.

This company will automatically reinvest dividends each quarter, and there are no commissions or other charges. The company absorbs them for you. That's one great benefit of participating in DRPs. Many companies pick up the entire commission tab. Even if they don't, using a DRP is still a good deal because the commissions (and other charges) are far less than you'd pay a broker, especially on a small amount of money like $86 per quarter.

Most companies with DRPs also offer OCPs—optional cash payment plans. The company in this example does, too. About one-third down from the top of the form note the sentence "To make an optional cash payment, please detach and mail with your check." You tear off the top of the form and send it in with your money. OCPs have minimum and maximum amounts that can be contributed each quarter. The minimum is typically $25–$50 while the maximum can be $1,000, $2,000, and more.

Each quarter when this statement comes in, we have the option (but we don't have to exercise it) to mail as little as $25 or as much as $3,000 to the address shown and buy more shares of stock for Will. As with reinvested dividends, this company also pays the commission. If we send in $1,000 the entire $1,000 goes to work for my son, not a broker. If we buy more shares through the lowest-cost broker we can find, we're looking at $25 or more in unnecessary commissions.

Because of DRPs and OCPs, it's possible to begin a portfolio with as little as $500 and still invest in five different companies. The technique I'm discussing here is especially useful for a young person or anyone else who can only afford to start small. Let's assume twenty-year-old Mary saves $50 a month for ten months to accumulate $500. She picks five companies with dividend reinvestment plans, each in a different industry. For simplicity, let's also assume each company sells for $50 per share and the commission to buy one share is also $50. Mary plunks down $500, $250 of which buys five shares of stock. The other $250, half her money, goes to the broker. This is not a good deal for Mary if she keeps investing $500 at a time because the broker will be taking half. But it is when she utilizes the OCPs.

Mary makes sure the one share of each of the five companies is registered in her name (not in "street" name, meaning it is held by the broker) and delivered to her. She then signs on for each company's dividend reinvestment plan. After the companies pay their next quarterly dividends, Mary will receive five statements that look similar to Will's statement. Almost without question, all her companies will have optional cash payment plans, and those will show on the fronts of the statements.

Before making her initial purchases, Mary should call

each company (phone numbers are in the appendix) and ask for DRP and OCP information. She'll want to know about service fees and commissions, if any, and minimum-maximum limits for the OCPs. About 10 percent of the thousand companies offering DRPs charge a service fee. In most cases, they're capped at $3.00 and are little more than a nuisance. As the number of shares owned grows larger, the service fee shrinks as a percent of the dividends reinvested. Even so, if you're working with a small amount of money, the charges from some companies might make quarterly reinvestment a bad deal.

Mary will also want to inquire whether buying one share of stock is enough to open a company's DRP. If not, there are plenty that only require one share to begin. Those are the companies to stick with.

For years, one of the companies in America's Finest Companies, Bristol-Myers Squibb, would allow investors to begin a DRP with just one share of stock. They could also buy additional shares with their cash dividends without paying a fee or brokerage commission. Stock purchases up to $3,000 per quarter were also free of fees or commissions. Then the company had a change of heart. It set a fifty-share minimum to participate in the DRP and also initiated a charge on shares purchased through the plan, and another charge when the shares are sold.

Mary continues to save $50 per month. After two months she has $100 to be mailed to the first of the five companies for investment. After two more months, she mails another $100 to the second, and so forth. At the end of twelve months, $600 is invested—$200 in the first company and $100 apiece in companies two through five. The next $100 goes into the second company, and the cycle continues.

After two years, the portfolio will be out of balance because one or more of the stocks will have done better than the others. That's easy to correct. Mary adjusts her optional cash payments to buy a little more of the stocks that have gone up the least and a little less of the ones that have gone up the most. As she gradually increases her savings from $50 to $60 to $70 and more per month, she increases the size of the extra cash payments. All the while she's paying no commission dollars to a broker. Her companies are picking up all, or most, of the transactions costs. As Mary continues her dollar-cost averaging program through the years, she'll save hundreds, if not thousands, in commissions. All those saved dollars will be working for her.

When I started an investment program for Will in 1992, his mother and I invested roughly $5,000 in each of five different companies. Total commissions were $621 through our full-service broker. As we invest an additional $5,000 per company, we'll save the entire $621 because Will's companies will absorb the costs. Since Will is only five, the $621 we don't spend—and which should compound at 13–15 percent annually—will grow to a minimum of $950,163 and a maximum of $2,722,463 by the time Will is 65. Staggering, isn't it?

There are drawbacks to dividend reinvestment plans whether they have the optional cash-payment feature or not. One is you can't instantly sell the shares held in the plan. You have to detach part of the quarterly DRP form and mail it back to the company or the financial institution administering the plan. With one of Will's companies, you'd have three options: (1) a stock certificate in your name for some of the shares in the plan (you name the amount); (2) a stock certificate in your name for all shares in the plan and your participation terminated; (3) your plan participation terminated by selling all and partial shares at the next available date, then the proceeds mailed to you. If the shares were in a brokerage account, you could sell them and get the money in a few days, sometimes the same day. With a DRP it will take weeks.

I own shares in a DRP that won't sell them for me. They'll mail me a certificate for all or some of the shares if I ask. Then I have to take the certificate to my broker to sell them. All that takes time and effort on my part.

When you want to buy shares of a company, you simply call your broker and buy them. In an OCP it can take weeks for the company to invest your money. Why? Because the company pools everyone's OCP contributions and buys only at certain times of the year. Your money and everyone else's sits idle in an omnibus account without earning interest until investment day arrives. That's bad. What's good is buying in "bulk" allows a company to keep commission expenses minimal.

Another drawback to a DRP is you need to save the final quarterly statement of each company each year for tax purposes. It will show all four quarterly transactions and the amount of dividends reinvested. Otherwise you won't know how much you paid for the shares. One trap a lot of investors fall into is they pay taxes twice on reinvested dividends. First, they pay taxes on dividends in the year they were reinvested. If they fail to add those reinvested dividends back to the cost of the original shares and "step up" their cost basis, they'll pay taxes on the dividends again when the shares are sold because the capital gain will be larger than it should be.

If you participate in a lot of DRPs, as some investors do, you'll never have an accurate picture of the value or balance of your portfolio unless you calculate it. And you might not be able to use DRPs for your retirement plan. That's because a financial institution has to domicile the account and hold all your securities in street name. When they're in street name, you can't participate in DRPs.

It is possible to participate in individual company dividend reinvestment plans through retirement plans, but it's not for everybody. A lot depends on the current size of your account because the fees involved might end up being more than the commissions you save.

There are several financial institutions across the country that handle this unusual service, and the leader appears to be First Trust. You can call them at 800/426-6242 for more information and a free kit. First Trust advertises that "if you are looking for a way to save with minimal investment amounts, the DRP IRA is for you." They also say that if you have rollovers, transfers, SEPs, or account consolidations worth $100,000 and more, they offer a free jumbo IRA.

First Trust has no establishment fees, no commissions or transaction fees and a minimal annual fee for smaller accounts. For the jumbos, the annual fee is waived. If you try First Trust and like them, please let me know.

For investors seeking dividend reinvestment without having to open accounts with each company, a number of brokerage firms, both large and small, have come to the rescue and more are on the way. Firms including Charles Schwab, Smith Barney, and Merrill Lynch allow investors to participate in the DRPs of approximately four thousand companies, whether those companies have DRPs in place or not. One terrific benefit is that retirement plans are usually included. Schwab is the nation's largest discount broker, whereas Merrill Lynch is the largest full-service firm. Smith Barney is one of the larger full-service firms as well.

There are many advantages to reinvesting dividends through a brokerage account rather than company by company. First, you can add the awesome power of dividend reinvestment for your retirement plan as well as for a taxable account. Second, you'll get one monthly statement (rather than quarterly statements from individual companies) showing the value of each stock and the amount of dividends reinvested. It's much easier to keep your portfolio balanced when all your holdings are together. It's easier at tax time, too, because all transactions are on one statement, not several.

Third, if you happen to lose one of your brokerage statements, it's easy to get a replacement by calling your account executive. I can get a copy from my broker by fax the same day I request it. If you lose a company's DRP statement, it's sometimes difficult to get another copy. More than one phone call or letter may be required.

Fourth, there are so many more companies from which to choose. I don't know the exact number of companies offering DRPs, but there are estimates ranging from nine hundred to eleven hundred. I usually say about a thousand. By going through a broker for dividend reinvestment, you can choose from close to four thousand companies.

Since I want you to invest only in America's Finest Companies, having four thousand choices compared with one thousand isn't the optimum benefit. The optimum is you can reinvest quarterly dividends in virtually all the companies in America's Finest Companies in either a taxable account, a nontaxable account, or even better, both. There's an easy way to find out which qualify; just ask the broker before making your purchases. If one you like isn't in their group of four thousand or so, substitute another that is. Then tell the broker you think it should be.

The main disadvantage of a dividend reinvestment brokerage account is you can't participate in optional cash payment plans. You'll always have to pay a commission to add to your holdings. To me that isn't a great detriment, but it may be to you. Is the convenience and ease of record keeping worth more than the commission costs? Only you can decide.

One way to handle this dilemma is to make taxable investments through individual dividend reinvestment plans and use OCPs to save commissions. Make nontaxable investments through a broker offering dividend reinvestment for retirement plans. Even though you won't get the benefit of OCPs, you will be able to reinvest dividends and add compounding power to your portfolio.

Earlier in the chapter I mentioned that twenty-two AFC companies allow you to reinvest dividends and make optional cash payments at discounts to market value ranging from 1 percent to 5 percent. The discounts are taxable as ordinary income. The twenty-two are shown here alphabetically with their discounts.

American Water Works Co.   5%
California Water Service Co.   3
CNB Bancshares Inc.   3
Colonial Gas Co.   5
Connecticut Water Service   5
EnergyNorth Inc.   5
First Michigan Bank Corp.   5
First of America Bank Corp.   5
First Union Corp.   1
H.B. Fuller Co.   3
Household International Inc.   2.5
Huntington Bancshares   5
Mercantile Bankshares   5
New Plan Realty Trust   5
North Carolina Natural Gas   5
Piedmont Natural Gas Co.   5
Public Service Co. of NC   5
Southern National Corp.   3
Telephone & Data Systems   5
United Cities Gas Co.   5
Utilicorp United Inc.   5
Valley Resources Inc.   5

Thirty-five companies in America's Finest Companies allow you to buy initial shares direct without going through a broker. They have varying requirements about the number of shares you must buy to start your investment program. Some require that you be either a customer or a resident in their service areas before making your first purchase. For specifics contact the ones in which you're interested. Their phone numbers are in the alphabetical list at the back of this directory.

AFLAC Inc.
American Water Works Co.
American Recreation Centers
Bancorp Hawaii Inc.
Bard, C.R. Inc.
Bob Evans Farms Inc.
Brooklyn Union Gas Co.
Central Fidelity Banks Inc.
Central & South West Corp.
Connecticut Water Service
Duke Power Co.
Energen Corp.
Enova Corp.
Exxon Corp.
Johnson Controls Inc.
Florida Progress Corp.
Hawaiian Electric Industries
Home Depot Inc.

Madison Gas & Electric Co.
McDonald's Corp.
Minnesota Power & Light
Northern States Power Co.
Northwestern Public
 Service
Piedmont Natural Gas Co.
Procter & Gamble Co.
Reader's Digest Association
Regions Financial Corp.
SCANA Corp.
Union Electric Co.
UtiliCorp United Inc.
Wal-Mart Stores Inc.
Western Resources Inc.
WICOR Inc.
Wisconsin Energy Corp.
WPS Resources Corp.

Five companies offer IRAs: Connecticut Water Service, Exxon Corp., McDonald's Corp., SBC Communications, and UtiliCorp United.

CHAPTER NINE

How to Dodge Uncle Sam Outside Your Retirement Plan

You've got to hand it to the IRS. If you don't, they'll come get it.

—ANONYMOUS

Money inside a retirement plan receives preferential treatment because it grows without taxes until withdrawn. If you sell appreciated stock in your retirement plan, there will never be any capital-gains taxes to pay. Taxes are paid only when money is withdrawn, beginning as early as fifty-nine and a half and no later than seventy and a half.

Money outside a retirement plan is treated poorly by both Uncle Sam and all the states with income taxes. Taxes on dividends and capital gains must be paid in the years they're realized. Although losses can be used to offset gains, that's not much of a benefit, because taxes can knock an iceberg-size hole in your financial ship.

Capital-gains taxes can take a huge chunk out of profits in a taxable account. That's why it makes the most sense to lock away every investment dollar possible in a retirement plan. For one thing, the government makes it hard to get money out of a retirement plan without triggering a 10 percent penalty. If you're building a stock portfolio for something other than life after work, you'll probably do it in a taxable account. Then you can get your hands on your money penalty-free anytime you want to.

To minimize taxes, you have to build a portfolio of low- to no-yielding (2 percent down to 0 percent) stocks and sell rarely. Selling rarely (and therefore not paying capital-gains taxes) is what has allowed many self-made millionaires and billionaires, members of the Forbes 400, to establish such incredible fortunes—Warren Buffett of Berkshire-Hathway, Leon Levine of Family Dollar Stores, Leslie Wexner of The Limited, to name three.

Three years ago an attorney client, who's very well-to-do, flew down from Baltimore for one of my personal-coaching sessions. He already had a substantial buildup in his retirement plan and was making the maximum annual contribution each year, but he still could put a lot of extra money into his taxable portfolio. The portfolio contained a lot of low-quality stocks sprinkled with companies in America's Finest Companies like Merck. There were capital gains in some issues, losses in the others, and no particular rhyme or reason as to what would be purchased and sold. In addition, there were far too many stocks to keep up with. My recommendation was to sell most of the stocks, offset the gains with the losses, and assemble a portfolio of ten companies in America's Finest Companies, with 10 percent of the money in each. The client and I together chose the portfolio, and the end result was one we felt comfortable with.

Without revealing what he bought, I'll show you the thought process that went into picking the ten names. You may or may not be, but my client is in a high tax bracket. With state and federal taxes combined, dividend income is taxed at approximately 45 percent. Because the combined rate is so high, it will pay my client to focus on low- or no-yielding stocks and strive for capital gains rather than dividend income. If you want to invest in stocks for a combination of yields and capital gains (utilities, for example), those stocks should be in your retirement plan, where dividends won't be taxed. When you invest outside the retirement plan, the focus should be on capital application at the expense of yield.

A general rule of thumb is that companies whose stocks have low yields (McDonald's) or no yields (Citizens Utilities) grow faster than their counterparts with higher yields. This is not inviolate when applied to individual companies, but for our purposes it's a good guideline when applied to companies on the whole. The reason it works is faster-growing companies figure they can earn more for shareowners by plowing earnings back into the businesses rather than paying it in dividends. Said another way, faster-growing companies earn higher returns on reinvested dollars than the typical company or investor. Slower-growing industries like banking and utilities provide above-average dividend yields because their growth prospects aren't nearly so bright as for a Wal-Mart or a Nucor.

The twenty-five top-performing stocks in America's Finest Companies over the past ten years (from capital appreciation) were, as a group, very low yielding stocks. Several, including Clayton Homes and Biomet, paid no dividends at all. The rest had minuscule dividend yields. Since capital gains is what we're looking for in a taxable portfolio, below-average-yielding stocks must make up the portfolio.

It's easy to pick such a portfolio and takes no more than a couple of minutes. Turn to the alphabetical listing of companies in the appendix and start skimming the list. For this example I'm sticking with all companies yielding no more than 2.0 percent and want to end up with eight.

I see Automatic Data Processing, a computer software company, with a 1.1 percent yield. ADP is near the top of the heap, with forty-six back-to-back years of higher earnings and twenty-one of dividends, the sixth-best record of all companies. Even more amazing, the company has posted 144 straight quarters of double-digit earnings growth. Although I can't prove it, that has to be the best record in the world. I know it's the best in this country.

I don't want more than one company starting with an A (you can have more than one if you like) so I skip to the Bs and find Bandag (auto parts) is the first B company meeting the 2.0 percent yield criterion. Bandag has one of the strongest balance sheets of any company, with equity being more than 70 percent of total assets. Then I go to the Cs. There, Century Telephone yields 1.2 percent.

In the Ds I find Diebold Inc. with a 1.4 percent yield. The first company in the Es, Eaton Vance (financial industry), has a 1.9% yield and fifteen years in a row of higher dividends per share. FlightSafety International, a commercial-services company serving the airline industry, has a 1.2% yield and qualifies for inclusion in the portfolio.

Now I have six companies and need only two more to get eight. GAINSCO, an insurance company, is in the Gs and sports a 0.6% yield. To round out the list, I spot Hannaford Brothers, a grocery chain, with a 1.5% yield.

Now I buy the portfolio and invest 12.5 percent of my money in each. One year from the purchase date, I add additional money to the portfolio and bring the bottom two or three laggard positions into line with the others. If one stock, let's say it's Bandag, runs way ahead of the rest of the pack and becomes dramatically overweighted, I don't sell part of it to bring it into line with the other seven because I don't want to pay capital-gains taxes. I let my profits ride. As long as I don't realize them, my money continues to grow tax-deferred with the exception of taxes

COMPANY	INDUSTRY	YIELD
Automatic Data Processing	Computer Software	1.1%
Bandag	Auto parts	2.0
Century Telephone	Telephone	1.2
Diebold Inc.	Office Equipment	1.4
Eaton Vance	Financial	1.9
FlightSafety International	Special Services	1.2
GAINSCO	Property Insurance	0.6
Hannaford Brothers	Grocery	1.5
	Average	1.4%

I'll pay on annual dividends. That won't be a lot because the yield is a skimpy 1.4 percent.

If I want to pay no taxes, I need eight companies that don't pay dividends. They're just as easy to find as stocks with meager yields although there aren't nearly as many from which to choose. In this example I'll start with the As and skim the list alphabetically. The first no-dividend payer is Biomet in the medical products industry. Next is Buffets. They're followed by Citizens Utilities in the electric-utility industry and Digi International in computers.

Company number five is Forest Labs in health care. Number six is Franklin Quest in special services; number seven, Microsoft Corp., computer software; number eight, Thermo Electron in electronics.

What could be easier? I quickly assembled a great portfolio of eight companies, each in a different industry, and they pay no dividends. This is a totally tax-deferred portfolio—just like a retirement plan—so long as I never sell and take a capital gain. One big advantage is I have instant access to my money in case I need it. There's no early-withdrawal penalty as there is with a retirement plan.

In a taxable account, there are only two good reasons ever to sell one of your stocks. The first is if the stock is deleted from America's Finest Companies. In that case you sell the deleted stock and replace it with another in America's Finest Companies. The second reason to sell is that you need the money. Other than these, there isn't a good reason to sell unless one of your stocks has a loss, and you'd like to use the loss to offset other income. In a nontaxable account, the loss wouldn't be recognized.

COMPANY	INDUSTRY
Biomet	Medical Products
Buffets Inc.	Restaurant
Citizens Utilities	Electric utility
Digi International	Computers
Forest Labs	Health care
Franklin Quest	Special services
Microsoft Corp.	Computer software
Thermo Electron	Electronics

It's important for you always to picture yourself as a buyer, not a seller, especially in a taxable account. Once your portfolio is set up, you want to keep buying more of what you've got and keep all stock positions in as near equal proportion as possible. Sell only when necessary. Otherwise Uncle Sam (and probably the state where you reside) will come calling to claim his "fair" share of *your* profits. Why pay taxes when you don't have to? Avoid them by letting your portfolio continue to appreciate over the next five, ten, fifteen, twenty years or more.

Multibillionaire Warren Buffett is a buyer of quality, and he rarely sells. Since he's worth more than $16 billion and is one of the world's wealthiest individuals, what he knows is worth knowing. Buffett says, "Buying only the best is something that . . . is very simple and very obvious." He also says his favorite holding period is "forever."

If you invest strictly in America's Finest Companies and continue to buy more of what you own and rarely sell, then you are modeling Buffett, the finest example of a successful long-term investor. Maybe you won't be worth $16 billion before you die (then again maybe you will), but you could easily become a millionaire, even a multi-millionaire, if you have enough time and patience.

To start building a secure financial future with a portfolio of stocks in America's Finest Companies, to continue buying them, and to hold them for a long time is such a simple (I call it a no-brainer) strategy you have to wonder why everyone doesn't do it.

CHAPTER TEN

If You've Never Invested Before, It's Easy to Get Started

I f you've invested before, you've already got a brokerage account and know how it works and the commissions and fees involved. But if you're just beginning, the prospect of opening an account can be intimidating, particularly if you've got only a few hundred or a few thousand dollars to invest. You may think you're such a small investor nobody will want to do business with you. It's true a lot of brokers aren't interested in accounts that "small" because they think they don't make enough commissions. What a shortsighted view! These brokers fail to realize that large accounts usually don't start large; they start small. If one broker doesn't seem interested, hang up and try another one. There are plenty who will gladly accept your business, and they're not hard to find.

You can normally open an account with any stockbroker by phone. In just a few minutes you give the broker enough background information (nothing confidential or revealing) to activate your account and then place your initial order to buy shares of America's Finest Companies. Opening a new account is that simple, and costs nothing but a few minutes' time.

Discount brokers generally offer lower commission rates than full-service brokers because they're seeking investors who want to save money and who, like you, make their own investment decisions. Charles Schwab (800-435-4000) is the largest, but there are others with a national presence, including Quick & Reilly (800-221-5220), Olde Discount (800-USA-OLDE), Pacific Brokerage (800-421-8395), Waterhouse (800-765-5185), and Jack White & Co. (800-233-3411).

The good news about discount brokers is that more and more are cropping up around the country. Your bank may have a discount brokerage operation, as do quite a few of the banks in my hometown. If it does, you can get more information at any of the bank's branches. Many discounters are local, have rock-bottom commission rates, and advertise little if at all. They usually don't find you. You have to find them. A good place to start is the yellow pages.

Full-service national firms are led by Merrill Lynch (800-MER-RILL) and Smith Barney (212-698-6000), the two brokers with the largest sales forces. They're trailed by a number of smaller but high-quality regional firms scattered across the country in cities like San Francisco,

Dallas, St. Petersburg, Minneapolis, Atlanta, Charlotte, and Richmond. What all these firms have in common is they usually have the highest commissions and fees, but they also offer services the discounters don't offer, like stock and bond research. They also sell an array of financial products, including life insurance and annuities.

Since you're now your own money manager and are comfortable with your own decisions about what and when to buy and sell, where you open a brokerage account isn't nearly as important as it would be if you had no idea what you were doing. You do know what you're doing. You're in control, not the broker. There's no need to worry about a salesman selling you something you don't want because you won't let him.

What is important is that the firm is reputable and has the services you need. Just as important is how much they charge. Most brokers have a fixed minimum commission in the $25 to $50 range regardless of the transaction size. The average is about $40. If you buy one share of each of five stocks, total commissions could be as low as $100, as high as $250, and on average around $200. One of my clients wanted to buy $200 of stock for each of her four grandchildren and have the shares registered in their names. After a lot of shopping, she found the lowest commission rate at the discount-brokerage arm of her bank.

Since the first edition of this book in January 1995 there are now more options available for small investors than ever before. The financial newspapers and magazines are full of ads, and the ads change frequently so that some of what you're reading now may already be out of date. This is by no means a comprehensive list of what's available but it is a good overview of the choices investors have.

Charles Schwab introduced a program called "e.Schwab." in 1996 proclaiming "low commissions of just $39 for stock trades up to 1,000 shares and just three cents a share for additional shares." The firm gives you the software to access your portfolio, create charts and graphs, and get company reports and quotes twenty-four hours a day, every day. You also gain access to Reuters Money Network and S&P MarketScope. For information call 800/372-4922 ext. 126.

Smallish Kennedy Cabot of Beverly Hills (800/252-0090) seems to be a firm that will always help the small investor, even if he or she purchases only one share of stock at the time. Established in 1960, the firm runs big ads in many of the national financial media. They say they are the first brokerage firm to offer IRA/Keogh accounts with no minimum deposit requirements and no set-up or maintenance charges. They offer free dividend reinvestment and margin accounts (where you borrow money to buy additional shares). At press time their commission was just $20 for 1–99 shares of any stock at any price and $30 for 100–600 shares of any stock at any price. The cost to register and mail a stock certificate is just $3. Each account is insured for up to $50 million. That should take care of most of us.

Prudential Securities (800/654-5454 ext. 400) has been pushing its no-fee IRA with a yearly contribution of $250 or more. Ceres Securities (800/628-6100) advertises you can trade any common or preferred stock, any number of shares, for one flat rate—$18. But there is a catch—you must have $5,000 or more equity in your account. A free service at the Ceres web site is a daily commentary from business columnist Andrew Tobias.

Waterhouse Securities (800/590-8899) of New York offers a free brochure about the company's commissions and services. They're running a lot of ads touting touch-tone trading to save an additional 10% on commissions, free mutual-fund investing, free investment information, free dividend reinvestment, and free IRAs with no fees, no minimums. The firm will either hold your securities in custody or deliver them to you without charge.

Fidelity Investments (800/544-0003) has an Ultra Service Account with no annual fee, discounted commissions for all customers, brokers available every day, and a minimum investment of $10,000. As do many firms, they throw in unlimited checkwriting, a VISA checking card and one "easy-to-read" statement.

There are numerous other firms that advertise often, including E*Trade (800/786-2573) and National Discount (800/4-1-PRICE), but this may already be more than you ever wanted to know. If it's not, there are other sources you can check out, probably for free at your local library. See the December 25, 1995 *Fortune* article, "Get the Best Deal From Your Broker." You can also check into the American Association of Individual Investors' "Guide to Discount Brokerage Firms."

There's an outfit called the National Council of Individual Investors that ranks brokers (even those of banks) based on mathematical weightings of data from four areas: breadth of service, commissions/fees, disciplinary record, and stock-performance record. They found that on the whole bank brokerages are cheaper than full-service brokers. No surprise there. They also found that quite a few firms will charge $25 and more for registering and delivering a stock certificate. That adds up to a lot if you buy one share each of five different companies, pay a commission to buy each, and then on top of that pay $25 per certificate to have it mailed to you. NCII's number is 800/663-8516.

When you begin an investment program with as little as $500, commissions, transaction fees, and other charges can be a real burden because they can take a good chunk out of principal. But as you continue to add to your portfolio every six months to a year and your assets multiply, they become less and less of an albatross. Although it's important to reduce or eliminate every cost possible, it's of far greater importance to have your portfolio invested strictly in America's Finest Companies, keep the holdings properly weighted, and buy more of what you already own every chance you get.

In my twenty-six years in the investment business, I've seen people fail to make a lot of money because they spent so much time shopping for the best broker, or trying to unearth the best brokerage firm, or attempting to cut commissions to the bone, or all three. They were putting the cart before the horse, and that's not a profitable strategy. Investing for maximum profits requires patience, a simple strategy like the one unfurled in these pages, and at least a ten-year horizon to give the strategy ample time to work. Keeping costs minimal improves your overall return, there's no doubt about that, but it won't improve your return nearly so much as planning to beat Wall Street with America's Finest Companies, implementing your plan, and sticking to your plan.

How to Turn Your Children or Grandchildren into Savvy Investors and Make Them Millionaires in the Process

The day after my daughter was born in 1978, I opened a custodial account for her at the brokerage firm where I was director of equity research. A custodial account is as simple to open as a regular brokerage account. An adult signs on as "custodian" until the child is eighteen, at which time the account is under the complete control of the child, who, of course, by then is a young adult. Anyone can contribute up to $10,000 of cash, securities, or a combination of the two to a custodial account every year with no gift-tax consequences.

Once the account was set up, my wife and I contributed a few thousand dollars, and then I made three very important phone calls, to my father, my mother, and my aunt, who's like a second mother. Since this was their first grandchild by me, I told them I was certain they'd each want to help secure Gracie's financial future with gifts of cash or stock. Naturally they couldn't say no. It wasn't long before those gifts came in the mail, and I was able to add several thousand dollars of stock to Gracie's account. Before she was even six months old, she had a five-digit sum in her brokerage account, which I invested in a portfolio of growth stocks. There was no America's Finest Companies back then, but I could still pick stocks to beat the market. I knew Gracie was off on a sound financial footing.

Since then my father and aunt made some additional gifts of stock, but the account is worth what it is today (about $200,000) primarily because her portfolio has performed so well. I don't know how much money has been withdrawn to pay for private-school education, but she started in kindergarten and is now in college. Average tuition taken out per year must have been at least $9,000, so you see the portfolio has been a real winner.

When my son, Will, was born in 1989, I immediately opened a custodial account for him as I did for his sister. Although he didn't get off to a five-digit start as she had done, he's still in excellent financial shape for a seven-year-old. He attends a wonderful Montessori school, and his account is paying all tuition and miscellaneous expenses.

Once Will is eighteen, the money in his account is his to do with as he pleases. That's the law as long as he's legally competent, and I have no reason to think he won't be. I hope he'll let me help him manage his money until he gets through college, as I'm helping his sister, but he doesn't have to. Even though his account is for his education, he doesn't have to spend the assets for that purpose. He can dispose of them any way he wishes once he is of age.

I want both my children to have secure financial futures. There should be more than enough money left over in their accounts after four years of college (perhaps graduate school, too) to be able to achieve that goal. Gracie will graduate from college in the spring of 2000. (I went on record in my newsletter in fall 1990 saying the Dow will be at 10000 by then. Let's hope I'm right.)

Assuming college expenses at a liberal $20,000 per year and 13 percent growth (before taxes) in the portfolio, she ought to have about $250,000 to work with when she graduates. If that money grows at a modest 9 percent a year after taxes and she doesn't tap into it, it will be worth close to $2.8 million when she's 50 and well over $6.5 million when she's 60. At 10 percent after tax, which is certainly achievable, the numbers will be $3.6 million at age 50 and nearly $9.5 million by age 60.

I'll encourage Gracie to open an IRA and put every dime she earns into it (up to $2,000 annually) while she's in college. When I was in school, I was fortunate to have my father pay all tuition and other expenses. The $3,000 or so I earned working for the student newspaper was mine to save or spend. Had I known anything about investing, I probably would have set at least part of it aside. Instead I spent it. That's okay. I had a lot of fun. If Gracie earns $100 per month nine months per year during her four years in college, and she invests it in an IRA compounding at 13 percent annually, that little $3,600 investment will swell to nearly $500,000 by the time she's 60. Even better, if she contributes the maximum $2,000 annually from age 22 through age 60, her IRA will multiply to $2.3 million.

An IRA is a powerful wealthbuilder for anyone, especially a child. The younger the child the more valuable the IRA is. Suppose Will begins to do odd jobs like mowing lawns (as I did) when he's 10 and mows five each week during the summer (again as I did). I made $7 a week back in the 1950s. Will can probably make at least ten times that. Let's say he rakes in $75 weekly for ten weeks each summer, starting at age 10 and ending when he turns 16. At 16 he'll drive a car and be much "too old" to mow lawns. For each of the six years he works, Will will put the entire $750 into his IRA, which will earn 13 percent annually through age 65. That's only $4,500, but it will surge to $2.8 million over 49 years. Will will become a millionaire from mowing lawns for just six years. Since this money will be in an IRA, the principal will grow without being taxed until Will begins to withdraw it.

I assume Will will be like a lot of young people and want to spend most of his income. Or worse, he'll be like I was. I spent everything I earned and then asked (begged?) my parents and grandparents for more. The words *saving* and *investing* meant nothing to me. I want them to mean something for my children.

To offset Will's urge to spend what he earns while in high school, I'll offer to match it. It will be either a dollar-for-dollar match or a two-for-one match, probably the latter. Under a two-for-one match, for every dollar Will invests in his IRA I'll give him a dollar to spend as he wishes. I'll also invest a dollar in his custodial account.

While he's putting $4,500 from mowing lawns into his IRA, I'll be pumping $4,500 into his custodial account. Using a conservative aftertax return of 9 percent, the $4,500 from me will be worth $306,981 when he is 65. But if I invest all the money in non-dividend-paying stocks and sell rarely and the money grows at 13 percent like the IRA, it will grow to about $1.8 million. With my small gifts and Will's small contributions to his IRA, he'll amass close to $4.6 million by age 65.

If I were to sit in a room with parents and grandparents and we discussed whether they should provide for their children's financial security, assuming they are able to, there'd probably be a heated argument within a few minutes. Some would say providing financial security works to a child's detriment because the child doesn't learn how to fend for himself in the real world. I recently met a father, Eddie Graham, who feels exactly like that. He grew up poor and worked hard all his life to make ends meet. His house is paid for, he still manages to set aside a little extra money each month, and he and his wife like to junket to Las Vegas and Atlantic City regularly to enjoy, in his words, "the good life." When I asked Eddie about his children, he said he planned to leave nothing to them. It was up to them to "work hard and provide for themselves" just as he's done. That's one view.

Another is that parents and grandparents should offer some financial aid but should not try, even if they can afford it, to provide everything monetary a child needs. And still a third view is my view. I want to make my children as financially comfortable as I can before they enter the workplace, which I assume both will do eventually. Why? Because I'd like both of them to have the opportunity to enjoy the kinds of careers they can sink their teeth into and not have to worry about whether the job pays enough. I want Will to become a high school history teacher if that's what he really wants, even though teachers, in my opinion, are grossly underpaid for what they render to society. If Gracie wants to be an artist, I don't want her to "starve" while she pursues her dream.

Using my children as examples, I'm demonstrating the relative ease with which all children can build small fortunes, even large ones. They can do so without your help if they have the knowledge within these pages, but it will be considerably easier with your assistance. A custodial account at a brokerage is a great starting place. If you're worried that your children or grandchildren will be foolish with their money after they reach 18, you can, for modest fees, establish trust accounts that are very flexible yet have restrictions preventing the assets from being abused. You can be the trustee and invest the money however you like. In either a custodial or a trust account, you'll want to invest strictly in America's Finest Companies. If your child or grandchild is eight or older, he or she will most likely want to participate in assembling the portfolio. Sometimes children even younger than that willingly cooperate. All you need do is ask them.

Remember the example of my daughter, who invested in eight companies she chose herself in 1988. Through July 31, 1996, they've beat the S & P 500 by 98 percent. Gracie was excited about having the chance to pick companies. She wasn't interested in why she was doing it. She just knew it was fun. Money is fun to most children and young people (as it should be with us adults), so why not take advantage of that?

As I said in a previous chapter, I teach applied economics to juniors and seniors where my daughter went to school. I'm the real-life "consultant" who takes practical experiences and knowledge into the classroom to bring economics to life for these bright young adults. Junior Achievement writes its own economics text, which is revised and updated every three years. If you've ever hankered to learn more about the "dismal science" but couldn't find an interesting, readable text, JA's is it. It's the most useful economics text I've ever studied.

With every group of students, I spend two to three sessions on investing, using the principles outlined here. One exercise I emphasize is having them pick five companies they'd like to invest in. There are only three rules. One, the companies must be high quality. Two, they must have dividend reinvestment plans. The students don't know whether the companies have DRPs or not, so they keep picking until they come up with five that do. Three, they have to hold these companies for twenty years. They cannot sell (unless there's a buyout and they're forced to) during the period, but they can buy more of the stocks whenever they get additional money.

Each of the five classes I've worked with to date has picked a good portfolio. Not surprisingly, at least to me, they always choose five companies in different industries. I don't tell them to. They do it as if by instinct. Most of the companies over the past five years have been among America's Finest Companies, even though the students haven't known which are in the universe and which aren't.

McDonald's, PepsiCo or Coca-Cola, Wal-Mart, and Merck or Bristol-Myers Squibb have been popular choices. My latest class started with ten companies initially and then narrowed the list to five. Half the ten were in America's Finest Companies. Any of your children or grandchildren could come up with a similar list of ten to twelve names. All you need to do is eliminate the ones that aren't in America's Finest Companies and let the child buy five of the ones that are, as long as they're in different industries. If there aren't enough, keep working until you have five spread among five industries, each with a dividend reinvestment plan. It won't take long.

A five-stock portfolio is easily put together at very little cost. Let's say the child wants to buy Walgreen, Coca-Cola, Colgate-Palmolive, Kellogg, and William Wrigley Jr. All have DRPs and you need buy only one share of each to begin participating. One broker you can call to execute your orders is Kennedy Cabot (800)252-0090. The firm is good with small transactions. If you buy one share of each of these five, you'll spend about $285, plus total commissions around $125, based on prices at this date. Get the shares registered in the child's name, with you or another adult as custodian, and have them delivered to your home. Each company will mail a simple form so you can check the block required to participate in the company's dividend reinvestment plan. Additional share purchases can be made through the companies' optional investment plans (OCPs), which generally carry no commission, or a small one at worst.

To make the investing process even more fun for the child, you should know that some companies offer freebies to shareholders. Every December, Wrigley sends all shareholders a box of twenty five-stick packs of gum hand-picked by Mr. Wrigley himself. Hershey Foods has a toll-free number shareowners can use to order gifts for friends and relatives. Anheuser-Busch has a Theme Parks Club for shareholders allowing 10–15 percent discounts at the country's facilities scattered across the country. To be eligible for these perks, the shares must be registered in the name of the shareholder and cannot be held by a broker.

If your child or grandchild loves to bowl, consider American Recreation Centers. An investor has to own a lot of shares—five hundred—but that amount entitles the owner (who automatically becomes a Distinguished Shareholder Club member) to five free games of bowling per day at any of the firm's alleys. The company owns Right Start children's catalog, and club members get 20 percent off all merchandise.

Colgate-Palmolive's new shareowners get a packet of discount coupons, which may or may not be fun for a child to receive. This will depend on the age of the child and what the coupons are for, but I guarantee the parent or grandparent will find them useful. Ditto for H. J. Heinz. CSX owns the world-famous Greenbrier resort. Shareholders can stay there at discounted rates. Minnesota Mining & Manufacturing sends its new shareholders a variety of Post-It notes, tape, and other accessories, while Kimberly-Clark provides the chance to buy a bag of its products at well off the regular retail price.

I'd never suggest buying one of these companies just for its perks, but the perks do make ownership more fun, especially for children. Children have to have fun while they're learning to invest. Otherwise they won't be interested. And come to think of it, having fun while you invest isn't a bad idea for adults either. Beating Wall Street with America's Finest Companies is the most fun way I know.

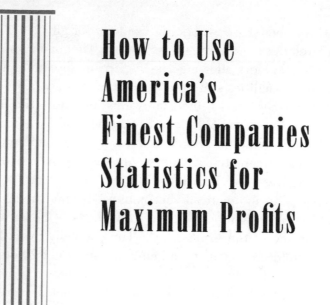

CHAPTER TWELVE

How to Use America's Finest Companies Statistics for Maximum Profits

This book shows you a simple, time-proven way to make your money grow at an above-average rate with practically no risk. By investing solely in America's Finest Companies, you can safely double your money every five to six years and beat 75 percent of all investment professionals 100 percent of the time.

As I pointed out in Chapter 1, a diversified portfolio in America's Finest Companies should give you a 13–15 percent compound annual return compared to 12 percent, the market's rate for the past fifty years. That 1–3 percent advantage over a long period of time is worth hundreds of thousands of extra dollars.

If you invest $50 per month at 12 percent for your child at birth and continue through age 18, his money will grow to $38,272 as the 19th birthday approaches. With no additional contributions from you or the child, that $38,272 will be worth $1,438,328 when he or she is 50; $4,467,228 at age 60; and $13,874,532 by age 70. These are staggering numbers, aren't they? You're probably asking yourself, "But isn't $13,874,532 at age 70 more than enough for anyone?" My answer is "It would sure be more than enough for me, by many millions."

My mission is to try to have you earn as much money as you can on your investments, as safely as you can, and in as little time as you can. I'd rather see you earn 13 percent per year than 12 percent. Fourteen percent would be even better and 15 percent even better than that. I believe 13–15 percent is reasonable. Beyond that, we go into the never-never land of returns that may never materialize, but are frequently promoted by others in the financial arena.

Why not earn as much money as possible? The more you earn, the more you'll have to spend on things you need, things you want, and for helping others, too. I'm not unreasonable or impractical. I know most of us don't save and invest every extra dollar and never spend it. We save and invest, or at least try to, in a manner that lets us spend part of our principal each year while leaving the balance to grow for the future.

Let's go back to the previous example, in which no money is withdrawn until at least age 50, and develop another example that mimics real life. In this instance, the young person is worth $38,272 when he's 18 and needs some money from his account for college, $8,000 per year for four years. The parents make up the difference. After taking out $8,000 for first-year expenses, $30,272 is left to grow at 12 percent, the market's historic return, until the next year, when another $8,000 is withdrawn, and so forth until the four years are complete. At graduation, the young adult is now 22 and his stockpile has shrunk to $17,399. This amount builds at 12 percent compounded annually. If nothing else is taken out, it will be worth $415,555 when he's 50; $1,290,651 when he's 60; and $4,008,569 when he's 70. But in reality, more will probably be extracted at some point. Maybe it's when he reaches 45 and buys the house of his dreams.

From age 22 to age 45, $17,399 at 12 percent will increase to $235,797. With $150,000 used to purchase the dream home (there'd be a mortgage for the balance), there's $85,797 to grow at a 12 percent annual rate. Five years later at age 50, it has grown to $151,204; to $469,616 at 60; and $1,458,554 at age 70. As a practical matter, money will likely be taken out at various other points from ages 45 to 70, so the end amount may or may not be close to $1,458,554.

If I repeat this illustration, using 13 percent and 15 percent returns, at the end of four years of college the remainder amounts are $18,559 and $20,999, respectively, compared with $17,399. At age 45, after $150,000 is used for the home, $158,574 and $372,696 are left over compared with $85,797. You can see what a huge difference these higher rates are making, even using 13 percent, a figure that's only one percent above the market's 12 percent.

In Chapter 8, I said I invested roughly $5,000 (plus commissions) per stock in five different stocks on February 7, 1992, for my son, Will, who was then nearly three. All dividends have been reinvested since inception. To date, Will's portfolio has knocked down a better return than the market. What I'm saying works in theory and, most important, in practice, too. I successfully invest for myself and my children and outpace the market virtually every year, using the companies in America's Finest Companies. You can do it, too.

Someone once said, "The easiest way to end up with a small fortune is to start with a large one." I've proved the opposite to be true. You can end up with a large fortune by beginning with as little as $50 each month and earning the market's rate of return. By outstripping the market, the fortune will be even larger.

Of course these "case-study returns" assume no taxes, but that's not uncommon. Taxes are excluded whenever returns are discussed, whether they be for the market, a mutual fund, or a portfolio manager. We all know taxes are impossible to avoid. They can be heavily reduced but never completely eliminated.

They also assume the investment program begins at birth. That's fine if you've got a baby or grandbaby, but it won't do you any personal good because you're almost certainly years, if not decades, behind. It's still not too late even if you're 50 and have done little or nothing for your future. Will an extra 1 to 3 percent per year really make a difference to your financial security? You bet!

To illustrate, you're already covered by a retirement plan at work but have extra money and decide to invest $2,000 each year in your IRA. If you equal the market and earn 12 percent annually, you'll have $39,309 after 10 years; $83,506 after 15; and $161,397 after 20. If you earn

13 percent, the numbers will be $41,628 in 10 years; $91,343 in 15; and $182,940 in 20. Using a 15 percent return, you'll have $46,699 at the end of 10 years; $109,435 in 15; and $235,620 at the end of 20 years.

Over a twenty-year period, the difference between a 12 percent and a 15 percent return is $74,223, 46 percent more. I'd say that's sizable, wouldn't you? The difference is even more dramatic if you have a SEP or Keogh and can kick in a lot more than $2,000 per year. What if the amount is $10,000 annually instead of $2,000 and you begin at age 50? At 12 percent per year, you'll build an $806,987 nest egg. At 13 percent, the nest egg will be $914,699. At 15 percent, it will be $1,178,101—$371,114 more than if you earned 12 percent.

Any way I've measured it, a diversified portfolio invested in America's Finest Companies has substantially outperformed the market over the past ten years. This means they've whomped most of the pros, too, since the market indexes beat three-quarters of them year in and year out. It's easy to see why they're market beaters. Each of the 406 companies qualifying for listing has increased dividends and/or earnings for at least ten straight years. Three hundred eighty-six have done it with dividends alone; 65 have done it with earnings; and a select 64 have done it in both categories.

It's easy to explain how America's Finest Companies are above-average performers. They're growing, and the value of their businesses is on a consistent uptrend. As the values of the businesses rise, the stock prices rise also. They have to. Here's why.

Look at this staircase. It begins on the left of the page and rises one step at a time until it gets to the right side,

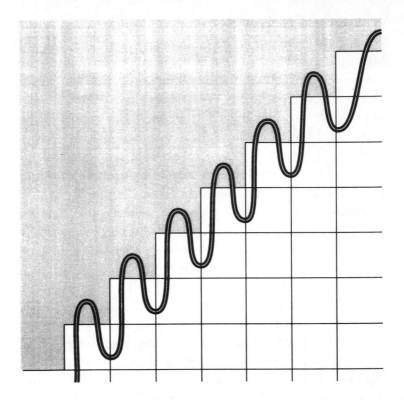

all the while getting taller and taller. This staircase could represent any of America's Finest Companies. Every step represents another increase in the value of the AFC company's business.

Now look at the curve. This represents an AFC stock price over the years. It goes up and down in value (randomly) in the short run, but the path is always in only one direction—upward. Sometimes the stock price is above what the company is really worth. At other times it's valued about correctly. And at still other times it's undervalued.

If you're dollar-cost averaging, as I strongly urge—purchasing the stock of an AFC company over five, ten, fifteen years, and more—you'll buy at different points along the stair steps. Maybe sometimes you'll pay too much. When you do, you'll buy fewer shares per dollar invested because the price is high. Often you'll buy shares on the cheap and for the same dollars invested will be able to load up. Given enough time, dollar-cost averaging will automatically produce superior results in contrast to a buy-and-hold strategy, as demonstrated in Chapter 7.

There are many ways to use the data here so that you end up with a well-balanced portfolio to meet your needs. You'll be a winner regardless of how you select your portfolio. Selecting can be as simple and easy as throwing darts. You could make copies of each of the statistical pages and post them on a wall you don't mind having a few holes in (in case you miss a throw or two). Next toss some darts, however many you require, one dart per company. Then buy the companies the darts strike.

One excellent portfolio you can buy outright or pick from is the eleven Dow stocks (there are thirty that make up the venerable Dow Jones industrial average) that made the AFC cutoff. These are some of the oldest, strongest, most respected names in American industry. They've been around a long time, and you can rest assured they'll be around a lot longer. All have roots stretching back decades before the Great Depression, with the exception of McDonald's, the rookie of the group.

This is not only a well-diversified group of companies, it's a high-caliber group as well. Six of the eleven are ranked A+ (highest) by Standard & Poor's, which establishes its rankings in a computerized system based on

COMPANY	YEARS OF HIGHER EARNINGS	YEARS OF HIGHER DIVIDENDS	S & P RANKING	DIVDS. PAID SINCE
Coca-Cola	21	33	A+	1893
Disney, Walt Co.	4	10	A	1957
DuPont	2	13	B+	1904
Exxon	1	13	A−	1882
General Electric	20	20	A+	1899
McDonald's	30	20	A+	1976
Merck and Company	2	20	A+	1935
Minnesota Mining & Manufacturing	4	37	A+	1916
J. P. Morgan	1	19	B+	1892
Philip Morris	2	30	A+	1928
Procter & Gamble	2	40	A	1891

earnings and dividend records over the past decade. Stability is a key variable. Two are rated A, one A− (above average) and two B+ (average).

From the end of 1985 through December 31, 1995, $1,000 spread equally among the eleven stocks grew to $6,727 (21% compounded annually) vs. growing to $4,010 in the Standard & Poor's 500 (14.9% annually). That's the 3 percent difference I've been talking about. Actually, in this case it's 6.1 percent. The performance of these eleven companies was so outstanding that only four mutual funds and the stock markets of two nations, Hong Kong and Singapore/Malaysia, did better.

Even if you'd owned the five or six worst performers out of the eleven (I bet you couldn't have done that if your life and all your money had depended on it), your return would have still beat the averages.

It's easy to get together a portfolio using any one, or an assortment of, variables. If you want stocks that yield at least 4 percent, you have 104 from which to choose. Do you like stocks selling for $25 or less? There are 129. Or maybe you'd feel better owning only the companies ranked A+ by Standard & Poor's. You can choose them from the list in the appendix. Other selection criteria are industry, the price/earnings ratio, and the number of consecutive years of higher earnings and dividends.

You might like to make up your own combination of several variables, i.e., stocks priced between $20 and $40 per share, with P/E ratios no greater than 20, yields of at least 3 percent, and at least fifteen years of higher dividends. It's up to you. The important thing to keep in mind is that however you build your portfolio, you're

(1) COMPANY/STOCK SYMBOL	(2) INDUSTRY	(3) PRICE	(4) PRICE/ EARNINGS RATIO	(5) YIELD (%)	(6) DIVD. REINVEST. PLAN
Abbott Laboratories/ABT	Health Care	44	19.3	2.2	X

(7) CONSECUTIVE ANNUAL EARNINGS INCREASES	(8) CONSECUTIVE ANNUAL DIVIDEND INCREASES	(9) S & P RANKING	(10) ADDRESS/PHONE NUMBER
24	23	A+	100 Abbott Park Rd., Abbott Park, IL 60064 847-937-6100

building it with the *crème de la crème* of corporations, the elite, America's Finest.

Now I'll tell you how to get more out of the data in the appendix. All the companies are listed alphabetically along with their stock symbols (column 1). An (A) follows a company's symbol if it trades, like Bowl America, Inc., on the American Stock Exchange.

After the stock symbol is the industry category in column 2. Regardless of the size of your stock portfolio—five, eight, ten, twelve, or more companies—each should be in a different industry. If you want to pick an eight-stock portfolio, there's no faster way than turning to any page of the company listings in the appendix and going down it company by company until you have the right number in diverse industries.

Column 3 shows the price of the stock when this book went to press. Column 4 gives the P/E ratio, which is the stock price divided by the latest twelve months' earnings. It's well documented that over longer periods of time a portfolio of stocks (culled from a large-enough group) with below-average price/earnings ratios consistently beats that group. For example, the eight lowest P/Es in the Dow Jones average regularly beat the Dow average of thirty stocks over one-, five-, and ten-year periods.

The first evidence I saw that this is true was in a paper written by Benjamin Graham, my financial hero. He cited research by the old brokerage firm of Drexel & Company in Philadelphia. Their 1965 study concluded that in twenty-two of the twenty-eight years since 1936 the ten lowest-P/E Dow stocks outdistanced the Dow.

If you'd like to track America's Finest Companies

yearly, including the lowest-P/E stocks, I invite you to become a member of The Staton Institute Inc. and receive my monthly newsletter, plus a host of other benefits. There's a membership application on page 251.

Column 5 shows the dividend yield for each stock if the company pays a dividend. Investing in stocks with above-average dividend yields is a conservative—but sound—way to make your money grow while simultaneously reducing downside risk and volatility. When you invest in the highest-quality companies like those shown in the back of the book and reinvest all your dividends, your returns will usually be equal to, or better than, the Dow Jones and S & P 500 indexes.

Column 6 shows whether a company has a dividend reinvestment plan. If the company reinvests dividends and optional cash payments at a discount to market price, the discount is shown in parentheses beside the X.

Columns 7 and 8 show the number of years of back-to-back earnings and dividend increases. Sixty-four companies, ranging from Abbott Laboratories and Albertson's to Wilmington Trust Corporation and William Wrigley Jr., have compiled double-digit increases in both categories. I haven't found any correlation between the length of a company's string of earnings and/or dividends and its stock price performance, but some people are more comfortable investing in companies with the longer records, like American Home Products, Emerson Electric, Johnson & Johnson, RPM, and Tootsie Roll Industries.

Column 9 provides the S & P rankings. The most consistent companies are ranked B+ and higher although Standard & Poor's has no ranking for some.

To contact a company for more information or to inquire about its DRP, use the address and phone number in column 10. If a toll-free number is available, it's included.

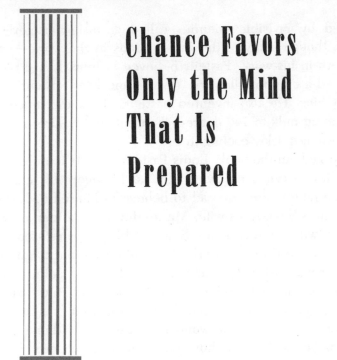

CHAPTER THIRTEEN

Chance Favors Only the Mind That Is Prepared

When my daughter was five, her favorite book was *The Value of Believing in Yourself: The Story of Louis Pasteur* by Spencer Johnson, M.D. (Few people know Johnson coauthored *The One-Minute Manager*.) It's one of my favorite books, too. I know his story almost by heart, having read it aloud several dozen times.

Pasteur (1822–95), as you may recall from your history courses, was a chemist and bacteriologist whose scientific exploits were widely ignored, since he was not a medical doctor. Pasteur had the firm conviction that diseases were caused by invisible enemies called germs or bacteria. Even though many of the finest minds in the world had no faith in his work, Pasteur believed in himself. He uncovered a cure for silkworm disease and later for anthrax and rabies. He also invented pasteurization, the process of heating milk to 140 degrees Fahrenheit for thirty minutes, then quickly cooling it.

Throughout the book, Louis Pasteur repeats to himself, "I believe I can, I believe I can," as he vigorously hunts for the rabies cure. He had to believe in himself because few others besides his wife, Marie, did. But Pasteur knew exactly what he was doing. Some of his critics refused to acknowledge his great works because they thought Louis Pasteur was just lucky. Pasteur knew luck had nothing to do with his outstanding accomplishments and said, "Chance favors only the mind that is prepared."

The average man or woman on the street thinks investing in stocks is nothing but a game of chance. The luckiest ones make money. The rest lose it. They don't realize that investing in stocks is the fastest way to accumulate wealth and that it can be done with virtually zero risk, as I've demonstrated. If you'll use the simple, rational method I've outlined, you'll have phenomenal success with your money regardless of the amount you begin with. In a sense, you'll be like Louis Pasteur because you'll ignore the advice commonly given by most financial experts, who want you to believe you need them to be successful. There aren't many of us who know you can do it yourself, have a lot of fun, and make a lot of money, too. Believe in yourself. You can do it!

In building a diversified portfolio of America's Finest Companies, you're doing far more than buying pieces of paper that change in price many times each day. You are actually buying pieces of American enterprises, the best this country has to offer. As these companies grow and thrive in the future, so will you by virtue of your ownership.

Does it really matter if the value of your shares goes down today and then bobs up tomorrow? Of course not. Value is not created in a day. Value takes years to build. Daily fluctuations in stock prices are meaningless. They do not affect the long-term value of the Finest Companies.

What does affect the value is growth in revenue, earnings, dividends, and the asset values of the businesses. If you continually add to your portfolio of first-rate companies, you can be certain that over the years the value will increase faster than from other investments—and keep you well ahead of inflation and the tax man, too.

There's nothing to wait for. You now have the knowledge you need for investing and stock-market success. Epicurus warned, "Life is wasted in procrastination." Procrastinate no longer. Start the steps to financial security today.

Happy investing!

Appendix:
List of the 406
America's Finest
Companies

Company Name/Stock Symbol	Industry	Price	P/E	YIELD	Dividend Reinvestment Plan	Consecutive EPS Increases	Consecutive Dividend Increases	S&P Rank	Address/Phone Number
Abbott Laboratories/ABT	Health Care	44	19.3	2.2%	X	24	23	A+	100 Abbott Park Rd., Abbott Park IL 60064 847/937-6100
ABM Industries Inc./ABM	Special Services	19	20.0	1.6%	X	8	31	A	PO Box 193224, San Francisco CA 94119 415/597-4500
AFLAC Inc./AFL	Insurance	30	12.8	1.3%	X	6	13	A	1932 Wynnton Rd., Columbus GA 31999 800/227-4756
Air Products & Chemicals/APD	Chemicals	53	14.2	2.1%	X	2	13	A	7201 Hamilton Blvd., Allentown PA 18195 610/481-5775
Alberto-Culver Co./ACV	Cosmetics	42	22.2	0.8%	X	4	11	A	2525 Armitage Ave., Melrose Park IL 60160 708/450-3005
Albertson's Inc./ABS	Grocery	40	21.1	1.5%	X	26	24	A+	PO Box 20, Boise ID 83726 208/385-6200
Alco Standard Corp./ASN	Ofc. Equip/Supp	41	19.9	1.4%	X	2	31	B+	Box 834, Valley Forge PA 19482 610/993-3608
Allegheny Power System Inc./AYP	Electric Utility	30	16.0	5.6%	X	0	37	A−	12 E. 49th St., New York NY 10017 212/752-2121
ALLTEL Corp./AT	Telephone	27	18.6	3.9%	X	4	35	A	One Allied Dr., Little Rock AR 72202 501/661-8999
American Brands Inc./AMB	Tobacco	44	14.7	4.5%	X	0	28	A−	PO Box 811, Old Greenwich CT 06870 800/225-2719

Company Name/Stock Symbol	Industry	Price	P/E	YIELD	Dividend Reinvestment Plan	Consecutive EPS Increases	Consecutive Dividend Increases	S&P Rank	Address/Phone Number
American Business Products/ABP	Ofc. Equip/Supp	20	14.2	2.9%	X	9	38	A	PO Box 105684, Atlanta GA 30348 800/227-3390
American Filtrona Corp./AFIL	Chemicals	31	10.3	3.6%	X	3	25	B+	3951 Westerre Pkwy. #300, Richmond VA 23233 804/346-2400
American General Corp./AGC	Financial	35	13.9	3.7%	X	2	20	B+	PO Box 3247, Houston TX 77253 800/242-1111
American Heritage Life/AHL	Insurance/Life	20	10.2	3.6%	X	20	26	A	1776 Amer. Heritage Life Dr., Jacksonville FL 32224 800/874-2532
American Home Products/AHP	Health Care	57	18.5	2.7%	X	43	44	A+	Five Giralda Farms, Madison NJ 07940 201/660-6936
American International Group/AIG	Insurance/Multi.	92	16.8	0.4%		11	10	A+	70 Pine St., New York NY 10270 212/770-7000
American Natl. Insurance/ANAT	Insurance/Life	63	8.2	4.0%		5	22	A	One Moody Plaza, Galveston TX 77550 713/763-4661
American Precision Inds./APR	Electrical Equip.	12	15.4	2.2%		2	18	B+	2777 Walden Ave., Buffalo NY 14225 716/684-9700
American Recreation Ctrs./AMRC	Leisure	6	33.3	4.2%	X	2	28	B	PO Box 580, Rancho Cordova CA 95741 916/852-8005
American Water Works Co./AWK	Water Utility	39	28.7	1.8%	X(5)	3	20	A	PO Box 1770, Voorhees NJ 08043 609/346-8200

Company	Industry								Address
Ameritech Corp./AIT	Telephone	55	15.5	3.9%	X	1	11	A−	30 S. Wacker Dr., Chicago IL 60606 800/257-0902
AMP Inc./AMP	Electrical Equip.	37	17.7	2.7%	X	4	42	A−	Harrisburg PA 17105 717/780-4869
AmSouth Bancorporation/ASO	Banking	36	10.9	4.4%	X	1	23	B+	PO Box 11007, Birmingham AL 35288 205/326-5807
Angelica Corp./AGL	Textiles/Apparel	21	300.0	4.6%	X	0	23	B	424 S. Woods Mill Rd., Chesterfield MO 63017 314/854-3800
Anheuser-Busch Cos. Inc./BUD	Alcoholic Bever.	37	19.6	2.6%	X	0	21	A	One Busch Place, St. Louis MO 63118 800/342-5283
Aon Corp./AOC	Insurance/Life	48	18.7	3.0%	X	3	44	A−	123 N. Wacker Dr., Chicago IL 60606 312/701-3000
Apogee Enterprises Inc./APOG	Auto Parts	28	19.9	1.2%		2	21	B	7900 Xerxes Ave. So., Minneapolis MN 55431 612/835-1874
Archer Daniels Midland Co./ADM	Foods	17	12.8	1.2%	X	1	21	A+	PO Box 1470, Decatur IL 62525 217/424-5200
Arnold Industries Inc./AIND	Transportation	14	12.2	3.1%	X	0	11	A	625 S. Fifth Ave., Lebanon PA 17042 717/274-2521
Associated Banc-Corp/ASBC	Banking	38	12.6	3.1%	X	4	25	A+	PO Box 13307, Green Bay WI 54307 800/236-2722
Automatic Data Processing/AUD	Computer Soft.	38	25.3	1.1%		46	21	A+	One ADP Blvd., Roseland NJ 07068 201/994-5000
AVEMCO Corp./AVE	Insurance/Multi.	15	13.2	3.2%	X	0	20	B	411 Aviation Way, Frederick MD 21701 301/694-5700
Avery Dennison Corp./AVY	Chemicals	51	17.3	2.5%	X	5	19	B+	PO Box 7090, Pasadena CA 91109 818/304-2000
Baldor Electric Co./BEZ	Electrical Equip.	19	15.8	2.1%		4	12	A	PO Box 2400, Fort Smith AR 72902 501/646-4711

Company Name/Stock Symbol	Industry	Price	P/E	YIELD	Dividend Reinvestment Plan	Consecutive EPS Increases	Consecutive Dividend Increases	S&P Rank	Address/Phone Number
Banc One Corp./ONE	Banking	34	11.0	3.6%	X	1	23	A+	100 E. Broad St., Columbus OH 43271 614/248-6889
Bancorp Hawaii Inc./BOH	Banking	34	10.7	3.3%	X	1	17	A	PO Box 2900, Honolulu HI 96846 808/537-8037
BancorpSouth Inc./BOMS	Banking	21	11.2	3.2%	X	8	13	A	PO Box 789, Tupelo MS 38802 601/680-2000
Bandag Inc./BDG	Auto Parts	45	12.5	2.0%	X	2	19	A+	2905 N. Hwy. 61, Muscatine IA 52761 319/262-1400
Bank of Granite Corp./GRAN	Banking	24	18.3	1.5%	X	42	42		PO Box 128, Granite Falls NC 28630 704/496-2022
Bankers Trust NY Corp./BT	Banking	71	11.2	5.6%	X	1	17	B	One Bankers Trust Plaza, New York NY 10016 212/250-3609
Banta Corp./BNTA	Printing	22	13.2	2.0%	X	5	18	A−	Box 8003, Menasha WI 54952 414/751-7777
Bard, C.R. Inc./BCR	Medical Prods.	31	19.3	2.2%	X	2	24	A−	730 Central Ave., Murray Hill NJ 07974 201/277-8000
Baxter International Inc./BAX	Medical Prods.	42	26.1	2.9%	X	0	39	B+	One Baxter Pkwy., Deerfield IL 60015 847/948-4550
Becton, Dickinson & Co./BDX	Medical Prods.	36	17.3	1.3%	X	13	24	A+	1 Becton Dr., Franklin Lakes NJ 07417 800/284-6845

Company/Symbol	Industry								Address
Bell Atlantic Corp./BEL	Telephone	59	13.3	4.9%	X	1	11	A−	1717 Arch St., Philadelphia PA 19103 215/963-6333
Bemis Co./BMS	Containers	32	17.9	2.2%		2	12	A	222 S. Ninth St., Minneapolis MN 55402 612/376-3000
Berkley, W.R. Corp./BKLY	Insurance/Prop.	40	13.4	1.3%	X	1	14	B+	PO Box 2518, Greenwich CT 06836 203/629-3000
Betz Laboratories Inc./BTL	Chemicals	43	19.0	3.4%		0	30	A−	4636 Somerton Rd., Trevose PA 19053 215/953-5550
Biomet Inc./BMET	Medical Prods.	15	19.5	0.0%	X	17	0	B+	PO Box 587, Warsaw IN 46581 219/267-6639
Black Hills Corp./BKH	Electric Utility	23	11.9	6.0%	X	2	24	A	PO Box 1400, Rapid City SD 57709 605/348-1700
Block, H & R Inc./HRB	Special Services	24	20.3	5.3%	X	1	33	A	4410 Main St., Kansas City MO 64111 816/753-6900
Block Drug Co. Inc./BLOCA	Medical Prods.	42	16.3	2.8%		2	24	A	257 Cornelison Ave., Jersey City NJ 07302 201/434-3000
Boatmen's Bancshares Inc./BOAT	Banking	40	11.5	3.7%	X	7	15	A	PO Box 14768, St. Louis MO 63178 800/456-9852
Bob Evans Farms Inc./BOBE	Restaurant	13	18.8	2.5%	X	0	32	A	PO Box 07863, Columbus OH 43207 614/497-4390
Bowl America Inc./BWLA(A)	Leisure	7	14.6	5.4%		0	23	B+	PO Box 1288, Springfield VA 22151 703/941-6300
Bridgford Foods Corp./BRID	Foods	8	11.4	3.0%		10	8	B+	PO Box 3773, Anaheim CA 92803 714/526-5553
Brinker International/EAT	Restaurant	13	28.3	0.0%		16	0	B+	6820 LBJ Freeway, Dallas TX 75240 214/980-9917

Company Name/ Stock Symbol	Industry	Price	P/E	YIELD	Dividend Reinvestment Plan	Consecutive EPS Increases	Consecutive Dividend Increases	S&P Rank	Address/Phone Number
Bristol-Myers Squibb Co./BMY	Health Care	87	22.7	3.4%	X	0	23	A	345 Park Ave., New York NY 10154 212/546-4000
Brooklyn Union Gas Co./BU	Natural Gas	26	13.3	5.5%	X	3	19	A−	1 MetroTech Ctr., Brooklyn NY 11201 718/403-3382
Brown-Forman Corp./BFB	Alcoholic Bever.	36	15.6	2.9%	X	6	11	A	PO Box 1080, Louisville KY 40201 502/585-1100
Buffets Inc./BOCB	Restaurant	12	14.6	0.0%		12	0	B+	10260 Viking Dr., Eden Prairie MN 55344 612/942-9760
California Water Service Co./CWT	Water Utility	33	12.1	6.3%	X(3)	0	28	A−	1720 N. First St., San Jose CA 95112 408/451-8200
Campbell Soup Co./CPB	Foods	67	21.9	2.1%	X	5	21	B	Campbell Place, Camden NJ 08103 800/909-7687
Cardinal Health Inc./CAH	Health Care	67	34.5	0.2%	X	1	11	A−	655 Metro Place So., Dublin OH 43017 614/717-5000
Carlisle Companies Inc./CSL	Building Materials	50	15.5	1.8%	X	4	19	B+	250 S. Clinton St. #201, Syracuse NY 13202 315/474-2500
CCB Financial Corp./CCBF	Banking	50	10.1	3.4%	X	5	31	A	PO Box 931, Durham NC 27702 919/683-7777
Central & South West Corp./CSR	Electric Utility	28	12.6	6.2%	X	2	45	A−	PO Box 660164, Dallas TX 75266 800/527-5797

Company/Symbol	Industry								Address
Central Fidelity Banks Inc./CFBS	Banking	21	11.4	4.2%	X	1	17	A	PO Box 27602, Richmond VA 23261 804/697-7038
Central Louisiana Electric/CNL	Electric Utility	26	12.4	5.8%	X	2	24	A−	PO Box 5000, Pineville LA 71361 800/253-2652
Central Reserve Life Corp./CRLC	Insurance/Life	6	0.0	8.7%		0	16	B+	17800 Royalton Rd., Strongsville OH 44136 216/572-2400
Centura Banks Inc./CBC	Banking	35	12.8	2.9%	X	4	29	A	PO Box 1220, Rocky Mount NC 27802 800/436-5898
Century Telephone Enter./CTL	Telephone	31	15.7	1.2%	X	6	21	A	PO Box 4065, Monroe LA 71211 800/833-1188
Chemed Corp./CHE	Chemicals	35	12.5	5.9%	X	1	24	B	255 E. Fifth St., Cincinnati OH 45202 800/224-3633
Chemical Financial Corp./CHFC	Banking	36	16.4	2.2%	X	21	21	A	PO Box 569, Midland MI 48640 517/839-5350
Chubb Corp./CB	Insurance/Prop.	43	11.1	2.5%	X	2	31	A	PO Box 1615, Warren NJ 07061 908/903-2000
Cincinnati Financial Corp./CINF	Insurance/Prop.	58	14.1	2.4%	X	6	35	A	PO Box 145496, Cincinnati OH 45250 513/870-2639
Cintas Corp./CTAS	Special Services	50	31.2	0.5%		26	13	A+	PO Box 625737, Cincinnati OH 45262 513/459-1200
CIPSCO Inc./CIP	Electric Utility	36	15.4	5.8%	X	0	17	B+	607 E. Adams St., Springfield IL 62739 800/710-7726
Circuit City Stores Inc./CC	Retail	33	18.1	0.4%		6	16	A	9950 Mayland Dr., Richmond VA 23233 804/527-4022
Citizens Banking Corp./CBCF	Banking	28	11.6	3.7%	X	13	12	A	328 S. Saginaw St., Flint MI 48502 810/257-2557

Company Name/Stock Symbol	Industry	Price	P/E	YIELD	Dividend Reinvestment Plan	Consecutive EPS Increases	Consecutive Dividend Increases	S&P Rank	Address/Phone Number
Citizens Utilities Co./CZNB	Electric Utility	11	14.7	0.0%		51	0	A+	High Ridge Park, Stamford CT 06905 203/329-8800
CLARCOR Inc./CLC	Machinery	21	13.6	3.0%	X	3	35	B+	PO Box 7007, Rockford IL 61125 815/962-8867
Clayton Homes Inc./CMH	Manuf. Housing	17	16.5	0.5%	X	15	0	B+	PO Box 15169, Knoxville TN 37901 615/970-7200
Clorox Co./CLX	Household Prods.	88	21.4	2.6%	X	4	19	A	PO Box 24305, Oakland CA 94623 510/271-2150
CNB Bancshares Inc./BNK	Banking	27	12.6	3.1%	X(3)	1	13	A	PO Box 778, Evansville IN 47705 812/464-3400
Coca-Cola Co./KO	Soft Drink	46	35.7	1.1%	X	21	33	A+	PO Drawer 1734, Atlanta GA 30301 404/676-2777
Colgate-Palmolive Co./CL	Household Prods.	82	82.8	2.3%	X	0	33	B+	300 Park Ave., New York NY 10022 212/310-3207
Colonial Gas Co./CGES	Natural Gas	21	10.0	6.2%	X(5)	1	16	B+	PO Box 3064, Lowell MA 01853 508/458-3171
Comerica Inc./CMA	Banking	42	11.0	3.7%	X	3	52	A-	PO Box 75000, Detroit MI 48275 800/292-1300
Commerce Bancshares Inc./CBSH	Banking	34	11.6	2.2%		9	27	A+	PO Box 13686, Kansas City MO 64199 816/234-2000

Company/Symbol	Industry								Address
Compass Bancshares Inc./CBSS	Banking	32	10.8	4.0%	X	7	14	A	15 S. 20th St., Birmingham AL 35233 205/933-3000
ConAgra Inc./CAG	Foods	42	53.2	2.3%	X	0	20	A+	One ConAgra Dr., Omaha NE 68102 800/840-3404
Connecticut Water Service/CTWS	Water Utility	25	11.6	6.7%	X(5)	5	26	B+	93 W. Main St., Clinton CT 06413 860/669-8630
Consolidated Edison Co./ED	Electric Utility	27	9.3	7.7%	X	0	21	A	4 Irving Place, New York NY 10003 800/522-5522
Consumers Water Co./CONW	Water Utility	17	14.2	7.1%	X	1	39	B+	PO Box 599, Portland ME 04112 800/292-2925
Cooper Tire & Rubber Co./CTB	Auto Parts	18	13.7	1.7%		0	16	A	701 Lima Ave., Findlay OH 45840 419/423-1321
Corestates Financial/CFL	Banking	38	11.0	3.6%	X	1	18	B+	PO Box 7618, Philadelphia PA 19101 215/973-6006
Corning Inc./GLW	Miscellaneous	36	24.3	2.0%	X	0	12	B+	Corning NY 14831 607/974-9000
CPC International Inc./CPC	Foods	66	18.3	2.3%	X	1	10	A+	Intl. Plaza, Englewood Cliffs NJ 07632 201/894-4000
Cracker Barrel Old Country/CBRL	Restaurant	21	18.8	0.1%	X	10	0	A	PO Box 787, Lebanon TN 37087 615/444-5533
Crawford & Co./CRDB	Insurance Brokers	18	15.4	3.3%		0	23	A	5620 Glenridge Dr. NE, Atlanta GA 30342 404/256-0830
Crompton & Knowles Corp./CNK	Chemicals	14	19.4	3.9%	X	0	19	A	One Station Pl., Metro Ctr., Stamford CT 06902 203/353-5400
CSX Corp./CSX	Railroad	45	11.1	2.3%	X	0	16	B+	PO Box 85629, Richmond VA 23285 804/782-1465
Dauphin Deposit Corp./DAPN	Banking	27	12.2	4.2%	X	0	19	A	PO Box 2961, Harrisburg PA 17105 800/458-0348

Company Name/Stock Symbol	Industry	Price	P/E	YIELD	Dividend Reinvestment Plan	Consecutive EPS Increases	Consecutive Dividend Increases	S&P Rank	Address/Phone Number
Dayton Hudson Corp./DH	Retail	30	21.0	2.1%	X	0	22	A	777 Nicollet Mall, Minneapolis MN 55402 612/370-6736
Dean Foods Co./DF	Foods	23	def.	3.1%	X	3	21	A	3600 N. River Rd., Franklin Park IL 60131 312/625-6200
Deluxe Corp./DLX	Printing	35	36.5	4.2%		0	36	A–	PO Box 64235, St. Paul MN 55164 612/483-7358
Diebold Inc./DBD	Ofc. Equip/Supp	49	26.5	1.4%	X	5	42	A–	PO Box 3077, N. Canton OH 44720 800/766-5859
Digi International Inc./DGII	Computers	15	12.8	0.0%		10	0	B+	6400 Flying Cloud Dr., Eden Prairie MN 55344 612/943-9020
DiMon Inc./DMN	Tobacco	19	def.	2.8%		0	21		PO Box 681, Danville VA 24543 804/792-7511
Disney, Walt Co./DIS	Leisure	54	28.9	0.8%		4	10	A	PO Box 11447, Burbank CA 91510 818/505-7040
Dominion Resources Inc./D	Electric Utility	37	13.5	7.0%	X	0	20	B+	PO Box 26532, Richmond VA 23261 800/552-4034
Donnelley, R.R. & Sons Co./DNY	Printing	30	def.	2.6%	X	4	24	A–	77 W. Wacker Dr., Chicago IL 60601 800/446-2617
Dover Corp./DOV	Manufacturing	42	15.6	1.4%		4	35	A	280 Park Ave, New York NY 10017 212/922-1640

Company/Symbol	Industry								Address
Duke Power Co./DUK	Electric Utility	48	14.5	4.2%	X	3	20	A–	PO Box 1005, Charlotte NC 28201 800/488-3853
Dun & Bradstreet Corp./DNB	Publishing	57	75.0	4.6%		0	44	A–	187 Danbury Rd., Wilton CT 06897 203/834-4200
DuPont Co./DD	Chemicals	77	13.1	3.0%	X	2	13	B+	1007 Market St., Wilmington DE 19898 302/774-1000
Eaton Vance Corp./EAVN	Financial	36	9.0	1.9%		1	15	A–	24 Federal St., Boston MA 02110 617/482-8260
Electronic Data Systems/EDS	Computer Soft.	49	57.6	1.2%		33	33	A+	5400 Legacy Dr., Plano TX 75024 214/604-6000
Emerson Electric Co./EMR	Electrical Equip.	82	19.0	2.4%	X	38	39	A+	8000 W. Florissant Ave., St. Louis MO 63136 314/553-2197
Energen Corp./EGN	Natural Gas	22	11.8	5.5%	X	0	13	A	2101 Sixth Ave. N., Birmingham AL 35203 800/654-3206
EnergyNorth Inc./EI	Natural Gas	20	10.5	6.1%	X(5)	0	13	A–	PO Box 329, Manchester NH 03105 603/625-4000
Engelhard Corp./EC	Chemicals	20	19.6	1.8%	X	2	13	B+	101 Wood Ave., Iselin NJ 08830 908/205-6000
Ennis Business Forms Inc./EBF	Ofc. Equip/Supp	11	9.8	5.6%		0	19	A	107 N. Sherman St., Ennis TX 75119 214/875-6581
Enova Corp./ENA	Electric Utility	21	10.8	7.4%	X	1	19	A–	PO Box 1831, San Diego CA 92112 619/696-2000
Equifax Inc./EFX	Special Services	25	25.3	1.3%	X	2	15	A–	PO Box 4081, Atlanta GA 30302 800/462-9853
Exxon Corp./XON	Oil	84	15.8	3.7%	X	1	13	A–	PO Box 2298, Irving TX 75062 800/252-1800

Company Name/ Stock Symbol	Industry	Price	P/E	YIELD	Dividend Reinvestment Plan	Consecutive EPS Increases	Consecutive Dividend Increases	S&P Rank	Address/Phone Number
Family Dollar Stores Inc./FDO	Retail	16	15.2	2.8%		0	19	A−	PO Box 1017, Charlotte NC 28201 704/847-6961
Fastenal Corp./FAST	Retail	39	48.8	0.1%		13	0	B+	2001 Theurer Blvd., Winona MN 55987 507/454-5374
Federal Natl. Mtge. Corp./FNM	Financial	31	14.6	2.5%	X	9	10	A	3900 Wisconsin Ave., Washington DC 20016 800/366-2968
Federal Realty Inv. Trust/FRT	RE Invest. Trust	22	12.3	7.5%	X	3	28		4800 Hampden Ln. #500, Bethesda MD 20814 800/658-8980
Fifth Third Bancorp/ FITB	Banking	51	16.3	2.0%	X	22	22	A+	Fifth Third Ctr., Cincinnati OH 45263 513/579-5300
Financial Trust Corp./ FITC	Banking	26	11.7	3.8%	X	31	31		PO Box 220, Carlisle PA 17013 717/243-8003
First Chicago NBD Corp./FCN	Banking	39	11.1	3.5%	X	0	29		Mail Suite 0460, Chicago IL 60670 312/732-4812
First Commerce Banc-shares/FCBIA	Banking	27	19.3	3.9%	X	0	11		1248 O St., Lincoln NE 68508 402/434-4110
First Empire State Corp./FES(A)	Banking	244	12.1	1.1%	X	6	15	A+	PO Box 223, Buffalo NY 14240 716/842-5138
First Merchants Corp./ FRME	Banking	23	11.6	3.5%	X	20	13	A+	PO Box 792, Muncie IN 47308 800/262-4261

FirstMerit Corp./FMER	Banking	30	18.8	3.6%	X	0	14	A–	III Cascade Plaza, Akron OH 44308 216/996-6300
First Michigan Bank Corp./FMBC	Banking	30	20.1	2.0%	X(5)	14	14	A+	One Financial Plaza, Holland MI 49423 616/355-9200
First Northern Capital Corp./FNGB	Banking	15	15.2	3.7%	X	1	11	B+	PO Box 23100, Green Bay WI 54305 800/999-3675
First of America Bank Corp./FOA	Banking	44	10.9	3.8%	X(5)	1	13	A–	211 S. Rose St., Kalamazoo MI 49007 616/376-9000
First Tennessee National/FTEN	Banking	29	11.6	3.7%	X	6	18	A–	165 Madison Ave., Memphis TN 38103 901/523-5620
First Union Corp./FTU	Banking	62	12.5	3.7%	X(1)	6	18	A	Two First Union Ctr., Charlotte NC 28288 704/374-6782
First Virginia Banks Inc./FVB	Banking	39	11.6	3.7%	X	0	19	A	PO Box 88, Falls Church VA 22040 703/241-4000
Firstar Corp./FSR	Banking	45	13.8	3.4%	X	6	17	B+	PO Box 2077, Milwaukee WI 53201 414/765-4321
Fleetwood Enterprises/FLE	Manuf. Housing	30	20.0	2.1%		0	13	B+	PO Box 7638, Riverside CA 92513 909/351-3500
FlightSafety International/FSI	Special Services	47	16.9	1.2%		2	19	A	Marine Air Term., LaGuardia Air., Flushing NY 11371 718/565-4100
Florida Progress Corp./FPC	Electric Utility	34	13.4	6.1%	X	3	43	A–	PO Box 33028, St. Petersburg FL 33733 800/352-1121
Flowers Industries Inc./FLO	Foods	17	25.8	3.5%	X	1	23	B+	PO Box 1338, Thomasville GA 31799 912/226-9110
Forest Laboratories Inc./FRX(A)	Health Care	35	16.7	0.0%		14	0	B+	909 Third Ave., New York NY 10022 212/421-7850

Company Name/ Stock Symbol	Industry	Price	P/E	YIELD	Dividend Reinvestment Plan	Consecutive EPS Increases	Consecutive Dividend Increases	S&P Rank	Address/Phone Number
Franklin Quest Co./FNQ	Special Services	19	10.8	0.0%			11	0	2200 W. Parkway Blvd., Salt Lake City UT 84119 801/975-1776
Franklin Resources Inc./ BEN	Investment Bank	56	15.2	0.8%	X		16	15	A	777 Mariners Island Blvd., San Mateo CA 94404 800/342-5236
Frisch's Restaurants Inc./FRS(A)	Restaurant	13	38.2	1.8%			0	21	B+	2800 Gilbert Ave., Cincinnati OH 45206 513/961-2660
Frontier Corp./FRO	Telephone	28	26.4	3.0%	X		0	36	B+	180 S. Clinton Ave., Rochester NY 14646 800/836-0342
Fuller, H.B. Co./FULL	Chemicals	32	17.2	2.1%	X(3)		2	27	B+	2400 Energy Pk. Dr., St. Paul MN 55108 800/214-2523
Fulton Financial Corp./ FULT	Banking	19	11.5	3.6%	X		14	14		PO Box 4887, Lancaster PA 17604 800/626-0255
GAINSCO Inc./GNA	Insurance/Prop.	9	10.8	0.6%			11	4	B+	PO Box 2933, Ft. Worth TX 76119 817/336-2500
Gallagher, Arthur J. & Co./AJG	Insurance Brokers	32	12.2	3.6%			4	11	A–	Two Pierce Place, Itasca IL 60143 630/773-3800
Gannett Co. Inc./GCI	Publishing	64	18.3	2.2%	X		4	25	A	1100 Wilson Blvd., Arlington VA 22234 703/284-6000
GATX Corp./GMT	Transportation	43	10.4	4.0%	X		3	10	A–	500 W. Monroe, Chicago IL 60661 312/621-6200

Company/Ticker	Industry							Address
General Binding Corp./GBND	Ofc. Equip./Supp	20	13.7	2.1%		2	20	B+	One GBC Plaza, Northbrook IL 60062 847/272-3700
General Electric Co./GE	Electrical Equip.	80	19.4	2.3%	X	20	20	A+	3135 Easton Turnpike, Fairfield CT 06431 800/786-2543
General Re Corp./GRN	Insurance/Prop.	148	14.0	1.4%	X	1	19	A	PO Box 10351, Stamford CT 06904 203/328-5000
Genuine Parts Co./GPC	Auto Parts	43	16.3	3.1%	X	13	39	A+	2999 Circle 75 Pkwy., Atlanta GA 30339 770/953-1700
Giant Food Inc./GFSA(A)	Grocery	34	19.1	2.2%	X	3	24	A–	6300 Sheriff Rd., Landover MD 20785 301/341-4100
Gillette Co./G	Cosmetics	63	30.3	1.1%	X	2	17	A+	Prudential Tower, Boston MA 02199 617/421-7000
Golden Enterprises Inc./GLDC	Foods	8	22.2	5.8%		1	24	B	2101 Magnolia Ave. So. #212, Birmingham AL 35205 205/326-6101
Golden West Financial/GDW	Savings & Loan	54	11.2	0.7%		0	13	A–	1901 Harrison St., Oakland CA 94612 415/446-3420
Gorman-Rupp Co./GRC(A)	Manufacturing	13	13.0	4.3%	X	9	23	B+	PO Box 1217, Mansfield OH 44901 419/755-1011
Graco Inc./GGG	Machine Tools	20	11.9	2.4%	X	2	10	A–	PO Box 1441, Minneapolis MN 55440 612/623-6672
Grainger, W.W. Inc./GWW	Electrical Equip.	70	17.9	1.4%		1	24	A	455 Knightsbridge Pkwy., Lincolnshire IL 60069 847/793-9030
Great Lakes Chemical Corp./GLK	Chemicals	57	12.6	1.1%		9	22	A+	One Great Lakes Blvd., W. Lafayette IN 47906 317/497-6100
Grey Advertising Inc./GREY	Special Services	218	13.1	1.7%		1	20	B	777 Third Ave., New York NY 10017 212/546-2279

Company Name/ Stock Symbol	Industry	Price	P/E	YIELD	Dividend Reinvestment Plan	Consecutive EPS Increases	Consecutive Dividend Increases	S&P Rank	Address/Phone Number
Hach Co./HACH	Pollution Contr.	15	15.2	1.6%		12	14	A	PO Box 389, Loveland CO 80539 303/669-3050
Hannaford Brothers Co./HRD	Grocery	31	18.5	1.5%	X	16	33	A+	PO Box 1000, Portland ME 04104 207/883-2911
Harcourt General Inc./H	Publishing	46	20.1	1.5%	X	1	27	B+	27 Boylston St., Chestnut Hill MA 02167 617/232-8200
Harland, John H. Co./JH	Printing	24	def.	4.3%	X	0	42	A−	Box 105250, Atlanta GA 30348 800/ 723-3690
Harleysville National Corp./HNBC	Banking	24	11.9	3.2%	X	20	21		PO Box 195, Harleysville PA 19438 800/423-3955
Hartford Steam Boiler Insp./HSB	Insurance/Prop.	44	14.1	5.2%	X	2	30	B+	PO Box 5024, Hartford CT 06102 203/722-5767
Hasbro Inc./HAS(A)	Toys	33	16.3	1.2%		0	17	B+	PO Box 200, Pawtucket RI 02862 401/431-8697
Haverty Furniture Cos. Inc./HAVT	Household Furn.	9	9.5	3.3%		0	20	B	866 W. Peachtree St. NW, Atlanta GA 30308 404/881-1911
Hawaiian Electric Industries/HE	Electric Utility	35	12.9	6.9%	X	2	32	A−	PO Box 730, Honolulu HI 96808 808/543-5662
Health Care Property Investors/HCP	RE Invest. Trust	33	11.5	6.9%		6	10		10990 Wilshire Blvd. #1200, Los Angeles CA 90024 310/473-1990

Company/Symbol	Industry								Address
Heilig-Meyers Co./HMY	Household Furn.	20	27.8	1.4%	X	0	20	A	2235 Staples Mill Rd., Richmond VA 23230 804/359-9171
Heinz, H.J. Co./HNZ	Foods	32	18.3	3.3%	X	3	29	A+	PO Box 57, Pittsburgh PA 15230 800/253-3399
Helmerich & Payne Inc./HP	Oil & Gas Drill.	35	29.7	1.5%		0	24	B	Utica at 21st St., Tulsa OK 74114 918/742-5531
Hershey Foods Corp./HSY	Foods	79	21.8	1.8%	X	1	21	A	PO Box 810, Hershey PA 17033 717/534-7556
Hillenbrand Industries Inc./HB	Medical Prods.	34	23.4	1.8%		1	23	A	700 State Rte. 46 E., Batesville IN 47006 812/934-8400
Home Beneficial Corp./HBENB	Insurance/Life	25	11.6	3.5%		1	32	B+	PO Box 27572, Richmond VA 23261 804/254-9602
Home Depot Inc./HD	Retail	50	32.5	0.5%	X	10	8	A+	2727 Paces Ferry Rd., Atlanta GA 30339 404/984-2776
Honeywell Inc./HON	Electrical Equip.	50	17.7	2.2%	X	2	20	B	PO Box 524, Minneapolis MN 55440 612/951-2122
Hormel Foods Corp./HRL	Foods	23	16.8	2.6%	X	11	29	A+	PO Box 800, Austin MN 55912 507/437-5669
Houghton Mifflin Co./HTN	Publishing	48	177.8	2.0%	X	0	13	B+	222 Berkeley St., Boston MA 02116 617/351-5000
Household International Inc./HI	Financial	69	14.7	2.3%	X(2.5)	4	43	B+	2700 Sanders Rd., Prospect Heights IL 60070 847/564-5000
Hubbell Inc./HUBB	Electrical Equip.	35	18.3	3.0%	X	2	35	A	PO Box 549, Orange CT 06477 203/799-4100
Hunt Manufacturing Co./HUN	Ofc. Equip/Supp	13	11.9	2.9%		0	28	B+	2005 Market St., Philadelphia PA 19103 215/656-0300

Company Name/ Stock Symbol	Industry	Price	P/E	YIELD	Dividend Reinvestment Plan	Consecutive EPS Increases	Consecutive Dividend Increases	S&P Rank	Address/Phone Number
Huntington Bancshares/ HBAN	Banking	20	11.4	3.7%	X(5)	5	29	A	Huntington Ctr., Columbus OH 43287 614/480-3803
Illinois Tool Works Inc./ ITW	Manufacturing	62	17.3	1.1%	X	4	33	A+	3600 W. Lake Ave., Glenview IL 60025 847/724-7500
Indiana Energy Inc./IEI	Natural Gas	24	11.9	4.6%	X	0	23	B+	1630 N. Meridian St., Indianapolis IN 46202 800/777-3389
International Dairy Queen/INDQA	Restaurant	19	12.9	0.0%	X	22	0	B+	7505 Metro Blvd., Minneapolis MN 55439 612/830-0200
Intl. Flavors & Fragrances/IFF	Cosmetics	42	23.5	3.2%		10	33	A+	521 W. 57th St., New York NY 10019 212/765-5500
Interpublic Group of Cos./IPG	Special Services	43	19.7	1.6%	X	1	12	A+	1271 Ave. of the Americas, New York NY 10020 212/399-8000
Jefferson-Pilot Corp./JP	Insurance/Life	52	13.6	2.8%	X	8	27	A	PO Box 21008, Greensboro NC 27420 910/691-3000
Johnson & Johnson/JNJ	Health Care	47	23.0	1.6%	X	37	33	A+	New Brunswick NJ 08933 908/524-6491
Johnson Controls Inc./ JCI	Manufacturing	67	14.0	2.4%	X	5	20	A−	PO Box 591, Milwaukee WI 53201 414/228-2363
K2 Inc./KTO	Leisure	24	17.4	1.8%		5	18	B+	PO Box 22252, Los Angeles CA 90040 213/890-5830

Company/Symbol	Industry								Address
Kellogg Co./K	Foods	75	32.2	2.1%	X	0	39	A	PO Box CAMB, Battle Creek MI 49016 800/962-1413
Kelly Services Inc./KELYA	Special Services	28	15.1	3.0%		4	24	A	999 W. Big Beaver Rd., Troy MI 48084 810/362-4444
Kenan Transport Co./KTCO	Transportation	20	14.3	1.4%		0	17		PO Box 2729, Chapel Hill NC 27515 919/967-8221
KeyCorp/KEY	Banking	38	10.7	4.0%	X	8	15	A+	127 Public Square, Cleveland OH 44114 800/539-7216
Keystone Financial Inc./KSTN	Banking	22	12.4	4.4%	X	7	11	A-	PO Box 708, Altoona PA 16603 814/946-6691
Keystone International Inc./KII	Machinery	18	32.1	4.1%	X	0	24	B+	PO Box 40010, Houston TX 77240 713/466-1176
Kimball International Inc./KBALB	Household Furn.	27	13.7	3.9%		2	24	A-	1600 Royal St., Jasper IN 47549 812/482-1600
Kimberly-Clark Corp./KMB	Household Prods.	76	105.6	2.4%	X	0	22	A	Box 612606, Dallas TX 75261 214/281-1200
KU Energy Corp./KU	Electric Utility	30	12.7	5.7%	X	1	14	A	One Quality St., Lexington KY 40507 800/786-2558
La-Z-Boy Chair Co./LZB	Household Furn.	29	13.7	2.6%	X	5	15	A-	1284 N. Telegraph Rd., Monroe MI 48162 313/241-4414
Lancaster Colony Corp./LANC	Foods	36	14.5	1.9%	X	5	33	A	37 W. Broad St., Columbus OH 43215 614/224-7141
Lee Enterprises Inc./LEE	Publishing	20	16.7	2.4%		4	35	A-	215 N. Main St., Davenport IA 52801 319/383-2100
Legg Mason Inc./LM	Investment Bank.	29	12.1	1.8%		1	14	B+	PO Box 1476, Baltimore MD 21203 410/539-0000

Company Name/Stock Symbol	Industry	Price	P/E	YIELD	Dividend Reinvestment Plan	Consecutive EPS Increases	Consecutive Dividend Increases	S&P Rank	Address/Phone Number
Leggett & Platt Inc./LEG	Household Furn.	26	16.9	1.7%			5	24	A	No. 1 Leggett Rd., Carthage MO 64836 417/358-8131
LG&E Energy Corp./LGE	Electric Utility	22	17.2	5.0%	X		1	41	B+	PO Box 32030, Louisville KY 40232 800/235-9705
Lilly, Eli & Co./LLY	Health Care	57	23.2	2.4%	X		2	28	A	PO Box 88665, Indianapolis IN 46208 800/833-8699
Lilly Industries Inc./LI	Bldng. Materials	17	27.9	1.9%	X		0	15	A-	733 S.W. St., Indianapolis IN 46225 317/687-6700
Lincoln National Corp./LNC	Insurance/Life	42	9.1	4.4%	X		1	12	B+	PO Box 7845, Ft. Wayne IN 46801 800/237-2920
Linear Technology Corp./LLTC	Electronics	27	15.9	0.7%			10	3	B+	1630 McCarthy Blvd., Milpitas CA 95035 408/432-1900
Lockheed Martin Corp./LMT	Aerospace/Def.	80	14.5	1.8%	X		4	24	A	4500 Park Granada Blvd., Calabasas CA 91399 818/712-2000
Loctite Corp./LOC	Chemicals	43	17.9	2.8%	X		2	12	A	10 Columbus Blvd., Hartford CT 06106 860/520-5000
Louisiana-Pacific Corp./LPX	Paper/Forest	20	def.	2.8%	X		0	19	B+	111 SW Fifth Ave., Portland OR 97204 503/221-0800
Lowe's Companies Inc./LOW	Retail	31	24.2	0.6%	X		0	15	A-	PO Box 1111, N. Wilkesboro NC 28656 910/651-4254

Company/Symbol	Industry								Address
Lubrizol Corp./LZ	Chemicals	28	13.7	3.4%	X	0	12	B+	29400 Lakeland Blvd., Wickliffe OH 44092 216/943-4200
Luby's Cafeterias Inc./LUB	Restaurant	24	14.5	3.3%	X	28	30	A	PO Box 33069, San Antonio TX 78265 210/654-9000
Madison Gas & Electric Co./MDSN	Electric Utility	21	14.9	6.2%	X	0	15	A−	PO Box 1231, Madison WI 53701 800/356-6423
Marcus Corp./MCS	Hotel/Motel	22	17.3	1.4%		8	11	A	PO Box 2077, Milwaukee WI 53201 414/272-6020
Mark Twain Bancshares/MTWN	Banking	36	12.0	3.4%	X	5	25	A+	8820 Ladue Rd., St. Louis MO 63124 314/727-1000
Marsh & McClennan Cos./MMC	Insurance Brokers	89	14.9	3.6%	X	11	35	A+	1166 Ave. of Americas, New York NY 10036 212/345-5475
Marshall & Ilsley Corp./MRIS	Banking	26	13.4	2.8%	X	1	23	A−	770 N. Water St., Milwaukee WI 53202 414/765-7801
Masco Corp./MAS	Bldng. Materials	27	22.5	2.8%	X	1	37	B	21001 Van Born Rd., Taylor MI 48180 313/274-7400
May Department Stores Co./MA	Retail	43	16.2	2.7%	X	21	21	A+	611 Olive St., St. Louis MO 63101 314/342-6300
McClatchy Newspapers Inc./MNI	Publishing	25	25.0	1.5%		0	12	B	2100 Q St., Sacramento CA 95816 916/321-1846
McDonald's Corp./MCD	Restaurant	45	21.7	0.7%	X	30	20	A+	McDonald's Plaza, Oak Brook IL 60521 708/575-7428
McGraw-Hill Companies Inc./MHP	Publishing	39	16.7	3.4%	X	2	21	A+	1221 Ave. of Americas, New York NY 10020 212/512-2000
Medtronic Inc./MDT	Medical Prods.	48	25.5	0.8%	X	12	18	A+	7000 Central Ave. NE, Minneapolis, MN 55432 612/574-3035

Company Name/Stock Symbol	Industry	Price	P/E	YIELD	Dividend Reinvestment Plan	Consecutive EPS Increases	Consecutive Dividend Increases	S&P Rank	Address/Phone Number
Mercantile Bankshares/MRBK	Banking	25	10.7	3.7%	X(5)	20	19	A	PO Box 1477, Baltimore MD 21203 410/237-5900
Merck & Co. Inc./MRK	Health Care	65	22.4	2.5%	X	2	20	A+	PO Box 100-WS3AB-40, Whitehouse Station NJ 08889 800/613-2104
Microsoft Corp./MSFT	Computer Soft.	115	33.5	0.0%		20	0	B+	One Microsoft Way, Redmond WA 98052 800/285-7772
Middlesex Water Co./MSEX	Water Utility	17	12.7	6.5%	X	6	14	A−	PO Box 1500, Iselin NJ 08830 908/634-1500
Millipore Corp./MIL	Manufacturing	35	16.7	1.0%	X	3	25	B+	80 Ashby Rd., Bedford MA 01730 617/275-9200
Mine Safety Appliances Co./MNES	Health Care	45	15.3	2.5%		2	25	B	121 Gamma Dr., O'Hara Township, Pittsburgh PA 15238 412/967-3000
Minnesota Mining & Mfg./MMM	Miscellaneous	63	20.1	3.1%	X	4	37	A+	3M Ctr. 216-2N-10, St. Paul MN 55144 612/733-3564
Minnesota Power & Light/MPL	Electric Utility	27	13.6	7.6%	X	1	25	B+	30 W. Superior St., Duluth MN 55802 800/535-3056
Mobile Gas Service Corp./MBLE	Natural Gas	21	8.9	5.3%	X	0	19	B+	PO Box 2248, Mobile AL 36652 205/450-4638

Company/Symbol	Industry								Address
Modine Manufacturing Co./MODI	Auto Parts	27	13.2	2.5%	X	0	11	A	1500 DeKoven Ave., Racine WI 53403 414/636-1361
Monsanto Co./MTC	Chemicals	28	8.3	5.4%	X	3	23	A–	800 N. Lindbergh Blvd., St. Louis MO 63167 314/694-8149
Morgan, J.P. & Co. Inc./JPM	Banking	85	10.8	3.8%	X	1	19	B+	60 Wall St., New York NY 10260 212/648-9446
Myers Industries Inc./MYE(A)	Auto Parts	15	13.5	1.3%	X	0	21	A	1293 S. Main St., Akron OH 44301 330/253-5592
NACCO Industries/NC	Machinery	51	7.0	1.5%	X	2	17	B+	5875 Landerbrook Dr., Mayfield Heights OH 44124 216/449-9600
Nash Finch Co./NAFC	Distributors	16	9.8	4.5%	X	2	27	A–	PO Box 355, Minneapolis MN 55440 612/832-0534
National Commerce Bancorp./NCBC	Banking	31	14.4	2.5%	X	18	21	A	One Commerce Sq., Memphis TN 38150 901/523-3434
National Fuel Gas Co./NFG	Natural Gas	33	12.6	5.1%	X	0	24	B+	10 Lafayette Sq., Buffalo NY 14203 716/857-7548
National Penn Bancshares/NPBC	Banking	28	13.3	3.3%	X	18	17		PO Box 547, Boyertown PA 19512 610/369-6291
National Security Group/NSEC	Insurance/Multi.	12	def.	5.3%		0	18	B+	661 E. Davis St., Elba AL 36323 334/897-2273
National Service Industries/NSI	Special Services	38	18.8	3.1%	X	4	34	A	1420 Peachtree St. NE, Atlanta GA 30309 404/853-1000
NationsBank Corp./NB	Banking	83	11.2	2.8%	X	4	18	A–	Charlotte NC 28255 800/521-3984
New Plan Realty Trust/NPR	RE Invest. Trust	21	14.3	6.7%	X(5)	3	20	A–	1120 Ave. of Americas, New York NY 10036 212/869-3000
Newell Co./NWL	Housewares	29	19.7	1.9%	X	13	3	A+	29 E. Stephenson St., Freeport IL 61032 815/235-4171

Company Name/Stock Symbol	Industry	Price	P/E	YIELD	Dividend Reinvestment Plan	Consecutive EPS Increases	Consecutive Dividend Increases	S&P Rank	Address/Phone Number
Nordson Corp./NDSN	Machinery	50	17.0	1.4%	X	5	32	A	28601 Clemens Rd., Westlake OH 44145 216/892-1580
Nordstrom Inc./NOBE	Retail	41	20.3	1.2%		0	21	A	PO Box 2737, Seattle WA 98111 206/233-6301
North Carolina Natural Gas/NCG	Natural Gas	28	11.8	4.6%	X(5)	1	17	A−	PO Box 909, Fayetteville NC 28302 910/483-0315
Northern States Power Co./NSP	Electric Utility	45	12.5	6.1%	X	2	21	A−	414 Nicollet Mall, Minneapolis MN 55401 800/527-4677
Northern Trust Corp./NTRS	Banking	59	14.5	2.1%		5	10	A−	50 S. La Salle St., Chicago IL 60675 312/630-6000
Northwest Natural Gas Co./NWNG	Natural Gas	34	12.7	5.3%	X	0	40	B+	220 NW 2nd Ave., Portland OR 97209 503/220-2591
Northwestern Public Service/NPS	Electric Utility	27	9.7	6.5%	X	3	13	A	PO Box 1318, Huron SD 57350 800/677-6716
Nucor Corp./NUE	Steel	47	16.8	0.6%	X	4	23	A	2100 Rexford Rd., Charlotte NC 28211 704/366-7000
Ohio Casualty Corp./OCAS	Insurance/Prop.	33	12.5	4.8%	X	2	49	B+	136 N. Third St., Hamilton OH 45025 513/867-3000
Old Kent Financial Corp./OKEN	Banking	37	12.1	3.3%	X	36	37	A+	111 Lyon St. NW, Grand Rapids MI 49503 800/652-2657

Company/Symbol	Industry								Address
Old Republic International/ORI	Insurance/Multi.	21	5.9	0.5%	X	1	14	B+	307 N. Michigan Ave., Chicago IL 60601 312/346-8100
One Valley Bancorp/OVWV	Banking	34	11.2	3.2%	X	13	14		PO Box 1793, Charleston WV 25326 304/348-7023
Orange & Rockland Utilities/ORU	Electric Utility	35	12.8	7.4%	X	1	20	A−	PO Box 3006, Pearl River NY 10965 914/577-2512
Otter Tail Power Co./OTTR	Electric Utility	33	12.9	5.5%	X	8	20	A−	PO Box 496, Fergus Falls MN 56538 800/664-1259
Pall Corp./PLL	Manufacturing	22	21.4	2.3%	X	2	21	A	2200 Northern Blvd., East Hills NY 11548 800/205-7255
Park National Corp./PRK(A)	Banking	49	14.3	2.9%	X	30	30		PO Box 3500, Newark OH 43058 614/349-3708
Parker Hannifin Corp./PH	Manufacturing	35	10.7	2.1%	X	1	39	B+	17325 Euclid Ave., Cleveland OH 44112 216/531-3000
Pentair Inc./PNR	Paper/Forest	25	16.0	2.0%	X	5	19	A−	1500 County Rd. B2 W., St. Paul MN 55113 612/636-7920
Peoples Bancorp Inc./PEBO	Banking	22	11.6	2.9%	X	22	30		PO Box 738, Marietta OH 45750 614/374-6136
Peoples Energy Corp./PGL	Natural Gas	32	15.2	5.8%	X	0	12	B+	PO Box 2000, Chicago IL 60690 800/228-6888
Pep Boys-Manny, Moe & Jack/PBY	Retail	30	21.4	0.7%	X	6	19	A+	3111 W. Allegheny Ave., Philadelphia PA 19132 800/737-0135
PepsiCo Inc./PEP	Soft Drink	32	28.8	1.4%	X	0	23	A+	Purchase NY 10577 914/253-3055
Pfizer Inc./PFE	Health Care	71	26.1	1.7%	X	2	28	A−	235 E. 42nd St., New York NY 10017 212/573-2323
Philip Morris Cos. Inc./MO	Tobacco	100	14.1	4.0%	X	2	30	A+	120 Park Ave., New York NY 10017 800/367-5415

Company Name/Stock Symbol	Industry	Price	P/E	YIELD	Dividend Reinvestment Plan	Consecutive EPS Increases	Consecutive Dividend Increases	S&P Rank	Address/Phone Number
Piedmont Natural Gas Co./PNY	Natural Gas	24	13.2	4.8%	X(5)	1	17	A–	PO Box 33068, Charlotte NC 28233 704/364-3120
Pitney Bowes Inc./PBI	Ofc. Equip/Supp	46	15.9	3.0%	X	14	13	A+	1 Elmcroft Rd., Stamford CT 06926 203/356-5000
Potlatch Corp./PCH	Paper/Forest	36	12.4	4.6%	X	2	12	B+	PO Box 193591, San Francisco CA 94119 415/576-8800
PP&L Resources Inc./PPL	Electric Utility	23	10.4	7.3%	X	1	26	A–	Two N. Ninth St., Allentown PA 18101 800/345-3085
PPG Industries Inc./PPG	Bldng. Materials	47	12.4	2.7%	X	2	24	A–	One PPG Place, Pittsburgh PA 15272 412/434-3312
Procter & Gamble Co./PG	Household Prods.	85	21.6	2.1%	X	2	40	A	PO Box 599, Cincinnati OH 45201 800/742-6253
Progressive Corp./PGR	Institute/Prop.	49	15.1	0.4%		0	26	B+	6300 Wilson Mills, Mayfield Village OH 44143 216/446-7204
Providian Corp./PVN	Insurance/Life	40	10.1	2.5%	X	26	33	A–	PO Box 32830, Louisville KY 40232 502/560-2391
Public Service Co. of NC/PGS	Natural Gas	16	12.2	5.5%	X(5)	0	25	B+	PO Box 1398, Gastonia NC 28053 800/784-6443
Quaker Chemical Corp./QCHM	Chemicals	12	15.8	5.7%		0	24	B	Conshohocken PA 19428 610/832-4119

Company/Symbol	Industry								Address
Quaker Oats Co./OAT	Foods	31	def.	3.7%	X	1	29	A–	PO Box 049001, Chicago IL 60604 800/344-1198
Questar Corp./STR	Natural Gas	32	26.4	3.6%	X	0	17	A	PO Box 45433, Salt Lake City UT 84145 801/534-5000
Raymond James Financial Inc./RJF	Investment Bank.	20	8.2	1.9%		1	10	A–	880 Carillon Pkwy., St. Petersburg FL 33716 813/573-3800
Raytheon Co./RTN	Aerospace/Def.	45	13.2	1.8%	X	1	12	A+	141 Spring St., Lexington MA 02173 617/860-2303
Reader's Digest Association/RDA	Publishing	41	74.5	4.4%		11	9	A–	Pleasantville NY 10570 914/238-1000
Regions Financial Corp./RGBK	Banking	44	11.1	3.2%	X	24	24	A+	PO Box 10247, Birmingham AL 35202 334/832-8493
ReliaStar Financial Corp./RLR	Insurance/Life	42	9.5	2.7%		4	24	A–	20 Washington Ave. S., Minneapolis MN 55401 612/372-5574
Republic New York Corp./RNB	Banking	62	12.9	2.5%		0	30	B+	452 Fifth Ave., New York NY 10018 212/525-6225
Rhone-Poulenc Rorer Inc./RPR	Health Care	63	25.2	2.0%	X	0	17	B+	500 Arcola Rd. 3C45, Collegeville PA 19426 610/454-3852
RLI Corp./RLI	Insurance/Prop.	23	20.5	2.4%	X	1	19	B+	9025 N. Lindbergh Dr., Peoria IL 61615 309/692-1000
Rockwell International Corp./ROK	Aerospace	51	13.2	2.3%	X	3	19	A–	PO Box 4250, Seal Beach CA 90740 310/797-5986
Rohm & Haas Co./ROH	Chemicals	56	11.7	3.2%		2	18	B+	Independence Mall W., Philadelphia PA 19106 215/592-3045
Rollins Inc./ROL	Special Services	21	20.2	2.8%	X	0	10	A–	2170 Piedmont Rd. NE, Atlanta GA 30324 404/888-2000

Company Name/Stock Symbol	Industry	Price	P/E	YIELD	Dividend Reinvestment Plan	Consecutive EPS Increases	Consecutive Dividend Increases	S&P Rank	Address/Phone Number
Roto-Rooter Inc./ROTO	Special Services	36	18.4	1.9%			10	A−	
RPM Inc./RPOW	Chemicals	15	17.4	3.2%	X	48	22	A+	PO Box 777, Medina OH 44258 330/273-5090
Rubbermaid Inc./RBD	Housewares	28	65.1	2.0%	X	0	42	A	1147 Akron Rd., Wooster OH 44691 330/264-6464
Ruddick Corp./RDK	Grocery	11	16.4	2.5%		1	10	A	2000 Two First Union Ctr., Charlotte NC 28282 704/372-5404
SAFECO Corp./SAFC	Insurance/Prop.	33	9.3	3.5%		1	24	A−	SAFECO Plaza, Seattle WA 98185 206/545-5000
St. Joseph Light & Power Co./SAJ	Electric Utility	16	11.0	5.9%	X	2	15	A−	PO Box 998, St. Joseph MO 64502 800/367-4562
St. Paul Companies/SPC	Insurance/Prop.	54	9.2	3.3%	X	3	10	A−	385 Washington St., St. Paul MN 55102 612/221-7911
Sallie Mae/SLM	Financial	72	11.2	2.2%		22	19	A	1050 Thomas Jefferson St. NW, Washington DC 20007 202/333-8000
Sara Lee Corp./SLE	Foods	30	18.0	2.5%	X	1	19	A	Three First Natl. Plaza, Chicago IL 60602 312/558-8662
SBC Communications Inc./SBC	Telephone	49	14.8	3.5%	X	11	11	A	PO Box 2933, San Antonio TX 78299 210/351-2044

Company/Symbol	Category								Address
SCANA Corp./SCG	Electric Utility	26	12.8	5.5%	X	3	44	A–	Columbia SC 29218 800/763-5891
Schering-Plough Corp./SGP	Health Care	58	18.8	2.3%	X	14	10	A+	One Giralda Farms, Madison NJ 07940 201/822-7000
Schulman, A. Inc./SHLM	Chemicals	23	21.5	1.7%		2	13	A	3550 W. Market St., Akron OH 44333 216/666-3751
Service Corp. International/SRV	Miscellaneous	27	27.8	0.9%	X	7	22	A–	PO Box 130548, Houston TX 77219 713/522-5141
ServiceMaster L.P./SVM	Special Services	21	8.2	4.6%	X	1	26	A+	One ServiceMaster Way, Downers Grove IL 60515 708/271-1300
Sherwin-Williams Co./SHW	Bldng. Materials	43	17.6	1.6%	X	17	16	A+	101 Prospect Ave. NW, Cleveland OH 44115 216/566-2000
SIGCORP Inc./SIG	Electric Utility	33	12.3	5.2%	X	0	36	A	PO Box 3606, Evansville IN 47735 800/227-8625
Sigma-Aldrich Corp./SIAL	Chemicals	49	18.1	0.9%	X	25	24	A+	3050 Spruce St., St. Louis MO 63103 800/521-8956
SJW Corp./SJW(A)	Comm. Services	37	9.2	6.0%	X	1	27	B+	374 W. Santa Clara St., San Jose CA 95196 408/279-7810
Smucker, J.M. Co./SJMA	Foods	18	17.8	2.9%	X	0	20	A–	Strawberry Ln., Orrville OH 44667 216/682-3000
Sonoco Products Co./SON	Paper/Forest	28	16.5	2.4%	X	3	13	A–	PO Box 160, Hartsville SC 29551 803/383-7277
SE Michigan Gas Enterprises/SMGS	Natural Gas	16	15.0	5.0%	X	0	19	A	PO Box 5026, Port Huron MI 48061 800/225-5647
Southern California Water/SCW	Water Utility	20	12.0	6.1%	X	1	42	B+	630 E. Foothill Blvd., San Dimas CA 91773 909/394-3600
Southern National Corp./SNB	Banking	27	10.4	4.0%	X(3)	0	23	A	200 W. Second St., Winston-Salem NC 27101 910/733-2000

Company Name/ Stock Symbol	Industry	Price	P/E	YIELD	Dividend Reinvestment Plan	Consecutive EPS Increases	Consecutive Dividend Increases	S&P Rank	Address/Phone Number
SouthTrust Corp./SOTR	Banking	26	10.4	3.4%	X	16	25	A	PO Box 2554, Birmingham AL 35290 205/254-5509
Standard Register Co./ SR	Ofc. Equip/Supp	27	14.2	2.8%		5	18	A	PO Box 1167, Dayton OH 45401 513/443-1506
Stanhome Inc./STH	Retail	27	12.9	4.0%	X	0	12	A–	Syms Way, Secaucus NJ 07094 201/ 902-9600
Stanley Works/SWK	Hdware. & Tools	29	67.4	2.5%	X	0	29	B+	1000 Stanley Dr., New Britain CT 06053 203/225-5111
Star Banc Corp./STB	Banking	71	14.3	2.6%	X	6	23	A+	425 Walnut St., Cincinnati OH 45202 513/632-4541
State Street Boston Corp./STT	Banking	48	21.2	1.6%	X	18	17	A+	Box 351, Boston MA 02101 617/786-3000
Stepan Co./SCL	Chemicals	18	12.9	2.6%		3	28	A–	Northfield IL 60093 847/446-7500
Stryker Corp./STRY	Medical Prods.	25	25.8	0.2%		19	3	A–	PO Box 4085, Kalamazoo MI 49003 616/385-2600
SunTrust Banks Inc./STI	Banking	36	14.0	2.2%	X	11	20	A+	PO Box 4418, Atlanta GA 30302 404/588-7711
Superior Industries Intl. Inc./SUP	Auto Parts	23	15.6	1.0%		0	12	A	7800 Woodley Ave., Van Nuys CA 91406 818/771-5906

Company/Ticker	Industry								Address
Superior Surgical Mfg./SGC(A)	Textiles/Apparel	10	22.7	3.6%		0	18	B+	PO Box 4002, Seminole FL 34642 813/397-9611
Supervalu Inc./SVU	Distributor	28	11.4	3.6%	X	1	24	A−	PO Box 990, Minneapolis MN 55440 612/828-4599
Synovus Financial Corp./SNV	Banking	23	20.7	1.9%	X	13	14	A+	PO Box 120, Columbus GA 31902 706/649-5220
SYSCO Corp./SYY	Distributor	29	19.6	1.8%	X	19	25	A+	1390 Enclave Pkwy., Houston TX 77077 800/337-9726
Tambrands Inc./TMB	Cosmetics	37	15.8	5.0%	X	0	44	B+	777 Westchester Ave., White Plains NY 10604 914/696-6000
Tasty Baking Co./TBC(A)	Foods	12	13.3	4.7%		0	14	B	2801 Hunting Park Ave., Philadelphia PA 19129 215/221-8500
TCA Cable TV Inc./TCAT	Broadcasting	25	19.7	2.2%		5	13	A−	PO Box 130489, Tyler TX 75713 903/595-3701
TECO Energy Inc./TE	Electric Utility	24	14.5	4.7%	X	9	36	A	PO Box 111, Tampa FL 33601 813/228-4111
Teleflex Inc./TFX	Electronics	45	15.2	1.4%		21	18	A+	630 W. Germantown Pike, Plymouth Mtg. PA 19462 610/834-6301
Telephone & Data Systems/TDS(A)	Telephone	39	36.8	1.0%	X(5)	0	21	B+	30 N. LaSalle #4000, Chicago IL 60602 312/630-1900
Temple-Inland Inc./TIN	Containers	48	9.3	2.5%	X	2	12	B+	Drawer N, Diboli TX 75941 409/829-1378
Tennant Co./TANT	Machinery	24	12.2	2.8%		2	24	A−	PO Box 1452, Minneapolis MN 55440 612/540-1209
Thermo Electron Corp./TMO	Electronics	34	29.1	0.0%		12	0	B+	PO Box 9046, Waltham MA 02254 617/622-1000

Company Name/ Stock Symbol	Industry	Price	P/E	YIELD	Dividend Reinvestment Plan	Consecutive EPS Increases	Consecutive Dividend Increases	S&P Rank	Address/Phone Number
Tompkins County Trust Co./TCTC	Banking	25	9.9	4.0%	X	6	13		PO Box 460, Ithaca NY 14851 607/273-3210
Tootsie Roll Industries Inc./TR	Foods	34	18.5	0.9%		14	32	A	7401 S. Cicero Ave., Chicago IL 60629 312/838-3400
Torchmark Corp./TMK	Insurance/Life	41	10.5	2.8%	X	1	44	A+	2001 Third Ave. S., Birmingham AL 35233 205/325-4200
T. Rowe Price Associ- ates/TROW	Financial	24	17.0	1.3%		5	11	A−	100 E. Pratt St., Baltimore MD 21202 410/547-2000
TRUSTCO Bank Corp NY/TRST	Banking	19	13.0	5.9%	X	20	19		PO Box 1082, Schenectady NY 12301 518/381-3601
Trustmark Corp./TRMK	Banking	21	11.7	2.3%	X	4	22	A	PO Box 291, Jackson MS 39205 601/354-5111
TRW Inc./TRW	Miscellaneous	84	12.4	2.6%	X	4	23	B+	1900 Richmond Rd., Cleveland OH 44124 216/291-7000
U.S. Bancorp Inc./USBC	Banking	34	14.1	3.3%	X	1	39	A	PO Box 8837, Portland OR 97208 503/275-5834
Union Electric Co./UEP	Electric Utility	39	13.7	6.4%	X	0	20	A−	PO Box 66887, St. Louis MO 63166 800/255-2237

Company/Ticker	Industry								Address
Union Pacific Corp./UNP	Transportation	69	22.5	2.5%	X	2	10	A−	Eighth & Eaton, Bethlehem PA 18018 610/861-3200
United Asset Management/UAM	Investment Bank.	22	19.5	2.9%		11	9	A	One Intl. Pl., Boston MA 02110 617/330-8900
United Carolina Bancshares/UCAR	Banking	22	10.7	3.3%	X	1	19	A−	PO Box 632, Whiteville NC 28472 919/642-5131
United Cities Gas Co./UCIT	Natural Gas	20	17.5	5.1%	X(5)	0	14	B+	5300 Maryland Way, Brentwood TN 37027 800/342-4413
United Dominion Realty Trust/UDR	RE Invest. Trust	14	11.9	6.9%	X	4	19		10 S. Sixth St. #203, Richmond VA 23219 804/780-2691
United Fire & Casualty Co./UCFS	Insurance/Multi.	33	11.4	1.8%		3	10	B+	118 Second Ave. SE, Cedar Rapids IA 52407 319/399-5700
UNITIL Corp./UTL(A)	Electric Utility	22	11.7	6.0%		4	10	B+	PO Box 25099, Richmond VA 23260 804/254-1303
Universal Corp./UVV	Tobacco	27	18.9	3.8%	X	0	25	B	PO Box 25099, Richmond VA 23260 804/254-1303
Universal Foods Corp./UFC	Foods	30	16.9	3.3%	X	0	24	A	Box 737, Milwaukee WI 53201 800/558-9892
USLIFE Corp./USH	Insurance/Life	30	13.6	3.1%	X	5	24	B+	125 Maiden Lane, New York NY 10038 212/709-6415
UST Inc./UST	Tobacco	33	14.5	4.5%	X	34	25	A+	100 W. Putnam Ave., Greenwich CT 06830 203/661-1100
UtiliCorp United Inc./UCU	Electric Utility	27	12.2	6.5%	X(5)	0	38	B+	PO Box 13287, Kansas City MO 64199 800/487-6661
VF Corp./VFC	Textiles/Apparel	57	23.6	2.5%	X	0	24	A−	PO Box 1022, Reading PA 19603 610/378-1151
Valley Resources Inc./VR(A)	Natural Gas	12	12.8	6.0%	X(5)	0	17	A−	PO Box 7900, Cumberland RI 02864 401/334-1188

Company Name/Stock Symbol	Industry	Price	P/E	YIELD	Dividend Reinvestment Plan	Consecutive EPS Increases	Consecutive Dividend Increases	S&P Rank	Address/Phone Number
Valspar Corp./VAL	Bldng. Materials	44	19.3	1.5%		21	18	A+	PO Box 1461, Minneapolis MN 55440 612/332-7371
Wachovia Corp./WB	Banking	43	12.2	3.7%	X	4	18	A	PO Box 3099, Winston-Salem NC 27150 910/732-5787
Wal-Mart Stores Inc./WMT	Retail	24	20.0	0.9%	X	34	12	A+	Bentonville AR 72716 800/438-6278
Walgreen Co./WAG	Retail	31	21.4	1.4%	X	21	19	A+	200 Wilmot Rd., Deerfield IL 60015 847/940-2972
Wallace Computer Services/WCS	Ofc. Equip/Supp	29	19.0	1.5%	X	5	25	A	4600 W. Roosevelt Rd., Hillside FL 60162 312/626-2000
Warner-Lambert Co./WLA	Health Care	54	18.3	2.6%	X	2	43	A-	201 Tabor Rd., Morris Plains NJ 07950 201/540-2000
Washington Federal Inc./WFSL	Savings & Loan	21	9.7	4.4%	X	0	12	A	425 Pike St., Seattle WA 98101 206/624-7930
Washington Gas Light/WGL	Natural Gas	21	10.6	5.4%	X	4	19	A	1100 H St. NW, Washington DC 20077 800/221-9427
Washington REIT/WRE(A)	RE Invest. Trust	16	15.1	6.5%	X	30	25		10400 Connecticut Ave., Kensington MD 20895 800/565-9748
Wausau Paper Mills Inc./WSAU	Paper/Forest	17	14.3	1.3%	X	0	12	A-	PO Box 1408, Wausau WI 54402 715/845-5266

Company/Symbol	Industry								Address
WD-40 Co./WDFC	Chemicals	43	15.8	5.8%		1	21	B+	1061 Cudahy Place, San Diego CA 92110 619/275-1400
Weingarten Realty Investors/WRI	RE Invest. Trust	39	13.5	6.2%	X	6	11		PO Box 924133, Houston TX 77292 713/866-6049
Weis Markets Inc./WMK	Grocery	31	16.4	2.7%	X	3	30	A−	1000 S. Second St., Sunbury PA 17801 717/286-4571
Wesco Financial Corp./WSC(A)	Financial	162	33.4	0.7%		2	24	B+	315 E. Colorado Blvd., Pasadena CA 91101 818/585-6700
Western Resources Inc./WR	Electric Utility	29	10.7	7.1%	X	0	20	B+	PO Box 750320, Topeka KS 66675 800/527-2495
Weyco Group Inc./WEYS	Shoes	39	9.6	2.3%		2	15		PO Box 1188, Milwaukee WI 53201 414/263-8800
WICOR Inc./WIC	Natural Gas	35	12.9	4.8%	X	3	12	B+	626 E. Wisconsin Ave., Milwaukee WI 53202 800/236-3453
Wilmington Trust Corp./WILM	Banking	31	11.6	4.3%	X	14	14	A+	Rodney Square N., Wilmington DE 19890 800/939-5066
Winn-Dixie Stores Inc./WIN	Grocery	34	21.2	2.8%	X	1	52	A+	PO Box B, Jacksonville FL 32203 904/783-5000
Wisconsin Energy Corp./WEC	Electric Utility	27	13.1	5.6%	X	1	35	A	PO Box 2949, Milwaukee WI 53201 800/558-9663
Witco Corp./WIT	Chemicals	29	17.2	3.9%	X	2	23	B+	One American Ln., Greenwich CT 06831 203/552-2263
Worthington Industries/WTHG	Steel	19	18.8	2.5%	X	0	27	A−	1205 Dearborn Dr., Columbus OH 43085 614/438-3210
WPL Holdings Inc./WPH	Electric Utility	31	11.5	6.4%	X	3	23	A	PO Box 2568, Madison WI 53701 800/356-5343

Company Name/Stock Symbol	Industry	Price	P/E	YIELD	Dividend Reinvestment Plan	Consecutive EPS Increases	Consecutive Dividend Increases	S&P Rank	Address/Phone Number
WPS Resources Corp./WPS	Electric Utility	31	12.7	6.1%	X	1	37	A–	PO Box 19001, Green Bay WI 54307 800/236-1551
Wrigley, William Jr. Co./WWY	Foods	50	26.5	2.1%	X	14	15	A+	410 N. Michigan Ave., Chicago IL 60611 800/824-9681

INDEX

ou are invited to join "The Staton Institute℠ – America's Finest Investors®" at a Spectacular Savings.

As our way of thanking you for buying this copy of "The America's Finest Companies® Investment Plan," please consider this your Personal Invitation to become a Member of "The Staton Institute℠ – America's Finest Investors®" at the <u>Special Rock-Bottom Bargain Introductory Rate</u> of *only $99, which includes* a one-year subscription to *The Staton Institute℠ Advisory* ($117/yr.) and a number of other wealthbuilding materials totaling $231.80. Yours for just $99.

Call toll free 800/779-7175 or clip and mail to The Staton Institute℠ Inc., 300 East Blvd. B-4, Charlotte, NC 28203. Or fax this coupon to 704/332-0427. You can also visit our Web site at www.StatonInstitute.com

☐ YES, I want to become a Member of "The Staton Institute℠ – America's Finest Investors®."

Name _____ Title _____
(please print legibly)

Firm _____

Address _____

City/State /ZIP _____

Daytime Phone (_____) _____ FAX (_____) _____

E-Mail Address _____

The Staton Institute℠ First-Year Membership	$99.00
NC Residents Add 6% Tax	5.94
☐ Check enclosed for $ _____ Shipping & Handling	6.95
☐ Charge to my credit card Foreign Orders add US $20	
☐ VISA ☐ M/CARD ☐ AMEX Exp. Date _____ TOTAL	

Signature _____ 97HY-1

Do Your Friends and Colleagues a Favor by Giving Them a **FREE** Copy of "The Staton Institute℠ Advisory."

So many people have benefited from the valuable insights and advice contained in each monthly issue of "The Staton Institute℠ Advisory" you will be doing your friends, relatives, colleagues – and yourself – a real favor if you send us their names so we can mail a no-obligation sample issue.

It will be sent FREE with <u>your</u> compliments.

And, "yes" we will be glad to send you a FREE copy of this newsletter so you can see for yourself just how useful Bill Staton's plain-English advice can be. There's no limit to the number of names you can send. Just be sure you submit a complete address in a legible way.

Your Name _____
(please print legibly)

Address _____

City/State/ZIP_____

Daytime Phone (_____)_____ Fax (_____)_____

E-Mail Address _____

Initial here _____ *if you want a no-obligation free sample issue of the "Advisory" for yourself.*

At no-obligation, send FREE sample issue of the "Advisory" newsletter to:

Name _____
(please print legibly)

Address _____

City/State/ZIP_____

Write below how you want each "gift notice" to read:

From: _____

Mail to "Sample Newsletter" c/o The Staton Institute℠, 300 East Blvd. B-4, Charlotte, NC 28203 or fax 704/332-0427.
Visit our web site at www.StatonInstitute.com

Praise for *Big Girls Don't Cry*

"Much, much more than another campaign book. . . . There are big ideas raised freshly. . . . Vitally important."

—Atlantic.com

"Traister [is] one of the most powerful voices in a new generation of American feminist writers."

—Walter Russell Mead, *Foreign Affairs*

"I ended up admiring Traister and loving her book. In its best parts, it is a raw and brave memoir of a journalist who discovered that all is not well for women in America, and a description of how she and other young women are laying claim to their rightful place in the fight. . . . Such a youthful embrace of the women's work yet to be done is exhilarating—for her generation and for mine."

—Connie Schultz, *Washington Post*

"A passionate, visionary and very personal account."

—*New York Times Book Review*

"[Traister's] main gift is for writing in a way that naturally blends storytelling, reporting, and commentary. The book is a mix of ethical journalism and emotional memoir, and she doesn't leave you wondering which pages represent which. She's [presented] level-headed, sane, intellectual reporting on an emotionally charged historical event, and she condenses the story in a way that produces real revelations you can take to the bank. . . . The 'a-ha' moments Traister delivers will pack a punch for many seasons yet to come."

—*Buffalo News*

"Traister's breezy style makes what might be a fact-filled slog read like feminism's coming-of-age tale. For those of us who were there, it's impossible not to relive the emotions; for those of us who were too young or distracted, this should be required reading."

—*Bust*

"Bludgeons conventional political wisdom by trenchantly exposing Palin's strange triangulation of mainstream feminism, Clinton's need to appear vulnerable in order to appeal to women, and the precarious position of black women—some of whom were conflicted between supporting candidates who mirrored their gender or their race. . . . Traister does a fine job in showing that progress does not proceed in straight lines, and, sometimes, it's the unlikeliest of individuals who initiate real change."

—*Publishers* Weekly

"[A] trenchant, entertaining analysis of the historic campaign."

—*Maclean's*

"Traister's mastery in reconciling her own thoughts and misgivings with the much larger and emphatic narration of her book speaks to her incredible prowess as a writer and researcher. A sharp observer of American culture, American media, and politically-minded women, Traister has produced an evocative meditation on modern feminism that is paired with the distinguishing voice of one woman voter— Traister. This enthralling and well-researched read is a tapestry of feminist voices, speaking from all the different corners of academia, media, and the blogosphere, all chiming in with an opinion worth hearing on America's most gripping election yet. "

—*Bookslut*

"A genuinely fun and provocative read."

—*Boston Globe*

"Reading *Big Girls Don't Cry,* I was often reminded how thrilling and infuriating much of that campaign was. The author takes a cold-eyed look at how America, wringing its hands about how race would impinge on the campaign, fumbled its way through an equally historic election for women."

—*New Statesman*

"If anyone was going to be up to the Herculean task of summarizing what went down in the 2008 elections with regard to gender, race, and class—and pointing the way forward—Traister was the one to do it. . . . I mean, when was the last time you read passages from a political book out loud because you found it so poignant and witty that you couldn't help but share?"

—Feministing

"Traister is a clear-eyed, whip-smart observer of the political scene, alert to the resurgence of identity politics as well as the recrudescence of feminism that marked the most recent presidential campaign. She has fashioned a remarkably engrossing page-turner of a cultural narrative, one which features outsize characters and unpredictable plot twists. *Big Girls Don't Cry* is a report on the 2008 election, but more important, it is a report on the way we think now. If you want to understand where we are going as an electoral entity—why Sarah Palin is the folk heroine du jour and why Michelle Obama has domesticated her freethinking persona—read this book."

—Daphne Merkin, novelist and critic

"Entertaining . . . a first-rate account of contemporary political warfare from an 'intersectional' perspective—one that regards racial, sexual, and class bias as equally pernicious."

—*American Prospect*

"Rebecca Traister's lively, insightful narrative discloses an underreported layer of the 2008 presidential campaign—and in so doing makes the subject fresh and vital again. An important and disquieting book, but also a pleasure to read."

—Robert Draper, author of *Dead Certain*

"In this riveting account of the 2008 election, Rebecca Traister negotiates the shoals of race and gender with exceptional grace and skill and establishes herself as one of the major younger journalists working today."

—Katha Pollitt, poet, essayist and columnist for the *Nation*

"The startling intelligence and graceful prose of Rebecca Traister's coverage of American cultural politics has been one of journalism's best kept secrets during the past decade. With *Big Girls Don't Cry,* she claims her place as heir to the tradition of Mary McCarthy and Joan Didion as she excavates the tectonic changes that lurked below the surface of most election reporting and illuminates events in a manner that will surprise political junkies and casual observers alike."

—Eric Alterman, author of *Why We're Liberals*

"Rebecca Traister is the most brilliant voice on feminism in this country. I was totally caught up in *Big Girls Don't Cry* from the first page and couldn't believe how much Ms. Traister captured and illuminated a story with which I had thought I was so well versed: the 2008 election. She told it as if for the first time."

—Anne Lamott, author of *Bird by Bird*

"I didn't know what I didn't know about the 2008 election until reading Rebecca Traister's smart, entertaining take on it. Well researched, well written, provocative and insightful, *Big Girls Don't Cry* is a high-spirited salute to feminism in its many forms."

—Curtis Sittenfeld, author of *American Wife*

BIG
GIRLS
DON'T
CRY

The Election That Changed Everything
for American Women

REBECCA TRAISTER

FREE PRESS
New York London Toronto Sydney

_f_P

FREE PRESS
A Division of Simon & Schuster, Inc.
1230 Avenue of the Americas
New York, NY 10020

First Free Press trade paperback edition June 2011

FREE PRESS and colophon are trademarks of Simon & Schuster, Inc.

For information about special discounts for bulk purchases,
please contact Simon & Schuster Special Sales at 1-866-506-1949
or business@simonandschuster.com.

The Simon & Schuster Speakers Bureau can bring authors to your live event.
For more information or to book an event, contact the Simon & Schuster
Speakers Bureau at 1-866-248-3049 or visit our website
at www.simonspeakers.com.

Designed by Mspace/Maura Fadden Rosenthal

Manufactured in the United States of America

1   3   5   7   9   10   8   6   4   2

Library of Congress Cataloging-in-Publication Data
Traister, Rebecca.
Big girls don't cry : the election that changed everything
for American women / Rebecca Traister.
    p. cm.
1. Presidents—United States—Election—2008. 2. Women in politics—
United States. 3. Women—Political activity—United States.
4. Feminism—Political aspects. 5. Clinton, Hillary Rodham.
6. Palin, Sarah, 1964– 7. Obama, Michelle, 1964– I. Title.
JK2762008 .T73 2010
324.973'0931—dc22
2010009631

ISBN 978-1-4391-5029-0 (pbk)
ISBN 978-1-4391-5487-8 (ebook)

"Obama Girl" lyrics by Ben Relles and Leah Kauffman

For two women
born before the 19th Amendment:
Eleanor Howard,
who always voted for Republicans,
and Betty Traister,
who often voted (in protest) for her cat

CONTENTS

*Yesterday, a beautiful day . . . I was talking to [an older]
woman who said that she wouldn't want to be me for
anything in the world. She wouldn't want to live today
and look ahead to what it is she sees because she's afraid.
Fear is always with us but we just don't have time for it.
Not now.*

HILLARY RODHAM, Wellesley
commencement speech, 1969

*The United States was said not to be ready to elect a
Catholic to the Presidency when Al Smith ran in the
1920's. But Smith's nomination may have helped pave
the way for the successful campaign John F. Kennedy
waged in 1960. Who can tell? What I hope most is that
now there will be others who will feel themselves as
capable of running for high political office as any
wealthy, good-looking white male.*

SHIRLEY CHISHOLM, *The Good Fight*, 1973

*I think we can all agree that it's a great time to be a lady
in America.*

TINA FEY, *Saturday Night Live*, 2008

BIG
GIRLS
DON'T
CRY

INTRODUCTION

THE FIRST TIME I entered a voting booth I was nine years old. It was 1984, and my parents had brought me with them so that I could pull the lever for the first woman ever to run on a major party ticket for vice president of the United States. I remember walking proudly with my father and mother and younger brother into the suburban Philadelphia firehouse five blocks from the house in which I grew up, where the poll watchers knew my parents by name because they were two of the very few registered Democrats in our district.

I remember the weight of the curtain closing behind me and my father lifting me up to turn the black lever to make the X appear next to Walter Mondale's and Geraldine Ferraro's names. I remember him putting me back down so that he could turn the buttons for the other Democrats, and then telling me to pull the rubber-covered metal bar back as hard as I could, until the machine made a clanging noise that meant my vote had been counted.

When we left the fire station my brother and I climbed into the back seat of our car and my mother turned to make sure our seat belts were fastened; my father looked at us through the rearview mirror. "I hope that someday you'll have the chance to vote for a woman at the top of a presidential ticket," he said before starting the car and driving us home.

Almost twenty-four years later, on Super Tuesday in February 2008, I walked into a cavernous school gymnasium in Brooklyn to cast my primary vote on Super Tuesday, for the first time in my voting life unsure of which lever to turn. It was the moment that could bring me closest to fulfilling my father's wish: I could put the X next to the name of a woman and bring her closer to the top spot on the Democratic ticket. But I had spent months saying that I would never vote for her, that she was not my kind of candidate, not my kind of woman. Even though I was beginning to change my mind, my distaste for her felt entrenched, and perhaps self-defining.

I spent fifteen minutes behind the curtain, shoving levers back and forth. I considered the other name on the ballot, a man who was also not exactly my kind of candidate, but whose potential place at the top of the Democratic ticket would put him close to becoming the first African American president, a possibility just as thrilling as that of electing a woman. I wished that I didn't have to choose between them. I wished that I could vote for them both. I wished that I could vote for someone else altogether. I mostly wished that it was a different woman's name in front of me, one that didn't fill me with ambivalence and vague foreboding.

I would never have imagined, as I stalled and fidgeted in that booth while a line of voters formed behind me, that four months later I would be ducking out of a cordoned-off press section in the National Building Museum in Washington, D.C., pushing my way through throngs of people in search of a place where I could cry in private. Behind a soaring column I gulped out sobs of exhaustion and disappointment at the end of the campaign of the woman for whom I had not been sure I could vote, even seconds before pulling the rubber-covered bar to seal my choice.

This book is an attempt to tell a story of change, change that came to me, yes, but also to the country, to the Democratic and Republican parties, to the women's movement, and to the White House. Over a period of just a few years, it seemed, the United States, its assumptions, its prejudices, its colors, shapes, sizes and vocabulary, had cracked open.

A woman, Hillary Clinton, won a state presidential primary contest for the first time in this nation's history. Less than a year later a candidate for vice president of the United States concluded her appearance in a national debate by reaching for her newborn baby. Whatever else there is to say about Sarah Palin or the reasons that her youngest son was on stage that night, that maternal reach was a roaring first in presidential politics. We have seen it once now. That means it is possible to see it again. In the first month of 2009 an African American woman moved into the White House, which was built in part by slaves, as the first lady of the United States. Michelle Obama is only the third first lady, though notably the third in a row, to have a postgraduate degree; she met her husband when she was assigned to mentor him at the law firm where she worked. He is now our first African American president.

These are not small things. These are changes that have piled up fast, creating a world that our grandmothers could barely have dreamed of, that many of our mothers thought they'd never live to see. They're also changes that our grandmothers and mothers made possible and that will in turn alter the landscape for coming generations. The events of the past few years provided a prism through which both past and future became briefly clearer.

Though a presidential election is by definition a political event, the cultural shifts made visible and made possible in 2008 took place well beyond the scope of purely presidential history. For a time it was very droll to credit Tina Fey with changing the course of the election and sealing John McCain's electoral fate with her deadly impersonation of his running mate. But Fey, who had made history some years earlier by becoming the first female head writer of *Saturday Night Live,* would never have had the opportunity to make this impact had there not been a woman running for vice president. Fey's most cutting sketches would not have been possible if another woman, Katie Couric, who had made history by becoming the first solo female anchor of a nightly news broadcast, had not been in a position to elicit unintentionally comedic material from Sarah Palin. And Palin, who had made history by becoming Alaska's first female governor, would not have wound up as a mark for Fey and Couric had she not been hired to sop up the tears and the votes of those who had supported Hillary Clinton's run for the presidency.

Political breakthroughs begat cultural breakthroughs begat comedy breakthroughs begat political breakthroughs. The country was in a steady revisionist conversation with itself, with voters, with candidates, with pundits, with entertainers. It was a wild, dizzying ride.

It is a poetic injustice that the drawn-out political marathon of 2008, a contest that at times seemed to drag on for decades rather than months, actually took place at breakneck media speed, and that it was narrated to us faster than we could absorb it. Once it would have taken years of retrospective investigative journalism to inform the American public of everything that had happened during a presidential election. In 2008 twenty-four-hour cable networks and the Internet offered hastily crafted daily tomes. We were fed sloppy synopses and cartoonish characters at rat-a-tat pace. Many of us, struggling to keep up, were happy to just get the Cliffs Notes version. But in the ceaseless cycle of revelation and analysis we lost depth, clarity and perspective on the story that was unfolding around us, as well as on how that story was itself changing and reshaping us.

My goal here is to tell the story of women and the 2008 presidential election, though not exactly the stories of the key women themselves. There are far better political reporters than I who have already begun to fill in the details surrounding why Hillary Clinton didn't fire Mark Penn in January, why Michelle Obama thought it was a good idea to be honest about *everything,* why Sarah Palin didn't just admit that she read the *New York Times* and move on. These women are at the heart of this tale, but insider campaign rehash is neither my talent nor my particular concern. The story I aim to tell is the one about the country and its culture, how we all reacted to the arrival of these surprising new figures on the presidential stage and what they showed us about how far we had come and how far we had yet to go.

Yes, there was misogyny, and I will describe some of it, but that is not the revelation of this book. To say that Hillary Clinton faced sexism is practically meaningless. She was the first woman in American history to get within spitting distance of a nomination for president; of course she faced sexism. It's far more interesting to examine the sometimes unlikely directions from which that sexism sprang, as well as the racism and classism that were often in high relief and aimed at other candidates, and why the manifestations of these prejudices still surprised us.

How ready were American voters for these women, and how ready were the women themselves? How prepared was the media to talk about them? How prepared were their political parties? What did their presence teach us about America's female voters—those who were hounded for supporting women candidates, those who were hounded for not doing so, those who reported on them and those who were still trying to sort out what feminism meant some ninety years after American women gained the right to vote?

In that last regard this book is not simply a narrative history but an argument, one that will not be popular with many who consider the 2008 presidential election as proof that feminism has failed. The political reporter Anne Kornblut has written that the contest was "a severe letdown, with damaging consequences" for women, and that it "set back the cause of equality in the political sphere by decades." And one particularly dour blogger proclaimed in the summer of 2009 that "2008 was when feminism, the women's liberation movement, ended up crashing." I believe the opposite, that this was the year—the years, really—in which what was once called the women's liberation movement found thrilling new life.

The impulse to declare social movements dead is as old as social movements themselves; the term *postfeminist* was used as early as 1919, a year before women gained the right to vote. The movement to increase liberties for women survived its first obit but has never lacked for premature mourners, or for critics eager to hold its wake. When people spoke, as they often did, about the state of feminism during the 2008 election, they mostly fell into one of two camps. One asserted that the women's movement of the 1970s was dead because its goals had been more than accomplished, and that modern women, no longer troubled by inequity, did not assign any larger symbolic value to the election of a female president. The other wailed at the expiration of a feminist dream, averring that the mixed fortunes of 2008's political women were emblematic of the unabated subjugation of women, and that not only had we not come very far at all, baby, but that perhaps we had slid backward.

Reality lay somewhere between, but also well beyond, these two diagnoses. The notion that we live in a world in which gender inequity has been satisfactorily redressed is about as persuasive as the proposition that Barack Obama's election proved that racism was a stage through which the country had successfully passed. But failing to recognize the vast distances women have traveled in the past half-century, let alone the past several centuries, was just as dishonest.

Progress does not happen in a straight line, as any historian of America's founding and revolutionary rupture, the abolition and suffrage campaigns, and the social movements of the 1960s can attest. The path toward perfecting our union has long been marked by semicircles and switchbacks, regress, tragedy and surprising forward bounds. Small advances spark resistance, resistance that in return provokes propellant bursts of reactive fury. The 2008 presidential contest electrified and enraged, radicalized and engaged us; it opened old wounds, and in doing so created new investments in the struggle toward equality. It recharged conversations—some ugly, some hopeful—that were perhaps in danger of going unfinished. The events surrounding the election did not provide a static snapshot of where women or feminism or America was; the events themselves were formative, catalytic, changing the positions and shaping the consciousness of American women and men at every turn.

The campaigns of Hillary Clinton and Sarah Palin, flawed and unsuccessful though they may have been, the arrival of Michelle Obama on Pennsylvania Avenue, the cultural shifts and uncomfortable exchanges these women prompted, the eye-opening revelations about the progress of women in early twenty-first-century America were in fact the most rejuvenating things to happen to the feminist conversation in many, many decades. They created and nourished a new generation of politically engaged Americans and left us with a story worth telling, hopefully far into the future.

☆ ☆ ☆

I am a feminist journalist allied neither with the generations of second-wave (or third-wave) activists that preceded me, nor with the online rabble of younger women who are revivifying and redefining the movement as I type. I was born in 1975 to a mother who taught me not by instruction but by example that it was not only possible for a woman to participate fully in academic, professional and economic spheres, but pretty much expected. She did not go to marches or talk to me about the patriarchy; her political activism had been forged during the civil rights movement and she spent more time telling me how she used to drive to Chicago to listen to Jesse Jackson preach on Sundays. An English professor, my mother worked throughout my childhood, but also did all the cooking, cleaning, laundry and child care in our house. My father believed fervently in the intellectual and political parity of women, but not so much in doing the dishes.

In adolescence I found a few friends with mothers whose consciousness had been raised more directly by the second wave; with them I attended the March for Women's Lives in Washington in 1992; I wore pro-choice buttons on my coat. In college I studied eighteenth-century literature from a feminist perspective and listened to the Indigo Girls.

But having been a teenager in the backlash 1980s and 1990s, when even the girls at my crunchy Quaker high school prefaced their feminist observations with the defensive caveat "I'm not a feminist, but . . ." and having held my first journalism job at a gloriously musty boys' club newspaper where any story pitch that smacked of gendered discontent would have been laughed out of the room, I assumed that although my interest in women's issues might shape my personal life, it would not find a public, let alone professional outlet.

By the time the 2008 election season kicked off, I was not only earning my living writing about gender, but I was doing so in an atmosphere in which looking at the world from a feminist perspective had, improbably, become hot. When I was hired by *Salon* in 2003 it was as a staff writer for the "Life" section, a squishy category that included stories about relationships, sex, children, religion, health: girl stuff. A few of my early pieces touched on gender politics. To my surprise and that of my editors, these pieces generated attention, page views and lots of florid comments. I wrote more about feminism; the comments and traffic kept rolling in. And so I had a new beat, a lens through which I could examine politics, the media, entertainment, and social and sexual conventions.

My approach was not doctrinaire. After covering a thirtieth-anniversary discussion of Erica Jong's *Fear of Flying* in 2003, I wrote a bratty review headlined "The Feminine Antiques." I played with verboten words like *battle-axe* and *bitch*; I dubbed Florida politician Katherine Harris a "chad harpy" and Ann Coulter a "thin political pundit." Fascinated by the often ham-handed attempts of second-wavers to make their movement meaningful to a younger generation, I wrote critically about the 2004 March for Women's Lives in Washington, where older leaders of big feminist groups were unable or unwilling to engage the thousands of eager young women who had shown up to march with them, as well as about the troubled history and shaky future of the word *feminism*. While reporting a story about incorporating questions of morality into the abortion debate, a piece that questioned the bland language of "choice" to which a generation of activists clung, I found myself on the receiving end of a tirade from Feminist Majority Foundation president Eleanor Smeal; she screamed at me over the phone, asking why I would write something so superficial and divisive when women around the world were dying of fistula.

Women around the world *were* dying of fistula, but I didn't believe that that should prevent young people from reassessing signifiers of what had become a badly dated movement. I didn't want to water down feminism or sex it up or dumb it down or sell it out. But I did believe that in order to be taken seriously by serious young women, the conversation had to be drained of some of its earnest piety. Talking about gender in the new millennium required us, I thought, to get over ourselves a little bit, to dispense with the sacred cows, to question power and cultivate new ideas and leaders.

My early tenure at *Salon* coincided with the development of a few online sites created by young women anxious to form a modern feminist community, women whose ideas echoed my own. The most prominent of these was *Feministing*, founded by a twenty-five-year-old Queens native, Jessica Valenti, who was busting her chops to reach people her age whom she believed were hungry for more coverage about women, power and politics. She was right. As the online world exploded in many directions, each month seemed to bring a new site with feminist content, with names like *Feministe, Shakespeare's Sister, Pandagon, Echidne of the Snakes, Angry Black Bitch, Angry Brown Butch, I Blame the Patriarchy, Writes Like She Talks, Majikthise, Pam's House Blend, Shapely Prose, Racialicious, Brownfemipower, Bitch PhD, Feminist Law Professors* and *Womanist Musings*. At various points there were about six publications calling themselves *The F Word*. My musty boys' club newspaper hired a writer who began to cover business and media through an unapologetically feminist lens. In 2004 the Center for

New Words hosted the Women, Action & the Media Conference for feminist journalists, which in its first year drew a hundred people, and five years later six hundred.

Funnily enough, as my youthful commentariat company got broader I found myself becoming a shade less irreverent toward my elders, nodding in agreement with some of the more traditionally old-school feminist figures, the ones whom younger activists sometimes railed against, among them Linda Hirshman and Leslie Bennetts, who exhorted wealthy, educated women to stop dropping out of the workforce to care for their kids, and Ariel Levy, a writer of my vintage whose book *Female Chauvinist Pigs* questioned the purported sexual empowerment of a "Girls Gone Wild" generation. In 2008 I gave an appreciative talk at the thirty-fifth-anniversary celebration of Erica Jong's *Fear of Flying*.

That's where I was when Hillary Clinton announced her campaign for the presidency: a feminist caught between old and new, senior and junior, retro and nouveau, wanting to poke my elders with a stick even as I found myself agreeing with them, and wanting to celebrate the achievements of my younger peers, even when I found some of their commentary short-sighted and overly self-celebratory.

The prospect of a Clinton candidacy was exciting to those of us who wrote about women and power, not least because it promised to be good copy: the story of a much loathed but highly competent woman boarding the presidential roller-coaster and making an unprecedented grab for the brass ring.

But I could not have predicted the kind of electoral rapture that was about to overtake us all. If I foresaw the fury Clinton would provoke, I had no idea of the loyalty she would rouse or the way her campaign would open so many eyes to the realities of sexism. I had no inkling that there would be both Obamas to consider, that the contest between two candidates vying to be the first woman or the first African American nominee would obsess the nation for the better part of a year. I could not have summoned Sarah Palin from my worst nightmare, nor imagined the way she would inspire women on the right to lay claim to what they saw as their share of the feminist legacy. I could never have guessed how many of the questions that bedeviled the feminist world—questions of generational difference, race, class, sex, sexism, abortion, choice, the place of feminism in a Democratic agenda and humor in a feminist agenda—would get so widely aired to an electorate that may never have considered these issues before.

Whether you were a devoted Hillaryite or a Feminist for Barack, a Republican who wore a "Kiss My Lipstick!" button or a self-identified patriot who could not believe that Michelle Obama wouldn't be proud of her country, you were thinking about women and power and perception. If you put an "I Wish Hillary Had Married O.J." bumper sticker on your car or wore a "Sarah Palin Is a Cunt" T-shirt, you were broadcasting messages about gender. If you hugged Michelle in a church basement in Indiana, lined up for a Palin rally in Pennsylvania, voted for Hillary in Guam; if you loved Rachel Maddow's commentary about the election or thought that Chris Matthews was kind of a prick; if you cheered when Campbell Brown defended Palin's expensive wardrobe or snarfed your beer when Samantha Bee forced Republican conventioneers to describe Bristol Palin's decision to keep her baby as a "choice"; if you were a young progressive guy who wished the Hillary supporters would shut up, a Hillary supporter who wished the PUMAs would go away or a PUMA who wished that everyone would just choke on it already, then you were talking and thinking about and making women's history in America.

1 HILLARY IS US

IT'S EASY TO forget that at the start it was feminists who weren't wild about Hillary Clinton.

I don't mean at the start of Hillary. Back in 1993, when she marched into the White House with her ill-tended hair, barren cookie trays and big ideas about health care, feminists thought her the bee's knees, the elephant's instep, the best thing to happen to the executive branch since Eleanor Roosevelt.

I'm talking about more than a decade later, when it was clear that Hillary was locked and loaded to do what Eleanor could not have done: she was the one who was going to make a go at the presidency, the one they'd been waiting for. You'd have thought that women who had dedicated their lives to improving professional and political prospects for themselves and their daughters would have been beside themselves at the prospect of a solid Democratic female presidential candidate. But the intervening thirteen years had made things between feminists and Hillary Clinton considerably more fraught.

In 2006 the country was fired up for midterms that would halt

Republican control of Congress and bring us one election cycle closer to a new Democratic ticket. As the possibility that Clinton was going to jump into the 2008 presidential race became increasingly distinct, it often seemed as though feminists were more distraught about it than the right-wing louts who'd been pressing their "Iron My Shirt" shirts since 2001.

That spring I attended a benefit for the Women's Campaign Forum, a nonpartisan organization dedicated to putting prochoice women in political office. It was a crowd of monied, Botoxed, electorally enthralled dames who, in the popular imagination of the time, should have had "Hillary '08" mown into their Hamptons house topiary, if not their bikini lines. But on that night, a few months before the election that would secure Clinton her second term as the junior senator from New York, discussion of her future beyond New York was as cool as the evening breeze. "I like her a lot more than my wife does!" an affable WCF supporter was telling me, mock sotto voce. His wife heard him and sidled up, eyeballing my reporter's notepad. "We *both* love Hillary," the woman corrected with crisp dishonesty. "I just hope she can *catch fire*."

It seemed a neat summation of how many politically engaged women were feeling about the woman poised to come closer than any before her to gaining Oval Office entrance. Clinton was on the brink, and though many of her would-be cheerleaders weren't eager to say it out loud, they were secretly hoping she would just catch fire. Literally.

Though it is often cited as the period during which Clinton's self-assuredness created the resentments that would later provoke lusty axe wielding, it remains remarkable, miraculous really, that there was a span of months, nestled between two centuries of uninterrupted white male presidential power and one long Democratic primary tussle, during which the nomination of Hillary Rodham Clinton to the Democratic ticket seemed inevitable. Not just possible or probable: inevitable. One of the strangest things about this moment, for which Clinton would pay dearly, was that when her victory was presumptive many American feminists did not cheer her on, but shrugged their shoulders, curled their lips in distaste, or simply kept their distance.

In my years writing for *Salon* I had witnessed the feminist hunger for a female president when it was still comparatively abstract. In 2005 I covered a premiere party for *Commander in Chief,* the short-lived network television show in which Geena Davis played the president. The program was a cliché-studded mess, chock-full of menopause jokes and aphorisms most frequently found in forwarded emails. ("If Moses had been a woman leading the Jews in the desert, she'd have stopped and asked for directions. They'd have been in Israel in a week!") The party for the show, hosted by the White House Project at Caroline's Comedy Club, left no Girl Power signifier unturned; chocolate bars were handed out while Shania Twain's "Man! I Feel Like a Woman!" played. The hokeyness of the affair made it all the more embarrassing that, at the moment in the otherwise dreadful pilot when the heroine entered the House Chamber to the familiar words "Mr. Speaker, the President of the United States" and the imposing Geena Davis—Thelma!—walked through the door, an unironic chill shot through the crowd.

Looking around at the gathering of mostly over-fifty women, some of whom had begun to sniffle, it dawned on me that some probably hadn't been sure they'd live long enough to see this, even on television. Gloria Steinem confirmed this realization later in the evening, when she took the stage and asserted, "One of the advantages of being an old person is that you see how far we've come." Steinem also hit on the thing that gave the evening its undeniable frisson: part of what made this silly program moving was the unspoken awareness that women were, for the first time, within striking distance. "We are so ready," Steinem told the crowd.

A year and a half later it was clear that although feminists may have been ready for the *idea* of a female president, they were not so ready for the candidate who was actually going to run. Even Steinem wasn't exactly throwing herself behind Clinton. In early 2007 she announced in a *New York Times* op-ed that she was supporting *both* Clinton and her newly hatched competitor, Barack Obama. The op-ed was very warm toward Clinton, but not a ringing endorsement. Far more damning were critics like Susan Douglas, who described the mood in a piece for *In These Times*: "We sat around the dinner table, a group of 50-something progressive feminists, talking to a friend from England about presidential politics. We were all for Hillary, weren't we, he asked. Hillary? We hated Hillary. He was taken aback. Weren't we her base? Wasn't she one of us? Why did we hate Hillary?"

Why did they hate Hillary? How had the candidate contracted this social disease, and why was it manifesting symptoms at such a crucial historical moment?

Perhaps women demanded authenticity from Clinton in a way that they might not have in another candidate, male or female. Ann Douglas, a Columbia University cultural historian who had profiled Clinton for *Vogue* in 1998, told me in 2006 that because of Hillary's long time in the public eye and her history as a flashpoint for issues political and personal, women saw—or more to the point, didn't see—in her what they wanted to see in themselves. She referred to an old Tony Curtis anecdote about a fan who approached him and asked, "Are you who I think I am?" It was the same with Clinton, Douglas said. "We say, 'I want her to hold up my own ideals of myself. I want her to be who I think I am.'"

Here was a woman who had been vastly overqualified for the traditional role of first lady, making feminist fantasy flesh by attempting a return to the White House as president. She wasn't the kind of woman you'd have guessed might be the first, some shellacked Republican whose politics made Margaret Thatcher look like Barbara Jordan. No, Clinton was a Democrat, with a lifetime of advocating on behalf of children's welfare, women's equality and universal health care; she was a woman whom her spirited conservative detractors had made the standard-bearer for feminism. To hear right-wing men tell the story, left-leaning women were already running through the streets, burning Bella Abzug's bra in ecstasy!

But they were not. By 2006 the discontent that some establishment feminists felt about Clinton's impending run had become the undercurrent of many political conversations. At a September awards reception for the Center for the Advancement of Women, I asked a smiling Jane Fonda what she thought of the idea of Hillary running for president. Fonda tensed; her grin faded. It was a celebratory, lady-happy night at the Waldorf Astoria; later the Washington comedy troupe The Capitol Steps would perform a *My Fair Lady* parody called "Wouldn't It Be Hillary?" Here were all these women celebrating advancement. And here was this unpleasant question. "I don't put so much importance on candidates," Fonda said, though two days later she would travel to Sweden to stump for female parliamentary contenders. "I want to spend my time and energy getting women to the polls. I would never vote for a candidate just because she was a woman, because we have had plenty of female presidents and prime ministers where I would rather have had a male feminist." A few months later Fonda would refine this point in an interview with *LA Weekly,* allowing, "It may be that a feminist, progressive man would do better in the White House than a ventriloquist for the patriarchy with a skirt and a vagina." (She later insisted that she hadn't been referring to Hillary specifically.)

⋆ ⋆ ⋆

When America first met her in 1992 Hillary Rodham Clinton looked like what she was: a working mother. She had recently chucked her Coke-bottle glasses but still sported headbands and weird amounts of ineptly applied makeup. Why should it have been otherwise? Clinton was a busy woman when her husband ran for president. Mind-bogglingly she would be the first first lady in American history to have maintained a full-time career outside her husband's political life prior to his presidency. In short, Clinton was the first candidate for the job of first lady to have a life that reflected post-second-wave America and the many working women who made their careers and raised their families here.

"I suppose I could have stayed home and baked cookies and had teas, but what I decided to do was fulfill my profession, which I entered before my husband was in public life," she famously said. She was responding to reporters at a Chicago diner who pressed her about Jerry Brown's charges that her law profits conflicted with her husband's political career. Her penitent follow-up was never as widely remembered. "I'm a big believer in women making the choices that are right for them," she told the reporters who'd been herded out of the diner as soon as she dropped the cookie bomb. "The work that I have done as a professional, as a public advocate, has been aimed at trying to assure that women can make the choices they should make—whether it's full-time career, full-time mother-hood, or some combination. . . . [That] is a generational change."

Amy Wilentz wrote about that famous remark, "What's wrong with baking cookies, Hillary, huh? Are you too good for that? But she did think she was too good for that, and so did hundreds of thousands of us. We were made for things that were better than baking." Hillary's statement wasn't radical for a certain class of professional women who had built careers in the 1970s and 1980s. But it was radical to hear it expressed by a woman whose task it was to win the hearts of American voters, some of whom had not yet adjusted to the idea of a woman who didn't consider tending home and hearth her highest calling.

"I got hundreds of letters about 'cookies and tea,'" Clinton wrote in her memoir, *Living History*. "One letter referred to me as the Antichrist, and another said I was an insult to American mother-hood." Clinton understood her position: "While Bill talked about social change, I embodied it. I had my own opinions, interests and profession. For better or worse, I was outspoken. I represented a fundamental change in the way women functioned in our society." Alluding to the many times during that 1992 campaign that she was called a Rorschach test for the American people, Clinton main-tained that neither the devotion nor the virulent rage she inspired was about her, but rather was about the still recent rupture in the American social fabric that she represented: "I had been turned into a symbol for women of my generation."

Everyone soon learned that Clinton had not changed her name after marrying her big-pawed law school swain, at least not until 1982, when advisors determined that her refusal to add her hus-band's last name to her own had cost Bill Clinton his second term in the Arkansas governor's mansion two years earlier. The sacrifice of her maiden name in the interest of her husband's political future always seemed to me to shed valuable light on Hillary and what she would eventually become. Whenever people claimed that she was a born shape-shifter, that political chameleonism was written into her genetic code, I would think of that last name and her pro-tracted insistence on keeping it independent. She hadn't wanted to be Hillary Clinton; she wanted to be Hillary Rodham. When faced with the assertion that doing it her way would result in her husband's loss, or at least blame for her husband's loss, she made the change. But it was a compromise, not a concession: she became Hillary Rodham Clinton. The question of her name would return, and on the campaign trail in 1992 it forced her to begin to grasp that although she "had worked full-time during [her] marriage to Bill and valued the independence and identity that work provided," she was now "solely 'the wife of,' an odd experience." Clinton described opening a box of stationery she'd ordered; embossed across the top was "Hillary Clinton." "Evidently someone on Bill's staff decided that it was more politically expedient to drop 'Rodham,' as if it were no longer part of my identity," she wrote, adding that she quickly ordered new stationery. But by that point, hers was a lost name.

There were still plenty of ways Clinton asserted her independence from hoary *femme couverte* practices, including her 1992 campaign trail claim, "[I'm not] some little woman standing by my man like Tammy Wynette." This was a gutsy thing to say. The fury with which the comment was greeted reflected a country unused to the idea that women are not obligated to stay in bad marriages and support their mates. It was the kind of statement that made millions of women, who may never before have identified with a political wife, look up at the television and take notice.

To many of those women Hillary Clinton was the real deal: smart and driven, with good politics. A Goldwater Republican kid who'd turned left at Wellesley, she gave a graduation speech so feisty that she received a seven-minute standing ovation and was featured in *Life* magazine as a student leader. She went to Yale Law School and worked for abused kids at Yale-New Haven Hospital, did research related to Walter Mondale's senate investigation into the treatment of migrant workers, and campaigned for George McGovern in Texas. She spent a summer working for the radical lawyer Robert Treuhaft, monitored the Black Panther trials for civil rights abuses and was one of a handful of young women on the impeachment inquiry staff that advised the House Judiciary Committee during its Watergate investigation. Clinton specialized in children's rights and in 1974 famously compared kids' legal rights to other unjust "dependency relationships," citing "marriage, slavery and the Indian reservation system." She would later be raked over the coals for aligning the institutions of marriage and slavery, but her point was legally and historically dead-on. Clinton was a rigorous social and political thinker.

In 1974 she made the loaded choice to give up her promising career in Washington to follow her boyfriend back to his Arkansas home, where he was planning to run for the U.S. House of Representatives. Her friend Sara Ehrman recalled the road trip the two women took together from Washington to Arkansas, during which Ehrman tried to persuade Hillary that she was making a terrible error; when they entered Fayetteville, Arkansas, they saw football fans hanging from lampposts making Razorback hog calls. A *Washington Post Magazine* piece from 1999 described Ehrman's realization "that her beloved Hillary Rodham, her high-powered hope for the future, was about to settle in a town full of frat boys wearing pig hats." "That," Ehrman told the *Post,* "is when I started to cry."

Clinton found a way not only to live her life in Arkansas, but to make herself heard over the "Woo Pig Sooie!" chorus. She became the second female faculty member at the law school of the University of Arkansas at Fayetteville. She cofounded Arkansas Advocates for Children and Families and was appointed by Jimmy Carter to the board of directors for the Legal Services Corporation, which she was the first woman to chair. Garry Wills would write in 1992 that Hillary Rodham was "one of the more important scholar-activists of the last two decades." As the first female partner at the Rose Law Firm in the years preceding her husband's run for the presidency she was twice rated one of America's most influential lawyers by the *National Law Journal.* Chelsea Clinton was born in 1980, and Hillary scored an Arkansas Mother of the Year award in 1984, an honor that might have surprised those who deemed her the cookie-eschewing Antichrist eight years later.

Hillary Rodham Clinton was a boomer lady of the left, successfully balancing work and life, and many women just plain admired her. As the late great columnist Molly Ivins joked when Bill Clinton was traversing the campaign trail in May 1992, "What this country needs is a candidate half as good as his wife." The filmmaker and feminist writer Nora Ephron, who had covered the nomination of Shirley Chisholm for president in 1972 and had attended Wellesley a few years before Hillary, marveled to *Newsday* in 1993, "Did you ever think that anybody like us would be in that job? . . . She has a career and a child and a husband, and she's doing it." In the same interview Ephron said, "I love her so completely that, honestly, she would have to burn down the White House before I would say anything bad about her."

Hillary didn't burn down the White House, though tabloids claimed that she broke a lamp or two in fights with her husband. But her tenure on Pennsylvania Avenue did not seal her place in the hearts of the American public. People who liked her liked her *a lot*. When she entered the White House her favorability ratings were higher than those of either Laura or Barbara Bush. But those who didn't like her really *hated* her. Bill Clinton had crowed about giving the nation a "two for the price of one" presidency, but the nation was not grateful. For those women who saw in Hillary a reflection of their own values and achievements, it was startling to witness the contempt that she inspired.

The hammering of Hillary was unrelenting. She was a bitch, a witch; she had big thighs, fat ankles. She was Shillary, Shrillary, Hellary Rotten Clinton. Together she and her husband were "Billary." Republicans sifted through her every business deal, tried to nail her on Whitewater and tie her to the death of deputy White House counsel Vince Foster. She was mocked bitterly after reports that she was having imaginary conversations with the spirit of Eleanor Roosevelt. By 1996 Nora Ephron was telling a graduating class at Wellesley, "Don't underestimate how much antagonism there is toward women and how many people wish we could turn the clock back. . . . Understand: every attack on Hillary Clinton for not knowing her place is an attack on you."

What juiced many of the most damaging early attacks on Hillary was her role in the failed effort to pass a well-intentioned and dismally received plan for universal health care. She and her husband, like many before them, understood that America's health care system was broken and needed to be rebuilt. Just after taking office in 1993, Bill announced that Hillary, who had led a successful effort to reform Arkansas's education system, would lead a task force to overhaul the national health system. Although her appointment provoked some early grumbling, her work initially earned positive reviews. Her lengthy testimony before five congressional committees in September 1993, weeks before the legislation was formally presented to Congress, was widely hailed as brilliant, though she would later write that she suspected the accolades were the product of "talking dog syndrome," a riff on Samuel Johnson's comment that a woman preaching was like a dog walking on its hind legs. "Some people are still amazed that any woman . . . can hold her own under pressure and be articulate and knowledgeable," Clinton wrote. "The dog can talk!"

Regardless, Hillary's barking testimony was soon forgotten; the Health Security Act was a political disaster. The reasons for Clinton's health care belly flop were varied and depended on who you asked. Many felt that the complex plan reached too far and too left, pushing for limits on spending and coverage requirements that the public and business employers were not ready to accept. Republicans knew that they could not afford to let health care pass and hand middle-class voters to the Democrats for generations; Republican strategist Bill Kristol had told them as much in a memo that urged them to kill the bill in any form. Both Clintons suffered from a hunted-animal, anti-Beltway complex; their early work on health care was done mostly in secret with their friend and business consultant Ira Magaziner, who did not have many Washington ties. By the time the Clintons trotted out the package they had a Congress full of Democrats who had been rubbed the wrong way and Republicans ready to pounce. Some have reported that it was Hillary's unwillingness to sacrifice the "universal" aspect of her plan, even when her husband was open to doing so, that helped seal the project's fate. Others, such as former White House senior health policy advisor Paul Starr, who worked under Magaziner, have written that Hillary's role in the plan's drafting was never as great as her husband, or history, led us to believe. But it didn't matter; she was too enticing a target for Republicans to resist. The plan was promptly dubbed "Hillarycare," linking her name with policy debacle, and its failure helped provide some of the fuel her husband's opponents needed to retake Congress in 1994, under the leadership of Newt Gingrich. Hillary's history-making role in the West Wing had been a fiasco.

She wasn't completely abashed. In 1995 she went to the United Nations Fourth World Conference on Women in Beijing and made the mundane but revolutionary statement that "Women's rights are human rights." At home she partnered with Janet Reno to support the creation of the Violence Against Women Office at the Department of Justice and told the United Nations in 1997, "In too many places, the suffering of women is defined as trivial, explained away as a cultural phenomenon; perhaps it is for this reason that women do not receive proper healthcare, including access to family planning." In a 1999 speech about pay equity she observed, "We know that women who walk into the grocery store are not asked to pay 25 percent less for milk. . . . It's not just a gap in wages, it's a gap in our nation's principles and promises."

But she did begin to tone it down, to smooth the unruly spikes of her personality. The hair, the makeup, the clothing: they all got fixed, patted down into some inoffensive template of first lady presentability. She also began to tame some of her political cowlicks, minimizing her role in her husband's administration and fulfilling more pro forma first lady obligations. (See *Dear Socks, Dear Buddy: Kids' Letters to the First Pets,* Hillary Rodham Clinton, Simon & Schuster, 1998.) Deducing that she was perhaps too much, too soon for the United States, Clinton took her show on the road, focusing on areas in Africa, Asia and the Middle East where she could talk about women's rights, child welfare and health care, often taking teenage Chelsea with her.

Clinton was seeking a middle path, where she could be heard and not reviled. But some of the directions in which she was willing to bend frustrated even her most devoted supporters. Gloria Feldt, who was president of the Planned Parenthood Federation of America during the second half of the Clinton administration and who would eventually become one of Hillary's most dedicated backers for the presidency, conceded retrospectively that at the start of Clinton's 2008 campaign she was unsure whether or not to support her. "I had had my ups and downs with her," said Feldt. "Knowing where her heart was, knowing where her intellectual understanding of things was. There were just so many times that she tried to appease people who would never be appeased anyway." Appeasing was a habit Clinton shared with her husband, a president whose hope-infused victory had filled the heads of his Democratic supporters with dreams of an energetic and progressive America, and then woke them rudely with "don't ask, don't tell," welfare reform, NAFTA and a second term lost to a blow job and a thong. For Hillary's army of early female adherents the let-downs were hard to take.

Feldt had been in Beijing for the women's conference. "I was in the room when she made that speech," she said, "and I was totally taken with her at that point." But when it came to reproductive rights in the Clinton White House, Hillary was best known as the rumored architect of Bill Clinton's famous assertion, anathema to pro-choice activists, that abortion should be "safe, legal, and rare," a formulation that cast abortion not as an integral component of women's rights and health, but as a regrettable last resort. In 2006 one of Feldt's predecessors at Planned Parenthood and later the head of the Center for the Advancement of Women, Faye Wattleton, told me with deliberate care that she hoped that as a presidential candidate Clinton would advance the notion that "unintended pregnancy should be rare and that abortion should be safe and legal."

As a team, the Clintons had often forced feminists to bob and weave. How many foreheads hit the desks at the National Organization for Women and the Feminist Majority when, less than three years after hammering the term *sexual harassment* into the American lexicon with their vocal support of Anita Hill's claims against Clarence Thomas, these organizations were being called on to respond to Paula Jones's accusations that Bill Clinton, the Democratic president supposed to be on their side, had committed the very same offense against her?

Feldt remembered with some horror the twenty-fifth anniversary of *Roe v. Wade* in 1998, which women's groups were marking together in a show of solidarity. Tipper Gore was scheduled to speak at a brunch for which President Clinton had been persuaded to make a video. In that video, recalled Feldt, Bill Clinton "was literally speaking from the playbook about the importance of family planning, connecting it to women's abilities to live their lives and be free. It was magnificent." At eleven thirty the night before the party someone called Feldt to say that Gore had the flu. "I knew something was wrong," Feldt said. At six the next morning she turned on the news, "and there was Monica." The video of Bill Clinton talking about family planning was never shown. "It was just devastating," said Feldt, "and kind of a metaphor for how the Clinton administration was for reproductive rights: your friends can do you in faster than your enemies."

☆ ☆ ☆

It was fallout from the Lewinsky scandal that did Hillary in with some feminists, at the same time that it made her history-making future a possibility. Throughout the endless rehash of White House intern Monica Lewinsky's relations with her husband, Hillary Clinton allowed the president to play her for a fool. She attacked the media for their prurience, described a vast right-wing conspiracy, stood by her man. She did *not* do what many women yearned for her to do: throw him out. In 2009 Gloria Steinem wondered if some of those women weren't angry at their own husbands, yearning for Hillary to be the better versions of themselves. "They wanted her to punish Bill on their behalf," she said, "in the way that they were unable to punish their own husbands." Some of them simply wanted her to put her money where that anti-Wynette mouth had been; some perceived a more complex feminist betrayal. Melissa Harris-Lacewell, a professor of politics and African American studies at Princeton, told me in 2009 that she thought Clinton made "an appalling choice as a feminist—not that she stayed with her husband, but that she did not speak out in defense of a barely-older-than-teenage girl who was harassed by her husband. . . . And then she used that experience to create sympathy for herself."

Suddenly Clinton was more palatable to those Americans who had previously despised her. What had made her so unlikable for so long was her power, but it turned out that she hadn't had any power over her partner's itinerant pecker. For some it was comforting to see mighty Hillary brought low; for others the scandal provided an antifeminist moral about professional women unable to keep their men satisfied. Some argued that America just prefers its women prostrate and suffering. Whatever the explanation, the Lewinsky scandal made people who had always hated Hillary love her, which made the people who had always loved her nuts.

Some steadfast Hillary defenders, such as Ann Douglas, tried to put a positive spin on the situation, arguing that Clinton's refusal to defenestrate Bill was a rejection of the Victorian notion that "women's real business was punishing masculine immorality" and a sign that she had more important things to do than fret over her horndog husband. But this was the kind of rhetorical high-wire act that feminists had been performing on behalf of the Clintons for years, and it was frankly exhausting. Especially when Hillary was watching her own approval ratings skyrocket and pursuing a spot in the Senate. All it took was a little martyrdom and a lot of humiliation to make the widely loathed Clinton politically viable herself. According to the columnist Maureen Dowd, the equation was depressingly direct: "She couldn't move up until she was pushed down." Suddenly it looked like Hillary's political boost had been leveraged by her husband's presidency, and by its damaging scandal, rather than by her own dynamism, calling into question the notion of her feminist accomplishment and offering instead the distinctly unprogressive whiff of dynastic privilege.

In January 2001, before her husband had even vacated the White House, Hillary Rodham Clinton was sworn in as the junior senator from New York, a state in which she had resided for just one year.

* * *

As she set about becoming the most popular girl on the Senate floor, Clinton was buoyed by startlingly high approval ratings and buzz about where her political career might go next. It went directly toward the center. Clinton's youthful work on behalf of migrant workers was replaced by her assertion on the radio in 2003 that she was "adamantly against illegal immigrants." Where she once fell on the sword of universal health care she now partnered on a health care compromise with Newt Gingrich himself. Where she once advocated passionately on behalf of children's rights she now pressed the reactionary Family Entertainment Protection Act, ostensibly protecting hapless kids from the dangerous effects of video games. Her positions shifted rapidly. She bid adieu to her longtime support of Palestine with a final wanton embrace of Suha Arafat in 1999. In its place was an unctuous devotion to Israel, embodied by the introduction of one of those convenient lost Jewish relatives. In 2005 she cosponsored a bill to ban flag burning.

After the 2004 election Clinton gave reproductive rights leaders worse heartburn than ever by joining the herd of Democrats distancing themselves from the pro-choice plank in the Democratic platform. Calling abortion a "sad, even tragic choice" for some, she told an Albany audience of family planning activists in January 2005, "I, for one, respect those who believe with all their hearts and conscience that there are no circumstances under which any abortion should ever be available." In the same speech she urged activists to shift their emphasis from abortion to prevention. "She's telling the people who invented prevention that they should get involved in prevention," Gloria Feldt said of the speech in 2009. "Honest to god!"

These gaffes were no longer the kind you could forgive or cheer, all knees and elbows and Tammy Wynette. They seemed not to be gaffes at all, but a preemptive shedding of her enlightened, liberal, populist impulses in favor of centrist agreeability. Clinton's political contortions radiated not independence or even a grim fuck-you attitude toward patriarchal, conventional wisdom, but a surrender to that wisdom. Unfortunately she had little of the ambrosial panache that her husband deployed to distract from his own obsession with likability. In January 2006, speaking at a black Baptist church, Hillary compared the House of Representatives to a plantation, adding with tone-deaf infelicity, "And you know what I'm talking about."

Most egregious for progressives, of course, was that not only had Clinton voted to authorize the use of force in Iraq, but she steadfastly refused to apologize for her vote and was late in condemning George W. Bush and his administration for taking the nation into a conflict as misguided as any since Vietnam, the war that had so obsessed her in her college years. Clinton voted for the Patriot Act, a bill that stripped away the kinds of civil liberties she had been so keen to protect as a law student. She resisted the idea of designing a timetable for troop withdrawal. She voted to categorize the Iranian Revolutionary Guard as a terrorist organization. She played it both ways in a crucial Connecticut senate race, backing her buddy Joe Lieberman in the primary and later lending his opponent, Ned Lamont, her communications director Howard Wolfson.

The galling thing was that it worked. Many predicted that Clinton would be a pariah in the Senate: an entitled, carpetbagging celebrity, a health care vampire whom no self-respecting moderate would come near without a garlic necklace and whom hard-right Mississippi Republican Trent Lott had publicly speculated might be struck by lightning before she set foot in the Capitol rotunda. Six years later Clinton and Lott were introducing legislation together.

In certain unexpected Washington venues Clinton went over like gangbusters. She became the first New York senator to sit on the Armed Services Committee. In New York she applied workmanlike hustle to addressing issues faced by her rural, conservative, upstate constituents. Her approval ratings in the state remained high, and she won reelection without breaking a sweat.

A cover story about Clinton in the *Atlantic Monthly* in 2006 opened with a scene from a 2001 Washington prayer breakfast, where she had become a regular as soon as she'd joined the Senate, during which anti-abortion, antigay Kansas Republican Sam Brownback asked her forgiveness for having hated her in the past. She and Brownback went on to cosponsor a bill calling for a study of violent television shows and video games. It was her willingness to play well with others, not simply by compromising with them politically, but by sitting respectfully at their knee, abiding by the hidebound traditions of seniority and spectacle that had long supported the Senate power structure, that paved her path to popularity.

As Joshua Green reported in his *Atlantic* piece, upon her arrival on the Hill, Clinton sought counsel from Robert Byrd, the aged West Virginia senator who had been in Congress for more than four decades and who had played a major part in blocking her health care plan seven years earlier. She asked him to lead classes for freshman senators on parliamentary rules and procedures. She brought her mother to meet him. Byrd told Green in 2006, "I guess I'm blowing myself up a little . . . but I think of her as a pupil of mine." Green reported that many prominent Republicans, including foresworn Clinton foes Gingrich and South Carolina Senator Lindsey Graham, warmed to Clinton in similar ways, and colleagues offered glowing reports of her willingness to move aside deferentially in photographs and to pour coffee for her (mostly male) colleagues, who approved of her efforts to be "a workhorse, not a show horse."

Clinton's curtseying was partly simple professionalism. Her reputation for being strident and chilly had been born mostly of sexist assumptions about powerful femininity, not reality. Expectations were upended easily when her archest of enemies actually worked with the woman most people agree is funny, warm, diligent and immensely likable in person. Clinton got major traction from a story about a trip to Estonia, during which she and John McCain threw back shots of vodka in a drinking contest. McCain told the *Atlantic*, "She can really hold her liquor."

Clinton was benefiting from the reverse of her "talking dog" formulation. The very fact that she was polite and civilized, that she was even kind of fun, was enough to impress her conservative male colleagues. The talking dog could heel! But the success of her ego-stroking strategy provided a disheartening lesson about how easily a powerful woman can change the minds of men if only she's willing to conform to power models that reassure rather than threaten them. Clinton was willing to do it, mirroring the process of abasement she underwent during the Lewinsky nightmare, to get what she needed. It was great for her presidential prospects, this comforting of feminist-frightened conservatives who had made her destruction their goal in the early 1990s. But it didn't put a spring in the step of the women who should have been her base, the ones whose initial admiration had been won by her refusal to kowtow to assholes.

Through an orchestrated willingness to manipulate parts of her belief system, Hillary Clinton became the world's most unlikely poster child for bipartisan cooperation and presidential potential. In the process she alienated many of the people who should have been cheering her on. She had become a one-size-fits-all likability machine who, in the minds of her detractors—the ones who used to be her supporters—would suck up to the bad guys, juggling freedom and flag burning if it meant winning the talent show.

★ ★ ★

This was the baggage weighing down those American women who had worked their whole lives to amend the single-sex history of the U.S. presidency but who no longer saw themselves or their political beliefs reflected in Hillary Clinton. As they headed into the 2008 presidential cycle they struggled with the question of whether to turn their backs on the disillusionment that was Clinton, or whether the rare, flawed opportunity she presented them was a better shot at progress than no shot at all.

Thirteen years after wishing in print that it were Clinton, and not her husband, battling for the White House in 1992, Molly Ivins wrote a column titled "I Will Not Support Hillary Clinton for President." "Sen. Clinton is apparently incapable of taking a clear stand on the war in Iraq, and that alone is enough to disqualify her," Ivins wrote. "Her failure to speak out on Terri Schiavo [an autonomic patient at the center of a political battle over the removal of her feeding tube], not to mention that gross pandering on flag-burning, are just contemptible little dodges." Ivins would not live to see Clinton compete in the primaries. Nora Ephron, who had sworn that Clinton would have to burn down the White House in order to earn her ire, wrote in 2006 that Clinton had "as much authenticity as Naugahyde."

The Pulitzer Prize–winning journalist Margo Jefferson recalled listening to Clinton's attempts to distance herself from feminist politics, even while counting on the support of feminists, and thinking, "'Bullshit! We're all feminists. What the hell are you talking about?' This would drive me mad. It enraged me. She seemed to have this way—all politicians do it, but I wanted more from her—of taking advantage with one group of being the embattled, patronized, terribly intelligent and competent woman, and with another group, being the loyal partner and wife. I found this very galling."

It seemed as if the strength of identification, idealization and self-idealization that many feminists had first directed at Clinton amplified the degree of discontent they felt as she developed as a political animal. Medea Benjamin, cofounder of the feminist pacifist group Code Pink, told the *Nation* that the group's anti-Hillary stance was born of the fact that people "expect more of a woman." Susan Douglas, who wrote that all her feminist friends hated Clinton, went on to point out, "We don't want the first female president to be Joe Lieberman in drag. . . . We expect something better." The actress and activist Susan Sarandon flayed Clinton as "a great disappointment." "[She is] not worse than other politicians," Sarandon said, "but I hoped she would be better."

So that was it, in part: women hoped she would be better. Perhaps her failure to hold fast her positions through political gales made them doubt their own strength. Or maybe it just made them sad, the recognition that someone so like them could never have gotten as far as someone who was willing to become unlike them.

The tragedy of stratospheric hopes destined to go unmet was one that no one would have understood better than a young Hillary Rodham. As she told her Wellesley classmates almost four decades before she ran for president, "We arrived not yet knowing what was not possible. Consequently, we expected a lot." She was referring to the high-minded dreams of young women who had come of age in a time when people walked on the moon, joined the Peace Corps, led the civil rights movement. But when these young women arrived at buttoned-down Wellesley, she said, they found "a gap between expectation and realities." What she argued for, even as a disruptive liberal student, was a kind of compromise: although Wellesley's strictures inhibited the progressive ambitions of its students, they would not abandon the school, but try to change it as best they could from within.

There were many who didn't question Clinton's slip-'n'-slide centrism, but appreciated it as her political career progressed. One was her longtime supporter and friend Ellen Chesler, who told me in 2006 that Clinton "has clearly shown herself to be a candidate who can carry the banner of women without making it offensive." This jibed with an anecdote reported by Joshua Green in the *Atlantic*. Many right-wing women on the Hill, he noted, had at first dutifully despised Clinton. "But many eventually went on to confess a grudging admiration for her, for reasons that initially struck me as bizarre. 'She wore slacks to her swearing-in ceremony,'" wrote Green, recounting the reaction of one Republican staffer. "'I mean, you just don't *do* that in the Senate.'" The staffer's point "was that Clinton has flourished in the male-dominated milieu without making the normal concessions demanded of women, and has done so—this is important if you're a Republican—without making a big feminist stink about it."

But—and this was important if you weren't a Republican—feminist victory was supposed to involve offense and stink making, wasn't it? As Anna Quindlen wrote, "The fantasy was that the first woman President would be someone who would turn the whole lousy system inside out and upside down. Instead the first significant woman contender is someone who seems to have the system down to a fine art." Then again, no true agitator would ever have made it as far as Clinton had. That, as Quindlen herself called it, was fantasy, not American reality. For some Clinton defenders it was time to dig in, butch up and stop being so damn picky. "The days of believing in any leader with your whole heart are over," the literary agent Sarah Burnes told me in 2006, fuming about liberal women who were turning up their noses at Hillary. Burnes suggested that it was "a political responsibility" for left-leaning women to support Clinton and stop wringing their hands about the authenticity of her feminism.

As she warmed up for her White House bid, Clinton regained some political ground with reproductive rights activists by pushing over-the-counter emergency contraception Plan B through the glutinous bureaucracy at the FDA. In the fall of 2006 she appeased some who had been disgusted by her refusal to support gay marriage by signing on to a bill that would provide insurance benefits for same-sex partners. These moves—late and somewhat limp, but good for women, good for underrepresented Americans, good for civil liberties—appeared to encompass the best of what Hillary Clinton had to offer the American left going into a presidential election: unreliable but intermittently effective action on behalf of the good guys.

"I see enormous progress right now," Faye Wattleton told me after expressing her hesitation about Clinton's abortion waffling. "We are a long way from Pat Schroeder, who was run off in tears because of pressure and ridicule." Schroeder, the former congresswoman from Colorado who had attempted a run for the presidency in 1987, was far from ambivalent; in 2006 she told me that she was delighted at the prospect of a run by Clinton, or even Republican Secretary of State Condoleezza Rice. Schroeder believed it was time to storm the White House bearing the slogan "We couldn't mess it up any more!" She understood better than anyone that women were a lot closer to the executive branch of government than they'd ever been. To her that was good news. But to others it meant the blighted prospect of Clintonian compromise.

By the time Clinton entered true front-runner territory for the nomination, some doubters, such as Feldt, were considering where they stood. "I still had reservations about her," Feldt said retrospectively, "but from a philosophical position, I knew that she would be the person I would be supporting because I did not believe there would be another opportunity like this coming for quite a while."

There had always been utopian visions of female leadership, perfect because they could not, until this point, have been real. There were the hopes, the dreams, the bumper stickers declaring that if women ran the world there'd be no war. But as Hillary Clinton became the first to close in on the fantasy, she was voting for wars and her journey was laying bare just how a woman's position on the inside of the power structure could result in, or more chillingly, could be made possible only by a paralysis of political idealism. As Clinton's longtime political advisor Ann Lewis told me in 2010, "There has always been a tension in the women's movement between the extent to which you can get things done and the purity of your issues." Lewis made reference to suffragist Carrie Chapman Catt, who as president of the National American Woman Suffrage Association supported Woodrow Wilson's entry into World War I and was denounced by her pacifist colleagues, but whose actions allowed NAWSA to retain influence with the U.S. government, greasing the passage of the Nineteenth Amendment in 1919.

Clinton was forcing women to ask themselves, *What did we have to give up to get inside? Did we have to bastardize our beliefs to do it? And were bastardized beliefs better than the alternative?* If Clinton could balance her political ambitions with the principles that motivated her to invest in politics in the first place, then she still had something in common with feminists: they were balancing their ambitions for her, and themselves, with the ideals that first motivated them to invest in her.

✳ ✳ ✳

I was not among those who had ever invested anything meaningful in Hillary Clinton going into election season. It's not that I didn't care about her at all. I was seventeen when Bill Clinton won the White House, and to my teenage mind he and his wife were superheroes. Too young to remember a Democratic president, I believed that the Clintons' arrival in Washington was going to change everything: we were going to have a new New Deal; education was going to be reworked from the ground up; everyone would get health care. I cheered when Bill and Hillary got out of their car at the 1992 inauguration; they were going to govern us benevolently and brilliantly. I believed the Fleetwood Mac song: I didn't stop thinking about tomorrow. I opened my eyes and looked at the day, and I saw things in a different way.

I was the perfect age for getting my political heart broken. Just as in young romance, the letdown—of welfare reform, "don't ask, don't tell," centrism—didn't make me any less likely to fall for the guy again four years later. All those compromises were just so he could get reelected, I reassured myself, so he could give us the new New Deal in his second term!

The political disillusionment of our youth casts particularly long shadows. I guess it can make some people very angry and cynical. It wrought in me a perpetual state of hopeful resignation. In my memory the Clinton years were two brief periods of high-octane campaign optimism bookmarking eight years of feeling like Charlie Brown on his back in the grass, trying to remember why it was that he'd believed Lucy this time.

I wish I could say that I ever truly got over Bill Clinton. But I fear he was imprinted on me as the president I would fall for again and again. I remember staring at him as he boarded the helicopter to fly away from the White House on the day that George W. Bush moved in. I couldn't believe that I wouldn't see my emotionally abusive, constantly disappointing, dissembling, philandering leader every day anymore. I was going to miss him so much! I have since wondered if I took out my steely fury, which I seemed constitutionally incapable of truly aiming at Bill, on his wife, who was beguiling but ultimately resistible in a way her husband never had been. Perhaps I chose to blame her for all the things I couldn't really stay mad at her husband about.

I admired Hillary well enough, but twenty-eight years her junior, I had none of the visceral reactions to her that my elders had. I saw in her no reflection of myself or my experiences, though I surely saw echoes of my mother: hard working, uncoiffed, practical, smart and reassuringly competent.

I understood that she was important, but for me her import was literally academic. In 1997, my senior year of college, I went with my roommate, who was writing an honors thesis on Hillary, to see her speak with Jesse Jackson in Chicago. I was mostly there to see Jackson, my mother's longtime oratorical hero, but nonetheless found Clinton impressive. I marveled at how awkward she was when she shook hands at the rope line afterward. It was like shaking hands with a textbook, a person we had already studied, considered, argued about and were perhaps a little bored by.

As she moved through the White House and into her own political career, I actually tried not to think about her. It was embarrassing, how everyone expected women to have such strong feelings about her. That wasn't me. It's not that I had completely tuned out; I just managed to remain cool about her. I took reasonable offense to the epithets hurled at her without ever becoming passionately interested in defending her. I noticed that her popularity rose after she was cuckolded, but I was not particularly bothered by it. I was appalled by her Iraq vote but not surprised by her unwillingness to play a lady dove. I certainly hoped that she would apologize for that vote but was perfectly aware that apologia and self-recrimination were signs of feminine fallibility she was not likely to flash. I got it. I understood what she was doing, the binds she was in, the deals she'd had to make. I just didn't have any intention of voting for her. For me, Hillary Clinton was Darth Vader, a candidate who might once have been skin and bone and female empowerment, but who was now practically mechanical, who didn't have anything to do with me or my women's movement.

In those languorous inevitability days, when there seemed no question that she would be the candidate, my Clinton disavowal was not exactly symptomatic of the attitude that would later be caricatured and attributed to young female Clinton-resisters. I was not beyond feminism. I was not over it. I was not immune to caring whether or not we had a woman president. In fact I really wished, to the tips of my toes, that there were a female candidate for whom I could cheer loudly and lustily, in part because she was a woman. Clinton just wasn't that person. But my distaste did not come without cost. I was sad that I couldn't enthusiastically get behind her, and many young women shared my melancholy. The journalist Allison Hantschel wrote in the fall of 2006 that although she

was "unexcited" and "indifferent" about Clinton, she was "nagged
by the feeling that this [made her] a bad feminist. . . . After all, a
woman president, any woman president, is a victory for woman-
kind, right?" Was it? I didn't know. Should gender have trumped
political ambivalence?

Before Clinton announced her candidacy, Kate Michelman, the
former president of the National Abortion & Reproductive Rights
Action League (now NARAL Pro-Choice America), told me, "If she
runs, it will have been a long journey." But, she cautioned, "even
though it will be historic, women want to be assured that they have
a candidate who will represent them." Me, I agreed with Faye Wattleton, who before anyone had officially entered the race told me
presciently, "Often, the pioneers who clear the paths do not have
the honor or privilege of running along them. If it's not Mrs. Clinton who becomes our first [female] president, she will have made an
enormous contribution."

2 SPOUSAL SUPPORTS

ALTHOUGH HILLARY'S BIG mouth and independent career were idiosyncratic departures when the Clintons hit the White House in 1993, the vision of the political wife was even more radically transformed by the brief presidential foray of North Carolina Senator Elizabeth Dole in 2000, and then by wives like Judith Steinberg Dean (who insisted that even if husband Howard became president she would not abandon her medical practice in Vermont) and Teresa Heinz Kerry (who listened to her husband's stump speeches with all the focus of a distracted tabby and greeted the Democratic convention in the five languages in which she was fluent). As the candidates geared up for the 2008 campaign America was greeted by Michelle Obama, who had met her husband when he was a summer associate and she his mentor at the corporate law firm where they both worked, and Bill Clinton, who was not a wife at all. The *Family Circle* cookie contest was not extinct, but when, in 2004, Heinz Kerry blithely admitted that a staffer had submitted a recipe in her stead, it was clear that the multicentury reign of happy first hausfraus was petering out.

The conga line of 2008's potential presidential partners reflected the broadly changed educational, professional, social and economic circumstances of women, especially American women of the class most likely to marry future presidents. In addition to the spouse who had already been commander-in-chief, there was Judith Giuliani, a divorced former Bristol-Myers sales manager, whose husband suggested that she might sit in on cabinet meetings; Cindy McCain, the founder of an international medical aid nonprofit, beer heiress, and recovering drug addict; and tongue-pierced sylph Elizabeth Kucinich, who had a master's degree in conflict analysis.

Elizabeth Edwards, an attorney and health care expert, copped one of the race's more traditional poses, as John's devoted spouse, unwavering in her adoration for him. That stance did not quite convey the centrality of her role, both within her husband's campaign and for the women deciding whether to support her husband.

Coming out of the 2004 election John Edwards did not appear to be going places. John Kerry had brought him on as a charismatic running mate and charged him with charming the pants off voters. Instead he was successfully tagged by the Bush campaign as a blood-sucking malpractice lawyer. As a vice-presidential candidate he had projected no coherent agenda and presented a résumé of slick and slightly dodgy jobs that only got dodgier when in 2005 he took a position at a firm with hedge funds incorporated in the Cayman Islands. The idea of Edwards attracting a following for a presidential run of his own seemed unlikely, especially with a Democratic field filled to bursting with female, African American, and Latino candidates.

But perhaps in part because he *was* a Caucasian guy who didn't have to worry about scaring other Caucasian guys with his difference, in competition with candidates who might attract their own progressive followings by dint of their history-making identities, Edwards had more freedom and more incentive to develop a broadly progressive agenda. When he wasn't working with the hedge fund, he was reinventing himself by talking about issues that no one else on the left would touch: poverty and the class divide in America. Edwards was rich; revelations about the size of his mansion and the price of his haircuts scratched his populist shell. But, as he was keen to remind anyone who asked, and everyone who didn't, he had grown up poor, the son of a mill worker. To those who believed in him, what mattered was that he was giving voice to a usually unspoken truth: that there were two Americas, one living above the poverty line and one below it, and that they offered their inhabitants starkly different scales of possibility. In this, Edwards was talking more about both race and gender than anyone else. Implicit in his calls for health care for every man, woman, and child, his insistence on better schools and on raising the minimum wage, were the facts that in 2007, 34.5 percent of African American children, 24.5 percent of all African Americans, and 21.5 percent of Hispanics were living in poverty, and that women were more likely than men to live below the poverty line.

I supported John Edwards going into the 2008 election because I agreed with him about the crucial place of poverty and class difference in the problems that ailed the nation. I liked what he said about the minimum wage and about rebuilding our education system. I believed that he had the most realistically progressive ideas about making the country a better place. And I really liked his wife, even if her earliest flirtation with women voters was not feminist-friendly.

In October 2006 Elizabeth was promoting her memoir, *Saving Graces*, which recounted her childhood as an army brat, the death of her sixteen-year-old son, Wade, in a car accident, the subsequent births of two children when she was close to 50 and her fight against breast cancer, which had been diagnosed days before the 2004 election and was then in remission. At a *Ladies' Home Journal* lunch she noted that she and Hillary Clinton were from the same generation of women: "We both went to law school and married other lawyers. But after that, we made other choices. I think my choices have made me happier. I think I'm more joyful than she is." The Edwards camp would later claim that her remarks had been inaccurately elided, but the rebuttal was not convincing, particularly because in her public apology to Clinton she reiterated a version of her earlier sentiments: "[Senator Clinton] holds a serious and demanding public office, while I am largely home, joyfully I must admit, with two lovely children."

Elizabeth Edwards had charged headlong into the battle royal referred to as the Mommy Wars. One of the most hotly debated subjects among well-off, highly educated feminists in the years leading up to the election was the purported Opt-Out Revolution, in which privileged heirs to the second wave had supposedly chucked their degrees (and their paychecks) in order to stay home with their kids. Studies would later demonstrate that the trend was largely invented, yet at the heart of the conversation was the concern that although feminism had created opportunities for some lucky women, it had not effectively redistributed or reimagined domestic expectations, leaving working mothers, still expected to cook, clean and manage children, to either take on the punishing "second shift" or leave the workforce altogether. On the other side were stay-at-home mothers who felt attacked and argued that feminism's goal was to give women choices, not dictums about how they must spend their days in order to qualify as feminists.

These brawls played out in magazines, newspapers and books about the pros and cons of working or staying at home: David Brooks's op-ed column in the *New York Times,* Caitlin Flanagan's pieces for the *Atlantic* and *The New Yorker,* Linda Hirshman's *Get to Work* and Leslie Bennetts's *The Feminine Mistake.* Mostly, however, invectives were slung in the mushrooming world of parenting and feminism blogs, where feminists, stay-at-home moms, working mothers and stay-at-home dads hashed and clashed until everyone's ears bled.

Well-known for the time she spent engaging in online debate, Edwards would have been acquainted with the hyper-self-righteous exchanges that took place on both sides of this discussion. Addressing a group of ladies who were literally lunching, Edwards chose to highlight one of the only discernible differences between her own professional history and that of her husband's prospective competition: that after the death of her son she had chosen to leave her law practice. She was sending a bat signal to mothers who might feel they had nothing in common with Hillary Clinton, a woman who not only had worked through motherhood, but was now fulfilling every conceivable dimension of her academic and professional promise by seeking the presidency of the United States.

Edwards's comments were, if technically true, wildly disingenuous. The "different choices" she and Clinton made after law school had come *a long time* after law school. Elizabeth had worked at the

North Carolina attorney general's office and then for a firm. During her cancer battle she had become an expert on the health care system and was one of its most zealous and inspiring public critics. She remained Elizabeth Anania until Wade's death, in 1996, when she became Elizabeth Edwards. But as she informed Ms. magazine in 2004, "I took my son's name; I didn't take my husband's name." In many respects the distancing of herself from Clinton was more performance than authentic self-expression. As dismaying as her Donna Reed feint was, it demonstrated that she understood something about the upcoming election: that in part it was going to hinge on women, and how they felt about other women. Even as she made digs at Clinton's less joyful choices, Edwards admitted that she remembered her congressional testimony on health care and that "as a woman, you couldn't help cheering from the sidelines." Edwards knew that there were others who would share her memories, and she was trying to figure out how to woo them to her husband's campaign. "That will be a factor for John," Elizabeth conceded. "She will be a formidable opponent."

Perhaps Elizabeth was so focused on Hillary not because of the differences she strained to manufacture, but because of how alike they were. Elizabeth Edwards was nothing if not formidable, another woman you couldn't help cheering from the sidelines. Her brains, her passion for policy and her brassy ability to endure hardship allowed women who were conflicted about turning away from Hillary the opportunity to invest in another dynamic political partner.

When the Princeton professor Melissa Harris-Lacewell, who would go on to be a vocal supporter of Barack Obama in 2008, initially said publicly that she thought he would make an excellent vice-presidential candidate, people assumed she meant as a running mate to Hillary Clinton. "I absolutely meant John Edwards," she told me in 2009. As a student in North Carolina, Harris-Lacewell had worked as an envelope stuffer for Edwards's 1998 Senate campaign. "I was just so impressed with him," she said in retrospect, "and with Elizabeth." She liked that John was a white southern Democrat, a profile she associated with Carter and Clintonesque coalition building. She liked in Elizabeth that, aside from her feminist credentials, she had a remarkable tale. "A fat woman married to a good-looking man is always a good story," said Harris-Lacewell, "particularly if she is a breast cancer survivor who has lost a child. There were so many different categories of women who could relate to those things and see themselves in her. When John Edwards looked at her lovingly, it was a way of valuing a whole group of women who are not typically valued in a public sphere."

In January 2007, just a week after Edwards declared his candidacy, Kate Michelman, former chief of NARAL Pro-Choice America, announced that she would be coming onboard as a senior advisor to the Edwards campaign. Michelman had spent her professional life fighting for reproductive rights, including running NARAL from 1985 to 2004. By 2007 she was struggling through a family health care crisis and needed a job, badly. Looking to work as an advisor to a presidential campaign, she would have been an obvious match for Clinton. But Clinton, trying her damnedest to pretend there was nothing unusual about her candidacy, certainly wasn't hiring feminists. John and Elizabeth Edwards were.

"It's rather unusual to have someone like me at a high level as a part of a campaign," Michelman told me soon after taking the job. Apart from Al Gore's depressing campaign dalliance with Naomi Wolf in 1999—*The Beauty Myth* author had famously advised him to wear "earth tones"—there was not an extensive history of presidential candidates taking on feminist advisors. Walter Mondale had solicited advice from the National Organization for Women, but that was because he was running the first female vice-presidential candidate, Geraldine Ferraro. Edwards had hired Michelman early, a full year before the Iowa caucus would kick off primary season. "It says a lot about his seriousness and commitment to addressing the experiences of women in society," Michelman said at the time. It also said something that he had not chosen just any old women's leader, but one who had specifically devoted herself to reproductive rights, one of the socially explosive issues away from which so many Democrats had swerved after the 2004 election. Her professional history, Michelman allowed, "could make a candidate feel somewhat reluctant or questioning. But it didn't with John and Elizabeth."

Michelman fielded questions from people who had assumed, or hoped, that she would work for Hillary. "I have three daughters and a granddaughter; I've been working for women's rights for nearly thirty years," she told me at the time. "Hillary's run is historic. . . . Part of me said, 'How could you not be a part of this given all you've worked for?' . . . But John's vision was very compelling." As Gloria Feldt later reminded me, "Kate had to live through the Clinton administration like I did, and it was not fun. They sold us down the river any number of times once Newt Gingrich had taken over Congress. And to get a budget through they'd sell their mothers."

What interested me more than Michelman's choice to work for Edwards was Edwards's choice to hire Michelman. Here was a male candidate's campaign preparing to tackle the challenges of facing a history-making female candidate by doing what she herself could not: making gender a centerpiece of his candidacy.

The month after Michelman signed on, the Edwardses added two even more surprising women to their staff, young denizens of the rowdy feminist blogosphere. Melissa McEwan, then thirty-two, was the founder of the online feminist site *Shakespeare's Sister* (later renamed *Shakesville*) and had written positively about Edwards on her blog; the campaign hired her as an Internet outreach consultant. McEwan supported Edwards because she was an economy voter, because she believed that Edwards was the most progressive candidate and because she loved Elizabeth. Though she would eventually move into the Clinton camp, she had a host of reasons for not initially supporting Hillary. "I bought into narratives about her that are just flatly untrue," McEwan told me in 2009. "Somehow I didn't think she was a great politician and was too focused on video games and flag burning—and she was. But those are little things. I wasn't careful enough to question things I normally question because the narratives about her are so pervasively negative." Despite the retrospective self-flagellation, McEwan maintained that she still would have been an Edwards supporter. "He had a good message that was prescient," she said.

Amanda Marcotte, then twenty-nine, had been writing about politics from a feminist perspective at the popular liberal site *Pandagon* since 2005. The Edwardses hired her as their campaign blogmaster. Marcotte, who would eventually become an Obama supporter, shared none of McEwan's self-recrimination about her decision not to support Clinton, a decision that many of the young liberal women at the forefront of online feminism would also make. "I always respected Hillary Clinton and thought she was kind of awesome," Marcotte said in 2009, but she added, "Hillary Clinton's flaw, at the end of the day, was that she voted for the Iraq war." Edwards had also voted for the war in Iraq but had bent over backward to assert that his vote had been a mistake. Marcotte liked Edwards because she believed he dragged his competitors to the left; she was also drawn to the campaign because they were drawn to her. "When they reached out to me, I thought, 'Here is a campaign that is trying to ground themselves in the netroots, and that obviously thinks feminism is viable and important.' The other campaigns struck me as play-it-safe types."

Hiring McEwan and Marcotte was anything but playing it safe. Though they had different writing styles, both were combatants in the skirmishes increasingly fought in the coarse vortex of the political blogosphere. For lefties and feminists furious at a warmongering and torture-condoning administration and incursions on reproductive rights and civil liberties, the unedited Internet meant no polite limits on discourse. Marcotte's and McEwan's posts on everything from birth control to popular culture often dripped with cynicism and outrage; they engaged in heated arguments with their readership and were profane with regard to institutions—the Catholic Church, the Bush administration, the right-wing media—about which many people still felt it inexcusable to be profane. Male-dominated liberal blogs tended to be wonky and politically aspirational, but feminist sites, dealing as they did with reproduction and body issues, were often raunchy and raucous in their embrace of carnal liberation and their rejection of sexual censure; feminist bloggers often made incisive but indelicate connections between sexual and other kinds of politics. Among the things Marcotte had written prior to joining the Edwards camp was a caption mocking the Catholic Church's position on birth control, posing the imagined rhetorical exchange, "Q: What if Mary had taken Plan B after the Lord filled her with his hot, white, sticky Holy Spirit? A: You'd have to justify your misogyny with another ancient mythology." McEwan, for her part, had a thoughtful and sharp-edged online persona and mostly engaged in old-fashioned cussing. She titled a 2006 post about a conservative Christian group's movement to ban gay adoption, "What don't you lousy motherfuckers understand about keeping your noses out of our britches, our beds, and our families?"

The choice to hire Marcotte and McEwan revealed either the campaign's prescient instinct that the election might lie in the hands of the young and the logged-on, or its short-sightedness with regard to some very old, creaky conservative machinery. The creaker in question was Bill Donohue, since 1993 the leader of the Catholic League (a league that may have included only Bill Donohue) and the erstwhile protester of every movie with questionably Catholic credentials since *The Last Temptation of Christ*. Donohue went to town on Marcotte and McEwan as soon as their hirings were announced, calling them "anti-Catholic vulgar trash-talking bigots" and stirring up easily purchased sympathy from conservative pundits like Michelle Malkin and Kathryn Jean Lopez. Even the *New York Times* dutifully reported Donohue's outsized ire against the bloggers, but failed to put it in the context of his history of outsized ire against *Dogma, South Park,* pop singer Joan Osborne and a 2005 episode of *CSI: Crime Scene Investigations.*

"It was Elizabeth Edwards who called to fire me," McEwan told me two years later. "That was the first time that I talked to her, and it broke my heart. It was so devastating that the first time I ever spoke to this woman whom I had so admired, I was getting fired." *Salon* was the first to report that McEwan and Marcotte had been discharged in stories I wrote with my colleague Alex Koppelman; our posts on their dismissals caused the liberal blogosphere to erupt. "I'm looking for a candidate who won't throw allies under the bus to appease opponents. Are you that candidate, John Edwards?" wrote Zuzu at *Feministe.* "Faithful flock of bitchitude, please take the time to contact the John Edwards Campaign in support of my blog sisters . . . who are currently dealing with all manner of bullshit because they had the audacity to be critical of the Catholic church," was the plea from Shark-fu at *Angry Black Bitch.* The respected liberal writer Ezra Klein blogged, "This will be a choice for the campaign. [Whose] respect do they care more about retaining? The netroots'? Or Bill Donohue's?"

In firing McEwan and Marcotte the Edwards campaign had affronted the online political community, the very progressives— young, brash and potentially influential—they had correctly surmised they needed to seduce. Scrambling to do damage control, the campaign denied to *Salon* (and every other media outlet) that the women had been fired; then they rehired both, though only after Edwards himself told them they needed to publicly apologize, which they did. Days later Marcotte included religious commentary in a film review on *Pandagon*; Donohue went ballistic and Fox News's Bill O'Reilly picked up the story, calling Marcotte and McEwan "Christian-haters." Marcotte resigned from the Edwards campaign first and McEwan left soon after. The Edwardses' great experiment in reaching the netroots had failed. But not before ensuring that one of the first campaign scandals of the election cycle involved young feminists.

About a month after McEwan and Marcotte quit, Elizabeth Edwards felt a pain in her ribcage and went to her doctor for X-rays. Within a few days the Edwardses stood next to each other for a press conference about Elizabeth's diagnosis. John talked in very matter-of-fact terms. She had gone to the doctor; there were further tests, a bone study. "The thing that is true is that her cancer will not be cured now. Elizabeth will have this as long as she's alive." They were both dry-eyed. No, they said, they would not suspend the campaign. "I expect to do next week all the things I did last week," said Elizabeth.

I found Elizabeth's commitment to chin-up fortitude almost chilling, but deeply admirable. To deal with a son's death by making two more children at fifty, to put off treatment of breast cancer until after a presidential election, not to let its return get in the way of continuing that quest—these weren't choices that many of us would likely have made, and I understood that perhaps they weren't all good ones. But the kind of person who would make them? To my mind, she was extraordinary. The next day, when I read Elizabeth's statement in the *New York Times* that she hoped to give her children wings so that they might "stand by themselves in a stiff wind," I felt as though a brisk, cold wind had just blown through me. It was an arresting image of what it means to survive and move forward.

As I watched the press conference it struck me that John Edwards did not look like a man who wanted to be running for president, but that Elizabeth Edwards looked like a woman who wanted to be doing nothing other than plowing toward the White House. It seemed clear that it was Elizabeth who was driving this, who herself might have been the candidate had she been born just a few years later, or perhaps if she were given more years than she likely had left. In my mind she was the motor, the candidate manquée. I was imposing a Clintonian model on the Edwardses, but it was not so outlandish: Hillary and Elizabeth were of a generation in which the only conceivable road to the presidency for a woman with political ambition was through a man. Hillary had maneuvered her way into her own political career, but her fortunes remained lashed to her preeminently powerful mate. Elizabeth was still steering the only vessel available to her—one later revealed to be terribly unseaworthy—with all her might.

Two years after the campaign McEwan recalled how much she had loved Elizabeth, before and even after she had called to dismiss her from her job. "I liked Elizabeth even more than John," she said, mentioning the most obvious comparison: "The two of them together—[John] would talk about the economy, and [Elizabeth] would talk about health care—in a weird way, it was Bill and Hillary all over again, wasn't it? It was two for one. God, the irony." She paused, and I assumed that she was referring to what would become John Edwards's own turgid sex scandal. But she was talking about something else: "I suspected that Elizabeth was the brains of the operation, and I'd thought the same thing about Hillary. But when I had the chance to support the brains of the operation, I chose the partnership. I literally went for the team that still had the dude on it."

★ ★ ★

Not every presidential spouse was thrilled about being on the road to Pennsylvania Avenue.

The tip-off that the lady sitting in the alcove of the Monticello Public Library in November 2007 would soon become a cultural lightning rod was that even in the dull safety of this standard-issue Iowa campaign setting, she was neither safe nor dull. Michelle Obama, the forty-three-year-old mother of two girls, was reading *Olivia . . . and the Missing Toy*. "Do you guys know Olivia?" she asked the rapt gaggle of children at her feet. "She's a pig. She's quite the personality." Told that there was time for one more story, Obama glanced at the preselected options. One was a hardback edition of *Our National Anthem,* the sort of starred-and-striped book that an aspiring first lady should read. "Not that one," said Obama quickly, discarding the patriotic pablum in favor of *Skippy-jon Jones,* the story of a Siamese kitten who, for reasons too murky to convey, used "his very best Spanish accent" to say things like, "My ears are too beeg for my head. My head ees too beeg for my body. I am not a Siamese cat. . . . I AM A CHIHUAHUA!"

The tale of Skippyjon Jones's trippy quest for beans (or something) required an increasingly incredulous Obama to utter lots of awkwardly accented Spanglish things like "Yip Yippee Yippito! It's the end of Alfredo Buzzito! Skippito is here, we have nothing to fear. Adios to the bad Bumblebeeto!" As she persevered, the kids went *loco,* rolling off their beanbags with belly-busting laughter. The wife of presidential candidate Barack Obama was laughing pretty hard herself, but on she forged, hollering "Holy Frijoles!" with great gusto. The next day one of Michelle's staffers overheard a photographer and me laughingly recall her rejection of the patriotic for the politically incorrect Mexican accent; the staffer half-jokingly, half-pleadingly said to me, "That was off the record."

The decision to read *Skippyjon Jones* was a minuscule one. But in Iowa in the months before the caucus the minutest of actions carried weight. Given that Michelle's husband had just been caught in a preposterous flap over his failure to put his hand on his heart during the "Star Spangled Banner" at Senator Tom Harkin's steak fry, the sound choice would have been the book about the anthem. But Michelle Obama, a Princeton and Harvard Law School graduate from Chicago's South Side, a woman who had quit a fancy law firm job to work instead for the city in which she was raised, a wife who had made known her reticence about jumping into the presidential fray, could not help but choose the book that was untested over one that was boring.

Michelle Obama, who was still working part time as the vice president of community and external affairs at the University of Chicago Medical Center, appeared determined to temper the near messianic expectations that greeted her husband's candidacy. In this she was, worryingly for some, reminiscent of Teresa Heinz Kerry, the troublemaker who had insisted on keeping the country's (already rather dim) appraisal of her mate in check. "I don't want to give [John] more [due] than he deserves," Heinz Kerry once informed Hardball's Chris Matthews, a sentiment that Michelle echoed in 2005 when she rolled her eyes at the entourage trailing her husband at his Senate swearing-in and said to a reporter, "Maybe one day he will do something to warrant all this attention."

Michelle Obama's particular impulse was to reject the mush of helpmate hokum in favor of candor and a good laugh. In the year-long windup to the Iowa caucus she had told various audiences about Barack's shortcomings when it came to putting the butter away and making the bed; that he was "snore-y and stinky" when he woke up in the morning; that she agreed to his presidential run only if he promised to kick his smoking habit. Perhaps most memorably, she had said, "He's a gifted man, but in the end, he's just a man." It wasn't like she was kneecapping the guy, whom she met at the Chicago law firm Sidley Austin in 1989. But so accustomed were we to hearing political mates in reverential mode that her remarks earned her an early reputation. The New York Times columnist Maureen Dowd wrote an April column in which she referred to Michelle, via an unnamed interlocutor, as "emasculating" and chided her for casting Barack "as an undisciplined child." Why, Dowd asked herself, if she liked the snap and twinkle of "a cheeky woman puncturing the ego of a cocky guy" in 1940s romantic comedies, did she not like it when the pinpricks were inflicted by Michelle, whom she referred to as a "princess of South Chicago," unwilling, in Dowd's colorful parlance, to polish her husband's pedestal?

It was hard to imagine that the theme of Obama as threatening to her husband's masculinity was born entirely of her cute jokes about putting away butter. But it was just as hard to discern whether its roots lay also with her height (five-foot-eleven), strength (her muscular arms would later become the subject of national obsession), or some combination of popular apprehensions of black femininity as angry, dominating and ultimately emasculating. Dowd's longtime specialty was making political figures into cartoons, but that proposition became problematic when political figures emerged from populations that historically existed in the white cultural imagination as cartoons to begin with.

Dowd's loopy characterization of Michelle was one of the first to depict her as perilously close to a stereotype of sassy, nagging, castrating black femininity, often referred to as a "Sapphire," in reference to one of its early popular iterations, the belittling wife on *Amos 'n Andy*. But Dowd wasn't alone in her concerns. The cultural critic Margo Jefferson told me in 2009, "There was a huge amount of discussion among black women, white women, all women, about [Michelle's approach]: 'Is this too much?' . . . Certainly some black women felt [she] was . . . not as extreme as a Sapphire, but a little too much 'Mmmm, hmmmm' and 'I'm gonna put you in your place!'"

Whether the anxiety Michelle produced in circles both black and white consciously or unconsciously had to do with her race, it was often expressed as concern that she might be hobbling her husband's presidential chances by making him either less of a man or too much of a black man. Barack Obama's mixed racial heritage, along with his Hawaiian upbringing and Kansas roots, helped to mitigate some of the racist assumptions about American blackness that might otherwise have been directed at him. But Michelle—darker skinned than her husband, descended like most African Americans from slaves, raised in a black neighborhood—was a reminder of all that was different and possibly scary about Barack. Melissa Harris-Lacewell told me in 2009, "Michelle is a representation of Barack Obama's choice to aggressively move toward blackness. He went to Harvard. He was editor of the *Law Review*. He could have actively made a choice to move toward whiteness or something else."

In a post on the women's pop culture blog *Jezebel* the writer Moe Tkacik counted among Obama's sins against her husband's reputation the time that she'd called him "the brother" even though "she knows it makes the white folks uneasy." In fact the reference to her husband as "the brother" was made not in front of white folks, but in a speech to a mostly black audience in Iowa, in which she had assured them, "This brother is smart!" Ironically this was also part of Michelle's job. For those Americans worried that Barack was not being black enough, she served as a reminder that he too was African American.

Marrying Michelle, who had strong ties to Chicago's black political community, had smoothed Barack's entrance into the circle from which he would build his career. According to her biographer, Liza Mundy, Michelle was clear about her role as his black credential in an interview with a Chicago public television reporter who asked about her husband's blackness in 1999, during his ill-starred congressional campaign against the African American incumbent Bobby Rush. "I'm as black as it gets," said Michelle. "I was born on the South Side. . . . We weren't rich, you know. I put my blackness up against anybody's blackness in the state, okay? And Barack is a black man. And he's done more in terms of meeting his commitments and sticking his neck out for this community than many people who criticize him. . . . And I can say that . . . because I'm black."

Eight years later she was taking a more subtle approach but hammering home a similar point. She told Steve Kroft of *60 Minutes* that she didn't stay up worrying about her husband's being assassinated because "the realities are, as a black man, Barack can get shot going to the gas station." In response, *RaceWire*'s Malena Amusa wrote that Michelle was "the saving grace" of the Obama campaign, both required and able "to be the typical Strong Black Woman," and thus present "a well-engineered counter to Barack's Black masculinity that has been attacked for being diluted."

An identification with Michelle was especially acute for black women, some of whom responded to her with the kind of intense recognition that some women had felt for Hillary Clinton a decade and a half earlier. Paula Giddings, an African American studies professor at Smith College, would later write in *Essence*, "Many of us [black women] began to take him [Barack Obama] seriously only after we saw and heard Michelle. . . . That Barack Obama would choose for his life partner a nearly six-foot-tall, incredibly smart, loquacious lioness of a woman told us virtually all we needed to know about his fundamental character—and the way he felt about us." Harris-Lacewell, who shifted her allegiance from Edwards to Obama in late 2007, echoed this sentiment: "[Obama's] open adoration for Michelle, a strong woman and a smart woman and a challenging woman and a tall woman [went] a long way toward generating a sense [among women] that 'We'll give Barack a chance.'"

Like Hillary before her, Michelle was walking smack into the high expectations of women who saw in her an independent woman with an education and professional history comparable to her presidential-caliber mate, a woman who was once his mentor and whom he often credited as being smarter than he. Harris-Lacewell explained that she became a professor at the University of Chicago in 1999 just as Obama was running against Bobby Rush. "He was smart, and terribly awkward at that point," she said. "I thought, here was a guy who was not terribly savvy. He picked a race he couldn't really win, he tried to intellectualize the whole race question, he tried to run against an incumbent, for god's sake!" Barack's political future might be maxed out, she thought at the time, but the one to watch was his wife. "The person who did have political acumen, who was capable of negotiating multiple communities, was Michelle. I don't mean as an elected official. But I thought to the extent that someone was really going to be the superstar, it would be Michelle, and Barack would be her competent partner. She was fabulous."

For Margo Jefferson, recognition of the Obamas' shifting balance of marital power explained some of Michelle's attempts to suck the air out of her husband's mythos. "It was not unlike what Hillary was faced with," said Jefferson, "a woman in an equitable intellectual relationship who was suddenly finding a huge divide of power. In Michelle's case, she did not consider herself a person who loved politics and saw nothing possibly to gain from it. I think this was really hard for her. What woman, including Maureen Dowd, wouldn't understand that?"

Some leaped in on her behalf, cranking expectations even higher. Upon learning that Michelle had reduced her workload at the University of Chicago Medical Center to devote more time to her husband's campaign, Debra Dickerson wrote in *Salon* about her "feminist fury" at seeing a successful and independent woman reined in: "She's traded in her solid gold résumé [and] high octane talent . . . to be a professional wife and hostess. Any day now, Michelle Obama's handlers will have her glued into one of those Sunday-go-to-meeting Baptist grandma crown hats while smiling vapidly for hours at a time. . . . I hate to add to Michelle's load, but . . . I hope she'll keep her role in women's history in mind." More specifically Dickerson hoped that Michelle would "confront dysfunction in the black community, . . . help America understand that black progress is American progress [and] . . . bring feminism to black women."

It was a colossal amount of pressure on a woman who hadn't wanted her husband to run for president in the first place. And yet, whatever competing or contradictory demands weighed on Michelle, they seemed in the early days of the campaign neither to slow her down nor dim her personality. "You've never seen anyone like us before, and that's a little freaky, isn't it?" she asked the crowd of grown-ups assembled at the Monticello Library after the *bangito* conclusion of *Skippyjon Jones*. "It's like, 'They're real!' Well, guess what? Real people can be politicians too. We as a country have grown suspicious of real. We take the fake."

Michelle Obama was aggressively not fake. Over burgers between events, she and four staffers reminisced about the Iowa State Fair. "All the candidates go to the fair," said Peter Weeks, Barack's staffer who was traveling with Michelle on this trip, but "we *went to the fair.*" What I gathered from this locution was that the Obama family had not attended the fair as a piece of presidential performance art: milk a cow, eat a corndog, pin a ribbon on a pig, and other assorted photo ops. Rather, they had stuffed their faces and ridden the rides like nonpresidential people whose lives had not been made into a camera-friendly tableau of fun, but were in fact *real fun*. As staffers recalled Barack and elder daughter Malia riding everything on the fairway, I asked Michelle why she hadn't been on the amusements herself. Was she scared? "Oh no, I love the rides," she said, explaining that she had to stay on the ground with six-year-old Sasha, having scared the bejesus out of her a year earlier by taking her on the Tower of Terror at Disneyland. One of Obama's aides, a mother, looked at Michelle reproachfully. "I know, bad mommy," conceded Obama. "Now I can't persuade her to go on any rides. She's like, 'You don't have good judgment.'"

Michelle hadn't completely laid off the "Take my husband, please" domestic complaints since her run-in with Dowd, telling one Iowa crowd, "I didn't marry [Barack] for all his degrees. Certainly he's made less money over the years, as my mother has pointed out."

But she seemed to be winning over Iowans, who in six short weeks would gather to caucus. It wasn't a given that Michelle, with her advanced degrees, her height, her grace, her killer Jimmy Choo boots and impeccably tailored bell-sleeved tunics, would connect so completely to the comparatively pale, squat groups of people who crowded restaurants and theater lobbies to hear her speak. But she did. As Margaret Blake, an eighty-one-year-old white woman, told me plainly in the back of a movie theater–cum–pizza parlor in Wau-kon, "I think she's one of our own. Our different heritage probably doesn't matter so much if her experience leads her to understand us." Forty-two-year-old Laura Hubka, an ultrasound technician, cried after embracing Michelle in a church basement in Cresco. She had never voted before but had become a precinct captain because of her belief in the Obamas. When I asked what she loved about Michelle, she said, "The strength that she has as a black woman married to a black man, running for president. The trust in the American people, that we can look past that, is such a courageous act. I would vote for *her* for president." At an old opera house in De Witt, Peter Weeks waited as Michelle embraced nearly every woman who approached her. "She's a hugger," he said, with weary appreciation.

The hugging, the smart speeches, the impact she had on people, the no-bullshit authenticity—it was all part of what led me, at some point during the three days I followed her around the rural towns of eastern and northern Iowa, to get on the phone with my *Salon* edi-tor and confess to him that I was a goner. "She's too awesome to be objective about," I told him, voicing a sentiment that critics would later hear in the press's coverage of her husband.

I did not feel that way about Barack Obama. Like others, I'd been captivated by the Illinois Senate candidate's keynote address at the 2004 Democratic convention, in which he had spoken of one America. And while reporting on the midterm elections in subur-ban Philadelphia, a year before I traveled to Iowa to write about his wife, I had heard him speak as part of a Democratic all-star tour that included Nancy Pelosi and Al Gore. Waiting in a six-block line in my hometown, the former blood-red suburb where my parents had once been among the only Democrats, I'd been blown away by the thirteen hundred people gathered outside the Keswick Theater. Some had been there for hours and come from great distances, just to see him.

I had wanted to love him as much as the long line of adherents did, but had been surprised and disappointed when his speech that day underwhelmed me; I found it derivative and thought that he lacked the charisma for which he was already being celebrated. But I was struck as I'd watched the crowd around me—old, young, black, white—practically levitate with joy. They were not underwhelmed; they were inspired by him. I felt like one of those people genetically incapable of tasting the deliciousness of cilantro. My first brush with Obamamania was also my first experience feeling immune to its thrilling energies.

His wife was a different story. I saw her on fire in Dubuque, giving a speech in which she said the United Auto Workers guys with whom she'd just shared a beer downstairs were like her city-worker father. Ron Hughes, a small-business owner, told me before her speech that he was a Joe Biden supporter and that his wife was apathetic about the political process. "She just comes for the socializing," Hughes assured me. By the time Michelle got to the part about how fear is used to bully and divide us, Hughes's supposedly apathetic wife, Suzette, a fifty-nine-year-old retired physical therapist, was nodding in assent. At the end of Michelle's address Suzette told me, "I think I found my candidate. . . . I hadn't been moved until tonight."

Part of what moved people, oddly enough, was what critics had been griping about: Michelle's gimlet-eyed view of her husband and the steady drumbeat of discontent about the process she was living through. "I'm not doing this because I'm married to him," she said again and again. "Because truly, this process is painful. If you have a choice, America, don't do this! Teach! Do something else. I tried to [tell] Barack—there are so many ways to change the world. Let's do them!" In another version, she said, "I [didn't] want to run for president! Life was comfortable! It was safe! Nobody was taking pictures of us!" This refrain went over well, in part because everyone in her audience could relate to it. Who among them would want to give up privacy, security, routine, all in a bid to watch their mate get verbally attacked and take on the most high-pressure, all-consuming job on the planet? She was telling the crowd, "You do what you say you're going to do in this life. Your word really matters. You put your *best* into everything you do." At the word *best,* emphasized through gritted teeth, eyes squeezed, it was all laid out for me: she had not wanted to do this; it sucked. But this woman who grew up on the South Side and went to Princeton and Harvard did not do anything halfway. So as long as she was here, she was going to sell it, and make clear that her exertions must be shared. "Don't ask if Barack Obama is ready," Michelle said, "because he is ready. The question is: are *we* ready?"

Watching Michelle reminded me of the chill I got from reading about Elizabeth Edwards teaching her kids to stand in a stiff wind. Running beneath the presidential foot-dragging, the perforation of her husband's hype, her calls to readiness, was an arresting sense of caution and realism. She might have been the only one making the sober estimate of how hard this was going to be, of what a leap people would need to take to make this happen. "Change is scary," she told the Iowans. "It was scary for me to say yes to this. So I know." It seemed to me that she was carrying many of the burdens for her husband. He had the hope, she had the fear; he had the enthusiasm, she had the reluctance; he had the high expectations, she lived on planet Earth. In many ways, for those who doubted a black man's ability to run successfully for president, be they cynic or racist, Michelle worked as an interlocutor, as a stand-in for what she presumed would be the larger national experience: she doubted, shook her head, said no. But then her experience and the country's became further aligned: she took a chance on the guy with the funny name and slim prospects for success, because, frankly, she fell for him, just as the country was beginning to.

Fifteen years after Bill Clinton promised a two-for-one presidency, Michelle hit a similar note on her own behalf: "[If you elect Barack] not only will you get to hang out with me—because I'll be there; I'll go to the White House with him—but we have a chance to fundamentally change this country." She was unapologetic about the fact that she, like Hillary, was not a housewife but a working mother. "I've felt so disconnected from Washington. You don't know me! As a mother, as a professional, as a wife, you can't represent me!" she said. Here was an unfussy assertion that her identity was multifaceted, and that in that formulation at least, her wifeliness came third to children and career. Over coffee in Monticello she told me her BlackBerry was the only thing that kept her connected to her job. "The one that *pays* me," she added, eyebrow arched.

As I left Michelle's Dubuque speech I spied hand-lettered signs advertising John Edwards's appearance that night at a bar where he would be visiting with the UAW members Michelle had greeted earlier. I followed the arrows. It was late, and Edwards was not part of my assignment, but I was a reporter and a voter curious to see my candidate up close. As I watched Edwards enter the teeming bar and moved as close as I could to address some questions to him, I felt my desire to speak with him evaporate. He was shiny and syrupy, pounding guys on the back and swigging beer, but somehow not really talking with anyone, and certainly not listening. He was tired, I told myself. It was past midnight. But I had spent two days watching a woman who, no matter how wiped out or disenchanted with her task, appeared to focus on every person who approached her. I slunk out of the bar, disgusted by Edwards, and then disgusted by myself. I was not someone who cared, or ever wanted to care, whether or not a candidate was someone I'd like to have a beer with. I liked John Edwards because of his platform, his policies. But, boy, did I not want to have a beer with him.

The next morning Michelle was an hour north of Dubuque, speaking to a crowd in a restaurant overlooking a broad stretch of the sinuous Mississippi River. While she was hugging after the speech, I overheard a group of four women gossiping about the Clintons, speculating rather ungenerously about why Hillary might be running for president. One, who was wearing a precinct captain button, boiled down the differences between the former first family and the Obamas: "Michelle and Barack are like us," she said.

It was this comment that provoked in me the reaction that is etched most clearly in my memory of this trip. Michelle and her team packed into their van, I got in my rental car, the photographer got into hers. It was November in rural Iowa, and between the Hopperesque towns in which we were stopping we drove through farmland, and brittle leaves blew across the road. I had thrown some CDs into my bag, and at some point on the drive to Michelle's next stump stop, on a crisp bright day following this crisp, bright woman, Bob Dylan's "The Times They Are A-Changin'" began to play. I was thirty-three years old; I had no memories of the 1960s, in which the modern civil rights movement took hold, or of the 1970s, in which second-wave feminism bloomed. But I felt for a few minutes as though, on some small highway east of everything urban in Iowa, I was living in the most powerful historic moment of my lifetime, as if the country I'd grown up in, with its rules and limitations and assumptions about who can do what and who can be what, was finally beginning to fulfill Dylan's decades-old promise. Elderly white women in Iowa felt they had more in common with Michelle Obama than they did with Hillary Clinton. Inhabitants of towns like the conservative rural Maine hamlet my mother had fled and the Republican Pennsylvania suburb where I'd been raised were crowding into church basements to listen to a black woman with advanced degrees tell them to elect her husband president. Mawkish as it may have been, I felt sure in that moment that everything was different. Anything was possible.

Though I would go on to feel great respect and appreciation for her husband, that trip with Michelle—the experience of watching one crowd after another fall head over heels for her, my own feelings of connection with and admiration for this powerful working mother who twenty years earlier might well have been a figment of our imagination—was the closest I would come, until November of the next year, to experiencing the optimistic fever caught by so many of my compatriots during Obama's campaign. And it felt fantastic.

※ ※ ※

During the Iowa trip I stopped with Team Michelle at a Hardee's restaurant in Allamakee County. As Michelle filled her medium soda cup, she was approached by an elderly couple, the woman wearing an American flag sweat suit. They were on their way to see her speak down the road and were beside themselves at their luck at catching her here first. "We just love you," they told her. When I told Michelle over lunch that I was surprised so many people who apparently had nothing in common with her managed to see themselves reflected in her, she looked unsurprised. She nodded, swallowing her bite of cheeseburger before saying, "They see beyond the surface to the core. We are so close to each other." It was campaign-issue political sentiment, but as she said it she made a small gesture with her thumb and forefinger that reminded me, in tone and content, of another political sentimentalist, and the other spouse on the campaign trail who was helping to turn history inside out.

For years Bill Clinton had been holding forth on genetic research showing us how much biology all human beings have in common, in spite of their outward diversity. While covering the former president's summer 2007 trip to Africa, I'd seen him make that thumb and forefinger gesture many times, in reference to exactly the same thing: how close we all are to each other regardless of our race, regardless of our sex.

Bill Clinton's wife was about to do something that no American woman had done before, and her efforts would involve asking Americans to rethink ingrained ideas about gender and power. That meant not only expanding the imagined bounds of traditional femininity to include authority (often coded as masculine and thereby monstrous when exhibited by women), but also stretching our ideas about masculinity to include subordination (coded as feminine and thereby pathetic when exhibited by men). The notion of a "first man" had always been seen as inherently comical. Television's *Commander in Chief* had eked knee-slappers from the fate of the female president's husband, played by Kyle Secor. In one episode a chipper amanuensis shows him around his new, pink East Wing office, asking him how big a staff he'd like and noting, "Mrs. Clinton had twenty. . . . That didn't go over very well." Would he like to confer on daily menus? "Mrs. Clinton, of course, shunned that. . . . That didn't go over very well." The humor was derived not only from the pathos of the neutered first man, but from the aberrations of a real-life former first lady.

For many, the suggestion that Bill Clinton could ever play second banana to his wife was ridiculous; he was the ultimate alpha male when it came to political achievement, charisma and sexuality. After the heart problems and memoir writing that took up his immediate post-administration years, Clinton had emerged from his presidential husk and established the William J. Clinton Foundation, a web of international projects that combined humanitarian interests with profitable enterprise. In this role he had persuaded pharmaceutical companies to lower the costs of medicines and provide drugs to a million people; his Clinton-Hunter Development initiative promoted sustainable growth in Africa, expanding access to clean water, fertilizer and irrigation systems. The Clinton Climate Initiative worked with banks to finance the reduction of carbon emissions in some of the world's biggest cities, and in the United States he had been bargaining with snack and beverage companies to get healthier food into schools.

Shuttling between hospitals and schools, hearing from rape victims and HIV patients, investing in education and training for women and girls, holding babies and watching schoolchildren skip rope, in the fall of 2007 Clinton published *Giving,* a book about his humanitarian work. Dana Milbank at the *Washington Post* sniggered that Clinton was "auditioning for two quite different honors: following Jimmy Carter to Stockholm as a Nobel Peace Prize recipient, and following Hillary Clinton to the White House as the first first gentleman." But the two paths were far from divergent. Whether by design or by accident, the work that Clinton had taken on dovetailed rather elegantly with his new role as campaign spouse. By plying the traditionally feminine art of giving, he appeared to be seeking an outlet for his immense ambitions and an angle from which his light could flatter Hillary rather than outshine her. As he told an audience at the Nelson Mandela Foundation in Johannesburg, "She helped me in every race I ran from 1974 to 2000. . . . I've got about twenty years to go before we're even."

"Even" was a tricky proposition if you were Bill Clinton, the former leader of the free world, one of the most recognizable people on the planet, a man who would joke to Jon Stewart after he returned from Africa, "I may slit my throat," when Stewart asked if he could handle trading places with his wife. "A First [Lady's] . . . power is derivative, not independent, of the President's," Hillary wrote in *Living History.* No matter how Bill contorted himself, his power was never going to fully derive from Hillary's. Persuading her ambitious and cocksure husband to curate a collection of letters to the White House family pets seemed about as likely as turning one of the lions we saw at the Ngorongoro Crater in Tanzania into the first house cat. In Ngorongoro the lionesses were the killers. Clinton watched one of them rub out a warthog in a neat metaphor for what he hoped might happen in November 2008. As he excitedly described the lioness kill over lunch in the crater, with zebras grazing in the near distance, he seemed to be gearing up to play his part in a social evolution—electing a woman president— that should have been tiny in comparison to the miraculous trek out of Africa and around the globe, but that had been unthinkable throughout American history. Perhaps Clinton's dominance was a boon, I thought as I watched him. Maybe only a man so sure of his power would be comfortable enough to give his wife a turn at the most public kind of supremacy. Or at least put on a show of it.

One day at the midpoint of the trip Clinton boarded the private plane that was flying the press from Malawi to Zambia and settled himself in a captain's chair. We reporters gathered on couches and at his feet, as if he were our favorite professor at the University of I Can't Believe I'm on a Private Plane with Bill Clinton, and he began to talk. He talked about ecofriendly bricks, ATM cards that could be activated by thumbprints, the aggregate impact of the Grameen Bank in Bangladesh and eBay philanthropy. He discussed his Middle East peace plan, explained why the Nigerian organized crime network was probably the most sophisticated in the world after the Mafia and the Russian mob and recounted the kidnapping and murder of Colombia's former culture minister Consuelo Araújo. The man appeared to remember every conversation he had ever had as president, and every conversation he had ever had *about* his presidency; his narratives looped and trailed back to his accomplishments, his regrets, his mistakes, his victories. It was easy to see why Bill Clinton might consider himself the most fascinating person in a room. I was gobsmacked by the sheer volume of words, his ability to nimbly and cogently jump from subject to subject. When his gaze swept his audience and caught mine, it felt as though my brain had been X-rayed, the flabbiness of my cerebrum exposed; I was overcome by a desire to please the whirring brain, to nod in sage agreement and chuckle wryly at his declamations about the expiration of the Multifibre Arrangement. I also could not help but wonder how this guy was ever going to stop talking long enough to let his spouse run for president.

Bill Clinton was made of words, and in the summer of 2007, though he was being held at arm's length by a Hillary campaign skittish about his rumored post-presidential peccadilloes, he was spilling a lot of them on the subject of his wife. Bill liked to talk politics and Hillary was the politician to talk about, but many of his references were also in the vein of easy camaraderie born of long-term partnership: "Hillary always tells me . . ."; "Hillary and I once knew these women . . ."; "Hillary thinks I'm nuts, but . . ." They spoke several times a day. An American raised on lurid speculation (and revelation) about the Clintons' marriage, I was taken aback by the apparently tight weave of the couple's dynamic. On our last night in Africa, in a small hotel in Arusha, with a 4:30 a.m. wake-up call ahead of him, Clinton and his aides stayed up all night so that he could call to wish Hillary luck and then watch her in one of the earliest Democratic debates. They seemed an almost spookily well-matched pair. In *Living History* she wrote, "Bill Clinton and I started a conversation in the spring of 1971, and more than 30 years later we're still talking." They sure were. Clinton fantasists had spent years unspooling conspiracy theories about the couple's power-mad pacts and dual presidential plans; a week in Africa offered a less malevolent and more persuasively affectionate vision of the couple's bond. But Bill was locked in on two subjects, his legacy and his wife, and I wondered whether he would be able to let go of the former in order that the latter might go it on her own. At the time I believed that he was giving it a thoughtful, studied try.

Clinton was spending his days holding babies, visiting sick kids, listening to stories of sexual assault, worrying about maternal health—work that had historically been marked as soft, feminized. "I never believed that those so-called soft power issues were unimportant," he said to me. "I always thought that [it was important] when Hillary did it; and Eleanor Roosevelt did the same thing all during the Depression." His favorite first ladies extended the reach of the Oval Office, tending to the international relationships that their husbands did not have time to focus on. "I didn't want Africa or India to believe I didn't care about them just because I couldn't physically go there in my first term," he said. So he sent his wife in his stead. In some ways he was still catching up to her. The reason we went to Ngorongoro was because Hillary and Chelsea had loved it back in 1997; Bill had been wanting to get there ever since, perhaps for reasons that were not simply geographic. When I asked Senator Clinton if she saw any of her own duties as first lady mirrored in her husband's foundation work, she replied, "I do, and he's even said that on a few occasions." When he finally traveled to Africa himself in 1998, the first American president to make an extended visit to the continent, Bill reaped the benefits of having dispatched an earlier avatar. He described meeting with Senegalese women who had previously talked with Hillary about their opposition to genital mutilation. "They saw America as actually caring about what happened to people like them, because Hillary had been there and met with them," he said. "Derivatively, they loved me and America." He also recalled the "brave men" who accompanied the women to their meeting with him. Shaking his head with remembered admiration, he said, "These few hardy guys there were so proud of themselves that they had been sticking up for these women and taking all this crap from the other guys, you know?" Taking crap from other guys was a position with which the former president was becoming familiar.

Two of Hillary's presumptive Republican opponents, Mitt Romney and Fred Thompson, got their jollies in 2007 with sissifying cracks about their wives making prettier, better first ladies than Bill. On Playboy.com's "Battle of the Sexiest" Bill Clinton had beaten Ann Romney; it was not meant as a compliment. A fall 2007 *New York* magazine cover story featured an image of the former president in drag, proving that the biggest hoots still came from putting a powerful man in women's clothes. The accompanying story opened with the question of whether Bill would hold the Bible at his wife's inauguration. It was a ludicrous query. Why on earth wouldn't he? In *Living History* Hillary described how moving this precise moment of role reversal felt at her Senate inauguration.

The leering speculation amplified how embarrassingly inconceivable such reversals remained—and how hard a time we were going to give the people trying to make them happen. A skeptical Barbara Walters later asked Bill, "If your wife becomes president, I don't suppose that you're going to participate in the Easter egg hunt or the Christmas decorations." "You know, I'd actually like doing that," Clinton assured her. "You're gonna do the Easter egg hunt?" asked a faintly mocking Walters. "If I'm asked to do it. I would love to do that," he replied. Walters still felt the need to ask, "Mr. President, is your wife really smarter than you are?" Yes, in some ways she is, he replied calmly, adding, "I'd rather spend the night talking to her than anybody I can think of." Hillary, predictably, told me she was not perturbed by the prospect of her husband's inevitable spaying. "We've been at this for a pretty long time," she said drily. "I don't believe that anything that is said will come as a surprise."

One of the great ironies of Bill Clinton, given his galling history with women, was that he appeared to be making an effort to stand apart from many men on the American left who talked the talk but would not walk the walk next to broads more powerful than they. When I asked Hillary if she thought Bill would have a difficult time adjusting to secondary power, she said, "I can't imagine a better partner. Obviously, this is my campaign and this would be my presidency. Neither of us would expect it to be any different. But I will count on him to be there for me just as I was there for him." He convinced me, in Africa, that he was genuinely unthreatened by the idea. I asked if he could conceive of inheriting the legacy of Hillary and Eleanor. "Yeah!" he replied. "And I wouldn't be ashamed to do it, either. I'd be proud of it."

In the months leading to the primaries, the question of whether he could follow through seemed less pressing than the question Michelle Obama was asking as she too dove into the breach of American history and prejudice on behalf of her history-making partner: Were the rest of us ready to follow their leads?

3 CAMPAIGNING
WHILE FEMALE

HILLARY CLINTON MUST have been as aware as anyone that by entering the presidential race she was kicking off a long-awaited social experiment. In 220 years of American presidential politics there had been no serious female major party contenders, though women had been campaigning for the presidency since before they could vote, starting with Victoria Woodhull in 1872 and Belva Lockwood in 1884.

In 1964 Maine's Republican senator and former congresswoman Margaret Chase Smith became the first woman to have her name placed in nomination and receive more than one vote at a major party convention. At the Cow Palace arena in Daly City, California, Chase Smith came in just behind Barry Goldwater, William Scranton, Nelson Rockefeller and George Romney on the first ballot, taking 27 of 1,308 votes.

Eight years later, New York's Democratic congresswoman Shirley Chisholm became the first African American woman to run for the Democratic nomination, and the first black major party candidate to run for the presidency (Frederick Douglass received one vote during the roll call at the Republican convention in 1888; the minister and civil rights leader Channing Phillips's name was placed in nomination at the 1968 Democratic convention). Chisholm, who in 1969 became the first black woman to serve in Congress, was a founding member of the Congressional Black Caucus and the National Women's Political Caucus and the honorary president of the newly formed National Association for the Repeal of Abortion Laws (which became the National Abortion Rights Action League, or NARAL). Chisholm won a nonbinding preference primary in New Jersey, though competitors George McGovern, Edmund Muskie, Hubert Humphrey and Eugene McCarthy were not on the ballot. Her run was more symbolic than realistic, and activists who might otherwise have backed her were anxious to curry favor with more powerful candidates. At a truly eccentric convention in Miami Beach, Humphrey released his black delegates to vote for Chisholm, helping her win 151.95 votes on the first ballot and ensuring that she would address the gathering at which McGovern and Thomas Eagleton received their party's nomination.

In 1984, when Minnesota Senator Walter Mondale chose another New York congresswoman, Geraldine Ferraro, to be his running mate, the idea was so exotic that Ferraro was treated more like a zoo animal than a politician. During a prenomination interview, Barbara Walters, a woman not known for her own professional timidity, noted that Ferraro had missed weekends with her kids because of her political career and wondered why she'd kept her maiden name. She also asked with wide-eyed incredulity, "Vice president, okay, fine. But do you think you're equipped to be *president*?" After her place on the ticket was official Ferraro met equally disbelieving interrogators, including one who asked during the vice presidential debate, "Do you think . . . the Soviets might be tempted to take advantage of you simply because you are a woman?" Her vice-presidential competitor, George H. W. Bush, offered in the same debate, "Let me help you with the difference, Mrs. Ferraro, between Iran and the embassy in Lebanon." Losing to Bush and Ronald Reagan in spectacular fashion, Mondale and Ferraro walked away from the election having won only Minnesota and the District of Columbia.

Recent elections had included marginalized runs by Pat Schroeder, Carol Moseley Braun and Elizabeth Dole. Had any of these women come into a race with the profile, momentum or money that Hillary Clinton had going into 2008, they might have been the ones to face the full-bore resistance of a white male establishment. Any plausible female candidate for the presidency was not simply offering herself up as a double-x interruption in the circle of white male faces that ring commemorative presidential plates. She was also presenting herself for cultural dissection, as a prism through which the country's attitudes about sex, power and the place of women in society were going to be projected. It was impossible for Hillary Clinton to have chosen a path to the White House that bypassed the loathing, jeering derision and gendered stereotyping built on two centuries of male power. What was interesting was how hard she tried to do just that.

As Clinton got closer to the race, a widely anticipated wave of resistance began to make itself apparent. This was the easy-bake misogyny of anti-Hillary men, but also of women eager to advertise their solidarity with and enthusiasm for traditional gender roles, like the one who entered a John McCain rally in Hilton Head Island, South Carolina, in November 2007 and asked the presumptive Republican candidate, "How do we beat the bitch?" McCain looked only momentarily uncomfortable before congratulating her on her "excellent question" and trotting out his most recent poll numbers against Hillary Clinton. He hadn't needed a proper noun to know to which bitch his supporter was referring.

Ideas about how to beat her came via truckloads of T-shirts, bumper stickers and urinal targets bearing Hillary's image—the crude calling cards of her most predictable foes: right-wing bullies. These guys had been spoiling to express their animus toward Clinton, whom they, if no one else, saw as a symbol of left-wing feminist politics. What better way to simultaneously neutralize her menace than by mocking, belittling, desexualizing and demonizing her while peeing on her likeness?

This population of Hillary antagonists produced a dizzying array of paraphernalia. Among the favorites were T-shirts from a group with a clever acronym, Citizens United Not Timid, and a related "I Love Country Music" rebus involving images of Hillary and of a tree. Anything that stood still long enough to be silkscreened bore lines like "Life's a Bitch So Don't Vote for Her," "Fuck Hillary: God Knows She Needs It," "Anyone But Her '08," "Even Bill Doesn't Want Me," "Stop Mad Cow" and "KFC Hillary Meal Deal: Two Fat Thighs, Two Small Breasts and a Bunch of Left Wings." More naked expressions of loathing included "I Wish Hillary Had Married O.J." and "Wanna See Hillary Run? Throw Rocks at Her." This brand of misogynist aggression was bracing, yes, but it also felt like the death rattle of a patriarchal culture, the last gasps from critics who had been spewing anti-Hillary bile for decades yet had failed to impede her rise to political power.

The most widely celebrated anti-Clinton effigy was a nutcracker. On the website that sold the implement (later to be joined by the Bill Clinton corkscrew) a thought balloon was attached to the Hillary figurine; it read, "I don't bake cookies. I crack nuts." After hearing Gloria Feldt complain about the nutcracker on television, its creator, Gibson Carothers, wrote her an email defending its production and sale. He concluded with the antifeminist chestnut, "Don't sell short the value of showing a sense of humor." Blogger Melissa McEwan, still an Edwards supporter, unknowingly took his advice, inaugurating a "Hillary Clinton Sexism Watch" on *Shakesville* (a series that would eventually comprise 114 posts). The September 6, 2007, entry showed the nutcracker with the hypothetical "Q: What's the going rate for indisputably proving to the world that you are a tiny little man who is profoundly afraid of women? A: $19.95."

Some men on television were antsy to get the Clinton bonfire started. One was Tucker Carlson, who seemed fixated on the possibility that the candidate might geld him. First he claimed, "Something about her feels castrating"; then "[When Clinton] comes on television, I involuntarily cross my legs"; finally he suggested, "The one thing we learned from the Lorena Bobbitt case . . . [is that] women are angry at men in a lot of ways." In one interview with Carlson, Cliff May, president of the Foundation for Defense of Democracies, called Clinton "a vaginal-American," prompting Carlson to ask, "Do you think that people who are voting on the basis of gender solidarity ought to be allowed to vote in a perfect world?" He seemed unaware that his gyno-obsession with Clinton, alongside his castration anxiety, revealed his very own commitment to gender solidarity.

In December, when a *CNN Headline News* guest observed to the conservative host Glenn Beck that most senators see a president in the mirror when they shave, Beck replied, "Does that include Hillary?" Then he mimed her shaving her chin and growling, "Gimme a pack of Kool cigarettes, will ya?'"

I was almost glad for this first, coarse wave of Hillary-hate; I practically wanted to buy a Hillary nutcracker myself. As someone who had written for years about the ambient antipathy toward ambitious women, I was more attuned to it than those who had been lulled by the myth of a peachy postfeminist world and were now aghast. These brazen expressions of threatened masculinity were gratifying, in part because they did not seem particularly effective, but also because they were loud, bright, incontrovertible consciousness-raisers. This stuff wasn't new, and it wasn't unearthed just for Hillary. For young women and men who had never seen blatant misogyny before, who had never heard a woman called a "cunt" or seen the size of a senator's thighs referred to on a T-shirt, these in-your-face examples of gender-based resistance to Hillary were eye-opening. They would later prove to be powerful talismans, tangible examples on which to call when the misogyny got more insidious, more complicated, more difficult to parse or name.

Far more curious, in the year of preprimary campaigning, was the unwillingness on the part of everyone *except* the bumper-sticker louts and right-wing windbags to address the thing that made Hillary different from the rest of the presidential candidates.

* * *

From the start, advertising the historic nature of Hillary's run was not high on the agenda of her campaign strategist, Mark Penn. A pollster and CEO of the public relations firm Burson-Marstellar, Penn had advised political candidates from New York City mayor Ed Koch to Israeli prime minister Menachem Begin and had become Bill Clinton's *consigliere* in the mid-1990s. Penn was the architect of one of the most irritating aspects of Clintonian politics: the overpolling, people-pleasing approach that was a hallmark of Bill's reelection and Hillary's campaigns for the Senate, on which he advised her. Months before she was to make her presidential bid official in January 2007 Hillary hired Penn as her chief strategist and pollster, to the consternation of many who had worked closely with her in the past. The socially inept Penn took a bloodless approach to the race. In an October 2006 memo outlining basic requirements for Hillary's upcoming launch, and later published in the *Atlantic,* he recommended that she develop such fundamentals as a "basic message," a "fundraising operation," policy outlines and a press strategy. He added one final and furtive reference to an "fwp (first woman president plan)." Although the memo went into some detail about the other requirements, Penn did not expand on the "fwp."

A month before Clinton officially declared her intentions, Penn offered further thoughts in another memo. He seemed to believe that she led "a movement of women looking to achieve the true promise of America—that a qualified woman could be president of this country." But three paragraphs later he advised, "Most voters in essence see the presidents as the 'father' of the country. They do not want someone who would be the first mama, especially in this kind of world. But . . . they are open to the first father being a woman." The model for which Clinton should aim, Penn believed, was Margaret Thatcher: "The adjectives that were used about her (Iron Lady) were not of good humor or warmth, they were of smart, tough leadership." He pointed out that the national press wanted to be kingmakers but that "Hillary [was] already the king."

Penn was the pollster who popularized the term *soccer moms* during Bill Clinton's reelection campaign in 1996. Alongside its descendants—*security moms, SUV moms* and *Sex and the City voters*—the phrase was one of many that pollsters had invented to describe large groups of women who they presumed would vote as a giant, ovarian bloc if they could just be convinced to go to the polls. In the months immediately preceding modern presidential elections, women were bombarded by politicians suddenly eager to talk about things they thought chicks dug—Day care! Work-life balance! Peace!—at least until the election was over and they could go back to gradually eroding reproductive rights. In recent campaigns the wooing had been particularly egregious, with both major parties and their boosters bombarding electoral quarry with preschool-reading-level slogans like "W is for women" (George Bush) and "V is for Vote" (Eve Ensler), a tactic that made most thinking women want to "S for self-immolate."

Penn assured Hillary that internal polling showed that 94 percent of young women would automatically vote for the first female president. It was perhaps this confidence that led him to shrug off concerns about reaching them. In one eleven-page memo he wrote just a few sentences advising Clinton to look into "set[ting] up separate fwp (first woman president) internet site and subgroup organizations as place to stimulate that vote. Check whether their [sic] can even be legally separate movement. Understand the life issues of young women." With strategies like this—act like their father, assume you're already king, set up a subgroup to stimulate their vote, and understand their "life issues"—it was not unjust to suggest that one serious problem with Clinton campaign leadership was that it did not think much of the women with whom it was supposed to be making history.

Hillary had traveled a lot of road with a group of bright, loyal, mostly female staffers, dubbed "Hillaryland" back when they'd helped her establish the first lady's office in the West Wing. These women knew her inside and out and many of them were deeply invested in her presidential prospects. But when it came time to run, first for the Senate and then for the presidency, she turned to an abrasive and contentious group of male advisors borrowed largely from her husband, installing only two Hillaryland veterans in powerful positions: Patti Solis Doyle as her campaign manager and Mandy Grunwald as her ad maker. Although many Hillaryland denizens—including Huma Abedin, Lissa Muscatine, Capricia Marshall, Cheryl Mills, Melanne Verveer and Maggie Williams—would ultimately work for Hillary's presidential campaign, they were initially placed in marginalized roles, a factor that may have accounted for the campaign's early disengagement with the question of how to present Hillary as a woman.

In charge of women's outreach was longtime Hillary advisor Ann Lewis, whom the political reporter Anne Kornblut claimed was not even present on the campaign's morning strategy calls, an account Lewis backed up in 2010, telling me, "They got smaller and earlier, and at some point I realized I was not on them anymore." At the time Lewis was sanguine about being shut out: "I thought, I can insist on getting back on the call and spend more hours in internal decision making, or get out there and do what I know how to do, which is reach women." Others within the campaign told me that Lewis had retrospectively reconsidered her passivity and wondered if she could have made a bigger difference had she worked harder to stay on the inside of Penn's operation. Lewis herself told me that she didn't believe Penn's error was necessarily in undercutting Hillary's feminist credentials. "She was presenting herself as 'I can be president,'" Lewis told me. "Here is where I think the strategy Mark developed missed it: Hillary Clinton has been a change agent all her life, certainly from the days in which she made the speech at Wellesley. Yet she wound up being presented as the candidate of the status quo. . . . What we missed, and what's painful, is that at a time when what the American people really wanted was change we had a candidate who had spent her life making change and we missed it."

Penn's suggestions for the language Clinton might use to address her gender in a kickoff letter to supporters were not electrifying: "Few thought a decade ago, a woman could be president—today we have 16 women senators and if we don't try we will never know if a woman can be president. It is a barrier that can mean a lot for a new generation wondering if we can overcome barriers of this new age, if we can again secure our prosperity and regain our footing in a more dangerous world." Clinton chose to sidestep mention of her gender altogether in both the videotaped announcement of her candidacy and in an email to supporters, in which sex was sucked right out of an oblique call to make history. "We can only break barriers if we dare to confront them," read the letter she signed, failing even to acknowledge what those barriers might be.

It was not crazy to avoid emphasizing womanhood on the road to the presidency. In 1987, when asked repeatedly why she was "running as a woman," Colorado's first congresswoman, Pat Schroeder, had a witty, if slightly baleful answer: "Do I have a choice?" Inasmuch as a female candidate *could* exercise choice in how to present herself, the decision was often to try to pass as masculine. To come across as traditionally female, and thereby not traditionally powerful, was to call into question an ability to command, to defend the nation, to be taken seriously by world leaders. "The conventional wisdom is that a woman cannot get elected president without being really, really tough," said Kim Gandy, former president of the National Organization for Women, in 2009.

This was part of what made untenable the pressure on Clinton to apologize for her war vote. In 2004 John Kerry's willingness to say he'd made a mistake had gotten him labeled a weak-kneed flip-flopper, and John Kerry was a tall, strapping Vietnam veteran. Clinton was a mother, a wife, a chick; the slightest overexposure of that reality put her at risk of ridicule. When she made her video-taped campaign announcement, placidly inviting America to begin a "conversation," Jon Stewart joked, "Look, Hillary, this may not be the most politically correct thing to say, but I don't think that slogan's going to help you with men. . . . You might as well get on your campaign bus, The-I-Think-We-Really-Need-to-Talk Express, to unveil your new Iraq policy: America, Let's Pull Over and Just Ask for Directions." Soon Clinton was emphasizing the bizarre and pugilistic slogan "I'm in it to win it!"

Even her rival's wife, Elizabeth Edwards, understood Hillary's quandary. She told *Salon*'s editor in chief Joan Walsh in a 2007 interview, "I'm sympathetic, because when I worked as a lawyer, I was the only woman in these rooms, too, and you want to reassure them you're as good as a man. And sometimes you feel you have to behave as a man and not talk about women's issues. I'm sympathetic—she wants to be commander in chief. But she's just not as vocal a women's advocate as I want to see." There was the rub: too dainty and she wouldn't have been taken seriously; too burly and she wasn't really running as a woman at all.

Mark Penn's breezy assumption that young female votes belonged to Clinton whether or not she extended a pinky toward them reflected his dismal estimation of young women's electoral impulses (They'll pick the girl!) and allowed him to pursue his plan to convince more discerning (male) voters that Clinton was not only not anomalous, but practically had been president already! Behaving as if he were running a candidate against George W. Bush, Penn was determined to hide Hillary's femininity under a bushel of boxing metaphors. Anyone who had known Hillary Clinton for more than two hours would tell you about her improbably sharp sense of humor, her devotion to her friends and strong relationships with children, her taste for a good drink and her visits to friends' sickbeds. But Penn was firm in his belief that voters did not want humanity and that they had no interest in entering into the inherently stirring covenant of changing American history with a groundbreaking candidate. He argued not only that forging emotional connections with voters should not be Clinton's priority, but that it was an enfeebling strategy to be avoided at all costs. As he wrote in one memo, "The idea that if only you were warmer and nicer so many more people would like you and [you] would be in the White House is wrong. True, more people would like you. Fewer would vote for you."

Occasionally Clinton broke down the wall. At the August 2007 AFL-CIO debate she barreled her way through a self-sell with the delicacy of a Sherman tank. "For fifteen years, I have stood up against the right-wing machine. And I've come out stronger!" she bellowed. "If you want a winner who knows how to take them on, I'm your girl!" At this final locution she looked momentarily surprised and almost pleased with herself, as if she couldn't quite believe she'd just pulled off such a perky line. More often her confessions of femininity came when she was talking to mostly female audiences. In an October appearance on *The View* she said, as she would many times throughout her campaign, "Women in their nineties come to my events. . . . When I'm going around shaking hands, they'll say something like, 'I'm ninety-five years old and I was born before women could vote and I want to live long enough to see a woman in the White House.'" But these moments were always couched safely amid assertions of swaggering brawn. On *The View* Clinton made up for her brief girl-power indulgence by railing against cowboy diplomacy and making a towel-snapping remark about how we "can't be patsies" when dealing with China.

On the stump Clinton would sometimes drop a reference to electing the first woman president, but practically trip over herself to reassure people that she was not running *because* she was a woman, but because she was the best qualified, the most experienced, the most prepared, the closest to an incumbent. Audiences and the media responded in kind: the language they used about her—that she was tough, ready to stand up to Republicans, inevitable, the front-runner, the establishment candidate, a hawk and part of a political dynasty—reinforced the notion that she was a competent masculine norm rather than a nut-cracking or lily-livered feminine exception.

✲ ✲ ✲

What Penn was not counting on was that voters and the media *were* responding to emotion on the stump. In Iowa Barack Obama's campaign was presenting the United States with one of its first African American candidates and trying not to overemphasize his racial difference, much to the reported chagrin of black leaders like Al Sharpton and Jesse Jackson. But Obama was eating Clinton's lunch when it came to feminine appeal. On the stump he was passionate and articulate; he connected and hoped and dreamed. If gender is performance, as disciples of the philosopher Judith Butler have long argued, then both candidates were engaged in some serious crossdressing.

Obama had help from Oprah Winfrey, an oracular presence for American women, who had endorsed him and was headlining rallies for him that drew tens of thousands of people. "Obama is the woman. . . . He is the warm candidate, self-deprecating, soft, tender, sad eyes, great smile," Clara Oleson, a former labor lawyer, told my colleague Michael Scherer before a Clinton speech in Iowa City. In Oleson's estimation Clinton was "the male candidate—in your face, authoritative, know-it-all." In *Salon*, Scherer described Obama rallies that featured the music of the Indigo Girls and Aretha Franklin and in which Obama promised, in a language spoken most commonly by Oprah-approved gurus, "We can discover the better part of ourselves as a nation. We can dream big dreams." Clinton meanwhile was described by supporters as the candidate who could "stand up to bullies" and would quite often tell audiences, "When you are attacked, you have to deck your opponent."

This surely gratified Mark Penn, who made no secret in his internal memos of his scorn for Obama's hope-y, dream-y speechifying or his assumption that racism and xenophobia would make the Illinois senator "unelectable except perhaps against Attila the Hun." But there were those who believed that Clinton was making a grave error.

Mary C. Kelley, a women's studies professor at the University of Michigan, told the *Los Angeles Times* in December 2007, "I strongly believe that it's feminism that made Hillary Rodham Clinton's presidency plausible. Therefore, I would like a candidate who is not simply running like another man, and that's what I see in her self-presentation again and again." Frances Kissling, the former president of Catholics for a Free Choice, wrote that Clinton had "missed the opportunity to talk about what it really means for women to be equal in this country. . . . A woman candidate who considered her gender a strength (as opposed to something she needed to overcome) would announce a series of measures specifically designed to ensure that women's needs and rights were at the forefront of her agenda. . . . We'd like to see a woman president, but more than anything we want to be able to say . . . that the first woman president did things no man would have done." Some women felt that Penn's insistence on stressing Clinton's toughness was misplaced. After all, it wasn't as if she had entered the race with a reputation for ditzy fragility that she needed to counteract. Ellen Malcolm, the founder of EMILY's List, an organization at the forefront of putting pro-choice Democratic women in political office, told me in 2009, "I understand [Penn's] concern about the credibility, but I don't think there's anybody in the universe who [didn't] think that Hillary Clinton [was] smart and tough, and I think it was clear that it wasn't working and that a pivot was needed, and it took way too long for the pivot."

Elaine Lafferty, a former editor of *Ms.* magazine and a Clinton volunteer, told me in a 2009 interview that when she arrived in Iowa she quickly concluded that the gender reversals were a serious problem. Lafferty believed the Clinton campaign had failed to take Oprah Winfrey's endorsement and coaching of Obama seriously enough as a threat to their base. In a memo, she wrote, "We believe Oprah and her organization has been closely advising Obama in terms of *message, vocabulary, and delivery.* Bottom Line: you are running against a WOMAN candidate. Obama's language and presentation is not just poetry. He employs the vocabulary of femaleness, the vocabulary of emotion that fills women's magazines and daytime television. He speaks endlessly of that which 'is deep inside of me.' (How many men speak that way?) . . . Everyone knows Hillary is a policy ace. They DON'T know she shows up in hospitals for friends."

Lafferty wasn't just hoping to jostle the campaign machinery; she was determined to roust Hillary's would-be female supporters, women who were still dragging their feet, and women's leaders she felt were not taking Hillary's precarious position in Iowa seriously enough. "I jumped up and down and yelled 'The sky is falling' and tried to sound an alarm," she said of her fears that Clinton was going to blow Iowa with no women behind her. Trying to deliver some recognizable feminists to Iowa for the Clinton campaign, Lafferty was not met with an energetic response.

The truth was, Penn's gender-masking strategy just hadn't fulfilled his vision. For the first half of her campaign it allowed women to see Clinton as representative of the masculine norm from whom they could feel distant or antipathetic without guilt. It alleviated pressures on them to either state their loyalties or disavow her. Why should they show up to support a woman who would barely reveal herself as one?

★ ★ ★

Despite the best efforts of the campaign to ensure otherwise, by the time Clinton had been on the trail for the better part of a year some people besides Republican T-shirt sloganeers were beginning to notice that she was a lady. It was the Pulitzer Prize–winning fashion critic Robin Givhan who first and most efficiently shattered the illusion of Hillary Clinton's hermaphroditism. In a July 2007 story in the *Washington Post* headlined "Hillary Clinton's Tentative Dip into New Neckline Territory," Givhan pondered the subtleties and political implications of a blouse worn by the senator as she spoke to Congress about the costs of higher education: "The neckline sat low on her chest and had a subtle V-shape. . . . The cleavage registered after only a quick glance. No scrunch-faced scrutiny was necessary. There wasn't an unseemly amount of cleavage showing, but there it was. Undeniable."

A surprised Clinton campaign, hoping perhaps to line the war chest by fanning a chest war, responded with an indignant email to supporters, provocatively titled "Cleavage." Ann Lewis, head of women's outreach, explained the email in 2010: "What became clear to me was that [Givhan's piece] had touched a nerve. I had underestimated the impact, but as the day went on, I started hearing from a lot of women." Lewis signed her name to the message that began, "Can you believe the *Washington Post* wrote a 746-word article on Hillary's cleavage? . . . I've seen some off-topic press coverage—but talking about body parts? That is grossly inappropriate."

I, for one, *could* believe that the *Washington Post* had published an article on Hillary's cleavage, and I thought it was pretty fascinating. There was merit to the campaign's complaints about "body parts" only in that many readers probably did not absorb the story as a nuanced consideration of the sartorial constructs of gender, but rather as a piece about Hillary's ta-tas. Otherwise the Clinton camp's charges were trumped up. Givhan had written an examination of how femininity and character were being communicated through clothes in this historic race. As she pointed out, it was not until the early 1990s that women staffers were permitted to wear pants on the Senate floor. To pretend that there were not questions to be asked about how Clinton was going to dress on a presidential trail was foolish. When Clinton herself found out about the email, she ordered a stop to any further promulgation of outrage.

Fifteen years of public futzing made attention to Clinton's self-presentation a reasonable line of inquiry. Mocking her hair had been one of the chief pastimes of those who wanted to express dislike for her ambition and her independence; her willingness to change that hairstyle was a handy metaphor for those who thought her politics were inconsistent. Her thighs and ankles and pantsuits had been thoroughly examined. In 2006 her Republican opponent for the Senate, John Spencer, allegedly remarked to a reporter, "You ever see a picture of [Clinton] back then? Whew. I don't know why Bill married her." He speculated that she had had "millions of dollars" of plastic surgery.

It's not that male politicians escaped related evaluation. During the primaries several shots of Barack Obama exiting the sea in swim trunks were published in celebrity weeklies. But those photos were admiring. Tellingly, when male politicians were jeered for their physique or their fashion it usually involved feminizing them: John Kerry was rumored to have had Botox injected in his patrician brow; John Edwards's pricey trims had gotten him labeled "the

Breck Girl"; Al Gore had been derided for turning to Naomi Wolf for clothing advice.

The scrutiny was much more intense for Clinton, because for women value is intrinsically tied to desirability and attractiveness. This meant that her advisors and her most vicious detractors had a shared goal: her complete desexualization. Those who supported her had to downplay her feminine attributes lest she be diminished by objectification. For those who hated her the goal was to humiliate her, and at the same time affirm that she held no alluring power over them. As Shirley Chisholm said decades before, "One distressing thing is the way men react to women who assert their equality: their ultimate weapon is to call them unfeminine. They think she is anti-male; they even whisper that she's probably a lesbian . . ." Sure enough, Clinton had long been called frigid, a lesbian, a wife who couldn't satisfy her husband. The *New York Times* had run a story toting up how many times a month she and Bill shared a bed. But now Givhan had destabilized everything by pointing to a garment that had given the impression, by one zillionth of an inch, that Hillary Clinton had breasts.

That same week, in an early YouTube debate between the Democratic contenders, one questioner asked each of the candidates to look to the person on his or her left and say one positive thing and one negative thing about the person. John Edwards cast his eyes on Clinton and said, "I admire what Senator Clinton has done for America, what her husband did for America. . . . I'm not sure about that coat." Barack Obama, dutifully playing Gallant to Edwards's Goofus, replied in turn, "I actually like Hillary's jacket. I don't know what's wrong with it." It was a startling moment: presidential candidates were discussing outfits in the middle of a debate for the Democratic nomination. *Politico*'s Roger Simon instructed in his debate wrap-up, "Write this down, guys: Attack her policies, attack her past votes, attack her personality if you want to, but don't attack what she is wearing. It looks sexist and cheap."

But this, for me, was part of the package, part of the fun, really, of what it was going to feel like to watch a woman run for president. They weren't treating her like the boys? That's because she wasn't a boy! Here at last was some sign of it. As a woman, Clinton had been able to don a coral blazer for the debate. How many

other presidential candidates' closets contained a rainbow of jewel-
toned jackets? In one sense it actually gave her an advantage: she got
to be the pretty flamingo in the sea of navy and gray, the one who
drew your eye, whether you liked her or not. On the other hand, she
was forced to suffer the indignity of having her clothes picked over
by her opponents, to have a positive assessment of her record—or
rather, her *husband's* record—lost in tittering over her ensemble.
These were not just the costs of being the first serious female contender; these were the realities of a candidacy that could never have
been as run-of-the-mill as her handlers were hoping. The awkward
revelation that one of these things was not like the others was actually freeing, kind of a hoot. As Helena Andrews wrote in *Politico*,
"First off, her coat was fabulous. . . . That color! . . . Clinton's got
the same exact coat in electric sky blue. I'm glad she didn't wear
that one, because she looks like a space alien in it. . . . [S]he managed to glow even standing next to Edwards. It was a statement
without words: I'm a woman; get used to it."

As tongues finally began to loosen on the subject of Clinton's
femaleness, some took nastier liberties than others. In December
2007 Matt Drudge posted a photo of Hillary Clinton in Iowa under
the headline "The Toll of a Campaign." Rush Limbaugh picked it
up in a radio segment titled "Does Our Looks-Obsessed Culture
Want to Stare at an Aging Woman?" The photo, taken at the start
of the final, grinding slog through Iowa, was simply of Clinton's
face. She had crow's feet, bags under her eyes; her brow was furrowed, and some of her neck skin had been pushed up around her
chin thanks to the unfortunate convergence of talking and scarf
wearing that was unavoidable when campaigning for president in
Iowa in December.

Limbaugh's take on the image was couched in oleaginous insincerity, what in Internet parlance is called "concerned trolling." Posing for the moment as a pseudo-feminist, he fretted to his estimated
14 million listeners that the public's thirst for a sexism-fed spring of
eternal youth would make it hard for Clinton to grow old in public. "As you age, and . . . women are hardest hit on this . . . America
loses interest in you," he said. "Will this country want to actually
watch a woman get older before their eyes on a daily basis?"

The radio host's main thrust, that "the appearance of perfection and good health . . . ties into the perception of mental acuity, stamina, being able to hold up to the job," reminded me of a bit of collegiate apocrypha, a legend about sorority sisters who made freshman bids stand on a table in their underwear while older sisters circled their physical flaws in magic marker. What had always struck me about this myth was not the social torture of it, but the idea that it was for the good of the initiates: before they could represent the sorority they had to rid themselves of distracting blemishes, lest their pocks or pimples distract from all their other excellent qualities. How, Limbaugh was innocently wondering, would Hillary Clinton represent the sorority of women? What if Americans never paid attention to her health care plan because they were so distracted by her wattle?

Limbaugh had successfully stirred the pot. The blogger Immodest Proposals asserted, "Whichever photog snapped this photo effectively ended Sen. Hillary Clinton's presidential campaign." The law blogger Ann Althouse wondered, "Did some treatment wear off?" before acknowledging, "A picture like this of a male candidate would barely register. Fred Thompson always looks this bad, and people seem to think he's handsome."

The freakout over Hillary's appearance was extreme; it provoked the kind of anxiety that an octogenarian candidate's senescence or physical infirmity might. This was especially strange because the picture was not that terrible. When it was taken Clinton was sixty years old and was about to commence a tour of all of Iowa's ninety-nine counties. An examination of former presidential candidates at exhausting stretches of a race would have turned up similar pallor, flappy necks and dry skin. In the weeks before Bill Clinton was elected in 1992 he had lost his voice. It was regarded as a mark of how many stump speeches he'd given, how many germy hands he'd clasped. Then there was the toll of the presidency itself: grayed heads and haggard faces on presidents from Abraham Lincoln to George W. Bush had long been evidence that being commander in chief was never a job for anti-aging enthusiasts.

In an age of lifts and injections and implants, and in a culture in which age confers on men authority and wisdom but makes women appear dried up and too lazy to maintain the illusion of youth, we had begun to forget what a sixty-year-old female looks like in nature. Here she was: a woman in late middle age. Wrinkled. Tired. She was getting pulled over for campaigning while female, and we were all witnessing the arrest.

Appearing on several Sunday morning talk shows in September, Clinton had laughed often, prompting a discourse on the sound of what some called her "cackle." Glenn Beck compared the laugh to the Wicked Witch of the West's; Bill O'Reilly's "body language expert" dubbed it "evil," Sean Hannity "frightening"; Frank Rich wrote that it had "all the spontaneity of an alarm clock buzzer." In fact Clinton's laugh, while occasionally overexuberant, was precisely the same breed of stalling tactic deployed for centuries by politicians trying to buy time before answering questions, to appear falsely relaxed or dismissive of criticism. Clinton's laugh sounded different in part because its register, high-pitched and female, was unfamiliar to those who no longer even noticed the low but equally fake rumblings of Bill Clinton, Newt Gingrich or any of Hillary's presidential adversaries. We were used to hearing old men chuckle long and deep while fielding questions from Tim Russert. A woman's voice sounded different, not old-man comfy and cocky, but witchy and crone-y.

None of us were above thinking about how Clinton sounded or looked or what she wore. We were like babies first encountering a new object: a potential president who had breasts and hips and a high voice, who was once pregnant and whose female skin changed as it aged. It was only natural that we were sometimes going to get tripped up and befuddled in how we talked about her. Noticing it, grappling with it, was part of accepting her presence on the stage. The notion that this was going to be easy and smooth and that Clinton's gender was going to go unnoticed had always been a false idea that took as its equally false premise that we were all totally comfortable with women in power.

Just as Clinton was dealing with undermining evaluations of her femininity, so was her opponent faced with criticism linked to his race. In December, former Nebraska governor Bob Kerrey, a Clinton supporter, took pains to emphasize that Barack Obama's middle name was Hussein; later, when defending his remarks on CNN, he said that Obama had "spent a little bit of time in a secular madrassa." Around the same time another Clinton backer,

Billy Shaheen, speculated, Limbaugh-style, that Republicans might ask questions about whether Obama had ever sold drugs. When Mark Penn went on *Hardball*, purportedly to disown Shaheen's aspersions, he instead sharpened them by using the word *cocaine* on air. Obama's youthful dalliance with drugs was not so different from Bill Clinton's half-admitted experimentation or rumors that had long dogged George W. Bush. But Obama's race allowed his opponents to push into the small-minded corners of the American imagination and try to peddle a factually implausible, shadowy suggestion of the candidate as drug dealer. These caricatures of Obama appealed to time-honored racial stereotypes, the still contemporary prejudices that for the previous two hundred years had prevented people with names like his from running for president. Barack Obama's father and paternal grandmothers had been Muslim; he had written openly about his experimentation with drugs in his memoir. These were things that had no presidential precedent, that made him an anomaly in the campaign.

The racist allusions that dogged Obama and the nastiness about Clinton's appearance testified to the endurance of certain stereotypes about black men and women. This was the oddity of both candidacies. They illustrated how far and how quickly the nation had progressed; no one would have appealed to sexist or racist stereotypes had there not been an African American and a woman running for president. At the same time they drove home how far we had to go.

★ ★ ★

As attention to Clinton's womanhood made Penn's gender-free strategy increasingly unwieldy, the campaign began to send out mixed messages. Clinton was still presenting herself as a patsy-decking leader in drag, except when her advisors were making badly aimed attempts to draw the attention of recalcitrant women supporters by portraying her as a victim of sexism. The worst misjudgment came after Clinton's poor performance in a debate in Philadelphia, during which she stumbled on a question about driver's licenses for illegal immigrants and her opponents pounced. Her campaign proceeded to portray her as an injured party, splicing clips of the debate and posting them as a video called *The Politics of Pile-on*. Ann Lewis told me in 2010 that the ad was not intended to play up a gender divide: "The only pile-ons I knew of were in football." But Clinton herself stoked a boys-against-girls reading of the response. Speaking at her alma mater the day after the debate, she said, "In so many ways, this all-women's college prepared me to compete in the all-boys' club of presidential politics."

As soon as she realized the message that she was sending, Clinton pulled back by telling reporters, "I don't think they're piling on because I'm a woman. I think they're piling on because I'm winning." It was true: she was winning in the polls, and this was partly why her opponents were teaming up to take her down. But the campaign could not shake the impression that it had been demanding special treatment for its female candidate by first obscuring her gender and then portraying her as the world's most improbable damsel in distress. At the time of the "pile-on" complaint, Kate Michelman said that Clinton was "disingenuously playing the victim card" and though she was speaking in her capacity as an advisor to one of Clinton's rivals, it was hard to disagree with her.

By and large, feminists seemed to be wary of intervening in this mess. EMILY's List was an exception, one of the only women's organizations to put boots on the ground in support of Clinton in Iowa. The National Organization for Women had issued a lengthy endorsement in March 2007, but was not a particularly visible presence later in the year. In fact, in the weeks before the first caucus, feminists were notable mostly for their absence from Iowa. One person in the Clinton campaign seemed to have noticed.

"Elaine, how are you?" volunteer Elaine Lafferty remembered Hillary Clinton greeting her in an Iowa restaurant a few weeks before the January 3 caucus. Clinton was talking with a lot of nodding eye contact, trying to communicate something but behaving as if someone with a tape recorder might be around any corner. "I'm good, Senator, how are you?" was Lafferty's reply. "I'm fine," said Clinton, pausing. "How's Gloria?" Clinton was referring to Gloria Steinem, the founder of *Ms.* magazine, which Lafferty had edited. "She's good," Lafferty said to Clinton. "Ah," replied Hillary. "*Where* is Gloria?"

"I said, 'She's in Bhutan, Senator.'" Lafferty remembered. "And Hillary said, 'Ah-ha. When is she coming back?'"

It was reasonable that the first woman to launch a realistic campaign for the American presidency might well wonder, as she tromped her way through the frigid Iowa winter, why Gloria Steinem, the most recognizable women's leader in the country, was nowhere in sight. Then again, Clinton could have summoned Steinem if she'd wanted to; she hadn't.

Steinem would later tell me that while she had always supported Clinton, whom she believed to be a strong and competent candidate, her initial reticence about throwing herself behind her campaign had stemmed from the fact that she had never believed that Clinton could win the nomination. Steinem initially endorsed neither Clinton nor Obama because she believed they were comparably great candidates. But she told me, "What was interesting was that white women, and black women . . . didn't think Hillary could win. And black people, men and women, didn't think Obama could win." The doubters, Steinem said, "were responding to the hurts of our lifetimes and assuming that they were going to be definitive."

If some feminists were doubtful that Clinton could win, others felt queasy at the prospect of a primary contest that would pit two histories of marginalization and disenfranchisement against one another. Still others cited the off-putting message they had received from the campaign itself. There was an offended *froideur* provoked by the distance the Clinton camp had put between the candidate and a feminist legacy. When I asked former NOW president Kim Gandy in 2009 whether there was pressure for her to go to Iowa, she responded, "The campaign wasn't pursuing it. . . . You never know who makes the decisions in a campaign like this, but Mark Penn, in my opinion, did not want an active feminist presence in her campaign." So there wasn't one.

4 FIVE DAYS IN JANUARY

HILLARY CLINTON DID not just lose the January 3 Iowa caucus to Barack Obama. She lost Iowa's women to Barack Obama, by a startling 5 percentage points. That night proved to be not simply the opening bell of primary season, but the kickoff to a surreal period between the Iowa and New Hampshire contests. Those five days were disconcerting for anyone who had gotten comfortable with the apparent ease with which America had made room for a female presidential candidate.

I was thrilled on that Thursday night, rushing to a friend's apartment to watch the results. It felt great to put an end to the election season windup, to learn how Americans were going to vote rather than how political prognosticators *thought* they were going to vote. The answer came fast and early: Barack Obama was the winner. I could not wipe the smile off my face.

It's not that I was an Obama supporter. I still planned to vote for Edwards. But the Iowa results were undeniably thrilling. Though he was not the first African American to win a primary or a caucus

(Jesse Jackson had won Louisiana, Washington, D.C., South Carolina and Virginia in 1984 and thirteen contests in 1988), Obama's
Iowa win had the shimmer and vibration of a history-making event;
his speech, which began "They said this day would never come,"
carried the promise of some future rapture.

There was also the invigorating bump of an upset: late polling
had shown Obama ahead of his competitors, but it was a surprise
that Clinton had come in a close third behind Edwards, and it was
big news that only 30 percent of female caucus-goers had supported
her, compared to the 35 percent who had rallied to Obama. Mark
Penn's presumed female constituency, underaddressed and undervalued by his strategy, had also apparently been underwhelmed,
and supported Clinton's adversaries.

This was a welcome reminder that in politics, as in baseball, anything can happen. If voters were veering away from the stale scripts
of pundits and strategists, I was all for it. I was sick of primaries
decided before Super Tuesday, by campaigns that devoted attention
and resources only to states with early contests. I wanted an election
that would engage voters and candidates beyond Iowa and New
Hampshire; it had never been more important. Here was an opening shot that got everyone's attention and presented a bracing array
of Democratic options.

Obama's triumph was definitive, with 38 percent of the vote,
but the remaining 62 percent had been divided quite neatly, with
Edwards coming in at 30 percent and Clinton at 29. Edwards had
put a lot of eggs in his Iowa basket, but I did not see this upset as his
death knell; similar numbers in 2004 had made him a strong competitor. Nor did I see Clinton's loss as determinative: Iowa, where
Bill Clinton had not campaigned in 1992 and ran unopposed in
1996, had never been a Clinton-friendly contest. Only six months
before the caucus a memo from Hillary's deputy campaign manager, Mike Henry, had been leaked, recommending that she skip
Iowa altogether since it was the campaign's "consistently weakest
state." Clinton had rebuffed the advice and sunk a lot of money into
the state, but it wasn't as though her Iowa showing came as a complete shock. The most exhilarating thing about January 3 was that
220,000 people had come to caucus, compared to 124,000 four
years earlier. That meant that Obama, Edwards and Clinton had

each drawn more supporters than 2004's definitive winner, John Kerry. As far as I was concerned, *this* was an election.

Apparently I wasn't seeing the same results that the men on television were seeing. It was my friend Geraldine who first pointed out how they were talking about Hillary Clinton. Geraldine, a political junkie and former news editor, had an investment in all the candidates; she was an undecided but dedicated Democrat. Her face grew ashen as Chris Matthews offered a mean little metric showing that Hillary's 30 percent share of the Iowa votes meant that seven out of ten caucus-goers had rejected her. Well, yes, that's what it means to get 30 percent of the votes. Seven out of ten voters had also rejected Edwards, six of ten had rejected Obama. "It's hard to call yourself the people's choice if two-thirds of the Democrats are voting against you!" Matthews said.

He was not alone in his glee. Before the caucuses had officially concluded, the *Washington Post*'s Eugene Robinson told us that if Clinton lost Iowa she would probably lose New Hampshire too. And South Carolina! She'd be lucky to scrape by with small states like Nevada, Matthews chimed in. Obama's victory wasn't even official yet when *Newsweek*'s Howard Fineman predicted, "If [Obama] wins this thing, even by one vote in Iowa, then that five-point lead of Hillary's [in New Hampshire] is going to disappear in a second."

On a night when Iowans old and young had come out in droves, on which Barack Obama had given one of his fine speeches, on which three strong Democratic candidates had carved up an unprecedented number of votes fairly evenly, all these people could talk about was throwing Mama from the presidential train. Geraldine was visibly upset. I realized that I'd never seen anyone my age react so strongly to Hillary Clinton, and she wasn't even a Clinton supporter. "I hadn't made up my mind," Geraldine told me in retrospect, "but I remember having a very strong reaction to how she was being treated by those guys on MSNBC. To have her unfairly torn down before I had the opportunity to vote was absolutely infuriating."

By the next morning, and the five mornings after that, what could have been written off as an overcaffeinated blitz on a briefly debilitated Hillary had transformed into a rowdy wake at which pundits were doing jigs on her freshly dug grave, speculating cheerily, practically drunkenly, about when, exactly, Clinton would pack it in. The night after Iowa Matthews proclaimed, "For Clinton, what was once considered inevitable is now barely likely." "Could New Hampshire end the Democratic primary race?" leered Keith Olbermann on January 7, during an hour in which he also speculated that the primary there "could be a blowout" and "the final score for the Democrats." Chuck Todd described for Olbermann the anticipatory certainty of the press in New Hampshire: "It's weird out here. . . . Everybody's already speaking in the past tense . . . about Senator Clinton's attempts to win the first two states."

Most discomfiting was that from my Democratic point of view these were supposed to be the good guys. For years MSNBC had stood up to the right-wing domination of Fox News. But some of its talking heads had long displayed a passionate investment in Hillary's demise. Matthews had made his career as a pundit in that heady era of Clinton bashing, the 1990s. That Hillary's political career had survived his wrath seemed to have incited him further, not just in the months leading up to the 2008 primaries, but for years preceding them. His fetishization of the threat posed by Hillary had led him, often, to imagine her strategy and imaginatively discredit it before it unfolded, or to offer helpful tips to her opponents.

When, in 2000, the Utah financial advisor Howard Ruff had begun taking donations to bring down Hillary, then not yet even a senator, he had appeared on *Hardball* and explained to Matthews that in a battle against Hillary's nascent political power, "it's a lot easier to kill a twelve-inch snake than a twelve-foot cobra." Matthews expanded his metaphorical arsenal: "You want to destroy the missile in its silo, which makes sense to me." The night after the Iowa caucus Matthews spoke to Elizabeth Edwards and coached her directly: "Even if Barack has to win up here [in New Hampshire], it's better to knock Hillary out because if she is knocked out, then you two can fight it out, John Edwards and Barack Obama." As Melissa Harris-Lacewell said in retrospect, "Chris Matthews lost his damn mind. It was not normal, the way that he was talking about Hillary."

Matthews's premature jubilation after Iowa was infectious. So cooked was Clinton's goose that the *Washington Post* reporter Dana Milbank saw fit to make a droll little video called *Fired Up and Ready to Bore,* about how deadly dull her New Hampshire rallies were. Criticized in Iowa for not taking questions from supporters, Clinton had switched gears in New Hampshire by opening up the floor to questions. In a desultory voice-over, Milbank explained that after a "peppy" stump speech Clinton "engaged the crowd in more than an hour of torpid Q and A." The video showed audience members yawning and trickling out. She was *soooo boooring*.

Milbank's little funny was especially cutting next to media reports of the massive, adulatory New Hampshire crowds lined up to hear Obama speak. Never mind that Clinton's purportedly snoozy events were drawing huge and sometimes comparable numbers; Obama's gatherings were for a purpose loftier than outlining policy points or answering voters' questions. Richard Wolffe, an MSNBC political analyst, told Olbermann, "The crowds I see at Obama's events are not just there to pick a winner . . . or even to pick a president. . . . They're really there to be witnesses to what they talk about as being history in the making."

Obama was making history, while Clinton was putting supporters to sleep with her talk of what she'd do as president. This was the narrative that took hold of the media, even as some tried to dispute it. When the *Huffington Post* editor Roy Sekoff appeared on Dan Abrams's MSNBC program on January 7, openly rooting against Clinton and saying that her "product's not selling," fellow guest Rachel Maddow interjected, "I was in New Hampshire this weekend. I know that Hillary Clinton and Barack Obama were turning out similar-sized crowds at a lot of their events. So it's not patently obvious, it's not a factual thing that's necessarily being reported."

Maddow would tell me in an August 2008 interview that she'd been gobsmacked by the press's twisting of the electoral tale in New Hampshire: "I remember thinking, 'I can't believe the media narrative about these guys [compared to] what this is like in person! The difference is a hundred eighty degrees.'" After recalling a John Edwards event, which she described as "so emotional, and small *d* democratic," Maddow then described going to an Obama rally: "It was like, he's talking about himself! And he was three hours late! And there was a mile-long line to get in and now we're going to hear about how inspirational your campaign is? I just listened to John Edwards talk about how inspirational the American people who struggle through adversity and still succeed despite all the forces arrayed against them are, and I'm supposed to be inspired by which guy?"

Joan Walsh, the editor in chief of *Salon,* reported on the primary from New Hampshire after covering a September debate and the Iowa caucus. In the fall she had heard fellow journalists grumble about whether Obama had the fire in his belly, but by the time she got to Iowa covering his rallies from the press section was "like being at a Springsteen concert. It was like he had become the hottest ticket and they were not even trying to cover up their fervor." She particularly remembered two journalists, "sixty-something political veterans, white guys, old enough to know better," rocking back and forth during an Obama speech. "They were literally finishing lines of his speech," she said, "like 'There's that line again, I love it!'"

Three days before the primary Democrats held a debate in Manchester during which Hillary responded to the enthusiasm for Obama's "change" message by outlining her experience with getting things done, tallying, in loud numerical detail, the medical and military programs she'd fought for. The media reaction was that she had lost her cool, an assessment that perplexed some young journalists who didn't agree but were having their eyes opened to how groupthink press spin got made. "It's a bit astonishing to watch the real-time narrative construction that went on at last night's debate," wrote Ezra Klein on the website for the *American Prospect.* "I must have heard the term 'meltdown' in reference to Hillary 65 times. And I talked to reporters who would literally say, 'I thought she did okay, but I just misjudged it.'"

Covering Clinton for the *New Yorker,* George Packer swam against this tide of mutual hallucination, digging deeper at the popular characterizations of the former first lady and her opponent, describing how, at a New Hampshire rally, "whatever question the crowd threw at her, she had an informed answer, often accompanied by a multi-point plan: immigration, health care, global warming, student loans, small business, animal rights, Cuba," but that her answers were delivered in a uniform shout and did not have emotional resonance. As Packer described it, "She wouldn't risk the loss of control that it might take to energize the room with humor or anger or argument, or the sort of spontaneous human touch that everyone who spends private time with her notices and likes."

Hillary was aware of her communicative limitations. "I think that the world is only beginning to recognize that women should be permitted the same range of leadership styles that we permit men," she told Packer. But years of putting her (female) humanity in deep freeze to preserve an aura of (male) impermeability was a seemingly unbreakable habit that was now crippling her: she was unable to simply be herself in public. Meanwhile, Packer described an Obama rally at which the candidate "spoke for only twenty-five minutes and took no questions. . . . I walked outside and found five hundred people standing on the sidewalk and the front steps of the opera house, listening to his last words in silence, as if news of victory in the Pacific were coming over the loudspeakers. Within minutes, I couldn't recall a single thing that he had said, and the speech dissolved into pure feeling, which stayed with me for days."

The tightly wound gender constructions of Clinton and Obama were unraveling quickly. Gone was the image of Clinton as the defending heavyweight champ and Obama as the soft-touched ingénue. In defeat she had been feminized; in victory he had been lionized.

Where once Hillary's competence had made her a prepared and inevitable presidential standard, it was now the thing that made her a particular kind of female archetype. Like Harry Potter's Hermione Granger or Margaret from *Dennis the Menace,* Hillary was being portrayed as the hand-in-the-air, know-it-all girl, grating and unpopular in her determination to prove herself. By broadcasting their disdain for Clinton, pundits like Dana Milbank and Chris Matthews and Roy Sekoff were affirming their own social worth: *nobody* asked women like Hillary to the dance. Obama meanwhile had been cast as the swaggeringly underprepared cool guy, a characterization that may have been intellectually unjust and more than a little bit racially inflected, but that nonetheless won him the popularity contest that was the press's presidential coverage. Everyone wanted to hang out with this guy!

A *Slate* video from later in January summarized these classically gendered views of Clinton and Obama, splicing clips of Reese Witherspoon's Type-A overachiever Tracy Flick from the movie *Election* with clips of Clinton. Both women, whom we were to understand had been preparing for their political victories since they were in diapers, were fuming over the easy ascendency of the prom king, who'd decided on a whim to get into the race and was destined to beat them. The video was very funny, the comparison trenchant enough, but as I watched I realized that the neat overlap of Flick and Clinton was rooted in daunting truths about the avenues open to ambitious women in the wake of the second wave: understanding that being popular wasn't going to get a girl taken seriously, women had spent years toiling to prove their professional mettle, only to get passed over for guys whose masculinity allowed them to take a more relaxed, and thus more appealing approach to achievement.

Jonathan Alter wrote in *Newsweek* that Hillary was "substantive and strong and . . . a better debater so far than Obama." But, he continued, "like most women in politics, she lacks a critical asset. Male candidates can establish a magnetic and often sexual connection to women in the audience." In the New Hampshire debate Scott Spradling, a local news anchor, prefaced a question to Clinton by reporting that voters believed her to be "the most experienced and the most electable" candidate. But, he asked, what could she say to New Hampshire voters who "see a résumé and like it, but are hesitating on the likability issue, where they seem to like Barack Obama more?" Clinton replied with a one-liner—"Well, that hurts my feelings. . . . But I'll try to go on"—and acknowledged that Obama was "very likable." But she added, "I don't think I'm that bad." Obama, looking absently down at his notes, added coolly, "You're likable enough, Hillary," and in his next response made a joke about the Washington Redskins.

Obama was a guy, a history-making guy who delivered addresses so powerful that they caused throngs of people to fall reverentially silent. Clinton, after all that inevitability, was apparently just a girl—and a nerdy, unpopular girl at that. As soon as her femaleness was established, other misogynistic characterizations began to fly: she was desperate, unhinged, melting down, hysterical. On ABC's blog the reporter Jake Tapper described her as "bickering" with Obama during the debate, and reported that Clinton, "well . . . she got angry." Tapper didn't see her as mad "about an issue, so much, as about the fact that Obama is beating her. . . . Pundits will say that her tone made male voters recoil. And led some female voters to sneer." Clinton, whose womanhood had until so recently been kept under wraps, was suddenly an example of femininity on the edge.

The eagerness to trash Clinton had been laid bare, and it reeked

of a particular kind of relief: relief from the guys who had thought
they were going to have to hold their noses and get pushed around
by some dame.

And then she cried. Sort of.

During a question-and-answer session with undecided voters
in Portsmouth on the day before the New Hampshire primary,
sixty-four-year-old Marianne Pernold Young asked Clinton, "As a
woman, I know it's hard to get out of the house and get ready. My
question is very personal. How do you do it? How do you keep
upbeat and so wonderful? And who does your hair?"

Clinton paused before replying, acknowledging the final query
by noting, "Luckily on special days I do have help. . . . If you look
on some of the websites and listen to some of the commentators they
always find me on the day that I didn't have help." Then she paused
again, returning to the more serious question. "It's not easy," she
said. "And I couldn't do it if I just didn't passionately believe it was
the right thing to do." She hesitated again, stammered briefly, and
said in a voice that sounded unusually reflective, "You know, I have
so many opportunities from this country." Then came the sound of
her voice breaking. "I just don't want to see us fall backwards. You
know, this is very personal for me. It's not just political. It's not just
public. I see what's happening, and we have to reverse it. And some
people think elections are a game. They think it's like 'who's up,'
or 'who's down.' It's about our country, it's about our kids' futures,
it's really about all of us together." This was what Packer and others
had surmised was impossible for her to do: ratchet down the defensive semishout, make the connection with voters. The spell broke,
and Clinton returned to politicking as usual, noting that some of us
(she) were ready to lead and others (Obama) weren't.

Around New Hampshire and around the country BlackBerrys
and emails began to ping. Hillary had cried! She'd *cried*!

Melissa Harris-Lacewell, by now an ardent Obama supporter
who had shepherded a group of Princeton undergraduates to New
Hampshire to volunteer for a variety of the candidates, was sitting
with the students in a restaurant when her phone began to buzz
with news that Clinton had broken down: "I was like, 'What? Hillary did *what*?' It didn't sound right to me." The immediate reaction from those around her was, "'It's over. A woman having shown

emotions? It's done.' There was a bit of glee on the part of Obama supporters."

The bulletin provoked similar assumptions of finality around the country. At *Salon*'s New York office it was just before lunch when an email arrived from the *Wall Street Journal* headlined "Emotional Moment for Clinton in N.H." The report of Clinton's remarks asserted that she was "softly crying, her voice breaking." My colleagues and I gathered around a computer screen, somber. Whatever we felt about her campaign, none of us wanted to see Clinton go out weeping. We found the clip and played it, staring intently as she discussed the personal, the political, the kids, the future. She sounded drained, her voice shot. We waited for the waterworks. Her voice cracked as if she might be about to lose it. We leaned in, squinted, but did not see a single salty teardrop fall.

That technicality didn't matter to those writing the congested headlines: "Clinton Fights Back Tears," "Clinton Gets Emotional," "Hillary Gets Leaky." She was leaky all right. As far as the media was concerned, she was leaking her feeble, funny femininity all over the place. Either that, or she had manufactured the whole episode, fulfilling yet another misogynistic expectation of manipulative femininity.

"Big news from New Hampshire tonight is, 'It cries,'" crowed Glenn Beck. "After spending decades stripping away all trace of emotion, femininity and humanity, Hillary Clinton actually broke down and actually cried yesterday on the campaign trail." Discussing whether the press was being unfair to Clinton, Dan Abrams asked Roy Sekoff to predict by how many percentage points she would lose New Hampshire. Sekoff sneered, "I give it a nine, and that's very personal to me," pretending to wipe a tear from his eye. John Edwards, the man who had built his candidacy in part on the support of progressive women, got in on the act, telling reporters with toothy opportunism, "I think what we need in a commander in chief is strength and resolve, and presidential campaigns are tough business, but being president of the United States is also tough business."

Such bliss was there at Clinton's journey from the front of the social evolution class back to the primordial stew of high-strung, overwrought femininity that even those who noticed that she had not actually wept could not help but tell the story as if she had. A blubbering Hillary Clinton was just too good an image to abjure. Olbermann opened his show promising coverage of "Senator Clinton . . . not crying at all, but close enough." But later in the hour he reported, "Today, Hillary Clinton, for whom I have the greatest possible respect, gets all emotional, a sentence later, attacking Obama and crying. By the way . . . after Ed Muskie, what Democrat cries in New Hampshire?"

Perhaps, on the verge of predicted electoral immolation, Hillary Clinton had had it. Maybe she felt the end was near and decided that there was little to lose. Maybe she was just too tired to be guarded. Maybe she was rebelling against Mark Penn, whom many speculated would be toast after her predicted loss. Ann Lewis said in 2010 that although Clinton had been conscientiously trying to follow Penn's campaign plan, in New Hampshire "she was true to herself. She forgot the plan and responded to the moment." In those few days, for the first time since the start of her campaign—and for the last time until the end of it—she let herself be Hillary. Answering questions in front of a New Hampshire crowd from a pushy Matthews, Clinton snapped, "I'm not on your show." "Please come on the show," Matthews immediately pleaded. "Yeah, well, right," she responded, getting a big laugh from the audience. Emboldened, she continued, "I don't know what to do with men who are obsessed with me. Honestly, I've never understood it." Matthews responded, "I'm not obsessed." And pinched her cheek.

The next day a man stood up in the middle of a Clinton rally holding a sign reading "Iron My Shirt." The guy and his companion turned out to be radio pranksters, but their presence provoked Hillary to blithely toss off a word she had not dared to utter in the gender-free calm before Iowa. "Ah, the remnants of sexism, alive and well," she said, adding, "As I think has been abundantly demonstrated, I am also running to break through the highest and hardest glass ceiling." She opened the rally to questions by cracking, "If there's anybody still left in the auditorium who wants to learn how to iron his own shirt, I'll talk about that." The crowd stood and roared its support.

Sexism! *That's* what this was! She hadn't whined about it, hadn't sent out a fund-raising letter about it, hadn't tried to capitalize on it. She had simply named it. And women had felt it, without having been directed to.

The night of the imaginary tears, the night before the primary, something changed. Spurred perhaps by the familiarity of Clinton's raw exhaustion, or a grim understanding of how she'd been persecuted for her lack of humanity and was now being jeered for revealing it, or a fury at the media hootenanny over her Iowa loss, or the obvious enthusiasm for embarrassing and degrading her, women began to break. They had had it, too. Suddenly feminists, missing in action for months, were sliding down the fire poles.

On primary day Gloria Steinem, back from Bhutan, published a *New York Times* op-ed provocatively headlined "Women Are Never Front-Runners," in which she laid out a litany of *Free to Be You and Me*–era rhetoric about women, race and politics, and declared her support for Hillary Clinton, concluding with a call to arms: "We have to be able to say: 'I'm supporting her because she'll be a great president and because she's a woman.'" EMILY's List's Ellen Malcolm, in New Hampshire campaigning for Clinton, recalled how the candidate's performance in the face of mortification sealed a personal commitment to what had already been her professional commitment. "She was so phenomenal I couldn't get over it," said Malcolm of the events in the last days before the primary. "She took questions for an hour, she had the audience in the palm of her hand, she so clearly understood what people were talking about. And the press was all *Obama Obama Obama*. I remember saying, 'I don't care, I'm in this now.' She so won me over."

Frustration with the Hillary pile-on was also gripping younger women. The cultural critic Cintra Wilson blogged that the spectacle of Clinton-hate was "a little witch-burny," and *Slate*'s Meghan O'Rourke questioned *USA Today*'s "Iron My Shirt" headline, which read, "Clinton Responds to Seemingly Sexist Shouts." "If these comments were only 'seemingly' sexist," O'Rourke wrote, "I wonder what, exactly, *indubitably* sexist remarks would sound like?" On *Feministing*, until now relatively quiet on Clinton, founder Jessica Valenti wrote that she had been "grossed out" by John Edwards's pouncing on Clinton's purported tears, and later that, "The last few days have really brought out some sexist assholery concerning Sen. Hillary Clinton."

Talking with MSNBC's Abrams the night before New Hampshire, Rachel Maddow said, "I'm not a Clinton partisan. If you had to put me in her camp or out of it, you'd put me out of it. But in doing media appearances talking about politics I have become somebody who praises Hillary Clinton, if only because I feel like I'm up against this scrum against her. I feel like, as a person who's not inclined toward Hillary Clinton's politics, I feel like somebody needs to defend her because it's such an onslaught of attacks on her."

I began to hear sentiments like Maddow's, often preceded by the phrase "I'm not a Hillary supporter, but . . ." uttered by friends and colleagues. Like its cousin, "I'm not a feminist, but . . . ," this utterance was invariably followed by an expression of its inverse truth, in this case, support for Hillary. Those who were "not Hillary supporters, but . . ." were downright horrified by the eagerness with which the media ridiculed her and declared her yesterday's news.

On the weekend preceding the primary I sat silent and surprised as my friend Merideth railed about Hillary's being questioned about her likability in a debate, about how she'd been written off so prematurely. Merideth was no Hillary loyalist, nor had I had ever known her to have a particular investment in gender politics. Meanwhile Geraldine was sending me lists of links to egregious slurs against Clinton on television and in newspapers. A banished memory came back to me, of an argument with my aunt, a feminist academic who thought I was crazy not to support Hillary. She'd warned me, in a near whisper, that I'd change my tune as soon as I realized how rare an opportunity Clinton presented for women.

I wasn't there yet, but I sure didn't like how much fun the media was having tearing down the girl who'd been called a tight-ass and was now labeled a basket case. A pattern was emerging, not academic or historicized, but live and right in front of me: the double binds, hypocrisies, impossibilities, and improbability of becoming, and being, Hillary Clinton, the first woman ever to get far enough to be taken seriously for the job of president.

The eagerness to oust Clinton from the race was not motivated purely by her gender. I understood that it was interwoven with enthusiasm for Obama, his promise of change. I knew what it was like to object to Hillary's centrism, her history of compromise. I knew that for fifteen years the Clinton team had behaved as if it had no use for the press, a press that had in turn become anxious to chomp the hand that refused to feed it. I knew that the prospect of two decades plus of Bush-Clinton-Bush-Clinton was not just unappealing, but almost un-American. I knew that Mark Penn's strategy was inane and that Clinton had chosen to listen to him.

But what centrist politics and flawed self-presentation should have gotten Hillary was a lost caucus, then a lost primary, and then more lost caucuses and primaries, until at some point she was out of the race and pundits could shake their heads and score her errors. But that was not what was happening in the first week of January. She had lost a single caucus, and instead of simply reporting on it her critics had rolled around in it, celebrated it, made it mean exponentially more than it ever should have. Their ardor for Clinton's abasement had reverberated with an unmistakable vibe, the loosening of a clenched resentment that it had been a chick who had dared be confident about her ability to win the Democratic nomination, who had exercised infuriatingly tight control over the press, who had for more than a year appeared to exert unrelenting dominion over her male competitors.

✳ ✳ ✳

On a subway to Geraldine's apartment to watch the New Hampshire results with friends, I couldn't fathom how I'd come to care so much. My heart was in my throat, my fingers crossed as if at a play-off game, my whole body pretzeled with the intense and irrational desire of someone madly hoping for an impossible upset.

I didn't want Hillary to win the Democratic nomination. I didn't want John Edwards out of the race. I didn't want Barack Obama to suffer a hope-squelching loss. But I knew with primal surety that if I had been a New Hampshire resident on January 8, I would have pulled a lever for the former first lady with a song in my heart and a bird flipped at Chris Matthews, Roy Sekoff, Keith Olbermann and every other guy who'd gotten his rocks off by imagining Hillary's humiliation. That humiliation had been almost assured by a last-minute Gallup poll placing Obama 13 points ahead of Clinton going into New Hampshire.

In baseball anything can happen. The results that began to roll in were not the numbers anyone expected. Women, it seemed, had come to the polls to vote for Hillary Clinton. By the end of the night she would win not only New Hampshire, but 46 percent of its women, compared to 34 percent for Obama.

On MSNBC Matthews recited like a catechism the numbers of every pollster who had forecasted Clinton's loss. Halfway through the night he had his arms crossed defensively across his chest like a shamed schoolboy and was proclaiming that he had been at Saturday night's debate and had thought it "a draw," but that apparently Clinton's performance had been "good enough here for women who wanted to root for her anyway." He said this as if it were obvious that a performance that was "good enough . . . for women" would not have been good enough for any rational political decision maker.

He was not alone in his estimation of female electoral impulses. Flailing for explanations for Clinton's strong showing, pundits soon settled on her purported crying jag. Suddenly the moment that had signaled her uproarious unraveling was being credited with saving her. "I never saw her like that before," said Jack Cafferty on CNN, "Sympathetic. Real." CNN's Gloria Borger informed the audience that "There is a lot of talk tonight about whether Hillary's tearing up made any difference." She noted that a striking percentage of female Hillary voters told exit pollsters that they had decided whom to vote for on that very day.

Tom Brokaw, retired from his NBC anchor spot but sitting in with Matthews for election coverage, was aware of the treatment Clinton had received in the grabby hands of his colleagues and seemed to relish the opportunity to spank them. "The end of the Clinton era—a lot of pundits saying that on this channel and on all the other channels," said Brokaw. "All of that conventional wisdom was turned on its head. This is one of the great triumphs in recent years in American presidential politics, . . . and the rest of us who were saying out loud that this was not going to happen, we've got a lot of explaining to do." Matthews barked back that he had relied on universities that devoted themselves solely to polling. Polling is "a lot less important than letting this process go forward in the way that it should," said Brokaw sternly. Even conservatives were doing some self-flagellating. "The press was dead wrong," said Pat

Buchanan. "We had virtually canonized Obama. . . . The press has been telling us she's gone and the women came out and said no, she's not. What New Hampshire did was stand up and body-slam the national establishment, the press corps, the pollsters, the whole bunch."

And then Rachel Maddow took it one step further. "Do you want to know who they're blaming?" she asked, looking as though she had canary feathers hanging from her mouth. Citing the online news source *Talking Points Memo,* Maddow continued, "They're blaming Chris Matthews. People are citing particularly Chris not only for his own views but as a symbol of what the mainstream media has done to Hillary Clinton." She later added, "People feel that the media is piling on Hillary Clinton. They're coming to her defense with their votes."

At eleven-thirty that night Matthews was finally forced to suck it up. Looking like he was chewing on a lemon, he confessed, "She stood there and took the heat under what looked to be a difficult time . . . I give her a lot of personal credit. I will never underestimate Hillary Clinton again."

The four of us watching at Geraldine's house, not one a Clintonite, cheered like mad.

For the first time in my life my reaction to a political news cycle was mirroring a larger national sentiment, and I was shocked by it. Notably it was also the first time in my life that my reactions as a woman and as a feminist had real-time application on a presidential stage, the first time that women had figured so large both as candidates and as voters. This was what it felt like to be relevant in a presidential contest.

If it surprised me, it was nothing compared to how the Clinton camp felt. A group of them had taken over their hotel's bar in Manchester to drown their sorrows on the afternoon of the primary. Mark Penn was sitting by himself. "No one would go near him at the table," said Elaine Lafferty, "because he was going to get fired." John Coale, a trial lawyer and friend of the Clintons, had brought Lafferty to the bar hoping that she would be able to personally deliver to Hillary her memo on new ways to reach women, strategies that might be useful since, after the predicted loss, the campaign was going to have to change course. Coale stuffed the memo into Hillary's hands as she passed through on her way to a radio interview. Returning briefly in the late afternoon, Hillary pulled Lafferty and Coale aside to say that she loved the ideas and would like to talk about them further, after she got through the night ahead.

Bill Clinton, suffering from a bad cold and looking, as Lafferty described it, "like hell on a biscuit," was the first to offer the sodden crowd any hope. "He walked in there at five o'clock and said, 'I think we're going to do better than they say,'" said Lafferty. As the results began to come in, all hell broke loose. "Mandy Grunwald was screaming. Capricia [Marshall] was having to pick [new] music. People were screaming at the television," Lafferty said of the reaction. Lissa Muscatine, a longtime speechwriter for Clinton, described her night in Washington, D.C.: "I was working on the non-victory speech, and then it was the 'it's going to be closer than expected' speech, and then it was the 'wow, this was really, *really* close' speech, and then suddenly it was the 'Oh! She won! Crap, we don't have a speech!' speech." Mark Penn would be keeping his job after all. Except for the demotion of overwhelmed Patti Solis Doyle, the Clinton campaign was not going to change its course.

As Clinton made her way from the stage at the Southern New Hampshire University gymnasium after her first victory speech of the campaign, she leaned in to Ellen Malcolm and grabbed her hand. "Ellen," she said, "I just became the first woman in history to win a presidential primary."

☆ ☆ ☆

The Wednesday morning quarterbacking was bleak. Many critics, it seemed, accepted an interpretation of the surprising results in which women had cleaved to a weeping Hillary like Golden Girls to cheesecake.

Judith Warner, blogging at the *New York Times,* wrote, "If victory came for the reasons we've been led to believe—because women voters ultimately saw in her, exhausted and near defeat, a countenance that mirrored their own—then I hate what that victory says about the state of their lives and the nature of their emotions." Returning to a Lewinsky-era refrain about Clinton, Warner continued, "I hate . . . that [women have] got to see a strong, smart and savvy woman cut down to size before they can embrace her as one of their own."

Obama supporters were dismayed and furious. Melissa Harris-Lacewell wrote on *Slate,* "Clinton cried about being attacked in the debates, but there are no public tears shed for the strain Obama must feel [about an uptick in death threats against him]." Even angrier was Moe Tkacik, a vividly irreverent writer for the women's blog *Jezebel.* Writing to a vocal readership that had shown Hillary leanings, Tkacik exploded: "Dear all you commentwhores who said Hillary's teensy little tear session had swayed your vote to Hillary: Fuck you. . . . Her narrow lead in yesterday's New Hampshire primary is entirely attributable to chicks like you, and you were allll111 chicks. . . . New Hampshire women, after telling pollster after pollster they were ready for change, went inside the booths and had a little cry."

If New Hampshire women had in fact voted for Hillary Clinton because they sympathized with her vulnerability, that was bad. It suggested that although the headline on Steinem's op-ed was patently inaccurate—a woman *had* been a front-runner for more than a year—an inverted version of it was correct: that front-runners were never recognized as women, and that other women jumped to their aid only when they were tied to a railroad track, a locomotive chugging toward them.

I supposed that there were women who recognized in Hillary a wounded, imperiled quality that they responded to as inherently, depressingly female. But I could not shake the feeling that there was something more complex than an appreciation for damp feminine excess or relief at seeing a powerful woman taken down a notch that had made New Hampshire's women rise up for Hillary.

In the days after the primary Harris-Lacewell pointed to a particular dynamic surrounding Obama's candidacy, and her observation felt more resonant than the media line we had been fed about Clinton. Appearing on *Democracy Now,* Harris-Lacewell noted that early in the campaign cycle there had been "a great deal of anxiety about Barack, because he had almost too much white support. . . . It raised some anxieties for African American voters, who were asking, 'Well, if there are all of these people in the media, if there are all of these white voters who are interested in you, does that mean that you're not with us, that you do not share our interests?'" What she was describing was the suspicion that plagued supporters of both Obama and Clinton: if you can win, then you cannot possibly be for real.

Referring to Bob Johnson, the founder of BET and a Clinton supporter who'd made derisive remarks about Obama's youthful drug experimentation, Harris-Lacewell pointed to the fact that support for Obama among black voters had begun, finally, to swell: "When that sort of attack occurs, it actually . . . increases the amount of support among most African Americans," whose reaction she summed up as "Oh, I see. Actually, [the establishment is] not completely for you."

The building volume and visibility of sexism aimed at Clinton post-Iowa, like the increasingly inescapable racism directed at Obama, was a stinging reminder that there was a system in place that had historically excluded anyone who was not white and male, and that those who challenged that system would not only meet with resistance, but would be pitted against each other. In New Hampshire two long-standing misapprehensions about gender had been corrected: the notion that there had never been antagonism to Clinton's candidacy from a reasonable (as opposed to right-wing crazy) male establishment, and that because Clinton had found a way to pass off her power as confident and thus male, she was no longer truly female.

Women who had spent months pretending that Clinton was not a woman suddenly could not help but recognize how she had been treated. Perhaps for some the moment of connection *was* her glistening eyes. But that didn't automatically indicate some lamentably drippy sisterhood. As Harris-Lacewell reported in retrospect, "If you sat at the [restaurant] long enough, you began to hear a ton of hard-working working-class and middle-class white women who said, 'I know what it's like when a young man comes in and takes your spot. You train him, and then he comes in and takes your spot on the job.'" You did the work on the science project; he got the credit. You voiced the idea at the meeting; he said it five minutes later and everyone complimented him. This was not about shared female essence; it was about a shared female experience.

Anita Dunn, who would go on to work as a senior advisor for Obama in the spring, later told the political reporter Anne Kornblut, "I was still neutral during New Hampshire . . . [but] I saw [Obama] walking into these adoring crowds like he was the Messiah. And I saw her out there sweating, with her political career on the line and then choking up because she realized that it was almost over. I would have voted for her."

Some women were voting in response to the humiliation of the media's fetishistic obsession with Clinton's supposed breakdown. "They played that thing over and over and over," said NOW's Kim Gandy. "I think that made women kind of angry. Like, why are they *doing* this to her?" Ellen Malcolm imagined women listening to the media characterization of Clinton's misty moment, and thinking, "*What?* This is the nicest thing I've ever seen Hillary do! I've always wanted to know that she really cared, and she's telling us that she does, and they're just pissing on her because she's crying. And she wasn't even crying!" Jessica Grose from *Jezebel* responded to her colleague Tkacik's rant against weepy women voters in a post that noted that men could be "just as emotional and capricious when choosing candidates as women are," citing her late grandfather, a quiet, mild yellow-dog Democrat who had had a "visceral, irrational dislike of" Hillary Clinton.

Some, like me, reacted to the gloating disrespect from the press. Pam Spaulding of the popular *Pam's House Blend* blog dubbed this phenomenon "the Tweety Effect," in reference to a popular nickname for Chris Matthews. As she defined it, it's "where the misogyny of a talking head in the MSM [mainstream media] so enrages a demographic that they go out and vote in a manner that will put egg on the face of the talking head." Even the liberal blogger Matthew Yglesias conceded, "I don't think pissing off Chris Matthews is a good enough reason to pull the lever for Clinton, but I can certainly understand the impulse."

These points of recognition were about identifying with a certain strain of ill treatment, something feminists are loath to do lest they be accused of capitalizing on victimhood. But feminism was born precisely *because* women faced gendered injustices. To identify and overcome obstacles and resistance was to advance the project of female empowerment. Did the sexism exhibited toward Hillary cast her as embattled and threatened? Yes. But that didn't mean that women responded to it because they themselves loved feeling threatened and embattled or believed that that was their natural pose, or because they loved seeing tough broads brought down. They might have responded because they *hated* that women were treated that way, and because in this instance they had the means to push back: voting for Hillary.

When someone made insinuations about Barack Obama selling drugs or emphasized that his middle name was Hussein, his blackness became accessible not because it was essentially black to sell drugs or have Muslim roots, but because blackness in America has long been an impediment to parity and acceptance, and because manipulated characterizations of blackness have been part of what has been used to enforce that impediment. So too with femininity. To see a woman get taunted for being simultaneously frigid and lachrymose and then get teased for her smarts was not to ascribe to her inherently feminine qualities of frigidity, sentimentality, or unsociability. Rather it was to witness femininity as it has historically been cast, especially when it threatened male power structures: as a laughable, silly, unpleasant, or devalued condition. Women had watched a popular vision of Hillary Clinton, a front-running candidate with whom they may have had a complicated or cool relationship but whose strengths, weaknesses, achievements, and mistakes had never been traditional or one-dimensional, manipulated to fit into retro molds of lightweight (peevish, unpopular, calculating, shrill) feminine illegitimacy. In a cartoon drawn by Pat Oliphant in the days after New Hampshire a blubbing Clinton is shown at a desk, facing Mahmoud Ahmadinejad, Osama bin Laden, Kim Jong-Il and other menacing men murmuring "Aww, she's sensitive—I had no idea"; "Was it something we said?"; and "Buy her flowers." A thought bubble above Hillary's head reads, "You guys are mean!" and in the corner, a miniature Bill remarks, "This is when PMS goes nuclear." In the face of plenty of good reasons to criticize Hillary Clinton, women now realized that for some it still came down to this: the same twisted characterizations used for centuries to bolster the idea that women were unfit to lead.

"We [human beings] like the underdog who is being unfairly attacked," Harris-Lacewell told me. "Part of the reason we come to like Hillary is watching her bear up under pressure, particularly sexist pressure, and we like to watch Barack bear up against the weight of racism." Those who were roused to Clinton's defense were roused not because she was a girl, but because she was being treated like one.

The remarkable thing about what happened in New Hampshire was that standing up for Hillary wasn't really about Hillary at all. "I'm still not voting for Clinton but I've been sickened by the behavior of the national media," commented DBR on *Feministing*, agreeing with a piece I had written for *Salon* to which *Feministing* had linked. Fellow commenter Gretchen wrote, "The night before the NH primaries, I said to my boyfriend, 'I hope Hillary wins.' And he said 'Why? You don't support Hillary.'" The attention women paid to Clinton in those five days was evidence that later media narratives equating support of Barack Obama with a rejection of feminist principles were hogwash. The women's vote in New Hampshire was not a sign of essentialist gynocentric solidarity; it was a show of political and rebellious feminist force more potent than any march on Washington.

But the press's nearly unanimous take emphasized only the impact Clinton's nonexistent tears had on voters' heartstrings. MSNBC's New Hampshire wrap-up included a rehash of how "Clinton's voice quavered." CNN's piece contained a mention of the "almost-tears," a description of how her "eyes welled up this week," and further analysis of whether her "emotions were sincere or faked as part of some strategy to diminish criticism that she is too steely, too cold." The *New York Times* referred to "Mrs. Clinton's unusual display of emotion" as a "galvanizing moment" for many voters, and quoted New Hampshire resident Elaine Marquis, who said, "Women finally saw a woman—perhaps a tough woman, but a woman with a gentle heart."

All three stories failed to include mention of the remarkable fact of which Hillary herself had been immediately aware: that on Tuesday, January 8, 2008, that steely, gentle-hearted woman had become the first in the history of the United States of America to win a presidential primary.

5 THE MOST RESTRICTING FORCES

GLORIA STEINEM'S OP-ED "Women Are Never Front-Runners" began with a description of a fictional female counterpart to Barack Obama, a figure reminiscent of "Judith Shakespeare," Virginia Woolf's imagined sister of William, who had "a gift like her brother's, for the tune of words" but no professional platform from which to express them. In Steinem's formulation "Achola Obama" was a mixed-race lawyer with eight years in the state legislature, a politician whose voice was a unifying force but who could never have been a political supernova like Barack. "Be honest," Steinem wrote. "Do you think this is the biography of someone who could be elected to the United States Senate? After less than one term there, do you believe she could be a viable candidate to head the most powerful nation on earth?"

Contextualizing the electoral fortunes of Hillary Clinton and Barack Obama, Steinem argued that although "the caste systems of sex and race are interdependent and can only be uprooted together," the gender barrier is not taken as seriously as the racial barrier.

She pointed out that "black men were given the vote a half-century before women of any race were allowed to mark a ballot, and generally have ascended to positions of power, from the military to the boardroom, before any women." The pull quote chosen by the *Times* was "Gender is probably the most restricting force in American life."

The response to Steinem's piece from many sectors was wildly positive. Dozens of friends sent me the op-ed, and many called to talk about it. It remained at the top of the newspaper's "most emailed" list for days and was reprinted around the world. Though it seemed unlikely that the piece changed many votes on the day of the New Hampshire primary, it was emblematic of the billowing resistance that Clinton's recent treatment had provoked. "Every once in a while a writer gets to name something that people are feeling that hasn't been named yet," Steinem told me more than a year after the publication of the piece. What she had named was sexism, the thing to which some women were beginning to respond instinctually.

I was surprised by my own reaction to Steinem's piece. It hadn't made me want to vote for Hillary, but it had made me nod my head in agreement that "anything that affects males is seen as more serious than anything that affects 'only' the female half of the human race," and that Obama "is seen as unifying by his race while [Clinton] is seen as divisive by her sex." Steinem observed that because children were still raised by women, some men feel as though "they are regressing to childhood" when faced with a powerful female, and that racist stereotypes of black men as hypermasculine prompt some white men to identify with them as a way of affirming their own masculinity. Yes! These things were true! I couldn't believe that I was having my eyes opened, perhaps even my consciousness raised, by a piece so old-school in its prose, so retro in its tone.

What I did not realize at the time was how many other people found the op-ed old-school and retro in ways that did not make them nod their heads in assent but shake them in fury and frustration.

The piece gave shape and language to an unprecedented moment in American women's history; it was also a grenade, exploding delicate bonds between women of different colors and ages. If "Women Are Never Front-Runners" was received in some feminist quarters with grateful relief, in others it was reviled with a comparable degree of intensity and viewed as a public reopening of deep wounds that had never fully healed.

Second-wave feminism had been riven, and partially unraveled, by divisions over whose interests it was representing. Most visibly emblematized by white middle-class straight women like *The Feminine Mystique* author Betty Friedan, New York Congresswoman Bella Abzug, and *Ms.* founder Steinem, the women's movement of the 1970s was dogged by criticism that it was an ultimately bourgeois project, one that did not take into account the perspectives of women of different colors, classes, and sexual orientations. While in reality the women's movement of the 1970s was powered by a diverse group of white, black, gay, straight, middle- and working-class women, *feminism,* as it was commonly portrayed and popularized, concerned itself most famously and (perhaps) most disruptively with getting women out of the home and into the workforce. This mission did not resonate for millions of women who did not suffer from Friedan's mystical stay-at-home ennui because they did not stay at home. Poor and minority women had always worked, and many were less concerned with sloughing off the repressive bonds of domestic drudgery than with winning economic and social freedoms that might afford them the choice to stay home with their family should they want to. When feminism did catapult some women into universities and professional spheres, women of color were often called upon to pick up the domestic slack, cleaning the houses and caring for the children of those who had reaped feminism's fruits. Through some lenses, privileged (and often racially privileged) women had advanced not by striking new, equitable deals with men, but by consuming those women below them on the power totem pole.

The perceived exclusions of the women's movement were part of what led the poet and activist Audre Lorde to argue that male-female gender distinctions were reductive, and that women themselves experienced such a divergence of identity that feminism failed most of them. The writer Alice Walker, one of Steinem's closest friends, coined the term *womanist* as an alternative for women of color in search of a way to indicate that their feminist perspectives and goals were more expansive than the word had come to suggest.

Competitive tension between female advancement and black advancement extended much further back than the 1970s. While suffragists and abolitionists worked in tandem before and throughout the Civil War—one of the earliest gatherings of the women's movement was the Anti-Slavery Convention of American Women in 1837, attended by both black and white women—alliances ruptured during Reconstruction-era battles over how best to secure rights of citizenship for America's disenfranchised populations. The Fourteenth and Fifteenth Amendments, which granted citizenship, due process, and voting rights to black men but not to women, drove a wedge between formerly cooperative activists. Some, including Frederick Douglass, Elizabeth Blackwell, Lucy Stone and Julia Ward Howe, supported passage of the amendments despite their exclusion of women. Douglass, a longtime advocate of female suffrage who participated in the 1848 Seneca Falls Convention, believed that white women's economic and social privilege put them closer to enfranchisement than black men, and that once black men could vote, black women would enjoy the same indirect empowerment. As he wrote in an 1868 letter to the suffragist Josephine Sophie White Griffing, "Woman has a thousand ways to attach herself to the governing power of the land and already exerts an honorable influence on the course of legislation. She is the victim of abuses, to be sure, but it cannot be pretended . . . that her cause is as urgent as . . . ours." Perhaps the more crucial argument was that, had the amendments included the rights of women, they would not have passed; many activists believed that enfranchising blacks, rather than no one at all, was the more broadly progressive choice. "We rejoice in every extension of suffrage," said Lucy Stone at the 1869 Women's Rights Convention in Chicago.

In staunch opposition were the suffragists Susan B. Anthony and Elizabeth Cady Stanton, who believed that their former allies had sold them out. They were particularly furious that the Fourteenth Amendment allowed the word "male" into the Constitution, surmising that its inclusion would make a future battle for women's rights only more difficult. Stanton's sense of betrayal was particularly rancorous and led her to overt racism. In 1869 she said, "Think of Patrick and Sambo and Hans and Yung Tung, who do not know the difference between a monarchy and a republic, who can not read the Declaration of Independence or Webster's spelling-book, making laws for [prominent suffragists]." Stanton and Anthony formed the women's-only National Woman Suffrage Association in opposition to the Fifteenth Amendment in spring of 1869. In turn Stone and Howe founded the American Woman Suffrage Association, an organization open to women and men who supported passage of the Fifteenth Amendment. More than two decades later the competing groups combined to form the National American Woman Suffrage Association.

Stanton's anxiety about women's progress being delayed by the abandonment of abolitionist friends was prophetic; it would be fifty years before the Nineteenth Amendment gave women the right to vote. Meanwhile blacks were not able to vote freely or safely for years to come. Stopped at the polls by property and residency requirements, literacy tests, and poll taxes, African Americans were beaten and lynched in their century-long struggle to exercise the rights they had been granted in 1870. Ninety-five years after passage of the Fifteenth Amendment, and forty-five years after passage of the Nineteenth, Congress passed the Voting Rights Act.

It was probably predestined that the race between Hillary Clinton and Barack Obama would so agonizingly recall the clashes of allies of the past, between people whose histories of discrimination were linked and, in the case of millions of black women, shared. In 2008 African American men and white women were once again set against each other, in a configuration that provoked a destructive tallying of oppressions, injustices, and suffering and left women of color caught in the middle. It was this explosive conversation that Steinem's op-ed kicked off.

"How can one compare racism to sexism—and if one tries, where do those of us who are disadvantaged both by our race and by our gender fit in?" wrote Jennifer Fang at *Racialicious*. Fang thought, "[Steinem's comparison] redirects our attention away from efforts to break the White male patriarchy that excludes all the Others, but towards in-fighting where we all compete to see . . . who's more oppressed. . . . Is it no wonder, then, that women of colour have long felt alienated by feminists like Steinem?"

"I was deeply, deeply offended," said Melissa Harris-Lacewell. "The part that took me over the edge was the imaginary black woman, Achola." To Harris-Lacewell's mind, Steinem's invented female version of Obama represented "the very worst of what second-wave white feminism does. . . . Instead of engaging with living, breathing women of color, it imagines us in these bodies. 'Imagine this black woman . . . ' But you don't have to imagine a black woman, we exist!" Conjuring one was not only unnecessary, but something that Steinem should have known better than to do. "This is Gloria Steinem, and she's been having these conversations for thirty years," said Harris-Lacewell. "The conversations in which people say 'White feminists: please don't do this.' It's not like Gloria Steinem doesn't personally know women who feel this way, that she hasn't worked with them and written with them and that she doesn't engage with them."

That Steinem might make an argument that women, or even that black women should vote for Hillary was fair enough. "It's not as though race should always trump gender," Harris-Lacewell said, or that blacks or black women vote as a monolith. But, she went on, "[Steinem] chose to make this point *not* by talking about the things that African-American women actually cared about that Hillary Clinton could address better than Barack Obama. . . . No, [instead she implied], 'Oh, you silly black women who are supporting Barack Obama, don't you see he means nothing to you because you are a woman, like me, and like Hillary Clinton, and your relevant issue is your gender, not your race?' I was livid about her use of black women in that way."

Steinem's argument, like so much feminist history before it, had rendered invisible (or imaginary) women of color, blithely presuming them to have the same perspective as the white women whose voices were given a prominent platform, in this case the op-ed page of the *New York Times*.

"[Steinem's piece] left me quite irritable," said Margo Jefferson, a journalist and professor. "But I just thought, 'Well, there goes Gloria.' She's such a good popularizer and always has these good points, but then misses something huge. I chose to take refuge in a certain kind of patronizing of her. It was very predictable. But I was also tired of being too sanctimonious. Yeah, this was an example of what we've been saying for years about feminists being bourgeois and racially exclusive, but I was also trying to check myself, certainly as a black person and also as a woman, because there was aggrieved sanctimony on both ends."

In 2009 Steinem explained to me that she had asked the *New York Times* to select a headline that did not make sex and race seem competitive. They complied, but then used "Gender is the most restricting force in American life" as the pull quote. Steinem said, in retrospect, "That was my fault, because at minimum I should have said 'pervasive,' because I meant that it was the most widespread, not that it was the most severe. They took that sentence and made it the slug on the Internet, and then it was . . . used as a theme for a whole weeklong series on CNN, asking 'Which is more important, sex or race?,' which I've spent my life trying to say are intertwined. They could have taken a sentence in the same piece that said 'The caste systems of sex and race are interdependent and can only be uprooted together.' If they had taken that sentence it would have been more fair. But it was my fault for creating this screwy sentence."

Steinem took the blame for another misleading sentence: "When I said that Negro men had got the vote on paper before women, black or white women." She said that a *New York Times* editor persuaded her that she did not need to delve into the history of black vote suppression because she had addressed it in her 2007 column expressing support for both Clinton and Obama. The editor, said Steinem, assured her that this earlier explanation would cover Steinem in her "Front-Runner" op-ed. "I shouldn't have fallen for that," she said in retrospect. When the fallout came, the *Times* would not let her run clarifications on its website, so she posted an explanation at the Women's Media Center website and withdrew the column from syndication. "Here is the important thing," she said to me later. "If you want to maintain racism, you have to restrict the freedom of the women of the ruling class, of white women, otherwise you don't have the means of reproduction and racial purity. That's how in the South, race and sex have always gone together. White women were restricted and like chattel, and black women were used as workers themselves and forced to produce workers and were everybody's sexual property. . . . It is not possible to be a feminist without being antiracist. It's not possible to be a civil rights person without being a feminist. It's all connected. And that's what made me craziest about this election, and that's what made me craziest about misinterpreting me."

In a *Slate* piece responding to Obama's New Hampshire loss Harris-Lacewell offered what appeared to be a fierce rejoinder to Steinem's piece, puncturing the myth of Barack Obama's postracial slide to victory. Making a point that mirrored Steinem's in some ways, Harris-Lacewell wrote, "What I know for sure is that if black Americans are going to be relevant to American elections, they must rally behind Obama now."

The progressive radio and television host Amy Goodman invited both women on to her show, *Democracy Now*. It was an intense conversation, with Harris-Lacewell hammering home points about the disparities between the ways America apprehends white female oppression and the oppression of African American men and women: "We have got to get clear about the fact that race and gender are not these clear dichotomies in which you're a woman or you're black; I'm sitting here in my black womanhood body, knowing that it is more complicated than that. . . . An anxiety for African American women feminists like myself is that we're often asked to join up with white women's feminism, but only on their own terms, as long as we . . . remain silent about the ways in which our gender, our class, our sexual identity doesn't intersect." Steinem accepted much of what Harris-Lacewell said, bristling only at what sounded like a suggestion that women who sympathized with Clinton and voted for her were acting on racist impulses. Harris-Lacewell responded briskly, "I would not disparage them by claiming they are racist. I would, however, say they're part of the American historical system that responds to white women suffering in very particular ways, and it cannot see African Americans suffering in the same ways."

It was a lucid, energetic exchange about the history of racial and gender politics. It was also painful to watch: two right-minded and quite like-minded women in tormented debate with each other about current and historical injustice. "When I got the phone call from *Democracy Now* I had just gotten back into town [from New Hampshire], and I was exhausted," recalled Harris-Lacewell. "My hair looked awful, I was up against an orange background. It was my least favorite television appearance in about four hundred different ways. But it was also my most favorite television appearance.

I don't think I've ever been angrier on television. I was pissed. And it came out in ways that I think led to very useful analysis." She admitted, "If I made a list of the top people I'd like to go on TV and tell how pissed I am about what they've done to my country, Gloria Steinem wouldn't make the top one hundred. I see myself as being very much on the same side as Gloria Steinem. So it was this weird moment, but one that speaks to the very heart of my political commitments about misrepresentations of African American women."

A YouTube clip of the *Democracy Now* episode circulated; young people saw it. What Harris-Lacewell heard afterward, she said, was that many of them had read Steinem's op-ed and felt uneasy about it but hadn't had the vocabulary, history or context to explain why. "College students and graduate students, other faculty, said, 'What was so useful about it was that you articulated why I have sometimes felt uneasy about feminism in general, or about that op-ed specifically.'"

Asked about whether the fracas reminded her of discord within feminism in the 1970s, Steinem said no, balking even at the inference of second-wave racial exclusivity. Noting that it was infuriating that the women's movement, which she called "more diverse than any other," was accused more often of a lack of diversity than other white, male-dominated social movements, she told me, "I learned feminism from black women. All my lecture partners were black women. They were so far ahead of us. It was true statistically that black women were, from the very first polls in the sixties, more likely to support feminist issues than white women. So this cherished idea that feminists are white middle class? They didn't say Stokely Carmichael was middle class. He was. They didn't say Martin Luther King was middle class. He was. They're always trying to disqualify women with all these adjectives, including trying to divide us from black women. There's certainly racism, God knows, in the women's movement. Of course there is. But in my actual personal experience it was the women of the National Welfare Rights Organization, it was Flo Kennedy, it was Dorothy Hughes, all these women from whom I learned."

Margo Jefferson took a different view. "Flo is a legend, but neither of those women profited at all from feminism and its popularization as much as Gloria did," she said. "And that is certainly because they did not have the background, race, and were not pretty young white women. Do I think Gloria Steinem is a racist? No. But so much of prejudice—gender and racial and class—has to do with the assumptions you're allowed to live with. I have class privilege, and sometimes I'm placed in that position toward people of my own race who have less privilege. Nobody is spared that kind of obtuseness."

Steinem acknowledged, "Yes, I became better known than most women of color I work with," but she pointed to the role of the media rather than the dynamics of the movement itself. Citing several examples in which she refused to participate in magazine stories or pose for pictures that would make her the poster girl for her diverse movement, Steinem recalled being approached by the *New York Times Magazine* for a cover story on pioneer feminists: "I said I couldn't do it unless they included Flo Kennedy, Eleanor Holmes Norton, Dolores Huerta, and others. . . . So they left me out of the cover photo and used Kate Millett, Susan Brownmiller—all white."

Opening up this conversation in 2008 allowed a new generation of women to weigh in. Latoya Peterson, then twenty-four, was writing at the blog *Racialicious,* calling herself a "hip-hop feminist," a term she said reconciled "an often-hostile term, 'feminism,' with a more embracing term, 'hip-hop.'" Peterson told me in 2009, "[Steinem's piece] minimized the balancing act that black women go through, because we're both racialized and gendered . . . and it manifests differently because our sexism is racialized and our racialism is sexualized. Feminists think they can gloss over these things. 'It's not that big a deal because we're still all women.' Well, we're not all women, because you've made it clear that my experience does not matter, [but] you still feel like you know what's best for me. It's that maternalistic streak in feminism that really turns a lot of women of color off. You don't know us, you don't know our culture, you don't know what we've been through, and I'm not going to sit here and be condescended to by a white woman when I could easily go and organize my own people."

One of the ironies of the dissatisfactions stirred by "Women Are Never Front-Runners" and the way the piece resurrected old impressions of a generation's blinkered approach to racial difference was that Steinem, the icon of the women's movement of the 1970s, did not initially want to write the piece at all. She had done so at the behest of a twenty-year-old friend.

As a teenager, Shelby Knox was the subject of an award-winning documentary, *The Education of Shelby Knox,* chronicling her political awakening in conservative Lubbock, Texas. Knox had been raised religious and taken a virginity pledge before launching a doomed battle against the local school board to get sex education taught in high schools. In 2007 Steinem offered Knox room and board in her Manhattan home while she found her footing as an activist and speaker. Upon moving in, Knox papered her bedroom with "Hillary '08" stickers. "I was putting them up by my bed, and I was like, I wonder what Gloria thinks of this, so I asked her," Knox said. Steinem's response was, "I don't think any woman can win—it's too soon." Knox was devastated. "Gloria Steinem cannot be telling me that Hillary Clinton has no chance of winning," she said. "I kept saying, 'But Gloria, don't you want her to win?' And she kept saying, 'I don't know if we want to go through all the ridicule and misogyny or put Hillary through it.'"

Both women were traveling the country, speaking at colleges, and reporting back to each other about the confusion they were hearing from female students disturbed by the animus directed at Clinton but unwilling to believe that the hatred was motivated by her gender since they'd been taught that sexism in America was a thing of the past. Knox in particular was alarmed by the inability of women her age to talk confidently about how they felt about Clinton. She understood why she was more thrown than her mentor. "[Gloria] has had seventy-five years of blatant sexism and talking about it," said Knox. "She told me in 2007 that this was what was going to happen, and that she dreaded it. So, to her, it was just coming true. Whereas my generation had been told we are equal our entire lives. I was hearing young women on campuses internalizing this and thinking they were crazy, that something was wrong [with them] for seeing [sexism]."

The night of the Iowa caucus Steinem returned home to find Knox crying in front of the television. "I was saying, 'This is *sexism,*' raving and ranting," said Knox. "'Yes, Shelby, this is sexism,' Gloria said. 'This is hard. This is what this is.'" Knox recalled that she "got a little pissed at Gloria": "Because I was like, 'Someone needs to say that this is sexism!' I [was telling her,] 'We're starting to feel like something's wrong with us, so *you* may know that this is sexism but you have to say it.'" Steinem responded by suggesting that Knox herself write a piece. "I said, 'No, Gloria, no one will listen to me. Everyone will listen to you, and if you don't do this then I will blame you on behalf of my generation forever for what this has done to us. It makes us think we're crazy. You have to name this, okay?'" After mulling her own growing anger at the media's misogyny, Steinem drafted her op-ed and showed it to Knox.

Knox, who is white, said that her only quibble was with a sentence about young women denying a gender caste system. To Knox's mind, Steinem's phrase "Gender is the most restricting force" was "a throw-away line that explained that white women and women of color experienced sexism and women of color experienced both racism and sexism but that therefore, statistically, more people would be affected by sexism. It was not a comparative statement of hardship at all." After some frenzied revisions the piece was published, and it was Knox who ventured online to check out the responses. "[Gloria] never looks at any of her things online," Knox explained, "because the comments often devolve into, 'Oh, that bitch is still alive?'" In this case, however, the initial comments were positive. "I ran downstairs and hugged her," said Knox, "and was like, 'Thank you for doing this for me and for my generation.'"

It was the next day, after Steinem had left for a business trip, that Knox heard from a former colleague: "[She] was calling Gloria a racist and a bigot and [said] she had no place talking about black women's lives and taking on the persona of a black woman. [Knox's colleague said that she] was there when people were getting lynched for voting, and how dare [Gloria] leave that out, it must not have meant anything to her." A startled Knox emailed the piece to a few of her African American friends to ask what they thought. They responded, "This is so insensitive and so devaluing and how dare she write this," remembered Knox. "The most painful ones were, 'This woman used to be my idol and now I hate her.' I was just like, 'Oh my god, this is bad.'"

Knox was particularly devastated because Steinem had often urged her to reach beyond her own white, college-educated perspective, to research how her cause, sex education, affected women of different colors and classes. "She was always talking about the inter-connectedness of oppressions," said Knox. "She says you can't be feminist without being antiracist. We had these conversations long before this op-ed was ever written." Knox, an emotionally transparent sparkplug, said over and over again how much she adored Steinem. "She gave me a home," she told me. "She is like my grandmother." Knox recalled watching Steinem on *Democracy Now:* "I watched it and I screamed at the TV for Melissa Harris-Lacewell to lay off, because I kept thinking of a dog fight. It's like you've already gotten her in the throat so many times, will you lay off? And Gloria didn't fight back." When Steinem returned home that night, Knox recalled, "she looked seventy-five, which is saying something, for Gloria to look her age. She physically looked devastated. And she said, 'I just can't believe that all of it leads up to this.'" Steinem told me later that after her appearance she thought, "I never should have gone on. I never do debates, and that's what it got turned into. It's crazy and bad for the movement for two women who agree on the issues and will both be for Obama in the general election to look as if we're opposed."

Soon, as Knox remembered it, the narrative became about second-wave women being out of touch. "I kept seeing these comments by young women like, 'They should just die, they should just shut up,'" Knox said. "Gloria was like, 'This crazy idea that you can be a feminist without being antiracist, or that you can be antiracist without being a feminist—Is this what young women are going to think of us?' The entire time I'm going, 'Is this what young women are going to think of her?' I asked her to do this. I felt incredible guilt."

* * *

Just as the seal on acknowledging Hillary's gender had broken, so too was Obama's protective postracial layer thinning as people increasingly considered his race and began to interrogate more thoroughly the language of both his opponents and the media. In an interview with Fox News, Clinton, voicing her refrain that Obama's unifying dreams could be made manifest only by someone who knew how to work the system, illustrated her point by stating, "Dr. King's dream began to be realized when President Lyndon Johnson passed the Civil Rights Act of 1964, when he was able to get through Congress something that President Kennedy was hopeful to do . . . but it took a president to get it done." This factually sturdy observation was met with offense by many: Was she minimizing King's role in the civil rights movement, subordinating it to the power of a white man? George Packer argued in the *New Yorker* that Hillary's remarks about Johnson seemed simply to reflect her workmanlike perception that the job of being president was "more about pushing difficult legislation through a fractious Congress than it is about transforming society." But a *New York Times* editorial portrayed the statement as coming "perilously close to injecting racial tension into what should have been . . . an uplifting contest between the first major woman candidate and the first major African-American candidate" as well as to "the distasteful implication that a black man needed the help of a white man to effect change."

What had been a friendly and self-celebratory Democratic field was becoming increasingly charged. Every remark was freighted, every statement of support electrified by anxiety over race and gender.

Jehmu Greene, then thirty-five, had headed up women's outreach at the Democratic National Committee and was the former president of the youth voting group Rock the Vote. She planned to remain neutral in 2008 as she pursued a career as a television pundit on Fox News and CNN. With her background in youth voting, Greene was not surprised by Obama's Iowa win but was shocked by the resulting Hillary-hatred. "Something in me flipped," she said in 2009. "All that shit that started being thrown at her? I took it personally." Greene's plan to stay neutral dissolved; she declared herself a Hillary supporter. "I knew that in coming out for her publicly it would piss people off," said Greene, "but I didn't expect for it to be as personal as it was. The level of animus was definitely surprising. I felt more of the anger came from the fact that I was black, that as a black person I was supposed to put being black before being a woman."

After New Hampshire came the January 26 South Carolina primary. Bill Clinton had been let loose on the state, both because the race was more hotly contested than anyone imagined it would be and because of his history of persuasive power in the South, particularly with African American voters. But as it became evident that Obama was ahead in South Carolina, the former president began to behave erratically.

A year earlier the Clintons had joined Obama and a group of civil rights leaders to walk across the Edmund Pettus Bridge in Selma, Alabama, to commemorate 1965's "Bloody Sunday" march for voting rights. A photograph of the event showed Bill Clinton, holding his wife's hand at one end of the line of marchers, leaning forward, grinning madly at Barack Obama, who was grinning back at him from the other end. I kept a copy of the photo above my desk and captioned it "The Love That Dare Not Speak Its Name." Had it not been for Hillary's presidential ambitions, Obama might well have been Bill Clinton's dream candidate. In many ways Obama was the natural inheritor of Bill's legacy of hope and youth-fueled politicking; he had the elder candidate's way with crowds, his ability to connect. Obama was a young man, as Clinton had been, with a brilliant wife and partner. Bill had been dryly dubbed "our first black president" by Toni Morrison and had worked his whole life alongside and on behalf of African Americans. In another universe Bill might have attached himself to Obama's project and busted a gut to be booster and political papa to the man poised to become the *actual* first black president.

But their union was not meant to be. Hillary's campaign put Bill on the opposite side of the fence from Obama. Instead of being an heir to the Clinton legacy, Obama's mission was to overshadow and discredit it, precisely what the hyperdefensive former president most feared. Obama-loving voters of South Carolina were forcing Bill to reckon with the fact that he was losing his never-fail Bubba charm, either due to old age or because it had been usurped by another compelling politician. After all the consideration about whether Bill would be able to stand up to being upstaged by a woman, what perhaps riled him more was having his legacy toppled by another man. Or at least that's what it seemed like as Bill Clinton talked to reporters in Columbia, South Carolina, on the day of the primary. One asked him about John Kerry, a question he declined to answer, calling it "bait" to get him to say something he shouldn't. Someone else asked why it was taking two Clintons to compete with one Barack Obama. "That's just bait too," he wisely replied. But the reporter had touched a nerve about the limits of Bill's persuasive powers. He got mad. He got a little bit crazy. He said, for absolutely no good reason, "Jesse Jackson won in South Carolina twice, in eighty-four and eighty-eight, and he ran a good campaign. And Senator Obama's run a good campaign."

Bill was, technically, correct. Jesse Jackson had won South Carolina in 1984 and in 1988. But the clear subtext of his words was that Jackson had won South Carolina only because African Americans had voted for him, that Obama was about to do the same, and that because of this, South Carolina didn't really count. Clinton was racializing and thereby devaluing Obama's impending primary success, as surely as anyone had feminized and thereby devalued his wife's victory in New Hampshire.

South Carolina was a landslide for Obama. The morning after his primary victory, George Stephanopoulos asked him to respond to the former president's Jesse Jackson comparison, and Obama killed Bill softly, excusing his remark by noting, "That's his frame of reference . . . that's when he was active and involved and watching what was going to take place in South Carolina." Bill Clinton called Barack Obama black, and Barack Obama called Bill Clinton old. In what should have been the most exhilarating election in modern memory, nobody was having any fun and everyone was pissed off. Bill would go on to accuse the Obama campaign of having played up his comments. He told a Pennsylvania radio station in April, "They played the race card on me," and attempted to reframe the context of his remarks, claiming, "We were talking about South Carolina political history and this was used out of context and twisted for political purposes by the Obama campaign to try to breed resentment elsewhere. . . . Do I regret saying it? No. Do I regret that it was used that way? I certainly do. But you really got to go some to try to portray me as a racist."

Two weeks before Clinton's Jackson remarks an internal Obama campaign memo had leaked; it listed instances of suspect utterances from people associated with the Clinton campaign, from Hillary's King-Johnson comparison to Billy Shaheen's drug insinuations to Andrew Cuomo's egregious assertion that inexperienced politicians would not be able to "shuck and jive" through press conferences.

The memo was evidence that the Obama campaign was indeed tracking, and perhaps looking to capitalize on racially questionable comments coming from their opposition, a strategy that drove lots of Clinton supporters, sick of hearing about the squeaky-clean tactics of the Obama campaign, around several sharp bends. "I don't think I had been as angry about a political tactic as I was at what they did with Bill Clinton," said Jehmu Greene. "Bill Clinton is not a racist. To accuse someone who has done so much for the African American community . . . I'm tearing up when I think about it. The way they turned just the facts into being a racist remark is unforgivable."

A handful of sentences did not wipe out Bill Clinton's history of engagement with African Americans; Jackson himself claimed not to be offended by his friend's diminishment of his historic victories. But the fact that those sentences caused offense to many was something that Bill could not undo, and the harder he tried, the worse off he made it for himself. "There always comes a time when whatever it was that worked for you doesn't work anymore," said Gloria Feldt, former president of Planned Parenthood and a Clinton supporter. "Here was a man who had been called the first black president, and suddenly African Americans were turning on him. He reacted in all the wrong ways. It was very pathetic to see."

Margo Jefferson was surprised by the Jackson remark. "I have had people tell me that it was really not meant to be racially double-edged or to have a signifying subtext," she said. "Some black people have told me that. But I was surprised that he let himself get out of control to that extent." No one likes to think of themselves as a bigot, Jefferson continued, "particularly if they think of their lives as having been progressive lives. Is Bill Clinton a hardcore racist? No. Did he allow himself to make calculated or uncalculated racialist-slash-racist-tinged remarks? Yes. Does that suggest that—hello, we're in America—his racial attitudes are a bit more *complicated* than we think? Yes. That he secretly hates black people? No. That he secretly feels more comfortable when the power is in his hands? Yes, I dare say it does. Sometimes that old-fashioned word of my youth, 'prejudiced,' is very useful. People are filled with prejudices that mutate and expand and disappear. It's all so colored, no pun intended, and inflected."

☆ ☆ ☆

The focus on Clinton and Obama became more pointed; they were the clear front-runners, but they were so interested in speaking only to one another that during a debate in South Carolina John Edwards had to remind them that there was a third person on stage. Though both camps would have been loath to admit it, Hillary and Barack had a powerful political chemistry; their every interaction drew the eye. On January 30, a few days before Super Tuesday, which would comprise twenty-four Democratic primaries and caucuses, Edwards dropped out of the race. Despite the fact that his departure left me not knowing who to vote for, I stared in shivering disbelief at the television the next night, as two candidates emerged to debate each other for their party's nomination, neither of them a white guy.

People had lots of critical things to say about identity politics; voting for someone because of who they were and not what they believed was an unsettling proposition for most thinking people. But it also seemed that those who most loudly deplored the corrosive impact of identity politics tended to be those whose identities had been adequately represented in their governing bodies. When the choice between Clinton and Obama became binary, especially given that the policy differences between the two candidates remained minimal, there was practically no way that personal histories, resentments, identifications and rejections could not come to bear; the choice seemed to become unavoidably loaded, emblematic of not only who you agreed with, but of who you were.

In the days before Super Tuesday, 1,000 "Feminists for Peace," including Katha Pollitt, Barbara Ehrenreich and Susan Sarandon, signed a petition supporting Barack Obama. Other feminists, including Steinem, Robin Morgan, Christine Stansell and Blanche Wiesen Cook, shot back with a petition supporting Clinton. Perhaps the most peculiar declaration came from Vagina Monologist Eve Ensler and academic Kimberle Crenshaw, who assailed not Hillary Clinton but her supporters, whom they saw as stark "either/or" feminist bullies who "interrogate, chastise, second-guess and even denounce those who escape their encampment" by voting for Obama.

Margo Jefferson was among the Feminists for Peace. "I was very aware of it as a source of tension with all my friends," she said, "of having to explain my reasoning very carefully every step of the way. One of my biggest struggles was with a childhood black friend who was becoming very pro-Hillary just as I was becoming more pro-Obama. It brought out a lot of old grievances. At one point this friend and I found ourselves arguing over whether Elizabeth Cady Stanton or Frederick Douglass had been the greater betrayer!"

So sharp was the pain of making a choice between Clinton and Obama that superdelegate John Lewis, a Georgia congressman and veteran civil rights leader, said in an interview that his late February change of support from Clinton to Obama, a change his constituents were clamoring for, was more difficult than walking across the Edmund Pettus Bridge in 1965. "All I had to do in Selma in 1965 [was] to put on my trench-coat and my suit, my back-pack and walk and look straight ahead," he told the NBC reporter Andrea Mitchell, who responded, "But Congressman, you got your *head* beaten in. Your face was covered in blood." "This is tougher," he responded. "I'm dealing with friends. People that I love. People that I admire. Part of my extended family." Clinton surrogate Stephanie Tubbs Jones, a congresswoman from Ohio and chair of the House Ethics Committee who would pass away in August of 2008, told the *Washington Post,* "Shame on anyone who . . . put that kind of pressure on John Lewis. I'm not trying to be a martyr. I think Senator Clinton is the best candidate. And the beauty of the United States of America is you have the right to have your opinion, and I have the right to my opinion. . . . If I change my mind, it will be because Senator Clinton said, 'Stephanie, let's make a move.'" But even the narrative of African Americans experiencing pressure was charged and destructive. Danielle Belton wrote on her blog *The Black Snob* that the story line fed another kind of racist fantasy: "'Sweet Jesus! What will happen if these *crazy darkies* don't get their way? *They're attacking their own people for just wanting to practice Democracy.* . . . *By golly there will be RIOTS IN THE STREETS,'* they shriek, as if our 22 million population . . . will choose this, of all things, to go *Rodney King* over."

"It was the most stressful time in my life," said *Racialicous*'s Latoya Peterson. "Because it's one thing to take hits from the outside; it's another if you're taking hits from your own. All of the old

wounds between women of color and white women who are trying
to work together in feminism, who don't understand each other, it
all bubbled up to the surface and it got very very ugly. . . . It was a
complicated history." Peterson said she tried to keep her blogging
space as neutral as possible. "Some of my very good commenters left
because they felt like the space was hostile to women and to feminism, which is really horrible to hear. It started pitting ally against
ally. And it didn't heal. Obama was elected. But that undercurrent
of suspicion is still there."

The emotional and historic pulls were felt, in one way or another,
by most Americans. But those who got most intensely fetishized,
whose loyalties provoked the most curiosity, were black women.
There were pressures on them to announce a presidential preference
and to extrapolate from that choice which oppressed part of their
identity was more essential.

Carol Jenkins, a newscaster and the founding president of the
Women's Media Center, found herself being quizzed by CNN host
Rick Sanchez about, in her words, "What's worse—being black, or
being a woman?" When Jenkins tried to explain that both identities
had an impact on her, Sanchez pushed her to choose. In response she
wrote a piece called "The Invisible Majority," explaining that "Hillary Clinton's run for the presidency has crystallized our stark unfamiliarity with women. . . . Never has our mainstream media been
so insanely obsessive—acting like teenage boys . . . who don't know
what to do when a woman enters the room." It was also apparent that
a white woman and a black man competing for the biggest job in the
world "[didn't] yet translate into possibilities for a woman of color."

In some cases black women themselves presented their political
loyalties as statements of comparative identification. Newsweek's
Allison Samuels described how her grandmother, "equipped with
just a fifth-grade education, sent each of her eight daughters to college (and beyond). . . . I doubt if she knew there was a feminist
movement or ever heard the name Gloria Steinem." In her grandmother's lifetime, as well as in her own, Samuels continued, "race,
not gender, [was] the defining narrative": "I know that a woman
president would change the course of history, too, and many might
even argue that gender is far more of an albatross than race. That
just hasn't been my experience."

Jehmu Greene's perspective was the inverse. "Sexism is something I've had to deal with my entire career within the Democratic Party," she said. "Speaking specifically from an African American perspective, [black women] are the ones always doing the work [while black men] got all the credit for it, going back to the civil rights movement and to this day. Look at the articulate, inspiring elected officials who are black women, and their trajectory within the party, and compare that to a Barack Obama and it becomes very clear. Carol Moseley Braun, the late, great Stephanie Tubbs Jones, Maxine Waters—we toil away and get the work done and when a microphone is put in front of someone it is usually the black man."

Some women, including superdelegate Donna Brazile, dealt with the constant tugging with humor. Talking with Stephen Colbert, Brazile cracked, "Look, I'm a woman, so I like Hillary. I'm black, I like Obama. But I'm also grumpy, so I like John McCain."

Others were just irritated. Melissa Harris-Lacewell said, "Every time [reporters] would ask me 'Are you going to support him because he's black or her because she's a woman?' I wanted to call them back and say, 'Why don't you call the white guy and ask him, "Are you going to support her because she's white or him because he's a guy?"'"

* * *

In early March, as Clinton was about to get creamed in Mississippi, former vice-presidential candidate Geraldine Ferraro told a California newspaper, "If Obama was a white man, he would not be in this position. And if he was a woman of any color, he would not be in this position. He happens to be very lucky to be who he is. And the country is caught up in the concept."

Ferraro would later state that she was describing a simple electoral fact, that Obama was winning with the help of black votes. But her defensive assertion that had she been named "Gerard" she would not have been tapped by Walter Mondale in 1984 confirmed that she was also suggesting that there was something faddish about the country's sudden eagerness to consider, much less vote for, a black man for president. There *was* an undeniable excitement among some Democratic voters about the fact that Obama was black, and his campaign knew it. To pretend otherwise was disingenuous. The University of Pennsylvania professor of political science Adolph Reed would point out later, "[The] hysterically indignant reaction to Geraldine Ferraro's statement that much of Obama's success stems from the fact that 'the country is caught up in the concept' of a black candidacy [was] no different from the campaign's touting its 'historic' character." But at the same time, in the context of U.S. presidential history, for a white woman to suggest that any black man was "lucky" to be black was a distressing stretch. The implication was that Obama was benefiting from tokenism, that his race was helping him gain a victory he would not have earned had he been female or white.

The Obama campaign justifiably bore down on Ferraro, asking Hillary to repudiate her remarks and remove her from the Clinton campaign finance committee. Hillary said only that she did not agree with Ferraro and noted, "[Both my campaign and Obama's] have had supporters and staff members who've gone over the line, and we've had to rein them in." This was not enough for Obama's campaign manager, David Axelrod, who said in a conference call with reporters, "When you wink and nod at offensive statements, you're really sending a signal to your supporters that anything goes."

Her back against a wall, Ferraro resigned from the Clinton campaign, but then amplified her remarks about Obama, suggesting with increased vigor that he was not only benefiting from his blackness, but that she was being attacked because she was white. Soon Ben Smith at *Politico* found a *Washington Post* story from 1988 in which Ferraro had said, "If Jesse Jackson were not black, he wouldn't be in the race." As more people began calling her racist, Ferraro became more enraged and sounded increasingly . . . racist. "Every time the campaign is upset about something, they call it racist," she said. "I will not be discriminated against because I'm white. If they think they're going to shut up Geraldine Ferraro with that kind of stuff, they don't know me."

In this instance there were few who would defend Ferraro. "Personally, I think Geraldine Ferraro should have apologized," said Steinem in 2009. "I don't think she meant her comments to be taken that way. I have never discussed it with her, so I'm just supposing. But I do believe she should have apologized." Latoya Peterson remembered, "Again, it was, 'Oh I don't think that was racist.' It was just, you know, white. Okay, so it was somebody expressing white resentment? What do you want to call that? You want to call it racism now? You want to call it something prettier today? It's the same thing."

Geraldine Ferraro had grown up in an Italian neighborhood in Queens to become a history-making Democratic politician. Her track was arguably more difficult than that of many liberals born into liberal worlds: she had emerged from an insular and historically xenophobic community, from a culture and a generation with ingrained attitudes about gender, race and religion, to become a liberal congresswoman and a zealous advocate of reproductive freedom. Though much was made of her 1988 line about Jesse Jackson, no one cited a 1984 interview in which Barbara Walters asked her, "The American dream has always been that any young boy can grow up to be president. . . . Are you now the American dream?" Ferraro replied, "If I am, it's not a complete one. Not until you can take not only the gender and remove it or include it in that dream, but also race. When you do that, then the American dream will be complete." Now, in her later years, in the midst of a decade-long fight with cancer, speaking about Hillary Clinton, the only woman in the twenty-four years since her candidacy to compete for executive office, she said things that at best sounded bad—and, truthfully, *were* bad. When she was challenged about them, it was as though her career and her beliefs got obscured, and she fell backward, over a precipice and into old ways of talking about race.

"I got tied in by the Obama campaign on being racist, which I probably will go to my grave with and will never get over," Ferraro told me in a 2009 interview. "And I wasn't, obviously. What I said was not racist. If Hillary had drawn black women the way she drew other women, she would have won. Black women had two choices: race or gender. They went with race. As a mother, if I were a black woman, would I rather have my kids see a black get elected president of the United States? I would, quite frankly. I didn't think there was anything wrong with that. So when this [reporter] said to me, 'What do you think is going on?' I said, 'It's black voters.'" Ferraro was still smarting over what she believed were the Obama campaign's tactics. "They came out against Bill Clinton," she said. "Bill Clinton, who has done more work in this country for African Americans, and people of color throughout the world. To turn around and call him a racist . . . and then me. I was so stunned, because of my record and because of my family's record. . . . I mean, ethnic Italians could be a little tough, but *never* with race. Never with race. So when I heard this stupid-assed comment by [David Axelrod,] who knew me, because I had supported Carl McCall when he ran for governor of New York. I was so active in Freddy Ferrer's campaign when he ran for mayor. And to call me a racist . . . I was like a lunatic."

The controversy over Ferraro opened up a media conversation about racism that extended beyond Clinton's campaign to her supporters. Instead of examining the intolerance of a nation still run by white men, suspicions were trained on the racialized resentments of older white women, increasingly viewed as Clinton's base. As some women expressed growing perturbation both at the sexism they felt Hillary was facing and at the way her triumphs were being ignored while her opponent's victories were being heralded, they found, as Steinem had before them, that it was difficult to express lingering resentments about whose advancements had come first, and at what cost to others, without sounding deeply suspect. The more women pushed to draw attention to Clinton as women's hero, the more comparisons they made between what she was experiencing and what Obama was experiencing, the more awkward the position they found themselves in, both with African Americans who registered their racial resentments and with a generation of young white women dismayed to detect in their elders the traces of racialized exasperation or even intolerance.

"It felt like all the stuff you were afraid might be out there was being made explicit," said *Feministing*'s founder, Jessica Valenti, recalling one incident that shook her. Some Hillary-supporting women were preparing a press conference about media sexism; one of the organizers asked Valenti to participate. Scheduled to speak elsewhere, Valenti recommended another *Feministing* blogger, Jen Moseley. "Jen is black, and had written something about race politics in the election," said Valenti. "The woman got back to me and said, 'We're really not looking for someone who trumps race over gender.' I said, 'I'm not sure what you mean by that,' and she said, 'Well, we want someone who understands that sexism is worse than racism.'" Valenti informed her that *Feministing* probably wasn't the right group for them. "I tried to be diplomatic about it, saying, 'That's just not along our lines of thinking,'" said Valenti. "But she got really upset, and was like, 'Don't you see?' She was clearly hurt and thought I was a big idiot. And I thought she was kind of racist. So it was a tough moment. It was crazy and really sad."

Many older white female Hillary supporters also felt sad that in this historical moment their progressive ambitions to put a woman in the White House were being tarnished, that the sexist stereotypes increasingly applied to them—that they were bitter, angry, desperate—now also included suggestions of racism. When Barack Obama gave his widely lauded spring speech in Philadelphia about race, he cited examples of white racial insensitivity by invoking two specific people, Geraldine Ferraro and his own grandmother, the white woman who had raised him and had confessed to him that she sometimes felt afraid of black men when she passed them on the street. He did not make reference to Bill Clinton, Andrew Cuomo, Bill Shaheen, or Bob Johnson. He did not talk about George Wallace or Strom Thurmond or about George W. Bush, who had left the city of New Orleans to drown. Instead he selected two Americans who stood in for the demographic that was increasingly associated with Hillary support. Critics would accuse him of throwing his grandmother under the bus in this speech, but he was simply playing out a history that, in some senses, had already been written, bringing the painful animus of Elizabeth Cady Stanton and Frederick Douglass back to vivid life.

"Comments that have been made and the issues that have surfaced over the last few weeks reflect the complexities of race in this country that we've never really worked through, a part of our union that we have not yet made perfect," said Obama. "Understanding this reality requires a reminder of how we arrived at this point. As William Faulkner once wrote, 'The past isn't dead and buried. In fact, it isn't even past.'"

★ ★ ★

In late February a group of women's leaders, journalists and academics, including Gloria Steinem and Carol Jenkins, Beverly Guy-Sheftall and Johnnetta Cole, gathered in New York to discuss the "race-gender split" among feminists. Patricia Williams recounted the meeting in the *Nation,* calling it a kaffeeklatsch at which "old friends broke out the good china for a light breakfast of strong coffee, blueberry muffins and fresh-squeezed orange juice." "We did not want to see a repeat of the ugly history of the nineteenth century," wrote Williams, "when the failure of the women's movement to bring about universal adult suffrage metastasized into racial resentment and rift that weakened feminism throughout much of the twentieth century." How, this group wondered, had this remarkable election been so badly damaged by "media depictions of white women as the sole inheritors of the feminist movement and black men as the sole beneficiaries of the civil rights movement? . . . What happened . . . to the last four decades of discussion about tokenism and multiple identities and the complex intersections of race, gender, sexuality, ethnicity and class?" The group agreed, "Everyone needs to refocus on the big picture. . . . [We wondered] how . . . to reclaim a common purpose, a truly democratic 'we': we women of all races, we blacks of all genders, we Americans of all languages, we immigrants of all classes, we Latinas of all colors."

But the breakfast did not cut it for we feminists who were not yet middle-aged. "I wasn't there, and I don't think anyone under the age of forty was there," said Shelby Knox. "So that was a problem, a problem that I registered at the time." Valenti was even less sanguine about the meeting: "'My friends gathered over china to have orange juice?' I was like, 'Are you fucking kidding me with this?' They declared it over. They declared it resolved. It was like, you don't get to do that! You and four other people don't get to declare this conversation over! That's not how it works, you know?"

For Valenti, the expressed desire to come up with a unifying solution was itself symptomatic of the worldview of another generation. "There is such a powerful desire for this imaginary utopian feminist universe that just isn't ever going to exist," she said. "I think it would be weird if all women connected on some womanly level." She described conferences at which women "want to talk about their vaginal wisdom and their feminine spiritual power." "My mom wants that," Valenti said. "She was like, 'Oh, I want to go to the panel that's about listening to your feminine intuition.' That's part of how they came to feminism, was this idea that being women was truly special and different in a certain way. I get that that's where they're coming from. But it's not where I'm coming from, and I don't think it's where the future is going, especially when you think about issues about people who are transgendered. Your entire movement is built on the idea of womanhood, but a new generation is mucking up what it means to be a woman. Something has got to change."

For many, though, airing the angers of election season, uncovering some forgotten, or repressed, history and forcing people to question where they stood on issues of race and gender was not only necessary, but positive. "It made me very thoughtful about my assumptions," said Margo Jefferson. "You intellectually got a little shaken up, and that was useful. If you didn't get shaken up, then your rages and your bad moods would have just settled back in a more calcified way. Your language and your thinking had to get sharper and more textured. That, I felt, was a potentially very good thing."

Some of the discussions proved instructive, even in climes assumed to be progressive already. Kim Gandy, former NOW president, remembered one conversation within her organization: "The white woman was saying, 'Don't you want your daughters to know that they can do anything?' And the African American woman said, 'What you don't understand is that of course I want my daughter to feel she can do anything, but for me, this would be the first time that I could see someone like me in the White House. Maybe not as president, but in the White House. I could see a family that looks like mine in the White House.' That was a discussion changer. The woman who had been arguing for Hillary sort of stepped back and said, 'Okay.' That was a completely different way of looking at it for her, something she hadn't thought of."

Harris-Lacewell found herself considering how she talked about gender with her daughter. "Sometimes it would get intense and I would grumble, 'I hate Hillary.' And then I would say, 'Oh, wait a minute. I actually don't want you to hate Hillary,'" she said. "I didn't want my daughter to be hating girls. I read to her a book called *Grace for President,* because it was about a little girl of color. It helped me work through what we were doing by not supporting the women candidates. As empowering as it is for me to have Obama in office, he had to beat a girl to get there, and beat a girl again [in] Sarah Palin. So I am keenly aware of them, because our socialization around race and gender is still not there."

Valenti believed that the election offered young women, who perhaps were unaware of the rifts over race that had ensnared their mothers and grandmothers and who perhaps thought their own generation was beyond the tensions, a chance to "lay it all on the table and discuss it." Latoya Peterson agreed that there was relief in the midst of all the tension. "Finally it's all out in the open. All these things that they acted like we were over," she said. "The questions of 'Why are women of color so sensitive?' Well, because racist stuff happens! And then you all make excuses! *That's* what happens. *That's* why we're so paranoid, because you never know who is going to have your back. It was ugly and it was hard and it's sad. [But] I think it will promote progress. Eventually. Everybody's got to get over their hurt feelings first."

Though I thought I understood something of the racially fraught history of the second wave, the election offered many moments of revelation about contemporary tensions. The negative reaction to Steinem's op-ed was one of them. I read and liked the piece; it wasn't for weeks, perhaps months, that I came across the commentary from women who had been angered and hurt by it. Watching the episode of *Democracy Now* made me miserable, realizing how much of this conversation had swept by me. In this instance I was learning about the privileged white perspective on social progress not from a textbook, but by embodying it, gliding approvingly through Steinem's piece without a thought of the voices it ignored. My post facto realization of how flawed the essay was was confusing in itself: I continued to agree with what Steinem said, at the same time that I came to agree with even her harshest critics. It was a lesson in how there were no correct answers.

"The biggest thing when you're trying to be in solidarity with other people who are different from you," said Peterson, "the first thing you have to acknowledge is that there is so much that you don't know and that you will never know. A lot of people don't do that. They feel like because they've read something, because they've talked to a few people, they can say 'Oh, I understand the black experience. Oh, I get it.' You don't get it. You all miss all the nuances because it doesn't happen to you."

This was the lesson that Shelby Knox took away: "I learned that you can never speak *for*. You can speak *about,* but you can never speak *for,* and even if you have a forty-year history with interracial cooperation and you think you understand a black woman's experience, you're denying people's lived experience by speaking for them. It's hard for me even now to say that [Steinem] made a mistake. If she made any mistake it was probably embodying a black woman at the beginning of the piece. . . . I realized that in order to not repeat the mistakes of the women before us, of some in the second wave and definitely the first wave, silencing the voices of women of color . . . we have to step aside and invite people to speak for themselves."

Steinem herself would later write about her unwilling debate with Harris-Lacewell, "Though at moments, I felt as if forty years of effort to link issues were going down the drain, even this human contact may have been better than none; I think we ended up on microscopically better terms than we began." She cheered herself up, she wrote, by conjuring the memory of her friend and lecture partner, the late Florynce Kennedy. "Flo would have found a purpose even in conflict," wrote Steinem. "I could hear her voice giving one of her wise lessons: 'The purpose of ass-kicking is not that your ass gets kicked at the right time or for the right reasons. It's that it keeps your ass *sensitive.*' . . . Suddenly, the hard things of the recent past had a purpose, and they weren't so hard anymore."

Valenti recalled seeing Steinem speak at a conference after the primaries: "I think the election must have made a real impression on her. All she was talking about was race. I was like, *damn.* She was *great.* Before that, I had never heard any mainstream feminists own up to the fact that the second wave was—not necessarily explicitly racist, but that it was a white, upper-middle-class straight woman's movement. Or that that's who got the most attention. The only people I heard talking about that were younger feminists or academic feminists. When I saw Gloria talking about all this stuff, I felt so heartened, not for her, but for me. Because she's fucking Gloria Steinem. She can say whatever she wants, right? But she's obviously still learning. That's a pretty great thing, especially in a movement that seems to be overwhelmingly stagnant on a lot of things. It was good for me to see someone who was obviously affected by this experience and has changed her tune a little bit. Like I can do the same thing."

6 ALL ABOUT THEIR
MOTHERS

DECIDING WHO TO vote for in the primary might have been easier if it hadn't been for my mother. Unsentimental, her politics listing left of Hillary's, my mom seemed barely interested in Hillary Clinton. I laughed when my friend Merideth brusquely chided me for my Edwards support by asking, "Are you going to call your mother and ask her permission to vote against Hillary?" It had never crossed my mind that my mother would care a whit if I voted for Hillary, let alone that she might vote for her herself. So I was floored when, the day after Iowa, I picked up the phone to hear her say, "I'm very sad." When I asked why, she replied, "Whether or not it's Hillary, any woman who is aggressive enough to make a go of it is going to be too aggressive to be likable."

The sentiment rattled around in my head for the weeks between Iowa and Super Tuesday, when I would cast my vote in New York. My mother's discouragement, which I think surprised her as much as it did me, was a reminder of how Clinton was lugging around questions about the future and remembrances of the past as she hauled herself from state to state. It was also my window on what was about to become a media fixation: the generation gap between women when it came to Hillary Clinton.

I had been resisting the idea that Clinton's presidential bid was a once-in-a-lifetime opportunity for women. I was confident that there would be many more female presidential candidates coming down the pike. But many older women clearly found this sort of optimism infuriating. They saw my generation's lack of enthusiasm for Clinton as naïve complacency. Sure, I knew that it was well past time for a female president, but I assumed that there would be loads more satisfactory models to choose from in the future. My mother created a flicker of worry that this was perhaps a careless bet. Her sadness, along with the torrent of ill-disguised resentment unleashed at Clinton since Iowa, shook some of the breeziness out of me, made me feel flashes of guilt for not having stood up for Hillary from the start.

But you don't vote for a candidate out of guilt. And you don't vote because your mother calls you. As primary day approached I didn't know what to do with these percolating qualms or, for that matter, with my political impulses. I had never had trouble articulating what I believed, but for the first time in my life I did not know what I believed. I did not know who to vote for.

I was not alone. *Feministing*'s founder Jessica Valenti told me two years after Super Tuesday, "Up to the day, I considered not voting at all. I didn't even know that I could do it. It was horrible. Horrible." Valenti, whose site did not endorse either candidate, finally voted for Obama. "But it was rough," she said. "I was not happy afterwards."

Valenti's experience was so like my own, and so different from Geraldine Ferraro's, who told me in 2009, "I didn't cry when I voted for myself [in 1984], but I went into that booth and I looked at [Hillary's] name . . . I'm beginning to well up now thinking about it. It felt like Susan B. Anthony was standing beside me saying, 'Pull that lever.' Which sounds so stupid. But I felt the struggle [for women's rights], and it just smashed me."

I would have given anything to feel that conviction, but I simply didn't. It was humiliating to be undecided in the weeks, days, hours before the first primary in my memory in which my vote would make one iota of difference. John Edwards's disappearance from the race had shown me that supporting him, while in general accordance with my political beliefs, had also provided a cop-out. Had I been able to vote for Edwards I would not have had to get my hands dirty by choosing between two similar candidates whose differences increasingly seemed to swirl around their race and gender. I would not have had to admit, or even consider, the role my gender and my feminist politics might have in my decision making. Now I had to face Hillary Clinton. Alas, she was my destiny.

I felt the pull of Obamamania, had considered how thrilling it would be to see the country come alive with excitement for a young person, a man beholden to few in Washington, who had lived around the world and took a reasoned approach to foreign policy. When I ran my own (useless, inevitable) calculus of oppression, I concluded that in the United States, race (especially when combined with class) remained a more formidable barrier to political and economic parity than gender. That meant that on some level, Clinton stood in for all those pushy white broads, the ones who were coming to steal college admissions letters and seats in Congress from the white men to whom they had historically belonged, while Obama could more comfortably be regarded as an exceptional black man, not the harbinger of a larger threat to established power. If Hillary's success was less exceptional—and there were certainly fewer African Americans of either gender in federal elected office than there were women—did she deserve my vote as much as Barack did?

But here was the part that I had been trying to ignore: Hillary Clinton was a woman, and so was I. I knew that my president didn't have to look like me, any more than she had to be a person I wanted to have a drink with, but I couldn't pretend that it didn't mean something to me, something more important than I'd realized, that we had never had one who looked like me before. Oddly, this realization didn't galvanize me as much as it gave me pause. However much I protested that I would never vote for someone just because she was a woman, I was realizing that a vote for Hillary would be an emotional decision as well as an intellectual and political one. And if that were true, then I would be conforming to every dismissive assumption about why and how women vote, fulfilling a feminized and thus devalued expectation of Democratic womanhood.

The morning of Super Tuesday I was reporting on primary voters at the ticker-tape parade for the Giants, who had just won the Super Bowl, when I came upon Brian Murray from Long Island, a young fan who had his fists in the air, frozen as if they'd been there since the last dramatic moment of the big game. I asked him if he was planning to vote. "No way," he said, lowering his arms. "But I wouldn't vote for Hillary Clinton, if that's what you were going to ask." I hadn't been going to ask. Brian and I blinked quizzically at each other for a moment. "I bet you voted for her, right?" he said. I didn't respond. I did not want to be the girl that everyone, from Obama-supporting progressives to a politically apathetic Giants fan, assumed I was, the one who chose the woman in part because she was a woman.

In fact, a few hours earlier, with a few final clicks of the levers and the pull of the big metal bar, I had emerged from the booth a shaky but now official Hillary Clinton supporter. I actually assumed my new identity would be short-lived. As the East Coast polls began to close on Super Tuesday it seemed likely that this would be the night that had been forecast since the Iowa caucus, the night that the senator from Illinois would halt Clinton's drive to the White House. When I walked into the grand ballroom of the Manhattan Center Studios that night to report on Clinton's Election Night celebration, the mood was practically funereal.

But when the first results showing Clinton leading in Massachusetts and New Jersey began to appear on the screen, the listless party began to swell and sway. The crowd, liberally studded with young people and with black and brown faces, cheered and yelped the news that Clinton had won Massachusetts, the state that liberal legend Ted Kennedy and 2004 candidate John Kerry had tried to secure for Obama by making surprise endorsements. "We know how badly Senator Kennedy and Senator Kerry wanted that state," Jonathan Mantz, Clinton's finance director, told me over the din. "The fact that we're winning it is very gratifying." It was gratifying in precisely the same way Clinton's New Hampshire win had been: after all the months of being treated as the establishment candidate, Hillary was being revealed as an outsider, providing thrills by escaping the fate to which the real establishment—guys who ran the media, guys who ran the Senate—was trying to consign her.

Clinton's Super Tuesday address was closer to lyrical than any she'd given to that point, full of rhythmic invocations of those Americans "on the day shift, on the night shift, on the late shift with the crying baby . . . all those who aren't in the headlines but who have always written America's story." There was also an increasingly progressive aura about her as she talked up the rebuilding of the American infrastructure and revamping of the GI Bill of Rights.

Clinton was learning, a little late, about establishing herself as part of a narrative of social progress. Early exit polling showed that once again it was women voters who were enabling her respectable showing, and she tipped her hat to them by mentioning her own mother, "who was born before women could vote and is watching her daughter on this stage tonight."

☆ ☆ ☆

> *I cannot wait, 'til 2008*
> *Baby, you're the best candidate*
> *Up in the Oval Office*
> *You'll get your head of state*
> *I can't leave you alone*
> *'Cause I've got a crush on Obama*

So went the hook of a brain-eating ditty that lit up the Internet in 2007. The viral *Obama Girl* video starred a pneumatic twenty-six-year-old model, Amber Lee Ettinger, who swung her hip-hugger Obama panties to the beat and presented America with its first vision of what youthful female support of Barack Obama looked like. Though the clip was meant to be comedic, the vision of Ettinger boogying in her bikini, inviting Obama to "Barack [her] tonight," came terribly close to how the media would portray one half of a generational divide among Democratic women: Obama Girls were the postfeminist sylphs who had fallen for Barack and cared not a bit for the earnest politics of their forebears, angry, punishing harpies who did not dance in their underwear but shook their pruny fists as young women rejected not just Hillary, but them, and the women's liberation they had given their lives for.

These characterizations reflected the wishful thinking of a

media hungry for any tale that might involve both a catfight and the implosion of feminism. But a white male press could not fairly be blamed for imposing a self-serving template on this tale of generational strife. Responsibility fell squarely at the feet of the ladies themselves, women on both sides of the generational chasm, who were airing their shrill differences and infusing them with a desperate gravity, as if they had been spoiling for a fight for years. In fact, they had been, and their conflicts had very little to do with Hillary Clinton, but swirled instead around the future and what remained of the women's movement.

From many angles the old-versus-young setup was grossly exaggerated. The briefest scan of any Clinton rally turned up teenage girls cheering for Hillary with a force that threatened to pop their heads off their bodies, high school guys offering restrained applause, demure twentysomething couples listening attentively. Even Obama Girl Amber Ettinger confessed that she was "very impressed with Hillary Clinton. . . . I watched the recent debates and I liked a lot of her answers." There were plenty of middle-aged women—including the well-known writers and pundits Barbara Ehrenreich, Katha Pollitt, Eve Ensler and Arianna Huffington—flocking to the Obama campaign. But the nuanced story was not as much fun to tell as the one in which the young women of America were thoughtlessly brushing off not only Hillary Clinton but with her their commitment to female political empowerment.

It was also true that throughout the primary season young people, including young women, turned out in unprecedented numbers to vote for Barack Obama, while Hillary's most reliable base consisted of white women over forty. The reasons for this dynamic began with the fact that the Clinton campaign was not good at addressing young people and the Obama campaign was great at it. If John and Elizabeth Edwards had been prescient in hiring bloggers as a way into the netroots, then Obama's use of technology, from blogs to Facebook to text messaging, was masterful. Obama did not assume that young voters were consuming the same culture or watching the same news that their parents were. He went to where they lived, where they socialized, to their phones and to their college campuses.

Jehmu Greene, who as president of Rock the Vote until 2005 was a specialist in youth voting, said, "He was doing all the right things that for the past ten years of my career we had been trying to convince candidates to do." Under-thirty voters had been regarded as unreliable, not worth the resources it took to reach them, ever since George McGovern's 1972 presidential hopes were undone when the young idealists who had made him the Democratic nominee failed to show up for him on Election Day. Most candidates, in Greene's words, assigned youth outreach to "some ghettoized cubicle" at campaign headquarters.

Barack Obama knew he could not rely on already registered Democrats, who appeared more likely to vote for Clinton, and so he took a chance on wooing new voters. Realizing that the Internet had reinvented the possibilities of political participation and provided candidates with a way of speaking directly into the ears of the young, his team made young people an integral part of its grassroots approach.

Greene said in retrospect that if Clinton's team "had targeted young women and incorporated them into their organizing efforts the way the Obama campaign did, she would have had way more support." The Clinton campaign instead took the traditional skeptical view of young voters, communicating with them tepidly and ineptly. Greene told me in 2009 of how the campaign had reacted when she'd called to offer her help after Clinton's Iowa loss. The thirty-five-year-old most recent president of Rock the Vote, an African American woman who had been in charge of women's outreach for the DNC from 1998 to 2000 and a former associate of Terry McAuliffe, Greene was precisely the kind of person Clinton's team should have been all over. The campaign could not seem to figure out what to do with her. "I ended up having to reach out to them I don't know how many times to say 'I want to *help*!'" Greene recalled. "'You have a *problem* with young people! This is my *expertise*!' It took a while for them to come around." Though Greene first contacted the Clinton campaign the day after the Iowa caucus in January, they did not officially announce her endorsement of Hillary or deploy her as a surrogate until mid-February, more than six weeks and many contests later.

Clinton often tipped her hat to the pre-Nineteenth-Amendment nonagenarians attending her rallies in wheelchairs. Only after her much derided Iowa concession speech, at which she was shown on television surrounded by a crowd of disconsolate dinosaurs, had her campaign cottoned to the fact that she had a little generational problem.

In the weeks before Super Tuesday Clinton engaged her deeply private twenty-seven-year-old daughter to speak at campuses. Chelsea was perhaps the sturdiest of all Hillary's personal credentials, and so effective a stand-in for her mom that, as the *New York Times* reported, at an hour-long February appearance at the University of Wisconsin–Eau Claire she nimbly held forth on "Medicare Part D, the distinction between the chronically and occasionally uninsured, health care premium caps, Pell grant allowance maximums, income contingency repayment programs for financial aid, sugar-based ethanol and carbon sequestration . . . Romanian reproductive policy and the design of the internal combustion engine." Oh, the Tracy Flick genes were strong, and Chelsea was a whiz.

But she could not compete with Obama, who had been beguiling undergrads for more than a year with limpid lines like "I've become a vehicle for your hopes and your dreams, but I can only carry it so far. . . . It's going to be you who carry it forward." He meant it, and he was proved right. The Obama campaign was so grassroots that kids themselves were self-starting campaign initiatives, making their own buttons and pamphlets. Clinton still shipped in the machinery from out of town.

In March, the young feminist Shelby Knox was dismayed when she arrived in her hometown of Lubbock as a Clinton volunteer and found no Clintonites in sight. Meanwhile, she said, "there were Obama supporters from the college on every street and Obama signs everywhere." A speaker at colleges around the country, Knox knew that there was an eager youthful following for Clinton, but when she walked into campaign headquarters "it was literally all older white women from out of town." The women explained that their unfamiliarity with Lubbock meant they weren't sure which thoroughfares to populate. Knox marshaled the feminist alliance from Texas Tech University, asking them, "Regardless of your political beliefs, can you please help me?" With her hastily recruited collegiate volunteers she canvassed Lubbock, holding signs for Hillary. Hillary wound up winning Lubbock, but as Knox learned, "Hillary campaigns around the country were being run by older white women, which was so unfortunate."

Younger women were there for the asking; it's just that nobody, besides Barack Obama, was asking. Worse, Hillary's older supporters were choosing to *tell* young women, in no uncertain terms, exactly what they thought of their electoral loyalties.

That the Clinton campaign was failing to seek out or address women under thirty did not seem to figure into the estimations of older Clinton supporters, who quickly worked themselves into high dudgeon over the perfidy of the next generation.

Steinem was gingerly dismissive with the sentence in "Women Are Never Front-Runners" that Knox had first objected to: "What worries me is that some women, perhaps especially younger ones, hope to deny or escape the sexual caste system; thus Iowa women over 50 and 60, who disproportionately supported Senator Clinton, proved once again that women are the one group that grows more radical with age."

Evoking an only slightly more cerebral version of the writhing Obama Girl, Steinem's characterization was doubly perplexing to young people who could not sense anything radical at all in Hillary Clinton. She was not selling herself as a history-making barrier buster or as an inheritor of a bold social project. Even as she absorbed more of John Edwards's populist message and economic policy ideas, she was still being cast as the conservative, allowing Obama to wear the progressive mantle as he coasted on his uncast war vote and allowed the young liberals he was so assiduously courting to project their every progressive fantasy onto his comparatively blank slate.

Steinem's discouraging take was polite compared to the can of censorious second-wave whup-ass that her Women's Media Center colleague Robin Morgan was about to open on young women. Morgan, then sixty-seven, had been a member of New York Radical Women and Women's International Terrorist Conspiracy from Hell (or W.I.T.C.H.). Sometimes credited with coining the phrase "The personal is political," Morgan in 1970 composed the blistering, movement-defining manifesto "Goodbye to All That," a venomous adieu to what she viewed as the sexism of left-wing male politics. On the day before the Super Tuesday primaries she published "Goodbye to All That #2" on the WMC website. This time she was not gunning for the liberal male establishment; she was gunning for everyone, *everyone* who was not supporting Hillary Clinton, taking particular aim at her jejune counterparts.

The piece had all of the retro flair of Steinem's op-ed with little of the insight. "Good-bye to a misrepresented generational divide," Morgan wrote, before ensuring that that divide was about to get a lot starker. "Goodbye to some young women eager to win male approval by showing they're not feminists (at least not the kind who actually threaten the status quo), who can't identify with a woman candidate because she is unafraid of eeueweeeu yucky power, who fear their boyfriends might look at them funny if they say something good about her." To those benighted young women, Morgan delivered from on high a famous statement by Harriet Tubman: "I could have saved thousands—if only I'd been able to convince them they were slaves."

Morgan would go on to tell the *New Yorker*'s Ariel Levy that the publication of the piece elicited more than eight hundred emails a day, and that only one in fifty were negative. That seemed a low estimate, given how many young women failed to warm to Morgan's characterizations of them as boyfriend-pleasing, power-averse dopes who didn't recognize their own servitude and used the word *yucky*.

"This is all incredibly offensive to me—not because of who I support in the presidential primary, but because of who I am, a younger *feminist* woman," wrote Ann Friedman at *Feministing*. "This crap is merely annoying when it comes from the mainstream media. It's *really* disappointing and hurtful when it comes from within the women's movement."

Jessica Valenti said in 2009, "[Censure from Morgan and her compatriots] was hardest because all of your fears about what older feminists thought about you were made extremely explicit. They just think I'm a mommy-hating idiot who's voting for Obama because my boyfriend is." Because *Feministing* did not support a candidate, Valenti said the site was inundated with hate mail from older women. "Ideologically there was a rift, because theirs was the idea that you have to support Hillary because she's a woman and if you don't that's not feminist."

This was the heart of the complaints about young women: they did not realize to what degree their gender was an impediment to parity, and had not considered that having a female leader would create a trickle-down effect that would empower all women. "Younger people don't get how the impact of having a woman in that particular office will have an impact throughout the world," said Geraldine Ferraro in 2009.

Michelle Goldberg, a young feminist and fervent Obama supporter, hit back at her elders and indulged in some generational characterizations of her own in a piece in London's *Guardian*. Calling Morgan's essay "a hysterical screed accusing female Obama supporters of being, essentially, blinkered bimbos," she bemoaned the fact that "otherwise admirable, even heroic women seem to identify with Clinton so profoundly that they interpret rejection of her as a personal rebuke," and in their responses were "lashing out in all kinds of counterproductive ways, doing far more damage to feminism than a Clinton loss ever could."

The hard truth, Goldberg asserted, was that the majority of young Democratic women were supporting Obama. "Maligning and disparaging them is no way to recruit them into a movement," she wrote. "[And] the more leaders of the movement insist on conflating their noble struggle for social justice with the fate of an uninspiring and nepotistic candidate, the less relevant [second-wave feminism] will be. Many progressives . . . see Clinton as cynical and narcissistic, pandering to interest-group sectarianism even as she compromises on important principles. It would be a hideous shame if they came to see feminism the same way."

But Clinton diehards continued to conflate support for their candidate with feminism itself, and to vilify anyone who opposed her. In February fifty-seven-year-old Marcia Pappas, the president of NOW's New York chapter, fired off a press release in which she called Massachusetts Senator Ted Kennedy's endorsement of Obama "the ultimate betrayal" of women and an "abandonment." Many feminist bloggers, and even other chapters of NOW, promptly repudiated Pappas's comments; *Feministing*'s Ann Friedman called the release "unhinged." The *New York Times* used the fracas as a peg for a column by Susan Dominus about escalating generational conflict between feminists, embodied by Pappas and Jessica Valenti.

The title of the *Times* piece was "Feminists Find Unity Is Elusive," a headline that could have run at any time in the past fifty years, or even the past hundred and fifty. The myth of a feminist monolith—some accredited synod that takes away your disposable razor and issues you a gift card for two free abortions—had been used against women's rights activists for years, by critics from Phyllis Schlafly to Rush Limbaugh to Katie Roiphe, antifeminists eager to paint themselves as gallant heretics, charging the forbidding fortress of the women's movement. In truth feminism was, at its cohesive best, a loose banner hoisted by women of different colors, classes, sexual identities, professional ambitions and religious affiliations, who sometimes managed to put their tussling aside to work for a shared goal; at its cannibalistic worst, it was a self-destructive mash-up of competing priorities and identities.

The story of the roiling, ever-evolving debate within feminist circles was as old as feminism: the National Woman Suffrage Association versus the American Woman Suffrage Association, womanism versus feminism, Betty Friedan versus The Lavender Menace, Betty Friedan versus Gloria Steinem, Catharine MacKinnon versus Ellen Willis. But for some in the media, hope sprang eternal that this would be the moment that the loose-knit coalition might unravel for good. The generational resentments made public during the primaries had been simmering for a long time. The election simply turned up the flame and made those resentments public.

For years Valenti and her cohort had been chafing against the older women who represented and ran institutional feminism, organizations like NOW, NARAL, Planned Parenthood, the Feminist Majority. According to many young women who began their careers banging on the doors of these umbrella organizations, institutional feminism treated them with the kind of disrespect against which women of the 1970s had bucked and strained. The young women did not feel listened to; they felt judged for their short skirts, as if their elders could not look past their piercings to their brains.

"The main reason I founded *Feministing*," Valenti told me in 2009, "was because I was working for a women's organization, and there was all of this lip service being paid to how important younger women were to the movement, but no one really wanted to hear what we had to say. They wanted us for photo-ops, and on their young feminist advisory boards that had no real power. When push came to shove, they were not interested in our opinions."

Valenti started *Feministing* not long before the April 2004 March for Women's Lives, a massive event that offered ample evidence that older feminists coveted young blood but didn't know what to do with it once they got it. I covered that march for *Salon*, and the feeling there was that a decades-old carapace of backlash had cracked. Tens of thousands of young women showed up, their faces open and expectant. I watched women in their twenties swarm a golf cart carrying an aged Betty Friedan, and saw one nearly pass out from excitement upon meeting Gloria Steinem. "Oh my god! I love you!" she gasped. The gamine crowd went nuts when Hillary Clinton made a surprise appearance. Here they were, aligning themselves with their elders, anxious to throw their fists in the air and be a part of the largest gathering of women since 1992, the year Hillary arrived in Washington and the unprecedented election of four women to the Senate made it the Year of the Woman.

Organizers had crowed happily as they gazed upon the sea of young faces, but could offer the juvenescent crowd only well-intentioned but sad displays of paleofeminism. *Cagney & Lacey*'s Tyne Daly and Sharon Gless, Wonder Woman Lynda Carter, *One Day at a Time*'s Bonnie Franklin and *Moonlighting*'s Cybill Shepherd ensured that there was full representation of television's primetime line-up from early 1980s. Ashley Judd, the Indigo Girls and *Saturday Night Live*'s Ana Gasteyer nudged the median age of entertainment acts toward forty, but what was there for anyone in their twenties? Heaping piles of condescension.

Whoopi Goldberg brought a hanger on stage with her, saying in an almost accusatory voice, "You understand me, women under thirty? This is what we used!" It was an attempt at communication, but it came out sounding like she was scolding a generation for its privilege, when that privilege was actually a right, a right that women had fought for and won, ensuring that the next generation might take it for granted. On the Metro the night before the march I'd overheard a young man in low-slung jeans ask what a coat hanger stood for. "That's how women used to get abortions," his young female companion replied. "Haven't you ever seen *Dirty Dancing*?" This was the world that the activists who organized the march had made, one in which comprehension of the atrocities of illegal abortion came via sixteen-year-old movies.

The women who had banished those hangers from the contemporary consciousness were not sure that forgetting they had existed was such a good idea. In part their distress was human: a keening desire for recognition, for appreciation and for credit due a generation that, as the columnist Gail Collins would suggest in a 2009 book, had changed *everything* for women.

Aging must have brought its own frazzled anxiety, creeping fears of irrelevance and invisibility, of not wanting to go softly anywhere, for the lives they lived had been loud. From this came the agitation and annoyance with young women: Would they treat so carelessly the freedoms their predecessors fought so hard for? Would they forget them? Would they undo them? The young ones, after all, were lucky, spoiled, their paths cleared by those who whacked through thickets of resistance. Older women sometimes sounded angry that young women's lives were easier than theirs had been, that they could afford to have more fun with their feminism, with their power, with their opportunities. Now those whippersnappers were going to push their worn-out progenitors aside just at the moment they might have taken their triumphant presidential bow.

This made some fanatical about Hillary in ways they would not otherwise have been. NOW's Kim Gandy, a strong Hillary supporter, remembered the surprise she felt watching some fervently liberal women who had sat out previous elections because the Democratic candidate was imperfect on issues like same-sex marriage or the war. When it came to Hillary, though, they were forgiving. "The hard-liners became apologists!" Gandy recalled. "They gave Hillary a pass. The historical commitment to seeing a woman president overrode everything." Gandy tried to reason with some of them, to remind them, "If you think she's going to make the ERA the number one priority as president, you're crazy." But for those who had given their hearts to Hillary there was no reasoning. "They wrote all their hopes and dreams on her, in the same way that other feminists who didn't support her wrote their fears on her."

This wasn't just about politics or policy. It was about mortality. "Older women felt this was their last chance to see a female president," Steinem pointed out in 2009, "and younger women knew they would have another chance." The sense that time was running out strengthened the older generation's identification with Hillary, a woman they thought was being pushed off-stage too soon. As Leslie Bennetts wrote, "Not only is Clinton well beyond the age when our culture deems women to have lost most of their value, but so are all too many of her supporters—and there are few things this country is less interested in than aging women." Robin Morgan's screed asked even more directly, "How dare *anyone* unilaterally decide when to turn the page on history, papering over real inequities and suffering constituencies in the promise of a feel-good campaign? . . . We are the women who changed the reality of the United States. And though we never went away, brace yourselves: *we're back!*"

They wanted so badly to be back, to lay claim to the most public, emblematic, political victory, and instead they were being reduced to carping mommies, the role they had worked so hard to break out of. In February Letty Cottin Pogrebin, one of the founders of *Ms.* magazine and a devout Clinton supporter, appeared on PBS with her adult Obama-supporting daughter, Abigail. "When a woman finally deserves to be where she is, somebody comes in and undercuts her," Cottin Pogrebin explained, while Abigail made the (dubious) claim that she had never experienced sexism growing up, in part *because* she was raised in a feminist environment. Cottin Pogrebin echoed Marcia Pappas's bathetic language when telling host Maria Hinojosa that Abigail's "abandoning Hillary" was a very serious thing, adding that younger women choosing Obama "hurts." Abigail ended the interview by wailing "Mommy!" in an effort to get Letty to stop kvetching at her about Hillary. It was all faintly embarrassing.

Perhaps because many of these conversations were taking place at kitchen tables, between actual mothers and daughters, women on both sides of the divide gave in to the impulse to lay out their differences about Hillary on the mother-daughter framework. Conversations were shot through with echoes of mothers who yearned for gratitude, or just the assurance that their children would be able to take care of themselves once they were gone. For many of the senior combatants there was a fear that younger women, so flip about the feminism that had landed them in law school and board meetings, would allow a roll-back that would condemn their own daughters to car pools and vacuuming.

Writing in *Slate,* the firebrand Linda Hirshman pondered the possibility that young women were supporting Obama as a way of flipping off their mothers, citing the respected young author Court-ney Martin, who had confessed one of the reasons she was not sup-porting Clinton: "Because she reminds me of being scolded by my mother." Hirshman also cited a piece of mine, in which I wrote that the pressure from elder feminists was like being told that I had "some kind of ovarian, fallopian responsibility" to vote for Hill-ary. "I suppose I must offer the obligatory reassurance that neither all women nor even all feminists need to march in lockstep to the polls to vote for Hillary Clinton," Hirshman wrote. "But I want to amplify that with the additional caution that *just because your mother did it does not make it wrong.*"

Hirshman had a beef with the next generation that would extend beyond the election. In 2009 she launched an attack on *Jezebel,* a blog aimed at young women, noting that although "from a certain perspective, the *Jezebel* writers look a lot like the natural heirs of feminism," their propensity to revel in their sexual emancipation by flaunting erotic triumphs and misfortunes, all in the name of good fun and an aversion to victimhood, contributed to an erosion of feminist principles. "Feminism was never only a liberation move-ment," Hirshman wrote. "It was a claim that liberation would open up a better life to women, a life of meaningful work and satisfying sexual relationships (among other things)."

Hirshman told me in 2010 that she had been initially thrilled to discover the feminist energies of the web, and believed young logged-on women to be rigorous political thinkers. "But then I started reading the blogs day in and day out," she said, "and [I saw] an absence and indeed a rejection of political thinking." Hirsh-man didn't object to the sexual focus of young feminist bloggers: "There was a tremendous amount of writing about our sex lives in the 1970s. But it was about how we wanted to have orgasms. How we wanted to try out our sexual partners before we committed to them for a lifetime. These are selfish things and the beginning of all politics." What she saw on the blogosphere was a self-interest of a different sort—personal revelation without much thought about the collective good of women. "It was the utter absence of the fundamental rules of social-movement politics: that you act collectively, identify your interest, and put it first."

The feminist journalist Debra Dickerson took a slightly less cerebral approach to her criticism of youthful activism, writing after the election, "Today's feminists need to blog less and work more."

Gripes about the feminist blogosphere were, from many perspectives, dead-on. The Internet featured an extreme openness about sex—good sex, bad sex, straight sex, gay sex, sex work and sex toys—indicating that feminism's inheritors believed that the personal was worth posting. Feminist bloggers treated their revelations with a crassness and nonchalance that sometimes seemed at odds with their serious-minded critiques about body image and objectification. Bloggers had a way of having it both ways, of firing off biting posts about the ill treatment or sexualized diminution of a female politician or actor at the same time that they published provocative photos of themselves or described sex acts—sometimes disempowering ones—in graphic detail. The self-exposure and self-celebration had all the hallmarks of a narcissistic Internet; it betrayed both an intellectual inconsistency and an eagerness to abandon the appearance of political self-seriousness. It was a transparent effort to contradict rusty but still damaging stereotypes of feminists as sexless succubi. And it made many second-wavers crazy. *Feministing*'s logo was the image of a mud-flap girl. Didn't these women know how hard their predecessors had worked to escape the mud-flap girl? But young women were eager to tip some of feminism's sacred cows.

As Ariel Levy reported, when the former child star Robin Morgan became involved in the women's movement and appeared on Johnny Carson's show in 1969 to talk about feminism, she marched off-stage when Carson tried to show clips of her pubescent television appearances, so vehemently did she object to the frivolous diminishment of her work. When Levy herself appeared on *The Colbert Report* to flog her book, *Female Chauvinist Pigs,* which picked apart many of the contradictions of purported sexual empowerment, she just laughed as Colbert hobbled toward her in high heels. When Valenti later appeared on the same show to promote her manifesto, *Full Frontal Feminism,* she gamely joked, "Nothing says feminism like a naked woman's body."

There were structural realities that shaped the tone and attitude of the feminist blogosphere. For many of the young women who ran independent blogs, women who lacked the boost of the feminist establishment to catapult them into (slightly) more remunerative spotlights as activists or writers, feminist criticism was something they produced on the side while working other jobs. Frequent posts and instant commentary written for little or no money often meant a decrease in intellectual heft. For those writers lucky enough to be paid for their work, their sometimes hourly enunciations had little in common with the deliberate, reported, long-form journalism and scholarship of the 1970s. An Internet maw demanded to be fed; posts had to go up, quick and often dirty.

But the Internet gave feminism something older women could not: an expansive new life and more abundant points of entry. When she first sought to get into feminist organizing, Valenti said, "you had to work for certain organizations, or have certain inroads with Gloria Steinem or Robin Morgan or Jane Fonda. The thing with the blogosphere was you could just build up your own audience and all of a sudden your voice was important."

Channeling their energy online, young feminists pushed the movement forward, making it more accessible to millions of women, reclaiming it for future generations who communed differently from those who had staged marches and sit-ins and consciousness raising in earlier decades. Models of activism that had once worked no longer pertained; women of the 1960s and 1970s did not have email, text messaging or the Internet, in effect a massive clubhouse in which to congregate, communicate and organize. This new wave of young people did not long for figureheads and spokespeople and megaphones—though if there was a young icon, Valenti was it. Gone were the days in which everyone read any one text or watched any one movie. Now everyone could produce their own texts and engage in multiple conversations without having to be geographically present or even visible. Online feminism afforded the option of pursuing activism in private. Young women, especially very young women, could explore feminist ideas without committing to a public brand, attending a meeting, wearing a T-shirt; they could read a feminist website at the same time that they played Beyoncé and shopped at gap.com. Perhaps it made feminism a less radical and less radicalizing choice, but it also made it far more available.

In turn, young women came aboard sooner. And because they did not have to go out of their way to seek a feminist community, many young people were coming upon online feminism by chance, not in reaction to instances of injustice or misogyny. What was often hard for older women to remember was that the young women creating a new feminist realm had not had the same experiences they had, both in broad poetic post-second-wave terms and also purely in terms of age. At the beginning of the twenty-first century women were surely still passed over for promotions, talked down to in meetings, sexually harassed, abused, asked to carry undue domestic burdens, paid less, objectified, disrespected and inadequately represented in government. But the younger a woman was, in any era, the fewer of these gendered data points she encountered, precisely *because* she was young and hadn't yet been exposed to them.

Debra Dickerson said it herself, even as she excoriated young feminists at *Mother Jones*: "Honey, you haven't seen sexism yet." Bingo. As Leslie Bennetts said in 2008, "We used to have a saying in the women's movement: 'It takes life to make a feminist.'" Much of what women learned about how their gender impacted their status—economically, socially, politically, professionally—came with time, with babies, with promotions and raises and marriages, with challenges that most young women had not encountered. That didn't mean that ten years later they would have voted for Hillary Clinton (though women over thirty did vote for her at higher rates than did their younger counterparts). It just meant that yelling at them about what they had not yet lived through was not going to do anyone any good.

✳ ✳ ✳

There was another serious, structural issue at stake in the disagreement between mothers and daughters: the youthful attempt to repair racial rifts within the feminist movement, an approach that academics and young women called "intersectionality." A new generation of feminists, acutely aware of what they perceived as the myopia of their predecessors when it came to racial, class and sexual variety among women, extended their gender activism to incorporate work around race, ethnicity, poverty, disability and sexual identity. Intersectionality meant not only stretching the feminist conversation to include new voices; it meant de-emphasizing gender as the single locus of oppression. Many young women saw this shift as unambiguously progressive, catalyzed by the diversity of the Internet and as an achievement of which they could be proud.

"If the blogosphere hadn't happened, we would still be in the same place we were in fifteen years ago," Valenti told me in 2009. "The only reason that intersectionality is talked about more often in mainstream feminist conversation is because mainstream feminists and national organizations were forced to take the issues on by blogs; they couldn't ignore it once so many people were talking about it." Online, conflicts about racial and economic and physical privilege continued to flare, but at least everyone was talking about it. The slow, imperfect move toward inclusion was the thing that earlier generations had failed to do effectively. That young women were aiming to correct it was seen in some quarters as a rebuke to traditional feminist organizations; crowing about the value of intersectional feminism sounded like an insinuation that young outsiders were more capable of improving the movement than the women who had created it, women who did not necessarily see the changes as improvements.

Until 2008 this conversation had been largely academic; it took place on blogs and in women's studies departments. But the election was bringing the differences of opinion into stark practical—and often personal—relief.

Latifa Lyles had worked at NOW since her early twenties, had been elected national membership vice president at twenty-nine and was an exception to a vision of the country's feminist organizations as forbidding to young women and women of color. During her tenure at NOW she had felt supported; she had been mentored and respected and believed that traditional feminist structures were inclusive. Until the election. "Despite how wonderful the election was in so many ways, it was a low point for me in the feminist community," Lyles told me in 2009. "The conversations that ensued—is sexism worse than racism, is racism worse than sexism, the sense [from older white women] that it was their time, the [voiced resentments about how] 'We had to wait for black men to get the vote!' Suddenly NOW felt like an organization and a culture that I did not know. I thought we had evolved into a better place."

Lyles began to see eye-to-eye with her outlying blogging sisters about the practical effects of intersectionality, of broadening and diversifying the conversation. "We had a progressive organization, but we didn't even have the language or the sensitivity to have these conversations!" she said. "You have to have diversity in your social justice work. Not just because it looks and feels good, but because [without an attention to issues besides gender] we harm ourselves and it's a detriment to our progress."

But older critics, the ones who saw their gender as the most central inhibitor of political parity, the ones who were weighing sexism against other oppressions and pointing out that women often came last in line, worried that the breadth of intersectional priorities thinned the interest in women, vilified older white women and left feminists too unfocused to move forward. "A movement that uses intersectionality as a lens but banishes white, bourgeois corporate older women might be a vehicle to glue what remains of feminism together, but it will struggle to achieve social change for women," argued Linda Hirshman in the *Washington Post*. She thought, "[The Clinton campaign] revealed what many in the movement know—that if feminism is a social-justice-for-everyone (with the possible exception of middle-class white women) movement, then gender is just one commitment among many. And when the other causes call, the movement will dissolve."

Hirshman regarded intersectionality as a step back into familiar patterns in which women put themselves last. "Everything is always a contest of one good against another," she told me in 2010. "You put your good against a competing good. Everyone since Hobbes has known these rules of social-movement politics. But you can't have politics if you don't take care of yourself. If you care for yourself first, *then* you make alliances with other people." The feminist movement, Hirshman argued, "had to be good girls and look after everybody but themselves. So when time came and people said 'It's more important to put a black person in the White House than a woman,' they said, 'Of course, you should go first.'"

Gloria Feldt recalled that at the 2004 march on Washington young, black and Latina feminist organizations insisted that the demonstration focus not just on reproductive rights, but on the kinds of social, economic and sexual challenges faced by poor women and women of color. "If we were going to build a coalition that would bring the women of color groups in, [they] made it quite clear that they needed the issues to be broader," she said. "So it became the March for Women's Lives. And then nobody knew what it meant. It diffuses everything."

Had that march taken place just four years later it might have looked very different. In 2004 the nascent *Feministing* had a minuscule readership. By 2008 Valenti had published two books and had more than half a million readers a month. In 2008 the march might have been covered by other blogs, such as *Racialicious, Salon's* women's blog *Broadsheet, Slate's* women's blog the *XX Factor,* or *Gawker* offshoot *Jezebel,* none of which existed in 2004. Celebrities might have included a generation of self-identified young feminists, such as Emma Watson, Andy Samberg, Adrian Grenier, Nellie McKay, Amy Poehler, Kate Winslet, America Ferrera, Lady Gaga, and Eliza Dushku, though a celebrity presence would likely not have been the galvanizing force. Conversation—and inevitable disagreement—about the impact of the march, the quality of the speakers, and the voices that were included and excluded might have been hashed out by young feminist journalists like Ann Friedman, Dana Goldstein, Ariel Levy, Amanda Fortini, Sheelah Kolhatkar, and Kira Cochrane, writing for the *American Prospect,* the *New Yorker, New York* magazine, *Portfolio,* and the *Guardian.* Maybe it was the early grab at Internet real estate by women like Valenti, maybe it was a backlash to backlash, maybe it was a swelling of the female media ranks related to Hillary Clinton's presidential run, but by 2008 feminism was not only far hipper than it had been in decades, but young people were taking control of the message. If the March for Women's Lives was a stilted mixer in which teenagers and mothers and grandmothers gaped awkwardly at each other, a matter of a few years would have seen emboldened youngsters turning up the music and owning the party.

But we didn't have a March for Women's Lives in 2008. We had a presidential election, and that was the event onto which the messiness of era, age and difference spilled.

☆ ☆ ☆

The yawning generational divides of 2008's election season were not exclusive to feminism. Time—and success—do funny things to social movements. Urgency gets lost; resentments build.

In July 2008 a live microphone caught Jesse Jackson, the revered civil rights leader, the man who was with Martin Luther King Jr. when he was assassinated in 1968, whose runs for the presidency in 1984 and 1988 helped make Barack Obama's candidacy possible, saying that he'd like to "cut [Obama's] nuts off" because he was "talking down to black people." Obama ran a race-light campaign, very different in tone from Jackson's earlier forays. Obama had not relied on Jackson for advice (though tellingly Jesse Jackson Jr. was one of his biggest backers), nor had he made much reference to the legacy of Jackson or his contemporaries. This fostered the perception of a lack of gratitude. To some Barack Obama's refusal to make his racial identity his priority was maddening, as was his distance from the history of black leadership. Obama carried none of the DNA of the civil rights movement; his political career had not originated at the pulpit; he did not rely on the counsel of leaders like Jackson or Reverend Al Sharpton.

In an entry on the *Huffington Post*, Brooklyn's Democratic congressional candidate Kevin Powell attributed Jackson's comments to a black generation gap, to the fact that while civil rights battles had made it possible for young African Americans to succeed in business and politics in ways that would have been unimaginable forty years earlier, their successes were often met with "a heavy resentment from the established black gatekeepers." Feeling frustrated and powerless, "some old school leaders have taken to chastising younger ones every opportunity they get," Powell wrote. Voicing sentiments that could have come from any number of young feminists, Powell continued, "The days of marching and protesting are over. The days of voting for someone just because they are black are over. . . . The multicultural legion of young Americans who've flocked to Obama's campaign suggest that we want leadership that builds bridges, not that is stuck in the rhetoric and realities of the past. . . . Yes, I must represent the concerns of blacks and Latinos in East New York. But I cannot ignore the Hasidic Jews in Williamsburg or the young white professionals in Fort Greene. They are all my people."

There were similar sensibility shifts within the gay rights movement, with some young people eager to move beyond the Stonewall-era, then AIDS-era history of their predecessors. In a 2009 *New York* magazine story Mark Harris described how online "there's no topic, from politics to locker-room etiquette . . . that cannot quickly devolve into 'What are you, 17?'—'What are you, some Stonewall-era relic?' sniping." Harris might as well have been channeling Robin Morgan in his description of what middle-aged gay men said about their youthful counterparts: "They reek of entitlement. They haven't had to work for anything and therefore aren't interested in anything that takes work. They're profoundly ungrateful for the political and social gains we spent our own youth striving to obtain for them. . . . They think old-fashioned *What do we want! When do we want it!* activism is icky and noisy. They toss around terms like 'post-gay' without caring how hard we fought just to get all the way to 'gay.'" Harris also reported on how youngsters perceive his plague-era compatriots: "We're horrible scolds. We gas on about AIDS the way our parents or grandparents couldn't stop talking about World War II. We act like we invented political action, and think the only way to accomplish something is by expressions of fury. We say we want change, but really what we want is to get off on our own victimhood. We're made uncomfortable, or even jealous, by their easygoing confidence. We're grim, prim, strident, self-ghettoizing, doctrinaire bores who think that if you're not gloomy, you're not worth taking seriously."

It all sounded so familiar, movement to movement.

A June 2009 Pew Research Center survey determined that the United States was experiencing the widest generation gap since the 1960s, when so many of the movements that were thrown into the spotlight by the 2008 elections had first coalesced. The Pew survey found that almost 80 percent of people polled believed that there was a major difference between what young people thought and what older people thought, the largest spread since 1969, when 74 percent of Americans polled saw major differences of opinion between older and younger generations.

Those young radicals from 1969 were now the elders, but it was their modern-day juvenile counterparts, the ones they bitched about being less radical, about being complacent, who were making manifest social progress that they could only have dreamed of forty years earlier. Products of this generational chasm included our first black president, a man whom eighteen- to twenty-nine-year-olds voted for by a two-to-one margin, and a widening acceptance of homosexuality and gay partnership, especially among young people. It also included the calm, if perhaps overly rosy assumption that women were so capable of winning the presidency that it was not incumbent on other women to support the first one to take a serious crack at it.

Anyone who lived through the 1960s should have known that the younger generation wins. The best anyone could hope for was that there would be some acknowledgment, some meaningful exchange before young women picked up their satchels and moved into the future.

And as difficult as it may have been, this election gave them exactly that. For all the kvetching and the carping, what didn't get reported was that many young women were not only listening to senior voices, but were expressing gratitude and acknowledging that their eyes had been opened to the challenges Clinton was facing, whether or not they were voting for her.

Some, like *Shakesville*'s Melissa McEwan, the blogger who had worked for John Edwards and initially dismissed Clinton as part of a corrupt political dynasty, described to me in 2009 her building "awareness of the ten metric fucktons of shit Hillary had to put up with to get where she was. . . . I just started admiring the hell out of her." Others admired her too, even without deciding to support her. Courtney Martin laid it out on *AlterNet*, explaining, "I . . . am an Obama voter, but was and will continue to be an avid Clinton supporter. I hate the sexist coverage that she endured . . . but that doesn't change my vote. My feminism is not just about gender equality in government, but also about racial justice, global security, community ethics, etc., and I resent being made to feel as if there is a 'right' way to vote if I am a feminist." In a *Nation* article excoriating those who assailed feminist Obama voters, Valenti wrote, "Let's focus on tangible goals: fostering youth leadership, working from the margins in and using intersectionality as our lens—instead of just a talking point. Let's use this moment, when our politics and emotions are raw, to push for a better, more forward-looking feminism."

The points that second-wavers seemed to think were falling on tender, deaf ears were actually being considered seriously. As twenty-five-year-old Jessica Grose wrote at *Jezebel,* "Hearing Abigail Pogrebin say that she has never encountered sexism makes me wonder if we do take the women's rights movement of the 60s and 70s for granted. . . . Have we stopped fighting a battle we didn't win?" And twenty-four-year-old Obama supporter Rebecca Wiegand told me in 2008, "[Going into the election] I felt very postfeminist. I felt like, I'm a woman and I'd love to have a woman president, but I also have many other issues I care about and the Iraq war is a big one, and I'm not going to make my decision just because I'm a woman." Over the course of the campaign, Wiegand said, "there has been a lot of anger toward Hillary that's felt really intense and misogynistic. . . . And it's made me realize we are still dealing with the gender issue. I don't think we know what to make of a woman in power, or make of Hillary. I don't think the world is as postfeminist as I was feeling that it was."

In some cases the sentiments of dissenting young women were practically love letters from a purportedly ungrateful generation. Responding to Linda Hirshman's piece about her mother issues, Courtney Martin wrote in the *American Prospect,* "I have gained an immeasurable amount from the wise, older women who have challenged my views on this election and other issues within a context of complexity. These women have made me a better thinker, a better writer, a better feminist, and a better human. And because of them, I will not cower, but I promise to be grateful. I will not forget, but I must also move on. I will not be a dutiful daughter, but I promise to be an impassioned, authentic, and brave inheritor."

What many of these young women were telegraphing was their willingness to see, to really see, through the prism of Clinton's campaign and their elders' reaction to it, that sexism was not a thing of the past. Whether it made them pull a lever for Hillary Clinton was practically immaterial—if not to Clinton's presidential prospects, then to the future of feminist engagement.

At least some older women heard this and shouted back. "I learn as much from them as they do from me," Steinem said about younger women. When I asked her if she thought the overzealous sex positivity and profanity of Internet feminism were weakening the movement, she replied, "As a person who walked around with a button that said 'Cunt Power' on it while I was wearing a miniskirt, I don't know that that's the case."

It was true, Steinem acknowledged, that many of her contemporaries "were not appreciated enough for the hard work and the sacrifice and so on. But you cannot now exact that price from your daughters. Even Susan B. Anthony said, 'Our job is not to make young women grateful. It's to make them ungrateful.'"

7 BOYS ON THE BUS

IN EARLY SPRING, in response to my *Salon* coverage of the election, I started receiving email messages from men who wanted to talk to me about Barack Obama. "Seriously . . . he's the bomb," wrote one friend from college. "To walk above the bitter bickering . . . to shoot straight, to continue to inspire, AND to continually remind us that we are responsible for our own democracy and future. . . . We need him." Another acquaintance expressed how much he admired "that Barack and Michelle Obama seem to have a very healthy thing going on with their family," and invited me for a drink by suggesting, "Yes We Can have a glass of wine."

This swollen-hearted adoration for the presidential candidate was startling coming from a usually ironic cohort. If my correspondents' bliss made me chafe slightly in those weeks after I cast my vote for Hillary, I believed it was because theirs was an enchantment from which I was now barred.

Then I began to get emails from a guy I'd been to dinner with six months earlier. "Hey, I don't mean to be confrontational," began his first missive, which went on to detail his hatred of the Clintons' political history, his dismay at how Hillary was conducting her campaign, and his fury at her front-running presumption. None of his antipathy had anything do with Hillary's gender, he assured me. In one of his notes he confessed, "Personally, I feel like vomiting every time I hear her hectoring voice."

My friend Geraldine, by the spring a strong Obama supporter, told me about a drink she'd had with a man who was ardent in his love for Barack and who made a series of legitimate complaints about Clinton before telling her that whenever he heard the New York senator's voice he was overcome by an urge to punch her in the face. Geraldine's date sounded chivalrous compared to one of my lifelong friends, a man with whom I had shared approximately one million beers and two million cigarettes as teens sorting through our nascent political beliefs. He said that when *he* heard Clinton speak he wanted to punch her in her uterus.

A pattern was emerging in the liberal, privileged, predominantly white climes in which I worked and lived: young men were starry-eyed about Obama and puffed with outsized antipathy toward Clinton. Swearing up and down that it wasn't because of her sex, they'd reel off dozens of reasons for not wanting to vote for her. But I was made uncomfortable by the persistent note of aggression that marked their reactions to Clinton, and puzzled by the increasingly cult-like devotion to Obama, a man whose policy positions were not so different, after all, from those of his opponent. Hating Hillary had for decades been the provenance of Republican blowhards, but now men on the left were spewing vitriol about her voice, her looks, her presumption—and without realizing it were radicalizing me in my support for Clinton more than the candidate herself ever could have. And it wasn't just me. I was hearing similar dismay not only from fellow Clinton voters, but from female Obama supporters put off by the Hillary-despising virus that had infected their progressive male compatriots.

On the morning of the Louisiana primary my friend Becca O'Brien, then a policy advisor in New Orleans, received five separate calls from male friends around the country. They were just campaigning on behalf of their candidate, Becca understood. "[But] the presumption was that I was undecided because I was a young woman and they could talk some sense into me. . . . With straight white male progressive friends, I feel something that makes me viscerally angry and afraid—the viciousness of the rebuttals to the suggestion that [Obama's and Clinton's] policies are roughly equal or that Clinton's have some benefits, the outright dismissal of any support of her . . . The whole 'Hillary Clinton is a monster' theme is so virulent."

After hearing from Becca I put out feelers, asking friends and colleagues to pass along the message that I was curious to hear from young women who were experiencing disturbing pressure from their Obama-supporting male friends. Within twenty-four hours I had an overflowing inbox; my voicemail was full; I had women practically climbing through my windows to tell me of their perplexities and aggravations. Those who contacted me were almost exclusively well-educated professionals, mostly white and very liberal, and they were complaining about their male counterparts. They described outright sexism as well as less well-defined suspicions that these men were uncomfortable with powerful women. The women who were supposedly rejecting feminism and diving deep into the embrace of the "Yes We Can" dude down the block were instead calling me out of earshot of their Obama-loving boyfriends, some expressing gendered discontent for the first time in their lives; more than one young woman voiced her own surprise, midlitany, at "sounding so feminist." Most contrary to the popular narrative of the election—that young women voting for Obama had no investment in Clinton—was that the majority of women who contacted me were Obama supporters, or at least Obama appreciators.

Dana Lossia, a twenty-nine-year-old labor lawyer in Brooklyn, called Obama "the most inspiring, amazing person, a different kind of politician." She was no fan of Hillary's and hated how she'd run her campaign, but she wrote, "I've been really bothered by what I perceive as sexism [among some male Obama supporters] and have spent hours defending [Clinton]. . . . It's the intensity of their irritation with her that disturbs me more than their devotion to Obama."

Thirty-one-year-old Maggie Merrill was an urban studies graduate student at the University of New Orleans whose anxieties were sown early, when a young family friend began talking as if every right-minded person would support Obama over Clinton. "I got the sense that this idealistic, highly educated, progressive man, regardless of the fact that he'd been raised by liberal women, was uncomfortable with the idea of a woman being in power," Merrill told me. She spoke with alarm about the Obamamania in Louisiana: "These young men get glassy eyes and start spitting out vague things about how Barack Obama is going to save humanity. Really, have you seen their eyes? It's this faraway look. It's scary."

Yes I had! In February, March, and April 2008 I saw that look on scads of scruffy volunteers lining the streets of Brooklyn and Manhattan, spreading the word. In grouchier moods I considered speaking with them about preaching, choirs, and possible relocation to suburban Ohio. In more sanguine moments I appreciated their ardor but wondered if the thing they thought Barack Obama might be saving humanity from was a threatening woman in the world's most powerful job.

Jessica Valenti, who spoke at fifteen colleges during the election cycle, told me in 2009 that in her travels she encountered "a lot of women who were voting for Hillary, and a lot who were voting for Obama. And *all* of them felt like their progressive male friends were sexist." Shelby Knox was also touring colleges, where undergraduate women told her things like "My boyfriend is so supportive of Obama and I guess I agree with him, but something about how much he hates Hillary feels mean." Some students, Knox recalled, told her about a banner at a fraternity that read "Bros before hos." "The girls told me, 'They say it's not sexism,' and when I ask them why they're calling her a ho they list all these things—her vote on the war, that he's more progressive, that she's a Clinton and she only got there because of her husband. But even if it's not explicitly misogynistic, it's just there."

Molly Cohen, a senior at Brown, fought with her boyfriend after he began telling her "about how, objectively, Hillary Clinton was a bitch," Cohen told me in 2009. She said other male classmates insisted that she watch the popular Will.i.am video, in which celebrities strummed guitar and sang along to an Obama speech. "It felt like they thought I needed to be converted or something," said Cohen. Anytime she said anything positive about Clinton her male friends attacked: "[They behaved] as if I didn't understand that I was siding with the bitch." At the same time they insisted that their distaste for Clinton had nothing to do with the fact that she was a woman. "These were liberal guys," Cohen said. "They were the guys fighting for Palestinian rights. And then it came to a woman and it was like, 'She's a bitch.' Wait, what about the sensitivity you just showed to all the people of the world?" Cohen wound up voting for Clinton. Why? "Mostly because I was so frustrated by the male Obama supporters."

Letters to left-leaning publications and blogs bubbled with enmity toward Clinton. As Katha Pollitt wrote, "Vats of sexist nastiness splattered across the Comments section of hundreds of blogs and websites. It's as if every obscene phone caller and every exhibitionist in America decided to become an amateur political pundit." Latoya Peterson, already dismayed by the racially inflected language of the feminist community toward Obama, was also troubled by the sexism coming from progressives. "Conservatives you expect it from," she said. "But when you look at liberal men, like black male pundits—I understand they [were] infuriated by this whole election cycle, but it is never cool to call somebody a cunt. It is never cool to tell somebody to shut up." Peterson stopped reading *Jackand-JillPolitics,* the blog cofounded by the comedian and *Onion* editor Baratunde Thurston, even though she agreed with much of what he wrote about Clinton's race baiting, because the atmosphere on the blog and in its comments section was "beyond sexist for Hillary." Peterson's blog, *Racialicious,* was often critical of Hillary. "But I never allowed anybody to call [Hillary] a cunt," she said. "I never allowed anybody to call her 'Shillary,' 'Shrillary.' . . . I can't allow gleeful misogyny to continue unabated."

The trouble was that because everyone was liberal and officially down with female empowerment, the many women who couldn't cite actual uses of the words *bitch* or *cunt* found themselves troubled by their inability to specify the sexism they sensed. "I don't think anyone in my peer group . . . would be comfortable saying, 'I'm not ready for a woman president,'" said Alex Seggerman, a twenty-four-year-old art history Ph.D. student. Seggerman was an Obama voter but noticed people making remarks like "She's had plastic surgery" or "Her attitude is off-putting," which she heard as "expressions of some deeper issues with the fact that she is a woman." "People can always come up with reasons they don't like the candidate they're not supporting," said Dana Lossia, the

Obama-supporting labor lawyer. "But no one disliked Joe Biden or Chris Dodd as much as they dislike Hillary." She'd never heard her friends say anything explicit: "[They never say] anything where I could say, 'That's a sexist comment.' It's just that I can't understand why they hate her so much."

It was a contemporary iteration of Betty Friedan's problem that had no name, a maddening cycle of vague hunches and self-righteous denials that left many of us feeling as though we were going insane. Even Valenti was disoriented by it; she was particularly hamstrung because, as she pointed out, she made her living identifying sexism. "You'd think I'd be able to find an example," she said, adding, "Because it's not [always] explicit sexism, it makes it impossible to argue with people, because if you say something, then you're the wackadoo feminist."

Those who did attempt to articulate their apprehensions about how Clinton was being discussed provoked defensive eruptions. The journalist Jessica Wakeman, an Obama voter, wrote that her commitment to pointing out the sexist treatment Clinton was receiving from the media was considered "really not cool" by her mostly male friends. Becca O'Brien, the New Orleans political advisor, told me that, after examining polling data indicating that white men were disproportionately breaking for Obama, she had posted the chat headline "National Gender Bias Puts Obama Ahead of Clinton." It prompted a phone call from a furious male friend and an argument that escalated, O'Brien said, to "a new territory of outrage. . . . [He told] me that it showed fundamental flaws in my judgment and ability to read polling data."

At least, as Gloria Steinem told me drily in 2009, the guys on the left were trying to deny any sexism. "It's a big step forward that they feel they have to hide it," she said. "In the old days, they did not."

✳ ✳ ✳

The reluctance to extend enlightened democratic thought to women's priorities, like so much else in 2008, stretched back hundreds of years, to Abigail Adams, who wrote to her husband in 1776, "Whilst you are proclaiming peace and good-will to men, emancipating all nations, you insist upon retaining an absolute power over wives." It recalled that terrible fissure between abolitionists and suffragists, and the words of Sojourner Truth, who observed at the meeting of the American Equal Rights Association in 1867, "There is a great stir about colored men getting their rights, but not a word about the colored women; and if colored men get their rights, and not colored women theirs, you see the colored men will be masters over the women, and it will be just as bad as it was before."

More immediately it evoked the 1960s, when women in antiwar, student, and civil rights movements realized that the freedoms and respect they were fighting for were not being applied to their own status within those groups in which they labored. The men gave the speeches, led the rallies, and wrote the manifestos, while women were called on for secretarial and sexual purposes. The 1966 annual meeting of Students for a Democratic Society was disrupted when women attempting to address gender inequity were pelted with tomatoes. The next year, when the vocal feminists Jo Freeman and Shulamith Firestone were among a group of women who rushed the stage to speak at the National Conference on New Politics, a male conference goer urged, "Cool down, little girl. We have more important things to talk about than women's problems." At a large antiwar rally organized to counter Richard Nixon's January 1969 inauguration, the SDS activist Marilyn Salzman Webb took to the stage and began, "We as women are oppressed." She plowed forward as rowdy lefties in the crowd heckled, "Take it off!" "Fuck her!" "Rape her in the back alley!"

The principles that guided the civil rights movement helped shape the feminism of many women, black and white. But in that movement too there was rampant sexism. Stokely Carmichael's infamous comment that "the only position for women in the SNCC is prone" may or may not have been meant seriously, but it nonetheless illustrated exactly what alarmed many women on the left in the 1960s and 1970s: in the civil rights and the later Black Power movement women were again the pamphleteers, typists, coffee brewers, and sexual outlets, while their radical brothers became the revolutionary heroes, a situation that, in conjunction with the racial exclusions of the feminist movement, helped give birth to womanism as well as predominantly female and black-run organizations like the

National Welfare Rights Organization, the National Black Feminist Organization, and the Combahee River Collective.

Robin Morgan's original "Goodbye to All That," published in the leftist paper *Rat,* excoriated "the male-dominated peace movement" and bid farewell "to the dream that being in the leadership collective will get you anything but gonorrhea." The groundbreaking rock critic and feminist Ellen Willis wrote in 1969, "A genuine alliance with male radicals will not be possible until sexism sickens them as much as racism. This will not be accomplished through persuasion, conciliation, or love, but through independence and solidarity. Radical men will stop oppressing us and make our fight their own when they can't get us to join them on any other terms."

Almost forty years after Willis's prediction, the generation of liberal thinkers that was reviving progressive activism online was finding contemporary gender resentments troublingly reminiscent of the 1960s and 1970s. In 2005 Markos Moulitsas, founder of the lefty blogging powerhouse *Daily Kos,* ran an advertisement on his site for the reality show *The Real Gilligan's Island*; the ad depicted scantily clad Gingers and Mary Anns throwing pies at each other. When some readers registered their opinion that the spot was degrading to women and therefore not appropriate for a progressive website, Moulitsas responded, "I find such humorless, knee-jerk reactions, to be tedious at best, sanctimonious and arrogant at worst." Claiming that he would not let "the sanctimonious women's studies set" control the content of his site, he continued, "Feel free to claim that I'm somehow abandoning 'progressive principles' by running the ad. . . . Feel free to storm off in a huff. . . . Me, I'll focus on the important shit." Moulitsas later withdrew his reference to "women's studies" but let the rest of his commentary stand. Here was a vivid expression of a modern online youth movement's attitude toward women, embodied by one of its most recognizable figureheads; it was a progressivism in which those who balked at the objectification of women were sanctimonious, humorless, and tedious, in which women's concerns about their representation did not count as "the important shit."

Former NOW vice president Latifa Lyles told me in 2009 about attending the 2007 Yearly Kos Convention. She was awed by the obvious importance accorded the gathering: every Democratic pres-

idential candidate save Joe Biden was in attendance. The netroots
movement had become so powerful that politicians understood they
had to woo the blogosphere, a remarkable development. Lyles was
impressed by the influence of a youthful, left-wing media that had
not existed just a few years before. But she said, "It was mostly
white men, even in this young group. It wasn't that [women] were
not welcome. . . . It just felt weird. Here were all these people my
age! This great power was being wielded by this incredibly powerful youth group. And there were so few women represented. It felt
like a missed opportunity."

Static between the online left and its female denizens was particularly fierce because the blogosphere was born during the period
during which the Democratic Party strategy for securing majori-
ties in the House and Senate hinged in part on running anti-abortion Democrats. The idea was that if women could just stifle their
impulse to prioritize reproductive rights, Democrats could stack
Congress with lawmakers who would pass broadly progressive
legislation that would benefit millions of Americans—*including
women,* proponents of this strategy always hastened to add. Party
loyalty would bar antichoice Dems from standing in the way of judi-
cial appointments, women were assured, so no actual reproductive
rights would be risked.

This scenario was not much fun for those who felt keenly that
hard-won, always imperiled reproductive rights were central to
women's freedom, equality, and ability to participate fully in the
democracy. The choices were either playing nice as those rights
got traded away, or raising a stink and getting cast as self-interested enemies of the greater liberal good. The scheme was possible only because it was assumed that Democratic women—thanks,
ironically, to their social progressivism and commitment to issues
of choice—would not leave the party; we had nowhere else to go.
When NARAL, a group built around the fight for reproductive freedom, chose to withhold support from the antichoice Democrat Jim
Langevin in the 2006 Rhode Island Senate race and endorse pro-
choice Republican Lincoln Chafee they earned the ire of the liberal
blogosphere. "NARAL, and many people here, whined and cried
about Langevin," wrote Moulitsas on *Daily Kos,* "the way they
whined and cried about Harry Reid, because of those Democrats'

personal opposition to abortion. Didn't we know, they demanded, that choice was a core principle of the Democratic Party? . . . The hell it is. . . . Single issue groups have hijacked [the Democratic Party] for their pet causes." This was how women with an investment in reproductive rights were cast by this new young left: as single-issue whiners too stupid and self-obsessed to understand the priorities of their own party. As Steinem told me in 2009, "Freedom of speech is also a single issue. Reproductive freedom is no less pervasive in its own impact than freedom of speech. A single issue is any issue not one's own, that's my theory."

In 2009 the impact of deemphasizing reproductive freedom in order to build a Democratic majority would be made manifest in the struggle to pass health care reform. Some of us had bought the line that if we just held our noses and voted for the antichoice Democrats, women and men of every stripe would benefit from the legislation they would pass. We were rewarded with purportedly "progressive" legislation that included proposals from both the House and the Senate for the sharpest curtailment of abortion rights since the Hyde Amendment, thanks to Democrats like Bart Stupak and Ben Nelson. The health care wrangling prompted some Democratic women to put their foot down at last. As Kate Harding wrote in *Salon* in 2010, "The party will not get a dime of my money as long as it could help a candidate who doesn't trust grown women to make their own medical decisions." Pamela Merritt, also known as the blogger Shark-Fu at *Angry Black Bitch,* told *Salon* at the end of 2009, "The woman of the year is the re-awakened feminist— the women who pulled together in coalition to protest Stupak and defeat Nelson, the women who are now organized to demand reproductive justice in a way that has never happened before." Women in the Senate threatened to vote down health care legislation if it included anti-abortion measures.

"I feel like individual women who were outraged [about Stupak] were a lot more engaged than they would have been prior to the 2008 election," said Women's Media Center head Jehmu Greene in 2009. Harding agreed, to some extent: "I think anti-Clinton bullshit woke some women up, though not enough." Even Moulitsas seemed to have thought further about the place of reproductive freedom in his party's politics. During the Stupak conflagration he urged readers to stop donating money to the Democratic Congressional Campaign Committee, in part because it was supporting Democrats who wanted to "get in the way of a patient and her doctor . . . on a LEGAL procedure." Instead, Moulitsas wrote, "give to those elected officials who best reflect your values."

* * *

In the spring of 2008 a conveniently nongendered campaign narrative was getting cemented: Obama was the progressive candidate, Clinton practically a Republican. This assuredness was slightly confounding. Yes, Clinton was hawkish as she continued to chew her way through primary states, but she had the better health care plan and was talking more about economic policies that benefited the working class. It may have been true, as her critics snorted, that Clinton's dive toward populism was an example of pandering to her increasingly secure blue-collar base. I failed to see how that differed from Obama's playing to his privileged, educated base. Both candidates appeared to be consummate politicians. But my friends continued to swear that Obama was different and to issue cutting renunciations of Clinton's supposedly more centrist centrism. In April Markos Moulitsas agreed with a commenter who wrote, "It's bizarre, but I don't really consider [Clinton] a Dem anymore."

That didn't make sense to Mia Bruch, a thirty-three-year-old writer who would have voted for Obama but was foiled by a voting-roll snafu. Even though she was supporting him, the liberal Bruch felt a "great distance" from her partisan peers. "You already see this idealistic longing projected on Obama," she said. "People talk about him as a secular messiah who will bring us political salvation. There's no sense of what is plausible." Bruch pointed to health care: "Hillary's policy is the more politically progressive one, but this has somehow been ignored, and Obama was projected upon as the progressive redeemer."

The image recalled George Packer's observation in New Hampshire that Obama shed a forgiving light on the country itself. "At times," Packer wrote, describing a rally, "Obama almost seems to be trying to escape history, presenting himself as the conduit through which people's yearnings for national transformation can be realized." National transformation, yes, and also personal transformation. As the Obama-love threatened to break the bonds of reason in some of my peers, I was reminded of a woman I'd met on Super Tuesday standing outside the legendary Manhattan grocery store Zabar's holding an Obama sign. Sixty-two years old, white, a teacher of English as a second language, Kathy Kline gestured to the young people standing around her. Beaming, she grabbed my arm. "One of the great things about Obama's influence is that not *once* have I felt like an old white woman," she said to me.

After eight years of the Bush administration I understood the longing to once again feel pride and inspiration. More than that, I understood the value of electrifying the electorate. The possibility of engaging generations and populations that had historically felt shut out of the political process was one of the only arguments that shook my strengthening Clinton support. But I wasn't sure that it was automatically more liberal than the mandated health care plan Hillary was proposing. It was fair and perhaps smart to prefer unifying inspiration over policy mechanics, but it was neither fair nor smart to pretend that the latter did not exist or didn't count. Obama's 2004 red states–blue states speech had been moving, but it was also a gracious invocation of centrism. His lyrical language made flesh would have looked a lot like Hillary's voting record. Kim Gandy, who was surprised by the often blind devotion to Hillary from some of her NOW constituents, was equally taken aback by others' idealization of Obama. "They're both moderates [but] they turned her into a warmonger and him into a peacenik," she said.

The *Sacramento Bee* published an article in January about a field organizer for Obama who instructed fellow volunteers to stay away from policy questions when talking to voters, instead focusing on "one of the campaign's key strategies: telling potential voters personal stories of political conversion." Campaigners were told "to hone their own stories of how they came to Obama." Kathleen Geier, writing for *Talking Points Memo* on the same day she cast her vote for Obama, nonetheless reported being put off by the slavish devotion of her compatriots: "How can we truly bring about real political change if the movement the Obama people are building is devoid of ideological content? . . . Such a movement becomes a cult of personality rather than [an] engine for social justice and

political transformation." Responding to the *Sacramento Bee* article, Geier observed that the language of "coming to Obama" was
"the language of evangelical Christianity. . . . But he's not Jesus!"

In late March Tom Hayden, Bill Fletcher, Jr., Danny Glover and
Barbara Ehrenreich wrote in the *Nation,* "All American progressives should unite for Barack Obama. . . . We take very seriously
the argument that Americans should elect a first woman President,
and we abhor the surfacing of sexism in this supposedly post-fem-
inist era. But none of us would vote for Condoleezza Rice as either
the first woman or the first African-American president." As surely
as Gloria Steinem had substituted an imaginary Achola for Barack,
these avatars of political enlightenment were simply sliding in one
woman, one whose politics were in stark opposition to Clinton's, to
stand in for another woman they didn't like. Just as underhanded
was their calling forth a younger, more radical Clinton—a woman
who could never have maneuvered her way to the presidency with
her politics intact—as enemy to her older self: "We believe that the
Hillary Clinton of 1968 would be an Obama volunteer today, just
as she once marched in the snows of New Hampshire for Eugene
McCarthy against the Democratic establishment."

In Democratic circles Obama loyalty, like white masculinity
itself, had become normative. If you were a liberal and you were
not for him, that deviation was always—in the spirit of the Condoleezza Rice comparison—linked to politically empty harebrained
femininity. As Amanda Fortini wrote in *New York* magazine, "A
woman I interviewed described the atmosphere of Obama-Fascism
in her office: '[My male colleagues] feel only idiots would vote for
Hillary. There's this kind of total assumption that of course any
thinking person is voting for Obama.'"

Ashley Johnson, a senior at Princeton, was an undecided voter
leaning toward Obama. She told me, "If I did end up voting for
Hillary, people are making me feel like I am making a superficial
decision based on her gender." But, she continued, aside from the
fact that a vote for Hillary Clinton was not exclusively attributable
to some dank, pheromone-driven sisterhood, she had a real question about why, if the candidates were politically comparable, it
would be so bad to be pleased to vote for a woman. "If I did end up
voting for Hillary," said Johnson, "would part of me be very proud

that I was voting for the first female candidate? Yes." Like Johnson, I wondered when it had become so half-witted to want the cycle of white male presidential power to be broken by a woman.

Though his supporters often made clear that they were not voting for Obama *because* he was black, his race had been a factor in his decision to run for president. Jodi Kantor reported in the *New York Times Magazine* that when the Obamas first discussed the campaign with David Axelrod in 2006 Michelle had asked her husband, "What do you think you could accomplish that the other candidates couldn't?" Although, in Kantor's words, "an Obama agenda would not look very different from that of Hillary Clinton or John Edwards," Barack's response was, "When I take that oath of office, there will be kids all over this country who don't really think that all paths are open to them, who will believe they can be anything they want to be. . . . And I think the world will look at America a little differently." This was true. This was crucial. To acknowledge that an Obama presidency would represent the beginning of an overdue correction in long-standing underrepresentation, that it would change the scope of possibility for the millions of American children who were not white, to admit that these ideas informed a vote for him—none of that invalidated a simultaneous appreciation for his policy ideas or his leadership style.

☆ ☆ ☆

If progressives were failing to give women's history its due, it was hardly to be expected that the mainstream media would do any better on this score. Chris Matthews announced in February that one of Obama's speeches sent a "thrill going up [his] leg," while open disregard for Clinton and her supporters among even left-leaning commentators became ever more common as she defied their prognostications by continuing her primary march and winning big contests. The more Clinton upended the expectations of the boys on the bus, the more those boys reverted to Moose lodge–style japery toward her and her sex. It was no surprise to hear the conservative strategist Bill Kristol, appearing on *Fox News Sunday,* observe that "the only people [supporting Clinton] are the Democratic establishment and white women" and suggest that while Democrats would be crazy to follow their establishment, "white women are a problem. . . . We all live with that." It was more jarring to hear the NPR correspondent Juan Williams, brought in as Kristol's nominally liberal stooge, chuckle heartily at the joke. When the former *Boston Globe* columnist Mike Barnicle appeared on MSNBC's *Morning Joe* and joked that Clinton reacted to Obama "with just the look, the look toward him, looking like *everyone's* first wife standing outside of probate court," Joe Scarborough, Willie Geist, and guest host David Shuster laughed and laughed.

Newsweek's Jonathan Alter had kicked off pleas for Clinton to leave the race in February with a column headlined "Hillary Should Get Out Now," suggesting that quitting her campaign before the March 4 Ohio and Texas primaries would be the "graceful" choice, since he predicted high odds of Clinton "looking bad" in the two big state contests. Clinton won Ohio and Texas and was now profiting from a new self-image: the resilient fighter who would not back down, even when media men were pushing her to give up. What those media men could not grasp was that their belittling, butt-slapping approach to her was actually fueling her robust new persona. The more states Clinton won, the more loudly they mocked her and called for her to quit, the more they looked like heavies.

On MSNBC's *Tim Russert* in April, Russert asked Andrew Sullivan and Christopher Hitchens to comment on remarks Clinton had made about how she was not going to be "bullied out [of the race] by a bunch of guys." Their responses—about Clinton's "self-pity and self-righteousness," about how Sullivan could not be a misogynist because he'd admired Margaret Thatcher, about how Thatcher was a real feminist "in the sense that we're post gender"—were like a *Saturday Night Live* sketch in which boorish midcentury patriarchs, soaked in martinis and cigar smoke, reassured themselves that women's lib was really a passing trifle. Hitchens took particular delight in his role as caveman provocateur, saying of Clinton's "welling up and sobbing," "if she knew how it made her look . . . alternately soppy and bitchy, she'd stop it." They were trying desperately to ruffle feathers; it was unclear whether they knew that by doing so they were only strengthening Clinton's position. At the end of the segment Russert thanked both men "for writing and thinking and talking with intelligence."

In a postprimary article Michelle Goldberg, the Obama supporter who had expressed such anger at older feminists who disparaged the next generation, would concede that the media reaction
to Clinton had been repugnant enough to catalyze female support.
She acknowledged that it was difficult to watch "professional media
types sing smitten fanboy hymns to Obama and, at the same time,
spend hours dissecting Clinton's laugh and cleavage."

None of this meant that young women were swaying in time to
the words of Robin Morgan; it merely demonstrated that the reactions to Clinton, especially from the left, were making as much or
more of an impact on women who had thought, in part thanks
to the liberal company they kept, that sexism was a thing of the
past. Even more than the exhortations of second-wave feminists,
the attitudes of Democratic men were eye-opening. As Fortini wrote
in *New York* magazine, "The past few months have been like an
extended consciousness-raising session, to use a retro phrase that
would have once made most of us cringe. . . . This is, admittedly,
depressing: *How can we be confronting the same issues, all these
years later?* But it's also exciting. It feels as if a window has been
opened in a stuffy, long-sealed room."

☆ ☆ ☆

As the candidates set up camp in Pennsylvania before the late-April
primary, the politics of gender, race, and class were proving ever
more complicated. Pennsylvania had a huge working-class population and was chock-full of seniors, two of Clinton's strongest demo-
graphics. In April the University of Pennsylvania scholar Adolph
Reed wrote a piece for the *Progressive* titled "Obama No," in which
he accused the Illinois senator of being "a vacuous opportunist, a
good performer with an ear for how to make white liberals like
him," and described the "disturbingly ritualistic and superficial"
enthusiasm of young Obama supporters. I didn't share Reed's harsh
perspective on Obama's candidacy, though I certainly agreed with
him about Obamamania, and about something else he observed:
"Increasingly, Obama supporters have been disposed to cry foul
and charge racism at nearly any criticism of him, in steadily more
extravagant rhetoric." As Obama supporters were ever more cer-

tainly avowing the progressive superiority of their candidate, they had fixed on another explanation (besides birdbrained female solidarity) for why people were still voting for Clinton: racism. Assumptions about the age, class, and whiteness of Clinton's base made it easy enough to assert that perhaps those who were supporting the woman were doing so in part because of an unwillingness to vote for a black person.

I hoped that Pennsylvania was a state that might challenge the ugly idea that Clinton's late-primary surges were fueled largely by racial intolerance. In eastern Pennsylvania Clinton support was multiracial, led by Philadelphia's then very popular African American mayor, Michael Nutter. Nutter wasn't just backing Clinton. Like Reed, he was openly disdainful of Obama. "This is not the Martin Luther King oratorical contest," he told *Bloomberg News* in late March. "It's a contest for president of the United States." But the Pennsylvania primary wound up challenging what was fast becoming my own idealization of Clinton and her supporters.

In April political reporters were running stories describing how exhausted the electorate was by the ongoing primary battle; Democratic pundits were agonizing over the money being spent by two Democrats working to expose each other's weaknesses. But on the weekend before the primary an improbably merry Hillary Clinton was shouting "Isn't this exciting?" to a crowded high school gymnasium in Bethlehem, Pennsylvania. "We love you!" came a young female voice from somewhere in the bleachers at the precise moment that paramedics wheeled in an empty stretcher. For one discombobulating second I wondered if the rally might have produced an Obama-esque scenario in which a twitterpated youngster collapsed in Beatlemaniac ecstasy for her candidate. The stretcher was actually for a middle-aged guy who'd had a brief diabetic episode, but the fact that the possibility had even crossed my mind was testament to the buzzing enthusiasm that characterized many of Hillary's spring events. This renewed exhilaration contradicted the fretful story line about how everyone was sick of the election and how John McCain was growing stronger while Democrats grew weary.

Clinton's packed Bethlehem gathering, on the heels of a rally drawing thirty-five thousand for Obama in Philadelphia, suggested that many people were actually thrilled that the choice was ongoing.

The mechanics of the primary system typically meant that presidential races were tied up after a few early contests. That was great for candidates who wanted to rest up and amass money before the general election, and for political parties eager to avoid the appearance of internal strife. But quick nomination battles were less salubrious for voters who lived outside of Iowa, New Hampshire, or perhaps, in a lucky year, the Super Tuesday states. Those people rarely had a chance to watch their votes make an impact on their party's nomination. This lengthy season was allowing voters to evaluate and engage with the candidates, arguably increasing their investment in those candidates for the general election. Perhaps more vitally it was forcing the candidates to engage with voters—to listen to them, visit with them, hold their babies, and hear their stories, and while they were at it lay down campaign apparati that would come in useful in the fall—all around the country, not just in the few states with early primaries.

The stretched race was transforming the candidates. Obama, something of a delicate flower going into the primaries, quick to pout and easily injured, was toughening up. And Clinton, who had approached her early campaign with the muscular determination of a Clydesdale, seemed to have recovered a bit of the freewheeling what-the-hell attitude that had served her well in New Hampshire. In early April she finally demoted Mark Penn; the well-liked pollster and strategist Geoff Garin was now at the helm alongside Howard Wolfson and Hillaryland stalwart Maggie Williams, who had taken Solis Doyle's job in February. Clinton was flashing snap and smile on the stump, plainly enjoying her role as plucky underdog. Losing the burden of inevitability had loosened her up and given her something to fight for: a nomination most people understood to be *just* beyond her grasp, that could in turn translate into a message about how she was fighting for people. She was making whooping campaign promises to big blue-collar crowds who cheered her on. She had also gotten better at appealing to women; she wasn't selling herself explicitly as a feminist champion, but her role as hard-working populist long shot offered female voters another way to embrace her as a symbolic heroine.

Roles had flipped somewhat, especially with working-class voters: now Clinton was the candidate with emotional appeal and

Obama was cast as the thinker. "She wasn't a cerebral 'have hope' candidate," said EMILY's List Ellen Malcolm. "She was conveying: 'I get it. I know what health care reform means to you. I know why you're scared about the college education system for your kids. I know that you want investment in jobs.' The Obama message of change in many ways was a very cerebral message that resonated with people wanting a different kind of politics. . . . But when it came down to brass tacks about who was going to make a difference, Hillary being scrappy and showing her expertise [made people believe] that she's the one who's going to fight for me."

"By the time we hit Pennsylvania, she was in charge of her own campaign," Ann Lewis told me in 2010. "We went out with less money [than Obama] and did a woman-centered campaign." Lewis said she was prouder of her work with women in Pennsylvania than anywhere else; rather than concentrating exclusively on the western parts of the state, Lewis and her team focused on the suburban counties surrounding Philadelphia that were tougher to take from Obama, playing up the campaign's "The Hillary I Know" approach, in which friends and associates testified to Clinton's humanity. It had been a fixture of the campaign since the start, but was put into full effect in Pennsylvania, bolstered now by a candidate who was increasingly comfortable showing off that humanity.

Much would be made of Clinton's negative campaigning in Pennsylvania, but I wasn't watching her television ads. I was listening to her address crowds, a warmer and more talented speaker than she'd been at the start. She was talking about ending tax cuts for those making over $250,000 a year, bringing back manufacturing jobs, going after student loan companies, forgiving school debt for those who went into nursing, teaching, and law enforcement. I wasn't just defensive about Clinton anymore; I was more excited than I could have imagined about her candidacy, her insistence on staying in the race, the fact that people all over the country were seeing a woman and a black man compete to be president.

On the night before the primary I heard Chelsea Clinton tell eight thousand people packed into the University of Pennsylvania's Palestra basketball arena that her mother would be a better president than her father because "she's not only more progressive but more prepared than he was." Someone in a presidential campaign was

crowing about being "more progressive"! My brother and I took my
mother to that rally, and we watched her watch Hillary speak; she
was so pleased to be seeing this woman run for president, so pleased
that she'd be able to vote for her the next morning. I wished I could
be less sentimental about how watching women's history refracted
through my mother's eyes made me feel, but I couldn't. It made me
so happy.

If my euphoria in April was comparable to the level of Obama
fanaticism I deplored, it came with the knowledge that there was no
good way for it to end. Obama-lovers could pray without equivoca-
tion for their candidate to fly straight on till morning. I could cross
my fingers all I wanted about Clinton's upward trajectory, could
celebrate her turn to the left. But I knew, on some level, that even if
she found a way to pull it off she would be hated for it. I also knew
that there was very little chance of a win that would be accepted as
legitimate. There was already too much rumbling from the Clinton
camp and Clinton supporters about the ethically bankrupt idea of
counting votes from unofficial primaries in Michigan and Florida.
Meddling with superdelegate counts and illegitimate primaries was
no way to win an election.

I also could not shake a memory of waiting to listen to Clinton in
Bethlehem. While most of the crowd had assured me that they loved
Hillary but would be thrilled to vote for Obama if he became the
nominee, a woman named LeeAnne followed up on her husband's
assertion that "Obama has some decent things to say" by noting,
"I don't even know what his name is. Bahama Mama? Osama?" As
LeeAnne spoke the crowd around her shifted uncomfortably. One
man said firmly, "His name is Barack Obama." LeeAnne looked
abashed. "Fine. I'll learn it," she said. "I just love Hillary. I love
everything about her. And I heard that what's-his-name doesn't
salute the American flag." At this about half a dozen people in line
corrected her misapprehensions about Obama's patriotism. "That's
just not the case, and you shouldn't believe gossip about him being a
Muslim, either," said a woman wearing two Hillary buttons. "Even
if he were Muslim, that's no reason not to vote for him," said a man
named Charles Johns, who said he was an Obama supporter but
was there to hear Hillary anyway.

After that, even in those weeks that I was feeling my most unrestrained appreciation for Hillary, I caught myself looking at some impassioned Hillary supporters with suspicion. On primary morning a thirtysomething white woman drove into the parking lot of the polling station where I was reporting, yelling out her car window, "I wanna vote for Hillary! I'm a Republican, but I want to vote for Hillary!" Instead of considering that this woman's zeal demonstrated that a hunger for female political leadership stretched beyond the Democratic Party, I stiffened. Maybe she was racist. Later that day, in a working-class Catholic neighborhood north of Philadelphia, Hillary voters told me that they would not vote for Obama because "there was something about him" they didn't trust.

Some of what I saw in Pennsylvania forced me to acknowledge that imputations of racism among Clinton supporters were as warranted as my own attribution of misogynistic impulses to some Obama voters. The very defenses I offered up about Clintonites—we were progressives who wanted the same things Obama supporters did, why should our commitments to social justice be called into question?— were precisely in tune with the "I can't be sexist, I'm a liberal" line coming from my uterus-punching Democratic compatriots.

The crucial question was how much Clinton and Obama themselves were stirring up, or capitalizing on, the prejudices of their supporters. Some of the charges thrown at Clinton strained the limits of credulity. In May she would defend her choice to stay in the race by noting, "My husband did not wrap up the nomination in 1992 until he won the California primary somewhere in the middle of June, right? We all remember Bobby Kennedy was assassinated in June in California." The reference was read by some as suggesting that perhaps Obama would be killed before the convention, an interpretation that I found implausible and unfair. But others were angry and bewildered simply at the fact that Clinton would unnecessarily summon the memory of Kennedy's tragic murder in the context of a fraught and historic political contest. "This is completely inappropriate in light of the fact that hate groups and white supremacists are . . . increasing the threat rhetoric," wrote Pam Spaulding at *Pam's House Blend*. "Why stoke the crazies even more with this kind of (presumably) careless remark?"

It was undeniable that some of the most egregious comments about Obama's race had come not just from Clinton supporters, but from her friends and associates, including Bob Kerrey, Billy Sha-heen and Andrew Cuomo. Clinton had not walked out of the room when Bob Johnson made comparisons between Obama and Sid-ney Poitier, and she had not harshly repudiated Geraldine Ferraro. Maybe she'd been reluctant to publicly excoriate an ill woman in whose footsteps toward executive office she alone had so far fol-lowed. But the fact remained that her gentle admonishment did not telegraph distance from or disgust with Ferraro's remarks. More-over the desire to profit from American racism and xenophobia had been written into the Clinton campaign's DNA, evidenced by Mark Penn's March 2007 memo, in which he wrote that he could not "imagine America electing a president during a time of war who is not at his center fundamentally American in his thinking and in his values." In May Clinton would comment to *USA Today* that her opponent's support among "hard-working Americans, white Amer-icans," was weakening. One of my favorite bloggers, Shark-Fu from *Angry Black Bitch,* wrote in response, "I've lost respect for this woman, her candidacy and the entire Clinton legacy. . . . I lift this vodka cran in a toast to the most amazing free fall from inspiring politician to complete gaping asshole of my lifetime. You've come a long way baby will forever have new meaning."

There were questions, though, about why Clinton was drawing so much flack for her missteps while Obama's gaffes drew so little. Paul Krugman wrote in the *New York Times* about "the inability of many alleged progressives to see that the news media created the narrative of Hillary Clinton as race-baiter in much the same way that . . . they created the narrative of Al Gore as congenital liar—by assembling a montage of quotes taken out of context and willfully misinterpreted." It may or may not have been true that some Clin-ton comments were taken out of context or misinterpreted. What was certainly true was that Pecksniffian sanctimony over the purity of Barack Obama's campaign glossed right over many of that cam-paign's own imperfections.

"The unctuousness, the holier-than-thou-ness of some of these people really annoyed me," said Gloria Feldt in 2009. "As if Barack Obama has always been totally pure. What are they smoking? The man came out of Chicago politics, for god's sake." It helped that Obama was a much better apologizer than Hillary was. When a memo from his campaign referred to Hillary as the Democrat from "Punjab" (a reference to her many Indian donors), Obama promptly apologized. When his advisor Samantha Power, the Pulitzer Prize–winning genocide expert, gave an interview to the *Scotsman* and said of Hillary, "She is a monster, too—that is off the record. . . . You just look at her and think, 'Ergh,'" the Obama campaign issued a statement decrying her comments and Powers resigned immediately. But apologia and self-correction flatter a man more than they do a woman. As the linguistics professor and writer Deborah Tannen pointed out in a 1996 essay, when it was reported in 1995 that Hillary had expressed remorse about the impact of her health care plan on her husband's administration, she was criticized by a political scientist who said, "To apologize for substantive things you've done raises the white flag," and by a woman in Florida's state cabinet who snipped, "I've seen women who overapologize, but . . . I believe you negotiate through strength."

Obama supporters legitimately attacked Hillary's infamous "3 a.m." ad, depicting vulnerable children in their beds, for its fearmongering negativity. But a January Obama campaign mailer employed those same alarmist tactics against Clinton's health care plan. The brochure showed a white couple sitting at a kitchen table, sorting through bills. "Hillary's health care plan forces everyone to buy insurance, even if you can't afford it," read the text. A few critics did notice; Ezra Klein pointed out that Obama had practically reanimated "Harry and Louise" from the deadly anti–health care ads of 1993, and Paul Krugman wrote, "I know that Obama supporters want to hear no evil, but this is really, really bad." On MSNBC's *Morning Joe* in March Zbigniew Brzezinski, an Obama supporter and former national security advisor to Jimmy Carter, compared Clinton's record of international diplomatic travel to the number of countries visited by his travel agent, and asked, "[If John Kennedy in 1960] had been running not against Nixon but against Mamie Eisenhower, would someone say that Mamie Eisenhower is better prepared to be president than John Kennedy?" Still, it was Hillary who was publicly branded as the negative campaigner with the rogue surrogates.

In February Obama gave a speech at Tulane in which he said of Clinton's campaign attacks, "You challenge the status quo and suddenly the claws come out," a characterization he might not have made about a man. Not long after that Obama told a reporter, "I understand that Senator Clinton, periodically when she's feeling down, launches attacks as a way of trying to boost her appeal." This evocation of a woman "periodically . . . feeling down" piqued the interest of some female television reporters, including Norah O'Donnell, who said, "It's getting a little personal," and Andrea Mitchell, who concurred and added, "Frankly, you know how deeply we interpreted every comment to look for some sort of racial motivation. . . . When you start describing a female candidate as being 'down' and 'striking back' . . . that's a little edgy, don't you think?"

One of the more ineffable complaints about Obama was that his team was a little too masculine, a little too fratty for comfort. Like Clinton's, Obama's campaign was designed by men; but unlike Clinton's, it was also largely staffed by men. With the crucial exceptions of Valerie Jarrett and later Anita Dunn, his closest advisors and strategists were men, and the vibe of the campaign, as described by both reporters covering it and those who did business with it, was clubby, sports-obsessed, and testosterone-fueled. Conversation within the ranks was dotted with "buddy" and "man"—dude talk, the kind of back-slapping repartee in which men, including some of the men in the media, could participate, but to which women found no easy entrance. There would be a spate of stories in September 2008 about how women working for Obama in the Senate made an average of 83 cents for every dollar made by men working in the same office. The numbers were misleading, but the explanation for the wage discrepancy was not particularly comforting: the average female salary was lower than the average male salary not because women were being paid less for the same jobs, but because they were not in the highest-level and best-remunerated positions. Of Obama's five highest paid staffers, only one was female, and only seven of his top twenty.

In May Peggy Agar, a reporter for a Detroit ABC affiliate station, approached Obama during his visit to the Chrysler LLC plant, asking, "Senator, how are you going to help the American autoworkers?" Obama waved Agar off, saying, "Hold on one second, sweetie." The clip gained YouTube traction, and within hours Obama left a message for Agar apologizing for failing to answer her question and for referring to her as "sweetie." He called his use of the word "a bad habit." His apology was timely and polite, but he was right: he had a "sweetie" habit. He had addressed a female factory worker in Allentown, Pennsylvania, by the same diminutive, and ABC soon found footage of him telling one female supporter, "Sweetie, if I start with a picture I will never get out of here," and another, "Sweetie, if I start doing autographs, I won't be able to get [out]."

The remark generated the opposite of outrage from the media: on *Good Morning America* a practically purring Diane Sawyer asked, "Don't you think it's going too far to care about that stuff?" Actually, no, it was not going too far to care about that stuff. To care about it did not mean that people should have changed their votes or their minds about Obama or his candidacy. But caring about that stuff was the only way to understand how language can convey diminishment, whether that diminishment is based on gender, race, age, or power. "Sweetie"—redolent of sugar and spice and all the rest of that stuff little girls are supposed to be made of—was an endearment. It was a warm word. Many women, myself included, enjoyed being called "sweetie" by people they cared about. That did not mean that we would have enjoyed being addressed that way by a presidential candidate, especially in response to a question about the future of American autoworkers, and especially when the word was part of a larger professional brush-off. Was it the most sexist thing a man could say to a woman? Certainly not. But whereas racially inflected remarks from Clinton had been pored over and parsed, the media seemed eager to sidestep the fact that Obama's reliance on the "sweetie" diminutive reflected some basic patriarchal attitudes. Much of the defensive maneuvering happened around the question of whether his elocution was premeditated or malevolent. Surely it was neither. As Whoopi Goldberg said on *The View*, the senator likely "meant . . . no disrespect." But good intentions don't render anyone incapable of disrespect or condescension, any more than a good record on race rendered Bill Clinton incapable of disrespect and condescension. Words are often both spontaneous *and* sexist.

The merry masculinity of Obama and his team was shrugged off as no big deal, but it was persistent enough to continue to draw attention after the primaries and into his administration. When, in

December of 2008, photos surfaced of Obama's wunderkind speech-writer Jon Favreau groping the breast of a cardboard cutout of Hillary, he apologized but was not publicly reprimanded or dismissed by his boss; he was hired to work in the White House. Less than a year into Obama's presidency the *New York Times* ran a front-page story about the president's habit of playing golf and basketball with high- and midlevel male staff members. The sports-heavy, lady-light vibe of an Obama White House made critics uncomfortable. While the choice of how and with whom to blow off steam might seem an awfully benign thing to get bent out of shape over, this was precisely the kind of pastime that throughout history had ensured the unceasing replication of patriarchal power structures. The ones who play ball, golf, cards, who smoke cigars and drink bourbon while speaking informally of power and policy are the ones who have the boss's ear, who understand him best and can manipulate him most successfully.

Barack Obama, the man with a silver tongue but a tin ear for lots of things having to do with women, should have known this but apparently didn't. He called the controversy about his all-boys basketball games "bunk," and in the words of reporter Mark Leibovich, he defended himself against the notion that the time spent with male advisors sent any kind of message in part by "point[ing] out that he is surrounded by strong females at home." This was an argument that not only echoed one made by George W. Bush's female adherents, who had equated respecting women with being henpecked by them, but also stank of long-entrenched sexism. Of course Obama was surrounded by women at home: that is one of the oldest gendered circumstances known to humankind; women at home are where they have always been. The question Leibovich and many of Obama's critics were getting at was where the women were *at work*.

My soreness over "sweetie" had less to do with the remark itself than with the determination to not acknowledge that it might reflect a societal approach to gender and power that was fundamental to why we had never had a strong female presidential contender before, just as comments about Obama's name signified the obstacles that long had come between African Americans and the presidency. But giving voice to these ruminations would only further flesh out an image of me as a finger-wagging L. L. Bean shopper affixing a Hillary '08 sticker to my Camry. Reciprocally, when I encountered odes to Obama's greatness, visions of dorm rooms humid with bong water and bedecked with Shepard Fairey posters floated into my head. We Democrats had become George Bush's soldiers, divided into "for us or against us" camps; nothing blurred our focus on our chosen candidates. I found myself fighting with Merideth, the friend who had first railed to me about how deplorably Clinton was being treated early in the race. Now Merideth spoke angrily about Clinton's answer to Steve Kroft's question on *60 Minutes*, about whether Obama was a Muslim. I had heard Clinton's immediate response, "Of course not," as definitive. Merideth had heard her later answer to Kroft's repetitions of the question, "No, there is nothing to base that on as far as I know," as equivocal.

I disagreed with the press's notion that the prolonged race was damaging the candidates, but I certainly noticed the toll it was taking on my affections for my fellow Democrats. American liberalism, unconsciously unfriendly to powerful women. American feminism, unconsciously unfriendly to African Americans. What was fascinating was the nearly identical rhythm of the unfriendliness in both camps: the vague doubts, something that the speaker could not quite articulate that made him or her distrust Obama or despise Clinton. There was the valid sense from Clinton supporters that people didn't sling racial epithets as easily as they called women bitches, that nobody joked about watermelons and fried chicken with the get-a-sense-of-humor brio attached to PMS and castration jokes. And the equally valid sense from Obama supporters that racism toward Obama was deeper, more insidious than what could be put on a bumper sticker, that Hillary's privileged racial and economic caste meant she could probably handle the period jokes. As Obama's former pastor Jeremiah Wright summed up, "Hillary ain't never been called a nigger." Both sides saw themselves in competition; they rarely realized how much they echoed each other. Baratunde Thurston, the blogger whom Latoya Peterson stopped reading during the primaries, wrote about his retrospective revelation that much of what offended him about how Obama was discussed closely resembled what offended female Hillary supporters. "I had an epiphany," he wrote, "*that which I most dislike about the*

*darker sides of her and her campaign is just what some people see
in me.* . . . I spent hours and days even, researching all the race-baiting
and ugliness going on in the media and among Clinton folks, but I
never bothered to try to find out what was driving some of Hillary's
staunchest supporters."

During the race, despite some agitation from within her camp
and much clamoring from her supporters, Clinton did not give what
was referred to within the campaign as "the women's speech," in
which she would address with depth and nuance her place in history
and women's relationship to power and public life. Clinton held
back because she and her advisors understood the risks. Ann Lewis
told me in 2010, "I just thought she was going to get beat up again.
No way was Chris Matthews going to say he's going to get a thrill
up his leg. They would just have said, 'Every time she's in trouble,
she plays the gender card.' It was painful because so many of our
friends and supporters hoped that she would do it. They wanted her
to speak up for them as only she could. But it wouldn't have been
in her best interest." Then there was the fact that Obama had given
his speech on race in response to controversy over the sermons of
Jeremiah Wright. "We didn't have a natural hook," Clinton advisor Lissa Muscatine told me in 2009. "We didn't want to do it in
response to the race speech. The struggle was how to do it in a way
that was compelling and substantive but also not regarded as 'Oh,
he did the race speech, now she's going to do a woman speech.'"

But during Clinton's victory speech in Philadelphia on April 22
she offered an almost Obama-style articulation of how this often
painful process was moving the nation forward. She noted that
her victory party was taking place in the city where the country's
founders had set down a vision for democracy's future, a vision
in which "neither Senator Obama nor I were fully included." Citing abolitionists, suffragists, unionists, and all those who had ever
marched and protested—the predecessors of those who were now
campaigning and fighting and yelling at each other—Clinton said,
"because of them, I grew up taking for granted that women could
vote. Because of them, my daughter grew up taking for granted
that children of all colors could attend school together." And now,
Clinton continued, children will grow up "taking for granted that a
woman or an African American can be the president of the United

States of America." She seemed to see the other side. This hell, she was saying, was worth it.

☆ ☆ ☆

True to form, the media did not react to Clinton's Pennsylvania win by sending her flowers. Instead her victory seemed to elicit an unprecedented wave of aggression. The calls for her to drop out became pointed, propelled now by serious alarm: her insistence on competing and winning against Obama was making him look bad. In *Time* Joe Klein criticized her insubstantial attack tactics against Obama, claiming that they had damaged her reputation, but that "that was nothing compared with the damage done to Obama, who entered the primary as a fresh breeze and left it stale, battered and embittered . . . no longer the darling of his party." In addition to the questions about his pastor and insinuations about his relationship with former Weatherman Bill Ayers, it was during the Pennsylvania primary race that Obama had been quoted at a fund-raiser saying that those Americans who clung to their guns and their religion were bitter. It was, by rational measures, an ultimately compassionate observation about those who had been economically devastated by Reaganism and then by two Bush administrations, but it had not gone over well with blue-collar folks, especially because on the campaign trail, as Klein noted, Obama "seemed to look on the ceremonies of working-class life—bowling, hunting, churchgoing and the fervent consumption of greasy food—as his anthropologist mother might have, with a mixture of cool detachment and utter bemusement." Obama's difficulty connecting with working-class America was beginning to cause Democrats concern about the general election. And they were blaming Hillary for it.

It was true that the Clinton camp had thrown some stones. But since when was it owed to any candidate that he or she escape the dents and dings of political competition? Just as voters and commentators had considered the impact on Hillary's electability of her abysmal strategic team, her personal and political baggage and her early trouble connecting with voters, it was now fair to evaluate how Obama performed as his opponent got stronger, as he accumulated baggage of his own, as he lost the glint of tender newness.

But pundits were sure it was incumbent on Hillary to drop out. When they fantasized about her exit in January it was because she had lost Iowa. When Jonathan Alter suggested she drop out in February it was because she was likely to be humiliated in upcoming big contests. Now that it was Obama who was losing and being humiliated, the prescription, oddly, remained the same: Hillary had to go. It was a media barrage that Melissa McEwan dubbed "Take Your Boobs and Go Home."

A *New York Times* op-ed castigating Clinton for running negative ads about Obama in Pennsylvania suggested, "It is getting to be time for the superdelegates to . . . settle a bloody race that cannot be won at the ballot box." Maureen Dowd nudged Hillary to take a cue from an old Dr. Seuss poem that the children's author had in 1974 applied to Richard Nixon. Dowd's verse went, in part, "The time is now. Just go. . . . I don't care how. You can go by foot. You can go by cow. Hillary R. Clinton, will you please go now!" On *Countdown,* *Newsweek*'s Howard Fineman suggested that it was time for "some adults somewhere in the Democratic Party to step in and stop this thing." Keith Olbermann agreed, saying, "Right . . . somebody who can take her in a room and only he comes out," a comment that led the *Huffington Post* columnist Rachel Sklar to headline an item "Olbermann's Idea for Beating Hillary: Literally Beating Hillary." Olbermann later apologized for his remark, calling it "a metaphor."

More arresting was an appearance by Ken Rudin on CNN *Sunday Morning* in late April, in which the NPR political editor said, "Let's be honest here, Hillary Clinton is Glenn Close in *Fatal Attraction.* She's going to keep coming back, and they're not going to stop her." In evoking Close's character Rudin was summoning a bunny-boiling virago whose bullet-riddled demise in a bathtub represented one of the most graphic cinematic punishments of aggressive femininity available to the American imagination. So outrageous was Rudin's comparison that it prompted *Sunday Morning* cohost Betty Nguyen to suggest, in response to Rudin's admission that he'd been partying all night at the White House Correspondents Dinner, "Maybe that explains the Glenn Close analogy." Rudin later apologized, claiming he wished he hadn't made the "facile and dumb comparison." But he had created a meme. Two weeks later Tennessee Con-

gressman Steve Cohen, an Obama supporter whom Nancy Pelosi
once called "the conscience of the freshman class," was asked about
Clinton's presence in the race and replied, "Glenn Close should have
just stayed in the tub." It was as if the id of every guy who had built
up resentments toward powerful women had staged a coup against
the superego, making it open season not just on Clinton, but on
all noncompliant women. Penn Jillette heartily joked on MSNBC's
Morning Joe in May, "Obama did great in February, and that's
because that was Black History Month. And now Hillary's doing
much better because it's White Bitch Month, right?"

Only a few people were calling foul. At *Media Matters* Eric
Boehlert wrote, "Looking back through modern U.S. campaigns,
there's simply no media model for so many members of the press to
try to drive a competitive candidate from the field while the primary
season is still unfolding. . . . Strong second place candidates such
as Ronald Reagan (1976), Ted Kennedy, Gary Hart, Jesse Jackson, and Jerry Brown, all of whom campaigned through the entire
primary season, and most of whom took their fights all the way
to their party's nominating conventions, were never tagged by the
press and told to go home."

The media was not presenting the fight between Clinton and
Obama as a norm for close presidential races. Instead we were being
told that in continuing to compete with him, in not letting him just
win, Clinton was behaving like a headstrong child or a demented
movie villain. Here were echoes of the strategies that in recent years
had bedeviled reproductive rights activists faced with one antichoice
Democrat after another. Couldn't they see that in prosecuting their
own self-interested aims they were imperiling the greater good?
That if they would just stand down, Democrats would win, which
would be good for everyone, *including women,* but that if they continued to make their self-serving stand we would wind up under
Republican control and everyone would suffer, because of *them?* As
with the siren song about antichoice Democrats, this argument was
painful for those of us on the other side of it. *Of course* we wanted
a Democratic president and a Democratic majority. *We were liberals,* or Democrats, or radicals, or progressives, or whatever we
called ourselves, who were invested in reproductive rights or in the
Clinton campaign precisely because we cared about liberal politics,

because we believed fervently in making the country a better place for more people. It felt almost sadistic, the maneuverings of those who would trade on our rights or dismiss our candidate early and then accuse us of undermining a progressive agenda.

* * *

My birthday, May 6, was the day Clinton lost North Carolina and won Indiana by a margin so slender that it was clear that this was, truly, the end. At a restaurant with three longtime girlfriends, conversation was strained; two of us were for Clinton, the other two for Obama. We would each start to talk and then cut ourselves off, not wanting to argue when we were supposed to be celebrating. Partway through the meal I checked my phone and saw the night's results. The reality of Clinton's fate began to settle heavy in my belly.

As we walked home after dinner, Geraldine, the friend with whom I'd started down this road four months earlier, tried to talk me out of my funk, explaining how much better I would feel once I made the inevitable switch of allegiance to Obama, how good it felt to support him, how much easier it was than backing Hillary. All I heard was a pod person, someone talking to me from the other side of the invasion of the body snatchers: Just give in; it's so much easier this way. I nodded, understanding that soon I would be a pod person too, that my frustrations would subside. I just wasn't ready to go there yet.

On the day of the last Democratic primaries, in Montana and South Dakota, Hillary Clinton was running for the Democratic nomination pretty much in name only. When my colleague Caitlin Shamberg, a video producer at Salon, and I tried to check in for her New York speech that evening—usually an arduous process of negotiating with officious campaign staffers—her press people practically threw our credentials at us. They were not laminated or hung on lanyards as per usual; they were simply pieces of paper on twine. I thought of Monty Python's dead parrot sketch: Hillary '08 had shuffled off its mortal coil, rung down the curtain, and joined the bleeding choir invisible. It was an ex-campaign.

When Hillary finally arrived at the lectern she gave her preconcession speech. She thanked South Dakota, which she had won. She congratulated her "friend" Obama, who she said "inspired so many Americans to care about politics and empowered so many more to get involved, and our party and our democracy [are] stronger and more vibrant as a result." She spoke of "mothers and fathers lifting their little girls and their little boys onto their shoulders and whispering, 'See, you can be anything you want to be.'" The crowd shouted, "Denver! Denver!" and she did not rebuke them. She said that the next day was her mother's birthday. She said she was going to take a day or two, confer with advisors. She suggested that her supporters visit HillaryClinton.com, a plea for help in paying down her monster campaign debt. There was a friendliness and a camaraderie about her speech, a weary but warm sense that those in the room had been through a lot together. Clinton was commencing the delicate process of turning her enormous ship around. As we walked out of the building, Caitlin, an Obama supporter from the beginning, said to me, "That speech made me like her more than I ever have before. It almost makes me wish she *would* take it to Denver. She's way more fun than I ever thought she'd be." I went home and went to bed, feeling flat and resigned, already pulling away from the campaign, distancing myself from the avidity I'd somehow generated for Hillary and her presidential project.

When I logged on to my computer the next morning there were three hundred emails from Obama-supporting readers, friends, and colleagues, all expressing barely cogent rage at Hillary. She had not conceded! She had not given Obama his night, his moment in the sun! She had held her speech in a building without cell phone service to keep reporters from learning that she had lost the primaries! She was plotting to use the superdelegate system to steal the nomination! She was going to destroy the party and the country in her preening bid for monomaniacal power!

This would be the last moment of the primary during which I felt as though I inhabited a different planet than everyone else in my party, that I had heard a different speech, seen a different person, been in a different room than everyone else. But I can't say that I was unhappy that they had heard what they did. If they thought Hillary was telling them to fuck off, that was okay with me. For just one last day, before I joined their ranks, I wanted them to fuck off too.

8 THINGS TO DO IN DENVER
IF YOU'RE FEMALE

FOUR DAYS AFTER Hillary Clinton's un-concession I dragged myself out of bed at the crack of dawn on a Saturday to travel to D.C. to watch her throw in the towel for real. I dressed in jeans and a ratty T-shirt, a sign of how much I didn't care about this event. But somewhere along the northeast corridor, as I began a draft of what would be my coverage of the speech, I wondered if maybe when I got to Union Station I shouldn't buy a nicer shirt. My sartorial reconsideration was not singular; when the train pulled in, several grouchy New York reporters hit Tiecoon and Express, searching for garments that conveyed something closer to respect than what they'd pulled on that morning. I can't say that my hastily purchased black button-down shirt (its material suitable for protecting human life during reentry into the Earth's atmosphere) will ever see daylight again, but it still hangs in my closet, and I think of Hillary whenever I catch sight of it there.

Clinton had spent days trying to figure out what she was going to say. Her advisors were split between those who believed she needed to emphasize her endorsement of Obama and those who felt she must, at last, truly address the women who had supported her. Speechwriter Sarah Hurwitz was caught in between. "I think [Hillary] was thinking it through herself," said Ann Lewis. "What she wanted to accomplish, what she wanted people to remember about her." Lissa Muscatine was arguing on the side of the ladies. "This was obviously a speech that was going to be parsed over and over again and psychoanalyzed by the press. . . . It was going to be a historic moment," she told me in 2009. "To me, the most important thing was that it be genuine, both in conceding to and endorsing Obama, and in conveying to the eighteen million people who supported her, especially women, that the end of her campaign didn't mean she was abandoning them. I felt you could do both in one speech." Muscatine continued, "I felt strongly—vehemently, actually—that she had to speak directly to women and let them know that she was not simply going to recede into the woodwork and become acquiescent about these issues because she lost the race." Muscatine was concerned that this had not been reflected in early drafts of the speech and wrote Clinton a long memo about it. "These people had come out for her in droves, especially in the last months of the campaign. Their hearts and emotions were tied up in the campaign, and her loss was shattering for many of them. They were counting on her. I really felt she had a duty and obligation to speak to those women even as she was endorsing Obama." There were big arguments within the campaign. Clinton's strategist Geoff Garin pushed strongly for keeping the emphasis on Obama; her aide Jim Kennedy contributed a sentence about 18 million cracks in a glass ceiling. At some point Hillary wrested control of her own speech, staying up all night to rewrite it and find the balance between Barack Obama and her campaign's place in women's history. The morning of her speech, hours before she was to give her address, some advisors were still pressing her to cut the parts about gender.

The National Building Museum was air-conditioned, but it couldn't keep the scalding heat from seeping in. The throng inside the large room glistened, their faces slick with perspiration and, even before Clinton began speaking, some tears.

When she took the podium Clinton issued a lengthy round of thank-yous before turning to her final task as presidential contender, rallying her supporters to her opponent's cause. She was, as she had always been, a good girl. She praised Obama, yelled "Yes, we can!" with a convincing show of enthusiasm, and did her damnedest to start a slightly lame and wordy chant: "We must help elect Barack Obama our president!"

But then she took a moment, the moment many of her supporters had been longing for since she entered the race, to unfurl some feminist plumage. "I know there still are barriers and biases out there, often unconscious," she finally said, and the room roared in relief and affirmation. "You can be so proud that, from now on, it will be *un*remarkable for a woman to win primary state victories, *un*remarkable to have a woman in a close race to be our nominee, *un*remarkable to think that a woman can be the president of the United States." She paused. People screamed. "And that is truly remarkable."

Clinton was making sure no one forgot that it was she who had made a footprint on history and then stamped up and down until her size 8½s made the mark indelible. "To those who are disappointed that we couldn't go all the way, especially the young people who put so much into this campaign," Clinton said, "it would break my heart if, in falling short of my goal, I in any way discouraged any of you from pursuing yours." I looked at the crowd of kids, the ones who had been sitting on their parents' shoulders all over the country for so many months, watching Clinton and Obama campaign. "As we gather here today," Clinton said, "the fiftieth woman to leave this Earth is orbiting overhead. If we can blast fifty women into space, we will someday launch a woman into the White House." Her crescendo was the line to which she will be forever tethered, a sentence far superior to any about not baking cookies: "Although we weren't able to shatter that highest, hardest glass ceiling this time, thanks to you it's got about eighteen million cracks in it."

Wary throughout the campaign of turning herself into too much of a symbol, Clinton had given the speech of her life, perhaps to her own surprise. Muscatine, who had worked with her since her days as first lady, explained that Hillary's particular brand of feminism had always been more focused on the nitty-gritty of policy issues than on soaring feminist rhetoric. "She was always about things like pay equity, breast cancer coverage, health insurance, or even going around the world talking about women and microfinance," said

Muscatine. "Her championing the cause was not emotional in the way you and I might feel about feminism. We might be motivated by an accumulation of all these little stupid obstacles thrown at us because we're girls, or women. . . . It's not that she's emotionally detached, exactly, but she doesn't come at these issues with a huge amount of emotion that other people try to project on her." Instead, Muscatine said, Clinton has always been focused on the practicalities of progress, what kinds of concrete improvements she could make. In their days at the White House they used to argue about it: "I used to tell her, 'You are not using the symbolic power of your position.' She would say, 'That's not going to effect systemic change, or make a lasting impact.' My argument was, sometimes you effect the change through the symbolic act."

In her concession speech Clinton gave in and made the symbolic gesture, and it was a corker, though as some of her advisors had predicted, the media wanted to hear only one thing: her enthusiasm for Obama. At MSNBC Rachel Maddow was moderating a panel discussion about the speech. Months later she told me that she heard the speech and knew the story was Clinton's embrace of her piece of American history, but all her colleagues wanted to talk about was the not-breaking news that Clinton had endorsed Obama. "The stuff about millions of cracks in the glass ceiling no longer being remarkable I thought was huge," Maddow said. "But look back . . . [and] see how much the commentary focused on [that part of the speech]. None of it. It was all 'She endorsed him!'" As a moderator rather than a commentator, Maddow had a mandate to direct conversation, not offer her own opinion, but she gave it a shot nonetheless. "I said something like 'Obviously what we saw here was an incredible statement about women . . . am I right?'" she recalled. "Everyone just replied, 'I think her endorsement of Obama was blah blah blah.' Even as a person who helped to decide what the point of discussion was in the mainstream media, I was alone."

I looked around at the people waving their flags, hoisting their kids, and cheering for her. My phone began to vibrate with calls from my mother, my cousin, my girlfriends, all watching from their homes. As Clinton stepped off the stage I saw a text from Geraldine. "I am completely losing it," she wrote. It was then that I lost it too. Sprinting from the press area, where Clinton's reporting squad were saying their good-byes after months on the road together, I found space behind a pillar. Next to me was Matt Drudge, who seemed not to realize or care that I was stupidly sobbing. I was so tired. Tired of caring so much about a woman I hadn't meant to care about at all. Tired of arguing with my friends. Tired of being angry at people I'd never been angry with before. Tired of being identified with Hillary even when I didn't like her. Tired of resisting the fact that maybe I did like her quite a lot.

Shelby Knox watched the speech alone at Gloria Steinem's house. Steinem had traveled to Washington for the address with batches of buttons she and Knox had made together; they read, "Hillary Supports Obama and So Do I!" She had discouraged Knox from attending the speech. "She knew I was going to lose it," said Knox in retrospect. Knox admitted that she had indeed cried through the whole concession and was still disconsolate when Steinem returned home.

When I asked Steinem in 2009 what she felt at Clinton's concession she answered without pause, "Relief." "I hate conflict," she said. "If I'd been [Hillary] I would have quit after Iowa. I know I'm in the wrong business." This jibed with the sentiment she voiced to Knox. "I asked her if it was as horrible in person as it was on TV," Knox recalled, "and she said, 'No, it was like a party.'" Knox was angered by Steinem's nonchalance, remembering that she said, "Think about it, Shelby: we don't have to talk about this anymore. We don't have to do this anymore." Knox tearfully pointed out that now we would also not have a woman president. "Gloria said, 'But Shelby, we will have a woman president. And you'll see it.'"

It was the young women who were supposed to have been optimistic and breezy about the future, the old ones who were meant to feel pessimistic, but here was Steinem, buoyant and dry-eyed in the face of a youthful lachrymosity. "Why are you crying?" Knox remembered Steinem asking her over and over again.

When Knox told me this story I remembered my own blubbing at the end of the concession speech. I remembered the message from Geraldine: "I am completely losing it." I also remembered a passage from a profile of Steinem that Nora Ephron wrote in 1972, at the Democratic convention in Miami. After watching the National Women's Political Caucus get sold out by the Democrats, including George McGovern, Ephron found Steinem in a hotel lobby and began to walk with her to her next meeting. Ephron described their conversation, "'It's just so difficult,' [Steinem] says, crying now. I begin babbling—all the pressures on you, no private life, no sleep, no wonder you're upset. 'It's not that,' says Gloria. 'It's just that they won't take us seriously.' She wipes at her cheeks with her hand, and begins crying again. 'And I'm just tired of being screwed, and being screwed by my friends. . . . They won't take us seriously.' . . . She is still crying, and I try to offer some reassuring words, something, but everything I say is wrong; I have never cried over anything remotely political in my life, and I honestly have no idea of what to say."

The intervening decades had provided Steinem with lots more experience in bucking up and carrying on. But Knox, her skin unthickened by age and repeated disappointment, and I, who like Ephron would not previously have imagined myself crying over any-thing political, and Geraldine, who had not even voted for Hillary—we were all momentarily gutted by the loss. There was certainly something to be said for the dignity and forbearance that came with experience, but I suspected that it had been Steinem's youthful intensity and sensibility, her impulse to cry over something politi-cal, that had helped affirm her dedication to staying in her business, despite her avowed discomfort with conflict.

There was something else at the heart of Knox's angst. "I couldn't say what I wanted to say," she recalled, until Steinem's repeated assurance that she would see a female president in her life-time finally made her blurt out, "But *you* won't. And I wanted *you* to see it." Reminded of her looming mortality by a twenty-year-old, Steinem looked slightly taken aback, Knox recalled. "Then she hugged me and said, 'I might, you know. It could happen in the next twenty-five years. But I also got to see Hillary run, and I got to see young women like you get angry about it and know that it was going to happen. I will get to see Sasha and Malia move into the White House. I got to see all of this happen."

* * *

As Clinton's threatening shadow began at last to recede, tributes started to stream in from feminist pundits who had backed Obama and were now comfortable extending some tepid "You go, girl" plaudits. Then there were those who were sticking to their anti-Clinton guns, reminding us that Hillary's loss was no one's fault but her own, that she may have been a woman, but she was no icon. Maybe if she hadn't voted for the war, maybe if she hadn't been married to Bill, maybe if she'd been more of a true feminist, maybe if she'd been more like them—then, maybe, these people could have gotten excited about her as a presidential candidate.

My gut reaction, as I recovered from my unexpected bout of emotion, was that though we all might wish that our groundbreaking leaders come in prettier packages, we get what we get. We got Hillary Clinton. In no small part we got her thanks to the reasons so many couldn't abide her: her ambition, her ruthlessness, her marriage, her centrism, her hawkishness. I couldn't think of many women of sterling liberal character who would have succeeded where she failed to satisfy all feminists while also winning Ohio.

It was all well and good that little girls might grow up knowing that women could run for president and break voting records; Clinton and Obama had each received more primary votes than any other presidential candidate in history. I was perhaps more gratified that those little girls would know they were not responsible for embodying the highest expectations for their gender's civility and decorum because one hellaciously difficult woman had been there before them and knocked everybody around pretty hard.

As each primary approached I was sure that Clinton was toast; again and again I got a thrill from watching the talking heads collapse into paroxysms of annoyance at this woman who would not quit. After one particularly wild election night, perhaps it was Ohio, I received an email from my cousin, a Clinton skeptic who had come to appreciate the senator's dazzling ability to drive her critics around the bend. "I hope she never stops running," my cousin wrote. "Even after he's elected." It had nothing to do with Obama. We were young women, drunk on the fun of watching an older woman refuse to concede to anyone's expectations. At the party after the Pennsylvania primary I bumped into a *New York Times* journalist who said, with great theatrical weariness about the fact that this primary had not clinched it, "Well, see you in Guam." But a smile played across her lips. This was funny. Actually, it was hilarious.

There was some hand-wringing about where the next female

contender would come from, but I did not feel particular alarm. Who knew the name Bill Clinton before 1992? Who knew the name Barack Obama before 2004? Who, ten years earlier, could have imagined that beleaguered First Lady Hillary Rodham Clinton would come so close to getting her own intern in the Oval Office? People came out of nowhere and surprised us. What turned out to be my dedication to—and, after all these years, my identification with—Hillary Clinton had surprised me.

To have voted for Hillary, to have deviated from my peers, had sometimes made me feel as though I wore a big red H on my chest, but learning to acknowledge and embrace my affinity for this woman proved to be not only an extraordinary political experience, but one that reshaped my appreciation for a certain kind of powerful woman.

But now it was over. Hillary had to let go.

Some of her supporters, however, did not.

* * *

In the bitterest days of the race there had been speculation that Hillary's flock would not go gently into the Obama campaign. It had seemed a silly prediction, born of the bad tempers and competitive antipathies of the primary. In the heat of things, Michelle Obama herself had said that she would have to carefully consider whether or not to support Clinton if she won the contest. Overblown prognostications about ornery Clintonites spoke to the vilification of Clinton's imagined coven and the eagerness to lay blame at their feet. They were going to ruin everything.

Five days after Clinton's concession I got my first inkling that the myth of the unforgiving Hillary die-hard had some basis in fact. I was in Washington, speaking on a panel at the annual convention of EMILY's List. My fellow panelist Katrina vanden Heuvel, editor of the *Nation,* was receiving a surprisingly chilly reception from the audience, largely, it seemed, because her magazine had endorsed Barack Obama for president. When she mentioned DNC chairman Howard Dean in her speech, the crowd booed. Was this, vanden Heuvel asked, about Dean's decision not to count votes from Michigan and Florida? Nope, they replied. It was about his behavior toward Clinton and her supporters.

It was true that Dean had not spoken up against sexism or about the historic nature of Clinton's campaign as soon as he might have. It was widely assumed, though never confirmed, that privately both he and House Speaker Nancy Pelosi were rooting for Obama, and that one or both of them exerted pressure on Hillary to get out of the race. "They were silent when it came to sexism," said Jehmu Greene, who had worked as the head of women's outreach at the DNC until 2000. "Nancy Pelosi should have spoken up; Howard Dean should have spoken up; Harry Reid should have spoken up."

After Clinton's defeat, Dean, who apparently did not watch a lot of television, claimed that he had not been aware of the misogyny directed at Clinton until a friend sat him down, around the time of Clinton's concession, and showed him back-to-back clips of some of the ugliness. Once he'd gotten a taste, several sources confirmed, he had been genuinely horrified. Within days of Clinton's concession he told the *New York Times,* "The wounds of sexism need to be the subject of a national discussion. . . . Many of the most prominent people on TV behaved like middle schoolers." But it was a strategic error: Clinton supporters only heard way too little, conveniently way too late. Dean would bring up the issue repeatedly in the months after Hillary's concession, asserting in a November panel discussion that sexism was the most "underwritten" story of the election. I made repeated attempts to contact Dean to speak about that underwritten story for this book, to no avail.

Dean's post-Hillary tip of the hat to misogyny was part of a larger trend among Democrats: a sudden, partywide enthusiasm for talking about gender. On some level this was terrific. But for those Hillary defenders who for months had been compiling and disseminating carefully catalogued lists of every talking head who ever called Clinton a castrating, cankled cauldron-stirrer, it was rather deflating to hear the people they'd been desperate to reach suddenly tumble to the idea that sexism was the most underreported story of the year.

Most of the women who were angry about Clinton's fate, the women at EMILY's List and beyond, were angry for some perfectly legitimate, and amply precedented, reasons. A period of recalcitrance was to be expected after protracted political battle. In 2004 it had taken Howard Deaniacs months to return to the Kerry fold. But their reluctance had not been monitored with the same lip-licking zeal, in part because the Dean-Kerry rivalry had not been plumped by the personal sting of identity politics. The length and ferocity of the Clinton-Obama competition had given supporters time to truly sink their teeth in and invest unreservedly.

Many of Clinton's staunchest supporters were women who had dedicated their lives to Democratic politics, had just had their hearts broken and now felt isolated and taken for granted by their own party, a party that was doing little to meet them halfway. Major Democrats were reacting to Clintonite bellyaching by broadcasting their assurance that once feathers were smoothed Clinton women would come back and vote like the good Democrats they were. In a profile of Keith Olbermann in the *New Yorker* MSNBC executive Phil Griffin described how Olbermann appeared to Clinton voters: "He turns out to be a jerk and difficult and brutal. And that is how the Hillary viewers see him. It's true. But I do think they're going to come back. There's nowhere else to go." The presumption that Democratic women's loyalty would ultimately not waver was historically sound, but it was precisely the attitude that most infuriated Hillary supporters in the aftermath of her campaign. Their party and their media, both kept alive in large part by female dollars and votes, had not treated them with respect, and then shrugged their shoulders at their anger, because they understood women to be strapped by their reproductive organs to the DNC.

Yes, there were suddenly lots of panel discussions, web forums, and newspaper stories devoted to the subject of sexism in the primaries. But the tendency to focus on two reductive questions—*Did Hillary face sexism?* and worse, *Did her campaign fail because of sexism?*—did not allow for much nuance or thoughtfulness. Of course she had not failed because of sexism. She had failed for a host of reasons that, sure, probably included sexism. Everything about Clinton's campaign was marked in some way by her gender, but the suggestion that sexism was exclusively or even largely to blame for her defeat was not only implausible, it was the kind of overwrought conclusion that did no favors to those who propagated it. There had been instances in which sexism had *helped* Clinton garner the outraged support she needed to remain in contention. But few in the media wanted to hear answers this complex. Few were interested in talking about sexism unless it could be made into a simplified game of aggrieved blame laying. And so it was those who were willing to simplistically and grievously lay blame—and even more, who were willing to jump up and down and point fingers—who attracted the media spotlight.

Thus were born the PUMAs, a small, loose collective of rabble-rousers who helped to fill the news void between primary season and the political conventions. With cameras and microphones trained on them after months of feeling dismissed, ignored or simply talked over, a tiny but vocal number of Clinton supporters—and as far as I could discern, some Republicans posing as Hillary Democrats—became the summer's media darlings by fulfilling every fantasy of affronted femininity, promising to make a scene at the convention in Denver and vote for McCain in November. They were the perfect foil for anxious Obama supporters who needed someone to blame everything on and found themselves short a Hillary.

PUMA stood for Party Unity My Ass. Those who rallied under its banner had a temperament distinctly different from that of the politically dedicated women I'd met at EMILY's List. The PUMA expressions of loyalty seemed tailor-made to corroborate every hoary, bigoted cliché about Hillary's defenders being irrational harpies. They damaged everyone who had ever supported her.

⋆ ⋆ ⋆

Meanwhile, despite a stagey "Unity" tour designed to show Clinton and Obama as a cheery team, Obama's campaign appeared not to be attuned to the more understated and rational distress of Clinton's following. In high-level meetings with Clinton donors, Obama advisors made precious little attempt to address her supporters' reservations or to entice them by asking what their concerns and priorities were. Instead, many donors reported, the sell was stupidly cold: *Sorry she's out, now please give us your money.* It made handing over the dough more difficult than it might otherwise have been.

Ann Lewis told me in 2010 of a phone conversation she'd had

with an individual donor. This was when she and other Clinton campaigners were "being good soldiers" over the summer, "talking to 'Women for Hillary' groups, getting them to get out and support Obama." "I used a line I had been using a little too easily, which was, 'Look, if Hillary can do what she's doing, which is so hard, then surely we can do this,'" Lewis recalled. "The woman said to me, 'Yeah, but she's a better person than I am.'"

Naturally some Clinton supporters harbored the hope that Obama would ask her to be his running mate, felt that it would be not only a courteous but a brilliant move that would deliver him her 18 million voters and unite the fractured party into an unstoppable whole. Obama supporters were understandably less thrilled by this idea. At a Unity breakfast at the New York Hilton in July I watched Clinton give one of her fulsome postdefeat speeches, with Obama befuddled next to her; he looked unsure of what to make of his once formidable opponent, now grinning widely beside him. In the ladies room after the speech members of a group called Women for Obama grumbled about Clinton's cat-that-ate-the-canary appearance. "You'd never know she lost," they said. "She makes him so uncomfortable," said another. "He better not choose her as a running mate," said a third. The whole ladies room line nodded in vigorous agreement.

Rumors swirled that Obama might pick another woman for the ticket, a choice that would suggest he understood the importance of having female executive leadership. Names began to float; Kansas Governor Kathleen Sebelius seemed the most serious possibility. The vocal PUMAs were not just unimpressed by this; they were steamed. Some remained so besotted by the idea of *their* woman as *the* history maker that they would not be satisfied unless Clinton or someone from her direct bloodline was the first female to breach the Oval Office. Even some of the more reasonable Hillary loyalists were dismayed by the more systemic problem that this imagined plan laid bare: the paucity of women in government left a pitiful few to choose from, and the names being bandied about seemed pallid substitutes for the steam engine Clinton had become.

Obama was in a bind. His smartest choice would have been to pick someone immediately, chilling the hopes of Hillary's monofocused flock. Instead he made a tone-deaf move: at just the moment he was supposed to be making nice with Camp Clinton, he appointed her estranged ex-campaign manager, Patti Solis Doyle, to his campaign's team as chief of staff for his yet unnamed vice president. To those who had paid attention to the power dynamics within the Clinton campaign, hiring the scorned Solis Doyle seemed a sure signal that her former boss was not even being considered as a vice-presidential pick. One of Clinton's top donors called it the "biggest fuck-you I have ever seen in politics."

Most discouraging about the Solis Doyle appointment was the degree to which it confirmed that neither Obama nor his advisors were hearing the reasons many women felt alienated from their campaign. Many sources within the Obama campaign reported that the organization was blindsided and mystified by the backlash over the appointment. This was the strategic problem with having a frat-house campaign, a dynamic related to the one that Latifa Lyles had described about the lack of diversity at NOW: beyond a failure of political correctness, the preponderance of men in the Obama camp meant that there was no one around to understand or explain that, intentions aside, hiring Solis Doyle was a nasty rebuke to those who had given their hearts and their pocketbooks to the Clinton campaign. So bereft was the Obama campaign of women that, John Heilemann and Mark Halperin would go on to report, it was Solis Doyle herself, once aboard, who would clue in the Obama team that picking another woman might not go over swimmingly with Clinton's supporters. Obama's announcement that he would be running alongside Joe Biden came late on the Friday night before the convention, getting things started with a flash of disappointment for Hillary's delegates who had perhaps held out some hope.

Clinton had not released her delegates, and in Denver many of them were hoping to make a symbolic gesture by voting for her on the first ballot. This made sense to me. They wanted their place in history, no different from Shirley Chisholm's or Ted Kennedy's delegates before them. They weren't threatening a takeover. Those I spoke to said they would vote for Obama on the second ballot. But their motives were made to seem nefarious thanks to the exploitive coverage of the small band of disruptive PUMAs.

"This is where you see the civil war!" said Chris Matthews from an outdoor stage in the sweltering Denver heat, while behind him two small but boisterous groups chanted "Obama! Obama!" and "Hillary! Hillary!" at each other. Matthews looked beside himself with happiness as he declared, "We're at ground zero!" He was in fact about six blocks away from the Pepsi Center, the crowd behind him probably no more than a hundred strong, and at least one of them was dressed as a toilet for reasons that appeared to have nothing to do with Clinton or Obama. Media mirages were made from miniature tableaux of political discord played out in front of a couple of well-placed television cameras. The PUMAs were making Chris Matthews's night. They held aloft Clinton signs and hand-markered cards reading "Stop Delegate Intimidation!" and "South Jersey PUMA." A small group holding "McCain" signs started a melodic chorus of "Clintons for McCain, sweetie, Clintons for McCain, sweetie," in reference to Obama's bad habit. Next to them a man in an Obama hat shouted, "You're all irrelevant! Jesus!"

The press, and especially MSNBC, thought the Hillary wraiths were relevant; in fact they seemed to think they were the most important story to be told about the convention, without regard for the fact that every national political convention in modern history had become a locus for agitators. The reporters did not take into account that during the convention antiwar protests drew thousands of people, compared to the dozens who made noise about Hillary. They did not take into account that on Monday of the convention Code Pink, the antiwar protest group, had hijacked a presentation by Nancy Pelosi, screaming "Liar! Liar!" "You said you'd impeach Bush!" "You lied to my face!" I had witnessed this demonstration, and it was far more disruptive and newsworthy than the people dressed as commodes milling around Chris Matthews's stage. No, Matthews and his colleagues were taking the grounded gripes with the way Clinton had been treated, the longer-standing concerns of liberal women about their place in their party, the simple desire of Clinton delegates to cast their symbolic votes, and representing it all via this small and overheated gathering. The media was putting a kabuki mask of unhinged wrathfulness over the saner impulses of most Hillary supporters.

In Denver Marie Wilson, head of the White House Project, told me, "There is such a fear of women coming into power that when they protest, they are given more weight. Just the fact of women saying they support their candidate and want to make their voices heard sounds more scary than it would be if it were guys. That's just part of backlash." Wilson saw the discord as a positive, though perhaps painful step in the right direction. "We are in the middle of a revolution," she said of the aftermath of Hillary's run. Her organization, which encouraged women to seek elected office, had enjoyed a 61 percent increase in participation in 2008.

Dana Kennedy, a forty-year-old Clinton delegate from Arizona, was one of three hundred signers of a petition to get a roll call vote for Clinton. "My hope is that in the first round of voting I get to vote for her, and in the second round, I will vote for Obama," said Kennedy. "A vote for Hillary is a vote for history and *not* against him." Another Clinton delegate, Rosina Rubin from New York, said, "This is not about anger. We all want to elect a Democrat in November. But why wouldn't her name be placed in nomination? She is the only woman who has ever come this far. Her achievement represents a giant moment in American history. We just want to celebrate that." The women would have a chance to celebrate it later in the week, when Hillary walked onto the convention floor, straight into the New York delegation, and symbolically suspended the roll call by saying, "I move Senator Barack Obama of Illinois be selected by this convention by acclamation as the nominee of the Democratic Party for President of the United States." The Pepsi Center, which had been buzzing with midday convention chatter, fell dead silent, then erupted in applause on the word *Democratic*. It was, to my ear, the most unifying and moving moment of the convention—genuine, surprising, and a world away from the story of discord playing out on cable networks.

☆ ☆ ☆

In all this, too few women were considering the pressures going into Denver for the most important woman still in the presidential contest. "This black woman is wondering," Mary C. Curtis had written in the *Washington Post* in June, "where are [Michelle] Obama's feminist defenders? . . . Just as you didn't have to be for Clinton to decry the sexism in the coverage of her campaign, you don't have to be an Obama supporter to defend Michelle Obama against similar treatment." Michelle Obama, the reluctant political spouse and inheritor of Clinton's trouble-making first lady legacy, had had a treacherous ride along the campaign trail. At a February speech in Wisconsin she'd said that her husband's political successes had taught her, "People in this country are ready for change and hungry for a different kind of politics. . . . For the first time in my adult life I am proud of my country because it feels like hope is finally making a comeback."

The response was damning. The next day Cindy McCain gave a speech in which she said, "I am proud of my country. I don't know about you, if you heard those words earlier [but] I am very proud of my country." The conservative columnist Bill Kristol told Fox News, "[Michelle Obama] was an adult when we won the cold war without firing a shot. She was an adult for the last twenty-five years of economic progress, social progress. . . . I don't think the American people think on the whole that the last twenty-five years of American history is . . . nothing to be proud of." Many reactions revealed a virulent current of race and class condescension. Jim Geraghty wrote on the website of the *National Review,* "America hasn't been good to her? What, opportunities to go to Princeton, Harvard Law, working for top-shelf law firms and hospitals . . . that's not enough?" Apparently Michelle was supposed to be damn grateful for her hard-earned achievements.

Maureen Dowd's original portrayal of Michelle Obama as an emasculating nag had gained a purchase on the public imagination. As the facts of her life became more widely disseminated they were often cast in a precise light: she had been the hard-driving lawyer, Barack's boss; she had been resentful when the domestic chores had been dumped on her when he took to a political life; like Hillary, she exerted tremendous influence over her husband. Her critics began to spin an elaborate narrative in which that influence was going to be threatening, in part because Michelle was angry and in part because she was black.

If Barack Obama had done a masterful job of conveying that he and his campaign were beyond race, his wife provided a counter-balance. Writing for *Slate* Christopher Hitchens used twenty-two-year-old Michelle's senior thesis, a research paper about being black at Princeton, to link Barack to a series of controversial Black Power figures, from Louis Farrakhan to Malcolm X to Jeremiah Wright: "How is it that the loathsome Wright married him, baptized his children, and received donations from him? Could it possibly have anything, I wonder, to do with Mrs. Obama?" Hitchens's dun-dun-*dun* accusation was like a real-life version of Dana Carvey's Church Lady: Could it be . . . *Satan*? Claiming that Michelle's thesis had made reference to her being "much influenced" by the separatist politics of Stokely Carmichael, Hitchens casually recalled that Carmichael had taken the name Kwame Ture, and that Hitchens had last seen him speak before Farrakhan in 1985, on the night that Farrakhan "made himself famous by warning Jews, 'You can't say "Never Again" to God, because when he puts you in the ovens, you're there forever.'" Black Power, separatists, Louis Farrakhan, Jews in the ovens, Michelle Obama—all neatly tied together in a piece that cast both Obamas as members of a club that Hitchens knew made both conservatives and liberals nervous. Ta-Nehisi Coates pointed out on his blog at the *Atlantic* that Hitchens lied about what Michelle had actually written in her thesis, which was that Carmichael and Charles Hamilton had "developed definitions of separationism in their discussion of Black Power which guided me in the formulation and use of this concept in the study." As Coates noted, Michelle made no allusion to any influence they had over her personally or politically. But whatever Hitchens's moral or ethical lapses, they were moot. By midspring Michelle was widely caricatured as the paradigm of angry black femininity.

In April the *National Review* ran a cover story featuring a photograph of Michelle, brow furrowed in what could have been concern or enthusiasm, but frozen in a snapshot, her expression appeared to be fury; the cover line was "Mrs. Grievance: Michelle Obama and Her Discontent." In June, celebrating the clinching of the nomination, Michelle gave her husband a fist-bump, or dap. On Fox News E. D. Hill played the footage, teasing it with the query, "A fist bump? A pound? A terrorist fist jab?" (Hill was taken off the air soon thereafter.) Less than a week later *Salon*'s Alex Koppelman, following a reader's tip, caught Fox News running a banner below a story about Obama that read "Outraged Liberals: Stop Picking on Obama's Baby Mama." Appearing with Bill O'Reilly, NPR's Juan

Williams compared Michelle to a black separatist. "She's got this Stokely-Carmichael-in-a-designer-dress thing going." By the end of the primaries a rumor was running rampant: there was a tape floating around on which Michelle could be heard saying the word *whitey.*

So broad was the brush with which she was being painted that she got half of Barry Blitt's July cover caricature on the *New Yorker.* Titled "The Politics of Fear," it was a sendup of all the paranoid, racially inflected slander being applied to the Obamas. There was Barack in a turban terrorist-fist-jabbing his wife, who had an Angela Davis–style Afro and was carrying a machine gun.

The Obama campaign was desperate to counteract the vision. Appearing on *The View* in June Michelle gabbed about pantyhose and confessed to buying her dress at the mall store called White House Black Market; she won over daytime audiences by being as girly as girly could be. The *Daily News* headline read, "With the Help of Off-the-Rack Dress, Michelle Obama Eases Harsh Image," a good tip for anyone looking to rid themselves of that pesky black radical aura.

When I settled into the press seats at the Pepsi Center on the first night of the convention and received a printed copy of the speech Michelle was about to give, I shouldn't have been surprised by its content, but I was. I knew that making herself as unthreatening as possible was what she had to do, but as I scanned the pages, looking for the Michelle Obama I had seen ten months earlier, I could find barely a glimpse of her. What I found instead was a woman turning herself inside out to emphasize her identity as a wife, a mother, a sister, a daughter—anything but a lawyer, a thinker, a person in her own right. Her speech was so comforting, so just-folksy, so daughterly and wifely and motherly that it made Nancy Reagan seem like an ambitious hussy with a wandering eye.

She was introduced in a video by her mother, who referred to her as "my baby," and then by her older brother, the basketball coach Craig Robinson, who called her "my little sister." Robinson's role was to lay down the evening's theme ("Black Potential First Ladies: They're Just Like Us!") with anecdotes about how as a child Michelle memorized every episode of *The Brady Bunch.* He explained that, though she eventually quit her powerful law firm job, she did take something from it: "a young lawyer by the name of Barack Obama."

A gifted orator, Michelle delivered her milquetoast address with such charismatic force that it almost made me forget it was an act of partial self-erasure. If it was slightly dispiriting to hear this smart and accomplished woman sum herself up in relation to the other people in her life—"a wife who loves my husband" and "a mom whose girls are the heart of my heart and the center of my world"—it was leavened by the fact that she was using every bit of her personal power to wrap the crowd around her little finger. She reminded the audience that during the span of this convention we would celebrate the eighty-eighth anniversary of women's suffrage and the forty-fifth anniversary of "that hot summer day when Dr. King lifted our sights and our hearts with his dream for our nation."

"I stand here today at the crosscurrents of that history," said Michelle in the best part of her speech, "knowing that my piece of the American dream is a blessing hard won by those who came before me." When she put her daughters to sleep at night, she said, she thought about the families they themselves would one day have. "One day, they—and your sons and daughters—will tell their own children about what we did together in this election . . . how this time, in this great country—where a girl from the South Side of Chicago can go to college and law school, and the son of a single mother from Hawaii can go all the way to the White House—that we committed ourselves to building the world as it should be." It was powerful and beautifully executed. But the speech itself was a sad indication that no matter how much we had done together in this election, the world we were committed to building still was not as it should be. It apparently would not warmly welcome this ambitious and dynamic woman until she was willing to briefly dim her own bright lights, downplay her autonomy, and present herself as an unthreatening wifely and maternal ideal. We had not sufficiently protected Michelle Obama against the race and gender inflected attacks she was now dodging, nor from the rigid expectations of "wife-of" femininity that Hillary had encountered sixteen years before, nor from the style-over-substance fate to which she was about to be confined.

* * *

On Tuesday, the night before she released her delegates, Clinton showed up at the Pepsi Center in a Phoenician orange pantsuit, appearing onstage after thunderous applause for the savviest ad she'd ever run, a video narrated by Chelsea, in which Hillary confessed her childhood dreams of being an astronaut while the Kinks blared "Girl, you really got me." "She was able to play with the boys, and yet sort of earn their respect," said Dorothy Rodham, identified as "Hillary's mom." "People who've worked with her feel I think a lot of respect and affection for her, and she unleashes people's energy," said Bill, identified as "Hillary's husband." In a photo negative of Michelle's speech on the previous night, everyone in the video was described in relation to Hillary. "It's so important for little girls to have someone to look up to," said a young woman in the video before a clip of Amy Poehler imitating Clinton's laugh. This was the message and the tone that her campaign had struggled and failed to achieve.

"It is time to take back the country we love, and whether you voted for me or whether you voted for Barack, the time is now to unite as a single party with a single purpose," said Clinton. Though some would accuse her of using her moment at the convention to fan the PUMA flames, she was in fact telling them to can it. She went on, "I want you to ask yourselves: Were you in this campaign just for me? Or were you in it for that young Marine and others like him? Were you in it for that mom struggling with cancer while raising her kids? . . . Were you in it for all the people in this country who feel invisible?"

"She went directly at the tension head-on," said Lissa Muscatine, who wrote the speech. "That was what Obama did so well throughout the campaign. He dealt with difficult issues by going straight into them."

"My mother was born before women could vote," Clinton bellowed one last time. "My daughter got to vote for her mother for president. This is the story of America." Later, outside the Pepsi Center, Clinton's former campaign chairman Terry McAuliffe stepped into the summer night, starry-eyed, smiling, shaking his head. "If she'd given speeches like that during the campaign, things would have turned out differently," he said.

McAuliffe wasn't the only one making this assertion. If she had appealed to people on an emotional level, presented herself as a candidate of change, been the feminist heroine so many had hoped she might have been, maybe it would have been different. Maybe, like Dorothy, she'd had to hustle all the way through Oz before realizing that she'd had the power all along.

Or maybe not. Had she taken the more emotive approach, let her feminist flag fly earlier, would she have made it to Texas and Ohio? More realistically, would she even have made it to Iowa?

It didn't matter now. For Hillary Clinton, the rousing speech in Denver was the end. Not the end of Hillary, but the end of her 2008 presidential story. What nobody knew, on that warm Denver night, was that from the ashes of her campaign, another woman, this one a Republican, would soon be rising.

9 ENTER PALIN

"McCain picked Palin." This was the urgent sentence that yanked me from sleep on a pull-out couch in the house *Salon* had rented in Denver. My colleague Alex Koppelman, conscious earlier than the rest of us the morning after Barack Obama's speech at Invesco Field, was standing above me, repeating, *"He picked Palin,"* as if, if he said it louder, I might better divine its meaning. On the AeroBed next to me, my colleague Caitlin sat up and started rubbing her eyes.

"Michael Palin?" I asked.

"No, *Sarah* Palin," said Alex, heading down the stairs to start writing, shouting over his shoulder, "She's the governor of Alaska. She's young and popular. Social conservatives love her because she kept her baby even though she knew he had Down syndrome. And oh," Alex turned around, "she's a woman."

The night before, America had witnessed Obama accept his party's nomination on the forty-fifth anniversary of Martin Luther King's "I Have a Dream" speech. The man had filled a stadium. It had felt like one of those rare occasions, ever rarer in the cable and Internet age, when the nation seemed, briefly, to be focused on the same thing. For an hour we were all looking in the same direction at the same time. Now the McCain team had dropped a bomb. In choosing Palin they had not only made a strategic appeal to disillusioned women in the Democratic Party; they had established their own claim to history. Palin was the first Republican woman ever selected as a vice-presidential nominee, and only the second woman in American history behind Geraldine Ferraro.

Later it would become clear that Palin's selection was not the carefully considered move it first appeared; it was in fact so impulsive a choice as to border on the accidental. John Heilemann and Mark Halperin reported in their book *Game Change* that the McCain campaign had been planning for most of the summer to make a splash by nominating former Democrat Joe Lieberman, the junior senator from Connecticut who had been Al Gore's running mate in 2000 and was buddies with McCain. The move would have been attention-getting, but Lieberman's pro-choice position and (tepid) support of gay rights would have imperiled Republican Party unity. The plan was scuttled at the last minute.

Former *Ms.* editor Elaine Lafferty, disgusted with the Democrats after Hillary's loss, was having meetings with Carly Fiorina, the former CEO of Hewlett-Packard then serving as an economic advisor to McCain. "She was encouraging me to get involved with the McCain campaign," Lafferty told me in 2009. Lafferty soon became part of a group that was pushing the Republican nominee to consider a woman as his running mate. Lafferty's friend John Coale, an attorney and the husband of Fox News host Greta Van Susteren, was also talking to McCain. "I went on his bus with him," Coale told me in 2010. Coale, a friend of the Clinton family, had campaigned for Hillary throughout Pennsylvania and had heard from many voters how much they wanted a woman to be president. "These were women with blue-collar jobs and they were passionate for Hillary," said Coale. "Time and again they told me it was because Hillary was a woman. I thought McCain could capture those voters." Coale brought some colleagues along with him to talk to McCain. "We urged him to pick a woman, big time," he said. "I always thought it would be Carly Fiorina or Meg Whitman. Carly and Meg were in the final running in his mind, as far as I could tell. He was talking about them."

But in the days leading up to the Republican convention in Minneapolis, before which McCain would be forced to select a running mate, his aides were not talking about Whitman or Fiorina. According to Heilemann and Halperin, McCain campaign manager Steve Schmidt and advisor Rick Davis had found a Charlie Rose interview with the forty-four-year-old governor of Alaska in July and had concluded that Sarah Palin was a star, and a socially conservative one to boot. As the Lieberman idea crumbled they began to fixate on the widely unknown governor, who could make their presidential ticket a history-making one. McCain spoke to her briefly by phone. The attorney A. B. Culvahouse, in charge of McCain's vetting process, asked another attorney, Ted Frank, to write up a report on Palin. The report, which came with a caveat that its hasty preparation meant that it might be incomplete, turned up criticisms of Palin's inexperience and an ongoing ethics investigation into accusations that as governor she fired Alaska's public safety commissioner after he'd refused to fire state trooper Mike Wooten, the estranged husband of her sister Molly. Schmidt and speechwriter Mark Salter met with Palin at the home of Bob Delgado, a McCain supporter in Flagstaff. Culvahouse spoke to Palin by phone, during which she told him that her sixteen-year-old daughter, Bristol, was pregnant. According to Heilemann and Halperin, Culvahouse responded by joking, "Is she getting married? . . . Is she getting married *tomorrow?*" Palin met with McCain in person at his ranch in Sedona; they took a walk by the creek and spoke for an hour. After conferring briefly with his advisors, McCain offered Palin the job.

As the reporter Anne Kornblut would point out in her book *Notes from the Cracked Ceiling,* there were very few women on McCain's lean staff to begin with, and none of them had been brought into conversations about having a woman on the ticket. No one asked campaign senior advisor Nicolle Wallace, a well-respected, savvy advisor who had most recently been a political analyst at CBS, working alongside Katie Couric, and who might have provided insight into the public presentation of powerful women. No one ran it by Fiorina, whose tenure at Hewlett-Packard had made her one of the world's best-known and most controversial businesswomen, and who might have had ideas about introducing Palin to the political spotlight. There were no women to mull in advance how voters regarded mothers of young children compared to fathers of young children (let alone how they might react to a mother whose young daughter was pregnant out of wedlock), no comprehension that Palin's beauty was anything other than an asset, no one to remind McCain that his new running mate would have to meet a higher bar of expectation than a man would, or to weigh whether or not she was strong enough to clear it.

Wallace would tell a 2010 panel convened by Kornblut that she learned about Palin only when her candidacy was already a done deal, late on the night before it was to be announced. "Were we ready for anything? No!" Wallace said. "I was the first woman I think to learn her identity, I think the fourth breathing human to learn her identity." Wallace remembered stressed-out speechwriter Mark Salter asking her if she thought it was a problem that Palin "sort of believes in Creationism." "I said, 'I don't know. I'll have to Google that,'" said Wallace. "Steve Schmidt said, 'And her daughter's pregnant, what do you think of that?' And I said, 'Um, I'll be right back.' . . . We were ready for nothing. . . . Three boys picked her. So they didn't ask, you know, girl questions." The biggest problem, Wallace told Kornblut's panel, was that "no one was prepared to defend her. . . . If you picked Jesus Christ, you have to be able to defend him. If your nominee is perfect and known and vetted, you have to be able to defend them. The early problems had less to do with her looks or her gender; it was that everyone was Googling her to find out who she was and what she believed in. Where she lived and how many kids she had."

In Denver we were Googling her too. Palin's gubernatorial campaign website advertised that she was pro-life and believed "that marriage should only be between a man and a woman." She belonged to a conservative women's group called Feminists for Life and had said in her campaign for governor that she was opposed to abortion even in cases of rape and incest, though she did believe in an exception for the life of the mother. She was a longtime member of the National Rifle Association, and when it came to health care she had said, "I support flexibility in government regulations that allow competition in health care that is needed." But there were other more unexpected things, like her reported willingness to stand up to crooked Alaska Senator Ted Stevens; the *Washing-*

ton Post's November 2007 report that outrage over Alaska's corrupt politics had "catapulted a reformer [Palin] into the governor's chair"; the catty political blog *Wonkette*'s post at the same time asserting, "We can never resist an opportunity to run a picture of the hottest Governor in all 50 states (and my total girl crush)." In the spring of 2008, Palin had enjoyed an 80 percent approval rating in Alaska. She had listed the state's private jet on eBay. A February 2008 *Vogue* profile had quoted an *Anchorage Daily News* reporter describing Palin's "small-town sincerity that voters found very appealing" alongside the editor of *Alaska* magazine, who said of Palin, "She really is a breath of fresh air. . . . It feels like a new era in Alaska." She appeared to be independent-minded and attention-getting, electrifying if combustible qualities on a national ticket.

In her introductory press conference Palin made it clear that she was not going to be bashful about celebrating her unprecedented place in presidential history. Noting—to big applause—that McCain had chosen her almost eighty-eight years to the day that women got the right to vote, she said, "I think as well today of two other women who came before me in national elections. I can't begin this great effort without honoring the achievements of Geraldine Ferraro in 1984 and of course Senator Hillary Clinton, who showed such determination and grace in her presidential campaign." Palin paused for the screeching affirmation of the crowd of fifteen thousand, the largest yet drawn by the McCain campaign, in Dayton, Ohio. My colleagues and I stared at each other dumbly in Denver; the Republican vice-presidential candidate was offering shout-outs to Democratic politicians in her first speech, and her Republican audience was eating it up. She wasn't finished. "It was rightly noted in Denver this week that Hillary left eighteen million cracks in the highest, hardest glass ceiling in America. But it turns out the women of America aren't finished yet, and we can shatter that glass ceiling once and for all!" The pinnacle of feminist self-congratulation to which Hillary had managed to ascend only in her losing moment was the place from which Palin launched her candidacy.

It was not crazy, in those days, to wonder if this scheme mightn't be a huge success. Though all of them would take it back within weeks, if not days, I knew women—Democratic women, liberal women—who told me that though they would never vote for Palin, they kind of liked her, and liked McCain for having put her on the ticket. It was a gesture that, at first, seemed to mean something. The actress and comedian Kristen Schaal, a devout Hillary supporter, would tell me in 2009, "I remember how when Palin first came on the scene I was so excited because there was a woman there, even if it was the worst woman I could imagine. It turned out she was a monster, but at first I was like, *Yes!*"

★ ★ ★

Palin's approach to political power was very different from Hillary's, and from Geraldine Ferraro's, and, for that matter, from any of the other women—Dole, Moseley Braun, Schroeder, Chisholm—who had made modern runs for national executive office. Palin was a governor, and before that a mayor. Instead of having worked within larger male-controlled local, state, or national governing bodies, she had been a boss; she had executive experience she would tout throughout the campaign as being vaster than Barack Obama's.

As of 2009 according to the group Equal Representation in Government and Democracy, there had been only thirty-one female governors in U.S. history, and they'd come from only twenty-three states. Among those who studied women's increased political profile, governorships were often cited as the most promising route to the White House. Barbara Lee, a philanthropist and feminist long obsessed with putting more women in office, in 1999 founded the Barbara Lee Family Foundation, an organization jointly dedicated to art and getting more women into politics, with an eye to examining and evaluating the paths of women governors. In 2010 Lee told me that Sarah Palin fit a classic model of female gubernatorial success in that she had won her office by selling herself as a clean politician; voters, Lee said, are often willing to believe a female candidate is more honest than a male: "When women become governors, voters really trust them." She also pointed out that though women running in gubernatorial elections face resistance when it comes to getting elected, once they're in office people tend to like them more than male governors, and they often enjoy high approval ratings, just as Palin did when McCain selected her. "We're tougher on women before they're elected," Lee said, "but once [women] get into these positions, voters . . . find them more believable, honest and trustworthy." Many states, including Texas and Arizona, that have had one female governor go on to elect other women more easily. "Women executives are powerful role models," Lee continued. "So when John McCain picked Palin, a woman who was also a mother with young children, to run on a presidential ticket, it was a good example, and really quite amazing."

For generations, largely because of the comparative sluggishness with which domestic roles had been reimagined and maternal expectations readjusted, the majority of women who could freely enter politics in the wake of the second wave were those who were single or childless. Most women with kids had to wait until their children were teens before diving into the electoral fray, limiting their opportunities to build the experience and support necessary to be taken seriously in a run for the presidency. At forty-two Palin had been elected not only Alaska's first female governor but also its youngest. She had shot from city council member to mayor to governor to vice-presidential candidate in twelve years, a timeline comparable to Barack Obama's. Even more unusual was that she had given birth to her fifth child while governor; her son Trig was four months old when Palin became McCain's running mate. Alongside women like New York Senator Kirsten Gillibrand, former Massachusetts governor Jane Swift and Arkansas Senator Blanche Lincoln, all of whom had young families, Palin represented a new generation of female political possibility.

Palin, who would etch herself into the American consciousness as "just another hockey mom" from Alaska, was one of those inheritors of feminist progress who had been taught to expect that she could do anything. She quickly shimmied up the professional pole while her husband, an oilfield production operator on Alaska's North Slope for part of the year, shouldered lots of the child rearing, with help from Palin's village of grandparents, aunts, and uncles who helped raise each other's children.

This was one of the most undeniably progressive things about Palin, perhaps most striking in the context of the hypereducated, prosperous segment of the left that was supporting Obama and in which the purported "Opt-out Revolution" was taking place. Predominantly liberal climes, in which privilege might ease the burdens of the work-life balance, had been the ones in which high-powered mothers had felt unable to escape old domestic responsibilities long enough to capitalize on or profit from their liberated and liberating career choices. But here was Palin, in her mid-forties, a baby on her hip, a seven-year-old at her side, and three more kids in various states of adolescent disarray; she was a governor, and now a vice-presidential candidate. Coale, the Democratic donor who had urged McCain to pick a woman, who would befriend Palin and go on to work with her after the election, told me in 2010, "I was around when the women's movement started in the early seventies, and if you take away the abortion issue, Palin is what everyone was fighting for, in the respect that she has a family and a husband who more than pulls his weight with the kids, the house. He is like the feminist dad that everyone hoped to achieve someday." Indeed in 2009 a profile of Todd Palin in *Esquire* included a scene in the hectic Palin family kitchen on an evening when he was about to sub for his wife at a corporate event and Sarah was teaching her daughter's then-fiancé Levi Johnston how to marinate and cook roast beef. This was the illustration of professional and domestic partnership, of household tasks freed from gendered expectations, of which feminists had long dreamed. The morning McCain announced her candidacy, Palin presented her oddly monikered brood—Track, Bristol, Willow, Piper, Trig, and First Dude Todd—to the nation as credentials, not liabilities. It was an instance in which it was impossible to ignore the social shifts that Palin represented.

Palin's arrival at McCain's side surprised everyone. As commenters began to parse the choice on CNN, John Roberts, who had previously held forth on how the major function of a vice president was "to go to funerals" and similarly untaxing ceremonial duties, changed his tune, telling correspondent Dana Bash, "Children with Down syndrome require an awful lot of attention. The role of vice president, it seems to me, would take up an awful lot of [Palin's] time. It raises the issue of how much time will she have to dedicate to her newborn child?" Bash sounded unmoved by Roberts's concern, countering with "If it were a man being picked who also had a baby four months ago with Down syndrome, would you also ask the same question?" Meanwhile at MSNBC Andrea Mitchell was consumed by the question of whether or not Palin would neuter big bad Joe Biden, an energetic debater. Apparently forgetting that the Delaware senator had not been paralyzed by chivalric courtesy while debating Hillary Clinton, Mitchell wondered whether Biden "can be tough against a woman. Doesn't it give her a gender advantage?" As I searched the web for further Palin information, I noticed that she had already been called a GILF (MILF—or "Mom I'd Like to Fuck"—for governors) and that the *Wall Street Journal* had quickly posted a piece about her workout routine and diet. "My ideal fantasy is to be running on a hot dusty road just wearing running shorts and some kind of top that wicks away sweat," she told the paper.

I didn't know which was worse: watching a grim cycle lurch once more into gear or acknowledging that the Republicans and John McCain, in their attempts to manipulate the female electorate, had walked through a door that had been left opened by my own party.

★ ★ ★

Less than two weeks later Sarah Palin—The story! The phenomenon! The pit bull in lipstick! The political superstar!—was eclipsing every other political story that had come before her. Every day there was some new twist. Putting the words *Sarah, Palin,* or *Wasilla* in a headline guaranteed blockbuster traffic online. She had an equally hypnotic hold on those who loathed her and those who loved her. In my liberal world she had burrowed deep into the psyche of every woman I knew, all of whom talked in jittering staccato about their bad dreams and imagined arguments with her or her supporters. A line kept running through my brain, spoken in the mid-Atlantic clip of *All About Eve*'s Addison DeWitt about that movie's titular, parasitic ingénue: "There never was, and there never will be, another like you."

Palin was simultaneously seductive and seditious, the kind of woman who spoke on behalf of other women but appeared not to like them very much. The kind of woman who, as Jessica Grose at *Jezebel* eloquently noted, gained her power by doing everything modern women had believed they did not have to do: presenting herself as maternal and sexual, sucking up to men, evincing an aw-shucks lack of native ambition. She met with such adulation because her posture reinforced antiquated gender norms. Her success made her the object of obsession for the women whose gendered goodwill she was trying to co-opt, and who saw how well her retro version of femininity was going over.

Within days of the announcement of Palin's nomination, news of Bristol's pregnancy broke. The Palins released a statement saying they were "proud of Bristol's decision to have her baby and even prouder to become grandparents," a statement that Palin would later claim, in her memoir *Going Rogue,* was not an authentic expression of family pride, but a move forced by campaign advisors. In actuality, she wrote, the family had been anything but pleased to hear of Bristol's pregnancy. McCain camp aides reiterated that "Bristol Palin made the decision on her own to keep the baby." Not lost on pro-choice Democrats was the fact that this "decision" was one that neither McCain nor Palin wanted to allow other American women to make were they to find themselves in Bristol's position. A pre-Palin piece in *In These Times* reported that McCain, who supported overturning *Roe v. Wade,* had said during his 2000 primary run for president, "[If our daughter got pregnant,] the final decision would be made by Meghan with our advice and counsel." When reporters pointed out to him that he had just described a pro-choice situation, McCain replied, "I don't think it is the pro-choice position to say that my daughter and wife and I will discuss something that is a family matter that we have to decide."

On the right, the pregnancy merely affirmed Palin's place in the pantheon of socially conservative heroines. Religious conservatives used Bristol's uterine condition as a chance to move their football down the field. Tony Perkins of the Family Research Council made the public statement "[Teen pregnancy] is a problem that we remain committed to reducing through encouraging young people to practice abstinence." He congratulated Bristol on "following her mother and father's example of choosing life in the midst of a difficult situation." Focus on the Family's James Dobson announced that the Palins "should be commended once again for not just talking about their pro-life and pro-family values, but living them out even in the midst of trying circumstances."

I didn't have a problem with Sarah Palin accepting McCain's nomination knowing that her young daughter was pregnant, but I found considerably less defensible her choice to turn Bristol into a living tableau of pro-life politics, and then to make those pro-life politics the crux of an argument that she and her family represented a "real" America, in which Barack Obama apparently did not live. At the Palin-smitten Republican convention the trick of wringing patriotism from an unplanned pregnancy was performed over and over. According to delegates interviewed by CNN, Bristol's pregnancy made Palin "a real person like the rest of us." A Texas delegate told the network, "If anything, it shows the Republican Party is a real American party." South Carolina Governor Mark Sanford told the *New York Times,* "People are looking for real. Real means blemishes, real means warts, real means real. These family imperfections make people say, 'That family isn't so different from my family.'"

This wholly mystifying definition of authenticity was crafted by the morally and religiously self-righteous faction of the right that had held sway in the GOP since Ronald Reagan began cultivating their allegiance in the 1980s. However illogical their rhetoric, the praise of Palin's imagined American realness reverberated with blue-collar voters. The economic and class divide, about which John Edwards had been so adamant, which Hillary Clinton had so advantageously addressed, and about which Barack Obama had been perhaps a touch too laissez-faire—and which he may have nudged a little wider with his comments about guns, religion, and bitterness—was now being crowbarred open by Palin and McCain, regardless of the fact that every bit of their agenda worked against working-class and poor people and on behalf of the champagne-swilling populations they claimed to disdain.

Some on the left legitimately noted that Bristol's pregnancy was a visible ramification not of some extra-American America but of what happens when you restrict young women's freedom, fail to provide them with ample sex education, and make birth control difficult to get. A few vainly tried to point out the hypocrisy of a party that for decades had been portraying itself as an exemplar of straight and straitlaced family values. But most of the attacks on Palin wound up being personal, sudsy, and slightly delusional.

The revelation about the pregnancy had come only in the wake of rumors about the circumstances of Trig's birth. Palin hadn't publicly revealed her own pregnancy until practically the moment Trig came into the world; reportedly she had gone into labor in Texas, where her water had broken—though she later claimed that her amniotic fluid was merely leaking—and then taken a long plane ride back to Alaska to give birth. Now there was a widely disseminated conspiracy theory that the baby wasn't really hers, but Bristol's. The allegation had found traction on, yes, generally liberal, Obama-supporting, Palin-hating blogs, a truth that the McCain camp was already flogging as persecution of their working-class female candidate by the elite.

The focus on and fetishization of pregnancy from both left and right was dispiriting. I understood that it was way more fun to cook up theories about the Palin family's quirks than it was to talk about policy. But it firmly resituated women's political prospects back in the realms of sex, scandal, and maternity, in a year and a presidential campaign that had so far managed not to be about female fecundity, but competitive ferocity.

To his credit Barack Obama held a very firm position on Bristol Palin's pregnancy, noting that if anyone in his campaign were to push the story forward they would be fired. Obama said that the pregnancy "has no relevance to Governor Palin's performance as a governor or her potential performance as a vice president." He also pointed out that his own mother had been eighteen when she gave birth to him. "How a family deals with issues and teenage children, that shouldn't be the topic of our politics," he said. But it was.

☆ ☆ ☆

Palin's speech at the Republican convention was astonishingly good. She lionized McCain, pointedly calling him "a true profile in courage." "Our family has the same ups and downs as any other," she said, pressing home her dysfunctional bona fides, talking about her son and nephew serving in the Middle East, and promising families of special-needs children that if she and her running mate were elected they would "have a friend and advocate in the White House." She thanked small-town America and her parents, noting, "Among the many things I owe them is a simple lesson that I've learned: that this is America, and every woman can walk through every door of opportunity." Especially one that had been sledge-hammered open for her in advance. Then Palin got mean, discussing her own experience. "I guess a small-town mayor is sort of like a 'community organizer,'" she said with a sneer, "except that you have actual responsibilities. I might add that in small towns, we don't quite know what to make of a candidate who lavishes praise on working people when they're listening, and then talks about how bitterly they cling to their religion and guns when those people aren't listening."

Palin's speech was delivered with an appealing calm that made me wonder whether, when she was done, she might enjoy some fava beans and a nice Chianti. I feared that I had just seen the future of gender politics, and that its name was Sarah Palin. Staring at her on television, all I could think was, *This is it. She's going to be the first woman president.*

That was when I began to have a series of persistent nightmares. I wish I could claim that they were sophisticated ones in which Palin led troops into Vancouver or led children in a recitation of "Sinners in the Hands of an Angry God." Alas, they were juvenile fear fantasies in which she kidnapped my cats and enjoyed brunches with my girlfriends while I banged on the restaurant window; in one tour-de-force she was an actual witch leering at me from a windswept hill, a baby doll grasped menacingly in her hands.

As these night terrors demonstrated, Palin's candidacy was testing my own beliefs about how I respond to women in power. My reactions to her were all tied up in her gender, a factor that I had always believed, as a matter of course and principle, should neither bolster nor dim impressions of a person's goodness or badness, smartness or dumbness, substance or lack thereof. When it came to Palin, I worried that my rules were changing.

I was perfectly capable of picking out and objecting to the sexism being leveled against the governor by the press, her detractors, and her own party. The liberalish radio host Ed Schultz, who had said on air that Palin set off a "bimbo alert," also asked, in conversation with Larry King and Republican Susan Molinari, "What kind of mother is she? Is she prepared to be the vice president? Is she going to be totally focused on the issues?" The *Washington Post*'s Sally Quinn asked if Palin was "prepared for the all-consuming nature of the job. . . . Her first priority has to be her children. When the phone rings at three in the morning and one of her children is really sick what choice will she make?"

That stuff was all familiar and sickening, and plenty of people on the left said so, from the linguistics professor Deborah Tannen, who called questions about Palin's ability to mother sexist, to the former Clinton strategist Howard Wolfson, who said, "There's no way those questions would be asked of a male candidate." Kim Gandy of NOW released a statement making it clear that though she did not support Palin and though her organization would be working to help elect Barack Obama, they would "monitor the media and call them out for their sexism directed at Palin. A woman slurred, regardless of her party or stances, is a woman slurred." The feminist writer and lawyer Susan Estrich weighed in, remarking, "No one would be asking these questions if she were a man. No one asked whether Arnold Schwarzenegger should run for governor because he has four children. . . . This is how the double standard works. . . . I have no doubt that Barack Obama can count on his fingers the number of times he has been home in the last 19 months to put his two beautiful daughters to bed. . . . Does this make him a 'bad father'? Should it undercut his claim to the presidency? Of course not."

But all that stuff was clean-cut. I was torn about the more subtle ways in which Palin's gender had me all disoriented. The rhetorical ground had shifted so quickly beneath the feet of feminists, that I was left with only a tenuous grasp on even the basic vocabulary of my beat. Palin, who initially referred to herself as a feminist, was being written about as one, including in a piece in *Adweek*, which called her "a classic third-wave feminist." Serrin Foster, the president of Feminists for Life, was on NPR crowing about the fact that Palin was "proud to say she is a feminist and pro-life at the same time."

During a panel at *Newsweek*'s Women & Leadership Conference in March 2008 Karen Breslau had asked Palin what she saw in the coverage of Clinton. Palin replied, "I do think that it's a more concentrated criticism that Hillary gets on so many fronts; I think that's unfortunate. But . . . she does herself a disservice to even mention it, really. You have to plow through that and know what you're getting into. . . . When I hear a statement . . . coming from a woman candidate with any kind of perceived whine about that excess criticism or a sharper microscope put on her, I think, man, that doesn't do us any good. . . . Work harder, prove to yourself to an even greater degree that you're capable, that you're going to be the best candidate . . . [it bothers] me a little bit to hear her bring that attention to herself on that level." But now that it was Palin under the microscope, she and her allies were perfectly willing to "whine."

Republicans were eager to talk about the sexism Palin was facing. Former Pennsylvania senator Rick Santorum not only opposed the use of birth control but had compared legal abortion to the institution of slavery and believed that radical feminists had forced women into the workforce against their will. Now he was talking about Palin as the "Clarence Thomas for feminists," by which he meant that feminists had an obligation to support her, just as "the African-American community obviously should have rallied behind Clarence Thomas and his achievement." Rudy Giuliani, the former mayor of New York who had famously used a press conference to let his second wife know he was leaving her, asked delegates at the Republican convention, "How dare they question whether Sarah Palin has enough time to spend with her children and be vice president? How dare they do that! When do they ever ask a man that question? When?" That morning, he'd taken his consciousness-raising roadshow to television, asking on CBS, "Where are the feminists?" and telling Fox News, "I'm at the point of [being] really angry!" McCain's advisor Steve Schmidt was painting any questions about Palin's vetting, or really any criticism of her at all, as an attempt "to destroy the first female Republican nominee for vice president of the United States who has never been a part of the old boys' network that has come to dominate the news establishment in this country."

Some days it felt as if I was watching a civics filmstrip about how much progress women made on the presidential stage in 2008 burst into flames, while in the back of the room a substitute teacher was threading a new reel into the projector. It had the same message and some of the same signifiers—Glass ceilings broken! Girl Power! Old boys' clubs!—but its meaning had been distorted. Hillary Clinton's 18 million cracks had weakened not only the White House's glass ceiling, but the wall protecting *Roe v. Wade*. The potential first female vice president in American history described her early career as that of "your average hockey mom" who "never really set out to be involved in public affairs." Teen pregnancy, once an illustrative talisman for sex educators and contraception distributors, now served those who sought to eliminate sex education and contraception.

In this strange new pro-woman tableau, feminism meant voting for someone who would limit reproductive control, access to health care, and environmental protections. It meant cheering for someone who supported the teaching of creationism alongside evolution, who had reportedly inquired locally about the possibility of using her position to ban certain books from the public library. Palin was the kind of feminist who by dint of her large family and load-bearing husband managed to juggle family and a burgeoning political career, but who would support no medical, health care, family leave or labor policies that would make similar paths possible for other women. In this *Handmaid's Tale*–inflected universe, in which femininity was worshipped but females denied rights, the CNBC pundit Donny Deutsch told us that we were witnessing "a new creation . . . of the feminist ideal," appealing because instead of being voiced by hairy old bats with unattractive ideas about power, it was now embodied by a woman who did what Hillary Clinton did not: "put a skirt on." Deutsch went on to say, "I want her watching my kids, I want her laying next to me in bed."

What Palin so beguilingly represented, not only to Deutsch but to the general public, was a form of female power that was utterly digestible to those who had no intellectual or political use for actual women: feminism without the feminists.

Although the Republicans would have us believe that Palin could simply stand in for Hillary Clinton, there was nothing interchangeable about these politicians. We had begun the election with one kind of woman and had ended up being asked to accept her polar opposite as a (cuter and beskirted!) consolation prize. Clinton's femininity, based on competence and an assumption of authority that upended gender expectations, was the kind that remained slightly unpalatable in America. It was a kind of power that had nothing to do with the flirtatious or the traditionally feminine. It was authority that was threatening because it so closely and calmly resembled the kind of power that the guys on the presidential stage had never questioned their right to wield.

The pro-woman rhetoric surrounding Palin's nomination, on the other hand, was a crafty bastardization of everything feminism had stood for. More than any of the intergenerational pro- or anti-Hillary arguments that had provoked such consternation during the primaries, I feared that Palin's candidacy and the faux feminism in which it was wrapped would actually imperil women's progress rather than speed it. If adopted as a successful narrative by the nation and its women, Palin's story would not just subvert but erase the meaning of what real progress for women meant, what real gender bias consisted of, what real discrimination looked like. It would put us all in reverse.

Perhaps that's why my reaction to Palin was so bone-deep, and why she was shaking some of my convictions about how to approach gender. When, on an early September Sunday morning, I picked up the *New York Post* with its front-page headline "Lady Killer: Hill to Check Hockey Mom" next to photos of Palin in porno-librarian mode and Clinton with her teeth bared, I did not roll my eyes in disgust at the imagined cage match. Instead I envisioned it. More than that: I enjoyed it. I wanted more than a hockey metaphor, hoping instead for a cinematic showdown, in which Clinton showed up, guns blazing Ripley-style, to surprise the mother alien just as she is about to feast on independent voters, shouting, "Get away from them, you bitch!"

Everything about the narrative surrounding Palin (and my fantasies of her defeat) was hypercombative and hyperfeminized, including the emerging media line about how it was, of course, the fault of Hillary supporters that she existed in the first place. Those who had raised their voice about sexism, those who had expressed an interest in female leadership, those who had made a fuss—they were somehow to blame for Sarah Palin and were therefore being implicated in the distortion of a feminist project.

This was the claim. And there was a germ of truth in it. But one could lay just as much blame at the feet of those on the left who failed to speak out about sexism when Hillary was running. For while it chafed to hear Rudy Giuliani and John McCain hold forth on the injustice of gender bias, part of what their running commentary threw into stark relief for anyone paying attention was the fact that we had never heard a peep or squawk or gurgle of this nature from anyone in the Democratic Party during the entire time Hillary Clinton had been running for president. If any of the Democrats had taken to defending her with a fraction of the zeal and bluster the right was now applying to Palin's cause, there might not have been so many angry people in the Democratic Party for Republicans to prey on. If there hadn't been so much stone-cold silence, so much shoulder-shrugging "What, me sexist?" inertia from the left, if there had been a little more respect accorded to the unsubtle clues being transmitted by 18 million voters that maybe they were interested in this whole woman-in-the-White-House thing, then the right would not have had the juice to charge this particular device.

Which led straight to my greatest nightmare: that because my own party had not cared enough to lay its rightful claim to the language of women's rights, Sarah Palin would reach historic heights of power by conforming to every outdated notion of what it meant to be a woman. I feared that she would hit her marks by clambering over the backs, the bodies, the rights of the women on whose behalf she claimed to be working, and that she would do it all under the banner of feminism, a banner that had essentially been handed to her by a party that was not proud enough to march under it.

10 POP CULTURE WARRIORS

IN THE DAYS following her Twin Cities rollout Sarah Palin agreed to a lone sit-down interview with ABC's Charlie Gibson, a demoralizing affair in which Gibson failed to disguise his pleasure at catching her out on her lack of familiarity with the Bush Doctrine. Gibson's condescension garnered Palin enough sympathy to neutralize the potentially candidacy-killing effects of the interview, but the conversation had exposed serious gaps in Palin's ability to discuss policy. The McCain camp quickly cordoned Palin off from the talking press, parading her silently in front of cameras at the U.N. and cultivating an air of inaccessibility that provoked suspicion among the media and the public. Under pressure the campaign at last agreed to let Palin sit down with CBS anchor Katie Couric. In her book *Going Rogue* Palin would write that she believed the interview was supposed to be "pretty mellow . . . short and sweet, about balancing motherhood and [her] life as governor," a cushy arrangement brokered by Nicolle Wallace, Couric's former colleague and Palin's advisor. Everyone else involved in the negotiations, including Wallace, denied Palin's version of events. Whatever the terms, the

Couric-Palin conversations that took place over a few days in late September turned out to be some of the most devastating and gripping television in the history of presidential politics.

Palin came off as bewilderingly flat-footed, ill-equipped even to bullshit her way out of tight conversational spots, and prone to bizarre enunciations that verged on self-parody. Observations like "The bad guys are the ones who say Israel is a stinking corpse and should be wiped off the face of the earth. That's not a good guy who is saying that," and that Alaska's "narrow maritime border" with Russia afforded her foreign policy experience made Palin sound politically infantile. Most damning was her inability to express herself clearly: her sentences were knotted, labyrinthine thickets from which she could not cleanly emerge without simply trailing off.

The interviews, when they aired, could have been set to the music from *Jaws*. "I'm just going to ask you one more time," Couric said at one point, smiling almost apologetically: "Specific examples in [McCain's] twenty-six years of pushing for more regulation?" Palin could only chirrup lamely, "I'll try to find you some and I'll bring them to you!" *Chomp!* Just like that, Couric totaled Palin's reputation, at least for the 2008 race.

Inevitably both Palin's supporters and her critics began to emit a bleating sympathy. The conservative pundits Kathleen Parker and Kathryn Jean Lopez wrote of their shuddering realizations that Palin was not ready for the spotlight. *Salon*'s Glenn Greenwald watched the Couric segments and confessed that he "actually felt sorry" for Palin. Judith Warner wrote a column on her *New York Times* blog called "Poor Sarah," about the wave of "self-recognition and sympathy [that] washed over" her when she saw a photo of Palin talking to Henry Kissinger. Palin, "a woman fully aware that she was out of her league, scared out of her wits, hanging on for dear life," reminded Warner of herself, and of what she dubbed "Imposter Syndrome," a condition she imagined was shared by women who watched Palin and felt, "She *can't* possibly do it all—the kids, the special-needs baby, the big job, the big conversations with foreign leaders. And neither could they."

The spectacle was disquieting. As it became clear that McCain's team had elevated Palin to a presidential ticket not because she was a woman with the experience and credentials to be a vice president, but because she was a woman, Palin's personal and professional shortcomings were being fused to her gender so tightly that even a clever critic like Warner projected upon her a spectral embodiment of her own grim self-estimation, and worse, a manifestation of some universal condition of female inadequacy.

I understood how terrible it felt to have one hand over your eyes and the other on the mute button while watching the second female candidate for vice president speak. But this misery moved me to anger, not to sympathy: anger at Palin, at the crassness of the man who had selected her, and at the misogynistic mash that had been made of an otherwise groundbreaking year. Why, after 18 million people voted for Hillary Clinton, was I reading about ladies who just couldn't imagine having a "big job" and "big conversations"? Even if the McCain campaign had been craven and sexist in thinking it could pass Palin off as an anemic Hillary substitute, she was in fact a grown woman, governor of her state, a candidate who averred that she had not blinked when asked to run for the vice presidency. I was willing to talk about the gendered double binds Palin faced, but not to feel sorry for her because she could not get through a television interview intact. She had made the choice to go on television in the first place.

I knew women like Sarah Palin, suburban mothers of my childhood acquaintances, savvy broads whose ambitions had been circumscribed by fate or economic circumstance but who believed, perhaps rightly or perhaps not, that they had been built for loftier opportunities than their world had so far offered them. Smart or stupid, gifted or lacking talent, these were women possessed of self-certainty as much as of vulnerability; they were survivors, not snifflers. I refused to be manipulated into another stage of gendered regress based on the assumption that Palin could not withstand the criticism she was earning.

This was a woman who took the national stage and sneered at the work of community activists. She told Couric that she did not get a passport until 2007 because she hadn't come from a family that handed out backpacking trips, thereby passing off incuriosity and lassitude as "regular people" qualities and doing a disservice to plenty of Americans who didn't come from privilege yet still managed to learn about the larger world. I did not feel sorry for a woman who used her special-needs child to garner support from Americans in need of health care reform she didn't support. I did not feel sorry for anyone whose project was reliant on the support of women whose rights she would limit and whose civil liberties she would curtail. Pity for Sarah Palin seemed disrespectful of every woman who had ever been unfairly dismissed based on her gender, because Palin's was a fair dismissal based on her willingness to take on a job for which she was not qualified. It was disrespectful of minority populations of every stripe whose place in the political spectrum had been unfairly interpreted as tokenism, because in Palin's case her presence on the ticket was tokenism of the basest variety. And Palin was tough. She could bite the head off a moose and move on.

* * *

What I did think was remarkable was that it had not been at the hands of Charlie Gibson—or Brian Williams, or Chris Matthews, or Tom Brokaw—that Palin had fallen, but at the hands of Katie Couric, who despite almost a decade as the highest-earning television journalist on the planet and a history-making arrival as the first solo female anchor of a nightly newscast, was still regarded as perky and unserious. And it wasn't just Couric who was turning in good work. Although the year in media bluster may have been owned by the frat boys at MSNBC, in those fall weeks the season's defining interviews, most fine-boned analysis, and buzziest commentary were coming from their newsroom sisters.

In her 2007 book *The Terror Dream* Susan Faludi points to the post-9/11 ardor for mission-accomplishin' masculinity as the cause of the decreasing frequency with which female journalists and pundits appeared on air and in print through the mid-aughts. Later in the decade, though, it was possible to detect an emergence from that gender depression, a shift surely catalyzed by the emergence of powerful female political players, including Condoleezza Rice, Nancy Pelosi, Hillary Clinton, and Sarah Palin. "You want African Americans around to talk about Barack Obama, right?" Couric said to me in a 2009 interview. "You want women around to reflect their experiences and see a female candidate through their particular prism."

To some small extent the media had to mirror the figures and stories it was covering. For generations politics had been male and white, and in turn the political media had been male and white. Frances Kissling, the former head of Catholics for a Free Choice, had often referred to *Meet the Press* as "Meet the Patriarchy." But the strides made by female political figures in the first decade of the twenty-first century created a corresponding appetite for female interlocutors who could make sense of their advancements. Female newscasters, long considered interlopers in the exclusively male domain of presidential politics, now had a choice perspective, not only on the women candidates, but on the world's reactions to them. By the blighted standards of its history, the American political media was crawling with women in 2008.

It would be reported in 2010 that NBC veteran Andrea Mitchell was the television reporter with the most evening airtime of the decade, clocking in at 2,416 minutes between 2000 and 2009. At CNN Candy Crowley was dominating coverage of Clinton's campaign, turning in such reliable reporting that Gloria Steinem wrote her a fan letter. Dana Bash admirably parried the sexist insinuations of John Roberts, and Gloria Borger and Donna Brazile were regular mainstays of the CNN politics panels. PBS's Gwen Ifill hosted the vice-presidential debate; 2004's most popular pundits, Arianna Huffington and Ana Marie Cox, remained a cable news presence, and a cast of new talking heads appeared, including Melissa Harris-Lacewell, Anne Kornblut, Leslie Sanchez and Joan Walsh, all of whom regularly duked it out on MSNBC and CNN. "It definitely had to do with there being a woman candidate," Walsh told me about her fast-multiplying invitations to be a cable guest in 2008.

Latoya Peterson, a writer at *Racialicious* who did some commentary on CNN, said, "The election allowed a lot of us to get a toehold where we wouldn't have before. . . . The need to have different types of people discussing these issues allowed so many more people [a] chance to be heard." Faludi herself was contributing op-eds about the gender politics of the election to a *New York Times* editorial page that now included not just the prose cartoons of Maureen Dowd, but also an incisive, funny political column by Gail Collins. In 2005 *Salon* had launched *Broadsheet,* a section of the magazine devoted to women's news, and during the election season *Slate* followed suit with its blog (later a short-lived stand-alone website) the *XX Factor*. *Texas Monthly* launched a political column called "In the Pink," and the *Washington City Paper* debuted a section called "The Sexist." At the same time, long-ghettoized girl zones like daytime television were providing political insight, and breakout stars like Couric, Rachel Maddow and Campbell Brown were asserting their perspectives on the unfolding election narrative and building audiences.

☆ ☆ ☆

One of the canniest questions asked of Hillary Clinton in all of 2008 came from Couric, during a webcast following the final debate between Barack Obama and John McCain: "Why do you think Sarah Palin has an action figure and you have a nutcracker?" Couric would later tell me what she believed the answer was: "Sarah Palin was less threatening than Hillary, it's pretty basic." But her exchange with Clinton never got that far. Instead Clinton replied with transparent insincerity, "I don't have any idea, Katie." Couric pushed her about whether she ever felt "the injustice of it all." No, said Clinton, before turning mock-serious: "Maybe someday I'll have an action figure. . . . I still have aspirations!" Couric flashed a grin—gummy, leonine—and joked, "A girl can dream, can't she?"

Apparently she could. Two years after having taken an inglorious nose-dive from NBC morning to CBS prime time, Couric found herself widely credited with having changed the course of a presidential election. An advertising generator for NBC during her *Today* tenure, Couric had been sold for years as America's sweetheart, at least when she wasn't in contract negotiations; then she was splashed across tabloids as a hard-bargaining businesswoman who chewed through producers. In 2006 she grabbed at the opportunity to become the first woman to sit alone at the nightly news desk; CBS would pay her $15 million a year for it. The move caused a media fracas about her lack of gravitas, in which critics emphasized that their qualms weren't about Couric being a *woman,* but about her being a woman who had spent her mornings reporting with gloss and bounce on fad diets and celebrity breakups. Few seemed to recognize that being glossy and bouncy before noon was one of the only avenues open to women in the television news business. The complaints were an early iteration of the "It's not any woman, it's *that* woman" line that would be deployed against Hillary Clinton by those who didn't stop to consider the factors that might lead a woman to become like *that*. The *Sturm und Drang* surrounding Couric's move might have been appropriate had it been 1943 and the Pentagon transferring stewardship of the Manhattan Project to Lassie. "The fact that networks seem willing to concede that the best man for the job is clearly a woman means that it just isn't the same job anymore," David Carr wrote in the *New York Times*.

After a nanosecond of boost upon its debut, Couric's nightly broadcast, indeed leavened with celebrity baby photos and chatty familiarity, plonked CBS right back into its long-held third-place berth. As Couric told me later, "People seemed to take some sort of perverse joy in it."

☆ ☆ ☆

Even before the Palin interview Couric had been making election season noise: she was one of the only journalists to voice her dissatisfaction with her colleagues' treatment of Clinton during the race, asserting at a June 2008 speech, "Senator Clinton received some of the most unfair, hostile coverage I've ever seen." In a later segment she noted, "One of the great lessons of [Clinton's] campaign is the continued and accepted role of sexism in American life, particularly in the media." Accusing her male peers of misogyny was a bold move in those overheated, hyperdefensive days. Keith Olbermann responded by naming Couric a World's Worst Person, huffing and puffing, "It is sad that Ms. Couric could not have . . . separated the hype from the news in her own promulgation of the nonsense that Senator Clinton was a victim of pronounced sexism."

But according to the critics, Couric turned in the best network coverage of the political conventions. It was made of the same stuff that had long powered her career: intelligence, approachability, and journalistic instinct. One incident, in which she nabbed Michael Dukakis in a Denver security line and got an interview that ended with the former Democratic presidential candidate apologizing to the American people for the Bush dynasty, was part of what prompted *Times* critic Carr to point out "what has been apparent for the last two decades to anybody with a television: Ms. Couric is a highly skilled interviewer, and people tend to tell her stuff." With the poll-rattling Palin interview, which got more airtime than *It's a Wonderful Life* on Christmas Eve and burned its way across the Internet, Couric's provocative critiques about her colleagues' sexism were forgotten. Her success was in drawing out Palin's inchoate sputtering by asking mostly very direct and mild questions, an approach reminiscent of Roger Mudd's 1979 interview with presidential hopeful Ted Kennedy, who had drawn a rambling blank when Mudd had queried simply, "Why do you want to be president?" Couric's straightforward approach was the sort that she had honed on morning television, where the goal was not to skewer, but simply to engage. "During the course of the interview I made sure I was as nonjudgmental as possible," Couric told me, "that I had no facial affect, that I didn't even cock my head when I didn't understand what she was saying." When I asked her whether she felt her gender had any impact on the way she approached Palin, she suggested that perhaps it was less about her approach than viewers' responses. "Charlie was criticized for having his glasses and being overly avuncular and condescending, which I frankly didn't think he was. But people project into whatever situation they're looking at. Perhaps the fact that I was female [made] people [feel] that it was less threatening. I don't know."

In 2010 CBS News would receive two Alfred I. duPont–Columbia University Awards, one for Couric's Palin interviews. The award committee pointed out that Couric's approach "prompted the most revealing remarks and had the greatest impact on the presidential campaign. . . . These were the interviews heard around the world." True, most people didn't watch their news at six-thirty anymore, but Couric's impact was significant: she had pushed the role of network news anchor beyond the confines of a televised half-hour, proved that the job still had the power to alter political story lines, and opened a door that other women might walk though—without having to fit themselves into anchor chairs that had been built for men.

Couric's former *Today* colleague Campbell Brown was also carving out new space at CNN. Brown, who moved to cable after having been passed over for Couric's *Today* job, was a frank and amiable television presence. She began appearing on her nightly CNN show, *Election Center,* in March 2008 and by fall was an Internet sensation thanks to a series of interviews and commentaries in which she displayed a short-tempered impatience with the dishonesties of a manipulative election season. It started with her demanding straight answers about Palin's experience from McCain spokesman Tucker Bounds, whose clock she cleaned so efficiently that McCain canceled an appearance on CNN's *Larry King Live* in retaliation.

When Palin was kept hermetically sealed from reporters during her visit to the U.N. Brown took to her anchor desk and went *Network* on the McCain campaign. "I have had enough of the sexist treatment of Sarah Palin," she began. Calling on the McCain campaign to "stop treating Sarah Palin like she is a delicate flower that will wilt at any moment," she went on, "She is strong, she is tough, she is confident. And you claim she is ready to be one heartbeat away from the presidency. If that is the case, then end this chauvinistic treatment of her now. . . . Free Sarah Palin." Brown told me in 2008, "I was [simply trying to point to] a degree of hypocrisy in accusing those of us in the media of being tougher on her than we would have been on another candidate because she was a woman. We would have been just as tough on any presidential candidate we had so little information about."

In late October Brown again let loose, this time on Palin's behalf. The press had latched on to revelations that Palin had spent $150,000 of the Republican National Committee's money on clothes for her and her family to wear on the campaign trail. The disparagement this information inspired on the left reflected a major comprehension gap about how much it cost to keep a woman looking well-groomed, especially by the harsh aesthetic standards of the modern celebrity (and political) media and especially when her appearance was not only part of the campaign's investment, but destined to be scrutinized by fans and detractors alike. It escalated into a point-and-hoot festival of Palin hate that became quickly misogynistic. Brown said on air, "There is an incredible double standard here and we are ignoring a very simple reality: women are judged based on their appearance far, far more than men . . . and look, I speak from experience here. When I wear a bad outfit on the air, I get viewer e-mail complaining about it, a lot of e-mail, seriously. When Wolf Blitzer wears a not-so-great tie, how much e-mail do you think he gets?" Brown said. There has been plenty of talk and plenty written about Sarah Palin's jackets, her hair, her looks. . . . There was plenty of talk and plenty written about Hillary Clinton's looks, hair, pantsuits. Compare that to the attention given to Barack Obama's fifteen-hundred-dollar suits or John McCain's five-hundred-twenty-dollar Ferragamo shoes." These were not issues that had historically been brought to bear on presidential elections. Now a dustup about the budget of a vice-presidential campaign was allowing women in news rooms to communicate careers-worth of marginalization.

✶ ✶ ✶

Women were also shaking up election coverage in another under-valued genre: the daytime talk show. It wasn't unusual for politi-cal candidates to appear on chat shows, but in 2008 they weren't always there just to share recipes (except when John McCain cooked ribs with Rachael Ray) or accept moony compliments (except when Barbara Walters told Barack Obama he was "very sexy looking"). In the lead-up to primaries throughout the general election it also became increasingly possible to see politicians, especially conserva-tives like McCain, made uncomfortable by the informal assertive-ness of daytime television.

Perhaps it was the product of a generation of post-second-wave female journalists, from Couric to Sawyer to Brown to Meredith Vieira, finding prime-time berths either unavailable or inhospitable and settling into female-friendly daytime slots. Or perhaps it was because daytime talk television had expanded to include women of different colors (Oprah Winfrey, Tyra Banks, Whoopi Goldberg, Sherri Shepherd), ages (Joy Behar, Barbara Walters), and sexuali-ties (Rosie O'Donnell, Ellen DeGeneres) than the more straitlaced white guy nightly news, creating a more diverse platform on which to casually entertain socially progressive issues.

Most likely of all was that 2008's energetic daytime engage-ment with the presidential election was a side effect of Oprah Win-frey's engagement with Obama's campaign. Winfrey had leveraged decades of cultural capital to endorse Barack Obama, giving him a boost that may have helped put him over the top in Iowa. But unwilling to exploit her platform on Obama's behalf, Winfrey was clear that she would not invite him or the other candidates onto her show, as had been her custom in past election years. This sent presidential contenders scurrying to reach daytime audiences via other chatty outlets that did not adhere to traditional templates for political discourse. Thus were born some of the most weirdly sophisticated and direct exchanges of the season.

In the year preceding the election Ellen DeGeneres was talking a lot about her wedding to actress Portia de Rossi, a union that had especially sharp political implications thanks to California's Proposition 8, which would reverse the state's legalization of gay marriage. In September 2007, when Hillary Clinton told DeGeneres that she supported equal benefits for gay partners, a repeal of "don't ask, don't tell," and an end to discriminatory hiring practices—an exasperating everything-but-marriage response—DeGeneres cut to the political quick by asking, "Do you think it would be possible for someone to run and openly say 'I support gay marriage' and win?" In May 2008 she opened her interview with McCain by saying, "Let's talk about the big elephant in the room," in reference to her forthcoming nuptials. McCain responded, "I think that people should be able to enter into legal agreements. . . . I just believe in the unique status of marriage between man and woman." DeGeneres replied, "We are all the same people. You're no different than I am. Our love is the same. . . . When someone says, 'You can have a contract, and you'll still have insurance' . . . it sounds to me like saying, 'Well you can sit [here], you just can't sit there.'" McCain could only say, "I've heard you articulate that position in a very eloquent fashion. We just have a disagreement and I, along with many many others, wish you every happiness."

By October DeGeneres was discussing Sarah Palin's support of Proposition 8 and telling viewers, "Maybe it's because I'm gay that I think we should all be equal, but . . . we need to learn to love [people] for who they are and let them love who they want to love." These were glimpses of what a daytime cadence made possible: a faux-breezy exchange as vehicle for a larger, sometimes genuinely moving conversation about justice and equality within the democracy.

Over at *The View* Barbara Walters and company were, as the *New York Times* reported, making "a conscious effort . . . to insert their daytime talk show forcefully into the nation's political conversation." And they did it to occasionally impressive effect, such as on September 12, when John McCain sat down with Whoopi Goldberg, Joy Behar, Sherri Shepherd (who had previously admitted that she had never voted before 2008) and Elisabeth Hasselbeck. Presiding was Walters, who after decades of barreling away in legitimate journalism, in her later years had put herself to pasture in the daytime lineup.

Walters and her colleagues began to quiz McCain about campaign ads misleadingly suggesting that Obama had used the phrase "lipstick on a pig" in reference to Sarah Palin. "We know that those two ads are untrue, they're lies," said Behar, using words that the press had been too polite to utter. "Yet . . . at the end of it [you] say 'I approve these messages.' Do you really approve them?" In the next segment Goldberg jocularly asked McCain if she was allowed to call him J-Mac, and then asked, "Do you believe in the separation of church and state?" When McCain said that "sure," he believed in secularism, Goldberg asked whether he was troubled by the fact that his running mate did not share this view; she was referring to Palin's expressed belief that the Iraq war was God's will and to her Christian-inflected opposition to abortion even in cases of rape and incest. "Judeo-Christian values were the foundation of our nation," McCain responded. Goldberg retorted that the nation was made up not only of Judeo-Christian disciples but of "Muslims . . . Zoroastrians . . . [and] Wiccans." Even Hasselbeck, the program's conservative bugaboo, after assuring McCain that he had her vote, asked if he would overturn *Roe v. Wade*. McCain replied that while he wouldn't impose a litmus test on Supreme Court nominees, "they would have to have a clear record of strict interpretation," which Walters promptly translated as "another way of saying 'people who would want to overturn *Roe v. Wade*.'" When McCain again talked up a strict interpretation of the Constitution Goldberg asked, "Do I need to worry about becoming a slave again? . . . Because certain things . . . in the Constitution . . . had to change." To this, all McCain could say was, "That's an excellent point. I thank you."

It was not only great television, but great journalistic interrogation from people unafraid to ask combative questions of a presidential candidate. *The View*'s hosts appeared so roused by the pelts hanging from the edge of their coffee table that they spent the rest of the political season wallowing in debate about the Weather Underground and the Keating Five like a *MacNeil/Lehrer NewsHour* that also included interviews with the likes of "the fabulous Alec Baldwin!"

☆ ☆ ☆

All this paled in comparison to the year's most improbable news media juggernaut, MSNBC's Rachel Maddow, whose combination of relatable zeal and high-brow smarts made her a television anomaly. Maddow kicked off the election season with her impish revelation to Pat Buchanan and Chris Matthews that bloggers were blaming Clinton's New Hampshire victory on Matthews's overzealotry. "I didn't mean it in a mean way at all," Maddow told me in a summer 2008 interview. "But I knew that it was just going to blow his mind."

Matthews was far from the first talking head to get the Maddow treatment. Before primary season began, clips of Maddow, an Air America host often invited to cable news shows as a ballsy gremlin of the left, had flooded the Internet. Her specialty was making Tucker Carlson's head explode and getting under Buchanan's skin until all he could do was gibber at her about socialism. But the election klieg lights that transform character actors into media leading ladies had made Maddow, at thirty-five, with fewer than five years of national broadcast experience under her belt, the explosive newcomer of 2008, landing her own nightly hour-long show just after the political conventions concluded.

Air America had taken a chance on her (her prior broadcast experience was as a part-time "newsgirl" at a local radio station in western Massachusetts) when it launched in 2004. Four years later love was too weak a word to describe how some people felt about Rachel Maddow. They lurved her, loaved her, luffed her. *New York* magazine's online "Intelligencer" column ran an item headlined "Why We're Gay for Rachel Maddow," and the blogosphere was dotted with similarly besotted posts.

What was remarkable about Maddow's ascension was not its

velocity—Anderson Cooper's coverage of Hurricane Katrina had made him a household name in less than a week—but the shifts in media it seemed to demarcate. Maddow was one of the few left-liberal women to have busted open the world of TV punditry, which had previously made icons of right-wing commentators like Ann Coulter and Michelle Malkin. Unlike her pneumatic, bilious female counterparts on the right or her cocksure male colleagues, Maddow had succeeded not through bluster, but thanks to a combination of brisk thinking and galumphing good cheer. She was neither a shiny matinee idol nor a smooth-talking partisan hack. She was a Rhodes scholar, a lesbian, and a policy wonk with a Ph.D. who had started as an AIDS activist focused on prison reform. Her rise seemed to signal a hopeful move away from the thuggish and angry and toward the lucid and nuanced.

Part of the hypnotic hold Maddow had on her audience was that despite her place in the "liberal media's" firmament, her election commentary was, in a funny way, nonpartisan. During the incendiary primary season she maintained an almost maddening equilibrium, expressing dismay and appreciation for just about every candidate. Weeks after Clinton's concession Maddow called the New York senator's war vote "unforgivable." But Maddow had also risen to her defense, especially in moments when no one else was willing to. She found herself "frequently underwhelmed" by Obama, and would go on to remain a critic of his administration, especially his ramping up in Afghanistan. "He got it right in opposing the war," she said to me in the summer of 2008, "but his war policy stuff now is bullshit." It was ironic that Maddow, perhaps Air America's most successful product (besides future senator Al Franken), had traveled through the looking glass of partisan journalism and come out the other side an electoral agnostic, a liberal in the purest, almost mineral sense of the word.

During the election Maddow was very often the only girl in the room. "It means I get dumb questions that I wouldn't otherwise get," she told me. "Anything about gender, anything about women voters, even if I really obviously have no expertise in the subject or it's not my turn to talk. I get that question." She smiled. "I love the idea that I am the voice of woman. Look at me! It's like, really?

The one woman in the room is really mannish!" She gestured at her baseball T-shirt and baggy jeans.

The segments that got Maddow the most traction out of the gate were, unsurprisingly, her bits on Palin, especially one about Palin's bizarro-world insistence that a legislative report on the Alaskan ethics scandal Troopergate revealed that she did not abuse her authority, when in fact it had found the opposite to be true. Maddow's commentary was direct: "She is lying. This is a person running for office who's been confronted with an uncomfortable and inconvenient fact, and her response to that is to look into the camera and lie to you. Enthusiastically and repeatedly." Like the other journalists I spoke to, Maddow didn't believe that her gender made her a better critic of Palin than she was of McCain or Obama or Biden. But the viral attention she got was often amplified after she said something pithy and cutting about the Alaska governor.

It was telling that the enthusiasm surrounding television's newswomen came not during Clinton's candidacy, but during Palin's. The dispiriting interpretation was that the willingness on the part of Couric, Maddow, Brown and other women to be tough on Palin fed an appetite for girl-on-girl combat. When I wrote columns critical of Palin they got more traffic than any other in my career, furthering my suspicions that viewers prefer their female journalists attacking other females.

But Brown had also made a splash defending Palin, and *The View* women had gone after McCain, not his running mate. There was clearly something else empowering television's women to come out swinging. Maybe it was months of bitten tongues, of sitting through Matthews and Olbermann and Joe Scarborough and Christopher Hitchens trying to explain how women think and vote and what they sound like. Now they had something to say for themselves.

☆ ☆ ☆

A year after the election some of the media surges by women had receded. After a maternity leave in 2009 Campbell Brown returned to lower ratings, and in May 2010 again showed off her knack for candor by announcing that because "not enough people want to watch my program," she was leaving it. Postelection, the obsession with Maddow began to cool, though she often beat her rival, Larry King, among viewers twenty-five to fifty-four. Enthusiasm for Couric's renaissance subsided, but she remained in the CBS anchor chair, dire predictions to the contrary. In December 2009 Diane Sawyer took over the evening anchor desk at ABC. The hosts of *The View,* for their part, made health care reform, troop escalation in Afghanistan, and gay marriage regular topics of their morning kaffeeklatsch. They had rediscovered what groundbreaking talk show host Phil Donahue had observed sixteen years earlier, when he explained his own success: "The usual idea of women's programming was a narrow, sexist view. . . . Women were interested in a lot more than covered dishes and needlepoint." According to the *Los Angeles Times* in February 2010 *The View*'s ratings were high, and producer Bill Geddie told the paper, "We realized [that political conversation] wasn't just for Sunday mornings anymore." Even Sunday mornings, long populated by Beltway-bound white guys jawing about the week's news, were changing. In 2010 Candy Crowley was named the host of CNN's Sunday show *State of the Union,* and ABC handed stewardship of *This Week* to the veteran CNN foreign correspondent Christiane Amanpour.

With the election over, female punditry became less ubiquitous, though MSNBC, and *The Rachel Maddow Show* in particular, continued to feature regular commentary from Ana Marie Cox, Melissa Harris-Lacewell, Joan Walsh and others. For some reason Walsh got the brunt of some marked male aggression. In January 2009 she was on MSNBC debating former House majority leader Dick Armey about the economic stimulus plan when Armey announced, "I'm so damn glad that you can never be my wife because I surely wouldn't have to listen to that prattle from you every day." Three months later, after she debated G. Gordon Liddy on CNN over the release of the Bush torture memos, Liddy said almost the exact same thing when he rehashed the debate on his radio show.

"I'd rather have it out there," Walsh said of these incidents. "Moments like that actually represent progress, because it was so shocking to so many people. It showed people what we're up against. Women are still judged on marriageability, and marriageability has a lot to do with keeping your mouth shut."

At the start of *The Terror Dream* Susan Faludi recounts a prophetic nightmare she had on the night of September 10, 2001, in which she was shot in the throat by a young man on a plane. She recalled, "[In the dream] I noticed that I was still alive but unable to speak"—an apt image for her argument about the silencing of the female media in an age of terrorism. Not ten years later the election allowed a lot of women to dislodge the metaphorical bullets from their throats. There still was not parity, but by refusing to keep their mouths shut women were regaining their voices and expanding their presence in the media.

☆ ☆ ☆

The increasing number of powerful women in politics and media during the election meant extended opportunities for the women who portrayed them in other pop culture venues. As Amy Poehler told me in 2008, "There are so many women . . . in politics and entertainment and in positions of power that you get to impersonate. It's really cool."

Predictably, there was still resistance to women gaining ground in terrain that had always been dominated by men. In a December 2006 *Vanity Fair* piece called "Why Women Aren't Funny," Christopher Hitchens offered not an argument so much as a provocation—a stew of Rudyard Kipling verse and some claptrap about how women find neither their "physical decay" nor their future of episiotomies inherently funny—alongside a photo of a lumpen, mirthless female whom *Feministing*'s Ann Friedman correctly observed resembled no one so much as Hitchens himself. It was the small and grating death rattle of a Rat Pack–era sentiment.

In April 2008 *Vanity Fair* published a winking mea culpa, putting comedians Tina Fey, Amy Poehler, and Sarah Silverman on its cover alongside an article by Alessandra Stanley asking, "Who Says Women Aren't Funny?" Stanley quoted Nora Ephron, who sensibly observed, "There is no question that there are a million more funny women than there used to be, but . . . there are more women in a whole bunch of places, and this is one of them." As Poehler told me, "The struggle as a female comedian was done for me by the women that were on *SNL* from the beginning, or the women who were on

SCTV, or the women in the films in the eighties when I was growing up."

The Hitchens flap was mostly a sideshow and a distraction from the truly compelling story about women and laughter at the start of the twenty-first century: the introduction of sometimes dry, occasionally side-splitting humor into what most would agree had not, until now, been an uproarious social movement. The news was not that women were funny; it was that they were making feminism funny.

★ ★ ★

It wasn't that women had never been witty about the oppressions and restrictions of their gender. Jane Austen became wildly popular, even with men, by transforming tales of the torturous fiscal and romantic constraints of Regency womanhood into social satire. But a century after Austen's death, as suffragists clamored loudly for greater liberties and extended rights, the weight of their project and the unlikelihood of its triumph did not lend themselves to whimsy. Neither did the social agitation of the 1960s and 1970s do anything to diminish feminism's prim reputation. In part that was because language that was offensive to feminists was often the sexualized language of objectification; any attempt to police it was countered with aspersions of frigidity. Gloria Steinem told me in 2009, "We were objecting to . . . guys in the street saying things like 'Why aren't you smiling, honey?' . . . When we objected, that probably gave us the reputation for being humorless." Then there was the practical reality that there were not many belly laughs to be harvested from the fight to break down prohibitive economic, social, and professional barriers. Talking with the thirty-year-old comedian Sarah Haskins in 2009, I ventured that feminism might be getting funnier than ever before. Haskins's initial response was to object, but then she paused and said, "Okay, actually, it wasn't ever funny. 'I want to work at your office.' 'Ha ha.' 'No, I'm not joking. I want to work at your office.'"

Certain individual feminists were funny, both in public and private. Covering the women's movement for *Esquire,* Ephron penned wry pieces about consciousness-raising and those parties where women used hand mirrors to look at their cervices. Erica Jong wrote sometimes hilariously about liberated female sexuality. Gloria Steinem, who worked as a television comedy writer before becoming a movement leader, was, Ephron told me in 2010, "much funnier than anyone remembers." In 1973 *Ms.* magazine ran a cover illustration of a Lichtenstein-style cartoon in which a man asks, "Do you know the women's movement has no sense of humor?" and a woman responds, "No . . . but hum a few bars and I'll fake it!" By and large, though, these chuckles were aberrations; feminism's straitlaced reputation was not altogether without merit.

But as conditions for some women began to improve, when they did not have to hold so fiercely to their convictions or fight as hard to get heard, women became increasingly likely to have a few laughs at their own expense, though often literally at their own expense; Phyllis Diller and Joan Rivers both succeeded in comedy's boys' club with brutally self-lacerating acts. The 1980s saw improvements in Hollywood, thanks to feminist comedies like *9 to 5* and later the emergence of Roseanne Barr and what Barbara Ehrenreich would call her "special brand of proletarian feminism." At the turn of the millennium Sarah Silverman's dirty act obliterated the assumptions behind Friars Club director Jean-Pierre Trebot's 1983 comment (in response to Diller dressing in drag to infiltrate the roast of Sid Caesar) that the club did not allow women because "the language gets kind of graphic." A 2007 episode of Silverman's eponymous Comedy Central series includes a nostalgic montage of her entering the same abortion clinic during the Reagan, Clinton, and Bush administrations while Green Day's lyrics "I hope you had the time of your life" plays in the background. Silverman's slightly less outrageous contemporary, Margaret Cho, crowed to Jessica Valenti in the *Guardian,* "Everything I do is about feminism," though that assertion was hard to reconcile with her joke, "Laura Bush is pretty but you know her pussy tastes like Lysol."

Increasingly, women were applying profane humor to politics, relationships and sexism itself. In a 2006 interview with Amy Poehler for *Bust* magazine the television writer Jill Soloway compared the still meager roles for adult female comedians to "a tiny pubic mustache." Poehler replied that female comedies should "be like full, giant '70s bushes." Wanda Sykes opined in her 2006 HBO comedy series about how great it would be "if our pussies were detachable." "You could do anything. You could go visit a professional ball player's hotel room at two o'clock in the morning. Sex? My pussy's not even in the building!"

Sykes made the most of 2008's political season, noting to Jay Leno in the fall of 2008, "I'm a feminist, but I'm sorry . . . [Sarah Palin]'s crazy!" Complaining that "they don't let [Palin] talk," Sykes continued, "They say, 'Oh, she's meeting with the world leaders,' but there's no reporters. I'm like, 'Is she meeting with the world leaders, or did you take her to the Epcot Center [and] let her drink around the world? Because I've done that! Maybe I should be secretary of state!" Months later Sykes returned to Leno's couch, mocking the press covering the about-to-be-inaugurated Obamas as "trying to dance around the race issue because they don't know how to do it without sounding racist. . . . 'Who's the real Michelle Obama?' . . . You know what they're saying is, 'When are we gonna see *this*?'" Here Sykes waved her finger in imitation of a black female stereotype. "They're waiting for her to throw all his stuff out on the White House lawn and [say] 'You get the hell out of my house!'"

"The power to make people laugh is a really big power," Steinem told me. "To come into a position where you can make people laugh not out of hostility but out of revelation, because you make people recognize something, is really big-time important." By 2008 women were yukking it up with a gut-busting abandon never before associated with gender and its discontents. Making jokes not necessarily (though sometimes) at the expense of other women, comedy was for the first time not just being embraced by feminism, but was serving a feminist agenda: making the circumstances of both liberation and lingering double standards laughably clear.

* * *

If Katie Couric was the nail in Sarah Palin's vice-presidential coffin, the hammer was Tina Fey. Fey's deadly impression of Palin was played out over half a dozen sketches for which Fey returned to *Saturday Night Live,* where she had been the first female head writer and where, in February, she made news with her comedic defense of Hillary Clinton, "Bitch is the new black." Her impression of Palin synthesized all that was mind-blowing about the vice-presidential candidate, crystallizing the improbability of her existence on a presidential ticket—and the hyperfeminized role she was hired to play there—with a (barely) amplified portrait of Palin's winking flirtatiousness, her rambling sentences, her dropped-g gerunds, and her penchant for trailing off midargument.

The Palin sketches, largely written by *SNL*'s Seth Meyers, contained indelible one-liners that captured Palin's self-assured vacuity and cheerful malevolence. As Fey's Palin described herself in a scene with Will Ferrell's George W. Bush, "I'm one part practiced folksy, one part sassy, and a little dash of high school bitchy!" They also communicated the hypocrisies and inconsistencies of her religious social conservatism. "I believe that marriage is meant to be a sacred institution between two unwilling teenagers," said Fey, portraying Palin in the vice-presidential debate sketch. The genius of Fey's impressions, which gave *Saturday Night Live* its highest rating in fourteen years, was that they boiled the reality of Palin down into its undeniable "You betcha"–studded essence. In the parody of Palin's conversation with Couric, the *SNL* team even included verbatim sentences cribbed from the interviews. This was what the show had done to political candidates for years. Gerald Ford's clumsiness, Michael Dukakis's diminutive erudition, Al Gore's waxen obsession with a "lock box," George Bush's menacing snicker—these outsized versions of real-life characteristics were the meat of the show's political play. In a profile in *Vanity Fair* Fey responded to griping that she had been mean to Palin: "What made me super-mad about [that criticism] was that it seemed very sexist toward me and her. The implication was that she's so fragile, which she's not. She's a strong woman . . . also, it was sexist because, like, who would ever go on the news and say, 'Well, I thought it was sort of mean to Richard Nixon when Dan Aykroyd played him.'"

Fey's take on Palin was serendipitous, prompted by the strong resemblance between the two women. But that likeness was part of what made it groundbreaking: a vice-presidential candidate looked like a famous comedian. A female comedian. And on it went. Hillary Clinton had been played by Poehler for several years. The interview that brought Palin low had been administered by Couric, a woman also played by Poehler. The vice-presidential debate had been moderated by Gwen Ifill, prompting a guest appearance by the inimitable Queen Latifah. Inasmuch as each of the impersonations relied on the amplification of feminine traits—Poehler/Couric's heavily mascara'd and incessant blinking, Poehler/Hillary's hyenic laugh, Fey/Palin's sexy librarianism—in ways that might indeed be sexist or reductive, those characteristics were ripe for amplification only because the objects of political and media parody had high-pitched laughs and wore mascara and pencil skirts. The heightened femininity of Palin's political persona also came in for examination; during the Couric-Palin sketch, Couric pointed out to a stumped Palin, "It seems to me that when cornered you become increasingly adorable." That little one-liner, accompanied by Fey's inspired shooting of fake finger guns, distilled a gender dynamic—wherein women infantilize themselves as a defensive strategy—it might otherwise take thousands of words to unspool.

When it came to analysis of presidential gender dynamics in 2008, few could have touched the textured acuity of Fey and Poehler's first Palin-Clinton sketch, in which the candidates give a press conference about sexism in the media (during which Fey/Palin crows the enduring line, "I can see Russia from my house!") and provided not just the first glimpse of Fey's embodiment of the Alaska governor, but a new vision of Poehler's Clinton.

Poehler did not bear any resemblance to Clinton; neither was she the world's most skillful mimic. From the start she had relied on the broadest possible identifying attributes in her performance: the big laugh and ravenous hunger for the presidency. But in comedy, as in real life, the arrival of Palin on the scene threw Clinton into new focus. Next to Palin, Clinton's good qualities—her brains, competence, work ethic, her belief in secular government and reproductive freedoms, her ability to complete sentences—became far more evident than they had been before there was another potential "first woman" to compare her to. Nothing conveyed these haze-clearing realignments of perspective as quickly and as firmly as Fey and Poehler did in five and a half minutes. The parodic depiction of the two women side by side exposed the complex dynamics of Palin's parasitism, their unwilling symbiosis, and their stark differences.

In the sketch, when Palin speaks of the "ugly role sexism is playing in the campaign," Poehler's Clinton notes dryly, "[It's] an issue

which I am frankly surprised to hear people suddenly care about."
More deft even than Couric's unanswered question about the nutcracker and the action figure, these two performers laid out the variety of ways that women's bodies could be used against them:

> FEY/PALIN: *Stop photoshopping my head on sexy bikini
> pictures!*
>
> POEHLER/CLINTON: *And stop saying I have cankles. . . .*
>
> FEY/PALIN: *Reporters and commentators, stop using words
> that diminish us, like "pretty," "attractive," "beauti-
> ful" . . .*
>
> POEHLER/CLINTON: *"Harpy," "shrew," "boner-shrinker."*

Next came a vision of how these two candidates' fates were tied
together, as Fey/Palin chirps, "Look how far we've come: Hillary
Clinton, who came so close to the White House, and me, Sarah
Palin, who is even closer. Can you believe it, Hillary?" Poehler/
Clinton, her eyes bulging, shouts back in disbelief, "I can not!"
before elaborating, "I don't want to hear you compare your road to
the White House to *my* road to the White House. I scratched and
clawed through mud and barbed wire. And you just glided in on
a dog sled wearing your pageant sash and your Tina Fey glasses!"
When Fey's Palin responds that it just goes to show that anyone can
be president if they want it enough, Poehler/Clinton lets loose with
crazed laughter and says, "Yeah, you know, Sarah, looking back, if
I could change one thing, I probably should have *wanted* it more,"
before ripping a piece of wood from the podium. This was the story
of these two women, told as directly and almost as honestly as anyone else had managed it, crescendoing with Poehler's ability to say
what Hillary never could have: "I invite the media to grow a pair.
And if you can't, I will lend you mine."

While Fey got all the credit for her work on Palin, the harshest comedic blow to the Alaska governor came from Poehler, who
on a later episode sat at the "Weekend Update" desk with the vice-
presidential candidate herself. After the setup, in which Palin declined
to perform a rap about herself, Poehler launched into the fevered routine on her behalf, bellowing lyrics like "I'm Jeremiah Wright 'cause

tonight I'm the preacher / I got a bookish look and you're all hot for teacher," as the real Palin bopped gamely at the news desk. Backed by two Eskimos and Jason Sudeikis as the First Dude, Poehler's verse got harsher; she sang, with sing-songy patriotism, "My country 'tis of thee, from my porch I can see, Russia and such." Amping it up further, Poehler mimicked Palin's animal blood lust, peppering a guy in a moose costume with imagined bullets, and snarling, "Now you're dead, 'cause I'm an animal! And I'm bigger than you!" As the enormously pregnant Poehler made her exit, she stopped very close to Palin, leaned in, and growled, "I'm Palin, I'm out!"

Poehler seemed to me incandescent in her willingness to exhibit such raw aggression in front of her mark. Making the moment even more sublime was the fact that Poehler was dancing around just one week before giving birth to her son. The layers of the act were remarkable: here was a woman in the last days of pregnancy, doing her public and nationally visible job—precisely the behavior that had helped to distinguish Palin as an anomalous mother-governor—appearing on television just fifty-five years after Lucille Ball's pregnancy could not even be mentioned on the air. Poehler had spent years impersonating the first woman to run for president, and here she was, throwing herself around the stage in front of the woman who had been sent to capitalize on her gains. In Poehler's exertions the strides women had made in recent decades became blindingly apparent.

It was culture as politics as comedy as culture as politics. It was goofy and grand.

✵ ✵ ✵

The fusion of feminism and funny wasn't just happening on *Saturday Night Live*. Improbably, Comedy Central's male-hosted double-header of fake news shows, *The Daily Show* and *The Colbert Report*, had also expanded the feminist conversation. In the years since his 2005 launch as a faux right-wing airbag in the style of Fox's Bill O'Reilly, Stephen Colbert had been one of the most reliable hosts of feminist writers and activists and had offered a friendly place for political women to be funny. Ohio Representative Stephanie Tubbs Jones made an appearance as a character called "Judge Tubbs" in a send-up of daytime legal shows. And it was on *Colbert* that Donna Brazile said, "I'm a woman, so I like Hillary. I'm black, I like Obama. But I'm also grumpy, so I like John McCain."

Colbert's own routines touched frequently on issues of gender. A June 2007 segment of "The Word" was dedicated to "Rodham" and the news that Hillary would be dropping her maiden name to campaign for the presidency. "You don't see the other seventeen presidential candidates dropping their maiden names!" blustered Colbert, shining an exaggerated light on the double standards plaguing Clinton. "For too many years women in public life have had an unfair advantage when it comes to media attention. If Hillary has a bad hair day, that's front-page news!" Colbert would do a bit in 2009 about the passage of the Lilly Ledbetter Fair Pay Act, complaining, "If you can't discriminate against women, what is the point of hiring them?"

Colbert's benighted antifeminist persona allowed him to mock misogynistic attitudes by playing them off his many feminist guests. Linda Hirshman explained the domestic inequities chronicled in her manifesto *Get to Work* after Colbert promised to explain to her that "a woman needs a man like a fish needs to be cooked and served to me for dinner by a woman on a bicycle." When Jessica Valenti, who gave Colbert a T-shirt with the slogan "Feminist Chicks Dig Me," suggested that she wrote her first book, *Full Frontal Feminism,* to empower young women, Colbert asked, "Why not just get *The Secret*? Because then they can just visualize equality and it will come to them!" Colbert gave young feminists the opportunity to dodge the uptight stereotypes of their forebears, and the forebears themselves a chance to disprove them. When Jane Fonda and Gloria Steinem appeared to advertise their women's radio network, they cooked an apple pie with Colbert in a segment called "Cooking with Feminists." Colbert got to say, "Gloria, if you'll grab some of those Macintosh apples and explain to me, what is the state of American feminism?" and to wonder, "How can you tell if a woman is a feminist or just angry?" So it wasn't Catharine MacKinnon, and maybe Colbert was declawing feminists, making them playful when feminism should be taken seriously. But the show also made the women's movement, its leaders and its writers, available and visible, an approachable part of popular cultural discourse, rather than being cast only in opposition to it.

On Jon Stewart's *Daily Show* the feminist edge came from the correspondents, especially Samantha Bee. In September 2007 Bee did a *Sex and the City* parody in which she swanned around New York in a tutu pondering the fact that women could now be "doctresses, body-buildtrixes, and firemenwomen," as the onscreen text asked, "Is America ready . . . for a catty, stacked, whorish, menstruating . . ." woman president? In 2007 Bee did a segment on busty and lusty cable newswomen, calling them NILFs, or "news I'd like to fuck," in which she reported that one CNN anchor's "screen says Baghdad, but her open neckline says 'Bag these,'" while another reporter "interview[ed] someone just back from Iraq in a skirt that barely covers *her* Sunni Triangle." Katie Couric cited the skit to me in 2009, noting that it "was so funny and so true," but that it had also thrown into perspective her own confusion: "Are we supposed to be fetching or are we supposed to be smart?" Couric continued, "I do look at some of those anchors on cable and I think, 'God, did I encourage this?' Because sometimes I'd show my legs on the *Today* show. And sometimes I look back and think, 'God, that skirt was a little too short.'" Here were larger questions of gender and self-representation, summoned by a piece on a comedy show.

"Feminism is important to me, women's issues are important to me, reproductive issues are very important to me," Bee told me in 2009. The idea that there was pointed comedy to be made from these issues was revolutionary, and occasionally moving. Bee recalled a segment she did at the Republican convention in which she asked conventioneers to talk about Bristol Palin's pregnancy, getting them to call her decision to have her baby a "choice." She was nervous watching the segment screen during the show. "This was close to my heart. . . . I think I cried when it screened and the audience loved it." Bee said, "I don't really know how it's possible not to be [a feminist]. I think people are coming back to it. For a decade nobody would use the word *feminism*."

In a piece in the *Guardian* about feminist humor Jessica Valenti wrote, "Most feminists develop a strong sense of humor—they have to. How else would we survive the daily sexism, a political climate that's hostile to our rights, and the general discrimination that comes with being a woman? If we couldn't laugh until we cried, we would probably spend all of our time sobbing." Such a grim assessment was nowhere more applicable than in Bee's laugh-or-you'll-weep take-down of John McCain's statements about late-term abortion during the final presidential debate. McCain had put air quotes around the term "health of the mother," calling concern with women's health the "extreme pro-abortion position." "Let's face it," Bee said in her *Daily Show* commentary, "women love abortions and will do anything to get one. The later the better. . . . Enough with the whining about rape, incest, and incest-rape. We're on to you, ladies. Those aren't the golden ticket to the abortion factory, okay?" John McCain, Bee said, "has finally put the concerns of women where they belong: in derisive air quotes."

"This place is very interested in gender and politics," Bee told me of *The Daily Show.* "There's a lot of vaginas around here, and we make our presence known." Another came aboard in spring of 2008, when Kristen Schaal, a thirty-year-old comedian and actress, pitched a piece about Hillary Clinton. "I really wanted Hillary to win," Schaal told me in 2009, "and I realized that she just wouldn't, and I couldn't believe it. She had everything in place to do it." Schaal did a piece called "Dear Madame President," in which she filmed a video to the future first woman president and wondered, "How did you do it? Did you have to be assertive? Were you a total bitch? Does that word even exist anymore?" Schaal made further appearances as *The Daily Show*'s "senior women's issues commentator," including one in which she stripped down to her Wonder Woman Underoos to protest the media sexism aimed at Clinton, and another with Bee in which the women fought over who would take over Stewart's anchor desk. Schaal parodied Palin with a flurry of accusations and excuses: "You are so sexist! . . . I'm not taking any questions! I'm still learning! This is a gotcha conversation! From my apartment I can see where they tape *Letterman*! I'm a maverick! I don't need the approval of the elites!"

Many of these comedy clips gained traction in part because they were posted on *Jezebel,* the pop culture website for women. *Jezebel* was founded in 2007 by Nick Denton, the bloodless British owner of the media site Gawker, to address women's media. It was a high-low hybrid that jibed with the cheekiness of the feminist blogosphere and was just serious enough in its feminist and political leanings to set itself apart from the cadaverous cynics dominating most pop culture sites. *Jezebel* cultivated a fan base of readers who called themselves "Jezebelles" and had an insatiable appetite for things that were feminist, things that were funny, and most especially things that were feminist *and* funny. As readership climbed— from fewer than 300,000 a month in the first three months to 1.4 million a month by the end of 2009—*Jezebel* became one of the most useful ways to disseminate clips. "You can really tell when something resonates with people," Bee told me. "I'm always excited when something of mine ends up on *Jezebel*."

The feminist comedian Sarah Haskins practically credited the site for her career. The twenty-nine-year-old Chicago native and Harvard graduate was touring with Second City when she was hired as a writer for the Current TV show *Infomania*. At home watching TLC's *Secret Life of a Soccer Mom*, Haskins noticed that a lot of the commercials were for yogurt; she proposed a segment about the common tropes of yogurt commercials: the assumption of constant dieting, women in gray hoodies (an outfit Haskins said indicated "I have a master's, but then I got married"), and spontaneous dancing over the deliciousness of dessert-flavored yogurt ("It's not real food, it's *yogurt!*"). Haskins's segment, in which she called yogurt "the official food of women," was the kickoff to a series called "Target: Women," in which she picked apart advertising aimed at women. Meant to be a short cycle of spots, the series extended through 2008 and all of 2009, and went on to include Haskins's commentary on the cultural fascination with Barbie, princess stories, underage pop stars, and the portrayal of Hillary Clinton supporters as angry ("You know what makes me angry? Watching you talk about how angry I am!").

Haskins told me in 2009 that she was "totally shocked" by the popularity of "Target: Women." "Women's identities are [often] constructed in ways that feel false, whether it's a bunch of pundits on MSNBC talking about Hillary and Sarah Palin or commercials that say that when you're cleaning, you should be wearing a snazzy outfit."

Paying attention to how culture addresses and represents

women, said Haskins, "has certainly raised my consciousness of the presence of a generation of women who are perhaps reclaiming the term. . . . There are all these sites on the Internet that I had no idea about, having a conversation that I certainly wasn't a part of when I was in school." Like me, Haskins described herself as a product of the "I'm not a feminist, but . . ." generation of backlash inheritors, and said her experience as an accidental feminist comic included "an education in, 'Oh, is this not a bad word anymore?'" and noted that that had a lot to do with the power of comedy to relax strictures and loosen ingrained attitudes. "A good joke lets you see things through a new lens without pushing you to do it," said Haskins, summing up many of the election year's lessons about feminism, pop culture and politics.

11   THE NEXT WAVE IS HERE

By mid-October Sarah Palin was receiving blame for McCain's expected loss from both Democrats and Republicans, and most pointedly from the people running her own campaign. Some inside the McCain camp, divided over its strategic errors and Palin's egregious performance, had opened fire on her in the press, anonymously telling reporters that her own advisors thought her an inexperienced prima donna who was sinking the ticket.

Whatever tight control the campaign initially had exerted over Palin's self-presentation had unraveled in her post-Couric spiral, and the distance at which the Republican presidential ticket was holding its vice president was alarmingly clear. When, in early October, McCain pulled his resources out of Michigan, Palin told Fox News that she disagreed with the strategy and admitted that upon hearing of the plan, she'd sent advisors an email that read, "Oh come on . . . do we have to?" Palin had obviously not been consulted or even officially informed of the decision to back out of the state. Her critics on the left and right were fixated on stories like her wardrobe budget. Her status as a McCain prop, a stunt gone terribly wrong, was ever more evident. And yet on the campaign trail she was drawing bigger and more frenzied crowds than ever.

It was no wonder that Sarah Palin was going rogue. As one unnamed Palin aide told *Politico*'s Ben Smith, Palin felt "completely mismanaged and mishandled and ill-advised" and made a decision to start trusting her own instincts. In addition to criticizing her boss's decision not to slug it out in Michigan, she openly criticized his unwillingness to attack Obama hard about his relationship with Jeremiah Wright. Hired as the pretty lady by the macho and ill-tempered POW, Palin was turning the Republican campaign strategy on its head by presenting herself as the pugilist and casting her boss as something of a pansy.

At a campaign stop in Colorado Springs in late October, Palin slipped the bonds of her minders and ambled over to a television news crew without permission or supervision; the *New York Times* reported that when campaign staffers noticed her in casual conversation with the press, they began shouting for her spokeswoman, who hustled to cut the interview off, but to no avail. On the same trip a reporter noted in the day's pool report that in her "continuing evolution from the least accessible to the most accessible of the four candidates," Palin took questions at a Cold Stone Creamery ice cream shop. The governor hadn't said anything particularly notable, but her steely insistence on talking at all demonstrated her conviction that she knew, better than John McCain or his team, how to campaign for office.

Whether out of courage or stupidity, Palin was a determinedly independent candidate and one who could see which side her bread was buttered on. In the weeks since her nomination had been announced the Rudy Giulianis and Rick Santorums had piped down a bit about the sexist rhetoric being thrown at her. Now conservative guys, anxious to fob off blame for McCain's poor showing onto his running mate, were sniggering about her outfits and calling her a lightweight. The women of the right-wing media had backed away from their support of her. Kathleen Parker wrote in late September that Palin was "clearly out of her league" and that she was tired of holding her breath every time she watched Palin being interviewed. She added, "My cringe reflex is exhausted."

But on the road Palin was becoming an ever greater sensation, with massive crowds of jubilant Republicans, many of them female, who had found in her not only a candidate to cheer, but an icon of female political empowerment. As the male-run campaign began to abandon her Palin turned to the people who still considered her the party's newest rock star: Republican women. She was committed to addressing her place in history and saw herself as a feminist heroine, even if most feminists didn't agree.

Palin's effect on female Hillary holdouts was the opposite of what McCain strategists had hoped. Her marked differences from Clinton prompted most of Hillary's faithful to throw their Clinton bumper-stickered cars in reverse and back Obama with a panicked energy. The introduction of Palin probably did more for Democratic unity than a month of awkward Unity breakfasts. Kim Gandy said, "I am frequently asked whether NOW supports women candidates just because they are women. This gives me an opportunity to once again answer that question with an emphatic 'No.' We recognize the importance of having women's rights supporters at every level but, like Sarah Palin, not every woman supports women's rights." Feminist excoriations of Palin did not stop there. Suzanne Braun Levine, the first editor of *Ms.* magazine, wrote, "Even behind the reportedly clear glasses she wears to play down her beauty-queen credential . . . she can't disguise her inexperience." A spokeswoman for NOW told *Politico* that Palin was "more a conservative man than she is a woman on women's issues," a statement so troubling that Gandy would go to lengths to disown it and clarify that it did not represent her organization's attitude toward Palin. At *Salon* Cintra Wilson wrote that Palin was a "Christian Stepford wife in a sexy librarian costume" and the "hardcore pornographic centerfold spread" for Republicans.

Other critics noticed the pile-on and didn't hesitate to point to its hypocrisy. The Libertarian columnist Cathy Young wrote, "Left-wing feminists have a hard time dealing with strong, successful conservative women in politics. . . . Sarah Palin seems to have truly unhinged more than a few, eliciting a stream of vicious, often misogynist invective." *Jezebel's* Megan Carpentier wrote a series of posts castigating feminists for their hypocritical fury; in one of them, plaintively headlined, "Please, People: Stop Making Me Defend Sarah Palin," she pointed out, "Sexism doesn't just hurt women when it's directed at liberal women. Being sexist to Sarah Palin hurts us by reinforcing stereotypes . . . and by allowing conservatives to point fingers at us and call us hypocrites." Melissa McEwan at *Shakesville* launched a Sarah Palin Sexism Watch with the tag line, "We defend Sarah Palin against misogynist smears not because we endorse her or her politics, but because that's how feminism works."

But there were still other Democratic women who believed that feminism worked differently, that it meant not just gamely defending Palin against sexist criticism, but supporting her full throttle. A small number of Democratic women, some livid about the florid ways the vice-presidential candidate was being dissed, some convinced that it was a feminist imperative to back any woman running for executive office, and a few still too sore to embrace Obama, were dissenting. They were angry at the national women's organizations for which some of them had worked and volunteered, and they wanted to make a public stand against them.

In early October Shelly Mandell, the president of Los Angeles NOW, a feminist organizer for more than three decades, and chief organizer of the March for Women's Lives in 2004, introduced Sarah Palin at a speech in California. Making clear that she was appearing personally, not on behalf of the National Organization for Women, Mandell told the crowd that she was there "as a woman's rights activist for thirty years who has worked for all those years to see this day." "I'm a life-long Democrat," said Mandell, "I don't agree with Governor Palin on several issues . . . [but] I know Sarah Palin cares about women's rights, she cares about equality, she cares about equal pay, and as vice president she will fight for it." Mandell did not mention that Palin's running mate had been vocal in his denunciation of the Lilly Ledbetter Fair Pay Act. "It is an honor to call her sister," Mandell said. "America, this is what a feminist looks like."

NOW's California president Patty Bellasalma hit back hard, issuing a statement that read in part, "The use of Shelly Mandell's Los Angeles NOW title was apparently intended to mislead the public, and indeed has resulted in local television outlets and internet reports misstating that LA NOW has 'endorsed' Sarah Palin or that she has a record of supporting women's rights. This in fact is not the case."

Mandell wasn't the only one to break with feminist opinion on Palin. Elaine Lafferty, the former editor of *Ms.* magazine who had volunteered for the Clinton campaign, officially signed on as a McCain consultant soon after he picked Palin. Lafferty, coauthor of a book with her friend and Fox News anchor Greta Van Susteren, had a complicated history with institutional feminism. Her two-year stint at *Ms.*, from 2003 to 2005, had been officially successful; under her stewardship the struggling magazine's circulation had jumped and she had published critically lauded stories. But behind the scenes there had been tension between Lafferty and the Feminist Majority Foundation, which had taken control of publishing *Ms.* in 2001, about her desire to move the magazine in a more broadly popular direction. At the time of her exit from *Ms.*, Lafferty told the *New York Observer*, "My vision of *Ms.* was that it would be a thinking woman's magazine—a feminist magazine for sure, but my vision of feminism is a big tent . . . as the original *Ms.* was; they didn't check membership cards at the door. I don't believe in dogma, in exclusion or rhetoric. I thought it could be a magazine that invites women into the conversation about how we live today."

Lafferty's words would resonate three years later, when criticism of feminism's exclusivity and elitism would be applied by people looking to stretch the movement's defining boundaries not simply outward, but rightward, and in doing so perhaps permanently explode them.

Lafferty came aboard the McCain campaign as Palin's unofficial *consigliere* on all matters feminist and began helping her with, as Lafferty would call it, "a speech that Palin had long wanted to give on women's rights." That speech took place on October 21 in Henderson, Nevada. Behind Palin stood Lafferty and NOW's Mandell, along with another NOW dissenter, former Oregon chapter president Linda Klinge, and Lynn Forester de Rothschild and Prameela Bartholomeusz, both vocal Hillary dead-enders and members of the Democratic National Platform Committee. Palin introduced and thanked the group for their bravery before asking the women in the audience, "Are you ready to break the highest hardest glass ceiling in America?" She next made a point lifted directly from the Obama-embittered PUMAs: "Somehow Barack Obama just couldn't bring himself to pick the woman who got eighteen million votes."

"American women, Democratic, Republican and Independent should not just let Barack Obama take their votes for granted," said Palin, sounding like the millions of Democratic women who had tried, with varying degrees of cogency or lunacy to express this very conviction to their own party peers. It would have been easy, in fact, to believe that Palin, a Republican hired by a Republican, was now doing the bidding of the knot of angry and unhealed Democratic women standing behind her, so closely was she adhering to what had been their own talking points during their party's nominating process.

Then came a part of the speech in which the interest of disenchanted Democratic women fused with what was unmistakably Palin's own experience of feminism. "When I was a kid Congress passed a law, that's come to be known as Title IX, and that law allowed millions of girls to play sports," she told the crowd. "Over time, that opened more than just the doors to the gymnasium. Along with other reforms, Title IX helped us to see ourselves and our futures [in] a different way. Women of my generation were allowed finally to make more of our own choices with education and with career and I have never forgotten that we owe that opportunity to women, to feminists who came before us. We were allowed to be participants instead of just spectators [of] the achievements of others." This was all pretty remarkable coming from a woman who opposed abortion even in cases of rape and incest. It was downright confounding given that she was running alongside a man who voted nineteen times against increasing the minimum wage, who voted against the Violence Against Women Act and against funding for the Office of Violence Against Women, who voted against expanding the Family and Medical Leave Act and to terminate funds for family planning. But she wasn't done.

Palin assured anyone surprised by her embrace of a feminist history that "equal opportunity is not just the cause of feminists. It's the creed of our country." Were she given the honor of serving, she said, "I intend to advance that creed in our own nation and beyond, because across the world there are still places where women are subjugated and persecuted as they were in Afghanistan, places where they're bullied and brutalized and murdered in honor killings. . . . No one leader can bring an end to all of those ills, but I can promise you this: these women too will have an advocate and a defender in the forty-seventh vice president of the United States." As her speech concluded, Shania Twain's power anthem "She's Not Just a Pretty Face" blared, and Palin embraced the rogue feminists standing behind her.

When I interviewed Lafferty in 2009 she said that just after the election, a teary-eyed Palin asked her, "Why does Gloria Steinem hate me? [She] was my hero. Why do they hate me? I'm a feminist." Lafferty was firm with me: "The woman I met during the campaign and that I was on the plane with was a feminist," meaning that she believed in the professional and economic potential of women, even if she didn't want to make policy to support it. She also believed in a redistribution of domestic work and had said, after giving birth to Trig, "To any critics who say a woman can't think and work and carry a baby at the same time, I'd just like to escort that Neanderthal back to the cave." Even I had to admit that the moment at the end of the vice-presidential debate at which she picked up her infant son had stunned me into silence. I knew the baby was there to advertise Palin's maternal allure, to protect her from criticism, to hammer home her anti-abortion bona fides, but still: seeing a vice-presidential debate in which one of the participants was holding her infant changed everything. As the feminist columnist Ellen Goodman wrote of Palin early on, "Mom to mayor to governor to veep nominee? There's one woman who didn't have trouble raising her hand in class. There's one woman who didn't think she had to be twice as good as a man to run. Be careful what you wish for." In many ways Palin embodied not only feminism's gains, but some of its still unmet aspirations.

The question of whether or not Palin "was a feminist" was one that obsessed and troubled lots of women. Katie Couric and I discussed it during our interview in 2009, during which Couric said, "I wrestle with this. . . . She's a successful woman. She's running the state of Alaska. She was a vice presidential candidate. Just because she doesn't believe in choice and she thinks abortion is tantamount to murder. . . . What is a feminist? Can you be a conservative feminist? I find this so interesting. . . . I think, 'Okay, maybe she is a feminist.' Then I think so many of her views indirectly or directly would hurt women. So I go around and around."

Some of the women associated with the earliest iterations of

American feminism had also been involved in the conservative Christian temperance battles. Gail Collins would remind readers in *When Everything Changed* that Republican women had been the strongest proponents of women's rights, while heavily Catholic working-class Democratic voters had been more reluctant to mess with gender roles. More recently those dynamics had been reversed by the liberal and radical Democratic women who led the midcentury social movements, and by Republican women who fought against modernization of the American family. Phyllis Schlafley opposed the ERA and pushed American women to stay home with their children, and Marilyn Quayle told the Republican convention in 1992, "Most women do not wish to be liberated from their essential natures as women."

Yet here was not just a candidate, but crowds of Republican women and a few Democratic ones, cheering on Palin's vision in which personal empowerment had no correlation to progressive policy, and beginning to agitate for a reevaluation of the meaning of feminism. On the day of Palin's speech about women, former Republican Massachusetts governor Jane Swift, the only woman before Palin to give birth while a sitting governor, told Greta Van Susteren, "There are some on the liberal left who believe that only they have . . . an ability to call themselves feminists. . . . I think a feminist is someone who believes that women should have equal opportunity to men. . . . It is someone like me, like Governor Palin, who hopes that our daughters, if they work hard and play by the rules, can do virtually anything they want to in their life."

When it came to bullying contests over language, it had never been difficult, historically, to get the feminist movement to hand over its lunch money. Perhaps in part because of its breadth and diversity, perhaps because of a lack of gumption that characterized many on the left in the fourth quarter of the twentieth century, perhaps simply because of the manipulative agility of the right, the women's movement lost almost every serious battle over words and imagery in the forty years following the second wave. The worst and most damaging defeats had come over the language of reproductive rights, in which abortion opponents had gobbled up the vocabulary of life, loss, morality, and emotion, while reproductive rights activists persisted with the limply fungible *choice*.

The word was meant to convey women's ability to make decisions regarding their own family and reproductive lives, but instead served most frequently as a baseball bat with which pro-lifers could hit feminism in its nuts. If *choice* was really the only word that feminists owned, then didn't that make every choice a feminist act? If the choice to have an abortion and the choice to continue a pregnancy were equally valid, then why, some women wondered, should the choice to give up a career, or stay in a bad relationship, or get breast implants be disparaged or dismaying? A year after Palin's appearance on the McCain ticket the conservative publication *Newsmax* ran a series of stories on "the newer feminism" that included one with the telling headline "Feminism Now Defined by Each and Every Woman." No one was quite sure how best to wrest stronger or more assertive language back from the other side.

The word *feminism* itself had not exactly inspired a ferocious defense by its own adherents. For decades the right had successfully demonized women who embraced the label as hirsute succubi, family-scorning and erotically disadvantaged old bags. In 2005 I wrote a story about old-school feminist organizations wondering whether to retire the much maligned word in favor of a new one, and a new generation of women determined to reclaim it. In recent years I had seen young women sporting "This is what a feminist looks like" shirts, and had read with surprise as teen and twentysomething celebrities identified themselves as feminists. Now that *feminist* was slowly clawing its way back to cool, Republicans wanted in. Sarah Palin, charismatic mascot of the you-go-girl spirit and the modern cross-party liberation she represented, had awakened in Republican women a desire to claim a piece of feminism as their own, but they were going to fight to remold it to suit their ideology.

Feminism's history of fluidity and combustibility, which originated with its impossible goal of adequately representing all of the interests of a population that came in innumerable shapes, sizes, colors, and identities, also made it legitimately vulnerable to incursions from those of a different ideological caste. The trouble here was that the intruding group was at odds with what was perhaps modern feminism's only truly immutable core value: a woman's right and ability to control her own reproduction.

Lafferty wrote in the *Daily Beast,* "Palin is being pilloried by the inside-the-Beltway Democratic feminist establishment. . . . Yes, she is anti-abortion. And yes, instead of buying organic New Zealand lamb at Whole Foods, she joins other Alaskans in hunting for food. That's it." Lines like this were practically enough to get thoughtful feminists—who, like Lafferty, *wanted* to expand the appeal of women's rights advocacy, who *wanted* more women to proudly celebrate equal opportunity, who *wanted* to move forward and away from the movement's reputation as exclusive, elite, white, and middle class—to say "Oh, that's it? Anti-abortion and no lamb from Whole Foods? Well, okay then, welcome!" before pausing to consider, "Wait, what was that first thing again?" That thing was at the heart of a very grave question for women's rights activists: could they work productively alongside women and men with anti-abortion stances? Could pro-lifers be feminists? As Couric wondered to me in 2009, "Should the feminist movement say, 'We have certain tenets but people who are pro-life, we can welcome them. Let's find our common ground to achieve things in other areas.'"

The trouble was that the goal of outlawing abortion (as well as desires to limit access to birth control and sex education)—not as a matter of personal belief, but as a legislative goal—was not compatible with feminism if feminism in fact meant supporting women's rights to pursue their life, liberty, and happiness on equal footing with men. Not believing in abortion personally was one thing. But preventing other women from exerting full control over their bodies and health, assessing their value as lesser than the value of the fetuses they carried, was, it seemed to me and many others, fundamentally antifeminist and antifemale.

Women like Lafferty, who had the stamp of being Democrats and professional women's rights advocates, were giving this effort a feminist, practically progressive imprimatur. And outside the feminist world they would fuel the assumption, so much in evidence with regard to Hillary, that female candidates appeal to female voters based only on sisterhood. In 2009, discussing her shock at seeing some NOW members support Palin after the struggles to communicate the fact that Clinton support and Obama support were *not* just about shared gender, NOW's Latifa Lyles told me, "Suddenly . . . everything [feminists had been saying] is out the window."

The hypercharged effect of this Woman Power fever, as well as the disjointed narrative in which Palin was the McCain campaign killer and also its biggest star, was obvious in Williamsport, Pennsylvania, on Mischief Night 2008. Five days before the general election, which she and her running mate looked increasingly likely to lose, Palin had drawn a crowd of thirteen thousand people to an outdoor baseball stadium in the near-freezing cold. How could she not have had supreme confidence in her future in politics when she was getting Lollapalooza-level turnout on an uncomfortably frosty night? On that same afternoon, in the same northern Pennsylvania town, her opponent, Joe Biden, the guy on the ticket that was lighting up polls around the country, managed to draw a crowd of only four hundred to a temperature-controlled school gymnasium.

People had been lined up since the morning at the site of the Sarah Palin rally; more than ten thousand tickets had already been distributed. There were hundreds of buttons for sale, reading "Read My Lipstick," "Hot Chicks Vote Republican," "We Love Sarah," and "Sarah-Licious." There were "You Go Girl" T-shirts and banners. As the line grew longer, eager attendees kibitzed and prepared for the big event. One woman held up an "I ♥ S & M" sign—for "Sarah" and "McCain"—and a man dressed up as Hillary Clinton explained why he/she was at the rally: "Obama ditched me."

"The media may not be portraying Sarah as popular," said Ellen Margraff as she waited in the line, "but look around." The polling on Palin was abysmal, but out in the world monster crowds with blankets and buttons, Christian literature and thundersticks in tow were willing to brave the cold for a glimpse of the woman they believed they would be cheering for well into the future. "I've come to see Sarah, our next vice president of the United States!" shouted Gloria Gordon, a sixty-four-year-old police officer. "Everything she says, I agree with one hundred percent of it." She added that should McCain and Palin fall short of their goals the next Tuesday, "she'll be president in 2012." On my way to report on Palin's last week of rallies I had been prepared to see Klannish, hate-spewing anti-Obama gatherings like the ones making the rounds on YouTube. But this crowd was not like that. These people were happy and pumped up, despite the fact that many of them knew Palin would most likely not be their vice president come January. They didn't care. Some of them were lifelong Republicans, some of them had found their enthusiasm for the right-wing ticket only through their enthusiasm for Palin. They believed that she would be president someday. And they really, really wanted a woman to be president.

"I'm a strong woman, and I really relate to strong women," said sixty-seven-year-old Gloria Stere, who wore a bright blue Palin Power T-shirt. Stere explained that she had just retired from running her own sewing machine business, and though a "dyed-in-the-wool Republican," she had considered voting for Hillary Clinton. But she was quick to add, "Palin is the one that absolutely made my mind up about supporting John McCain. I took one look at her, heard her speak, and thought, 'Oh my god, she is the one.'" Diane Ellis, a ninth-grade American history teacher, told me, "Even if they don't win the election I'll still be impressed by her. Hopefully in the next four years the Republican Party will realize what they have there, and maybe even bring her on as presidential candidate. She and Hillary going at it—that's what I'd like to see."

A security sniper ogled the crowd at Bowman Field with his night-vision glasses as a local minister took the stage to offer a benediction and pray for forgiveness "for so many [who] have shed innocent blood through the course of abortions, and so many [who] would stop the sanctity of marriage between a man and a woman." With these abominations in mind, he continued, "Thank you for raising up a woman like Governor Sarah Palin at a time like this. Bless her for standing against those who would remove the guns from our cabinets, and those who would want to remove the baby from the womb of her mother." In this version of the Newer Feminism the female heroine did not act on her own, but was raised up by God and selected by John McCain to work on behalf of enforced reproduction and restrictions on love. Before Palin took the stage the sound system blared Whitesnake singing "Here I go again / On my own" and "Like a drifter I was born to walk alone." The overture told the story: Sarah Palin was readying herself to ditch this suffocating campaign and assume her place as patron goddess of a socially conservative GOP faction and rebel feminist sect that worshipped women, at least from some angles, as vessels and caretakers. As the crowd got increasingly hot for Palin, I saw a sign that said, "Julianna's mommy is voting for Piper's mommy!"

When Palin walked onstage there was pushing and women

screaming, "Oh my god, Todd's so cute!" Palin gave a brief address. It resembled ingratiating vice-presidential boilerplate only in her assertion that the crowd must be "so doggone proud" of the local team and new World Champion Phillies. Palin wasn't in Pennsylvania to tell Pennsylvanians about themselves. She was there to tell them about herself, her husband, her family, and how she envisioned the country's future. She talked about the First Dude's snowmobile championships and made ample coded references to Ronald Reagan's 1964 speech endorsing Barry Goldwater, the white puffs of her breath in the cold night air making her repetition of the phrase "The time for choosin's comin' real soon" sound horror-movie eerie.

When I returned from Pennsylvania the weekend before the election I learned that Palin had been prank-called by a Quebec radio comedy team who had convinced her handlers that French President Nicolas Sarkozy wanted to speak with her. A recording of the embarrassing conversation was a big hit among Palin-haters, but it made me not just rationally defensive but viscerally angry on Palin's behalf. This wasn't political satire or parody or spoofing; it was a petty meanness that confirmed her admirers' worst assumptions: that the left applied the rules of civil discourse only to its own.

She was a bad vice-presidential candidate, like bad vice-presidential candidates before her, and her communications team had allowed a prank caller to get through. She was ill-prepared and inarticulate, and her chattiness about how much she liked Sarkozy's model wife, Carla Bruni, was cringey. But progress takes all sorts, and in the pantheon of political leadership there had been thousands of craven, ill-intentioned, pompous, and stupid men. There was no rule that said that in order to make history Palin had to be a decent, honest politician, nor that she be a rocket scientist. Were we to envision true equality in politics, it would involve as many Sarah Palins as it would Hillary Clintons. As Bella Abzug had said, "[The goal is not to see a] female Einstein become an assistant professor. We want a woman schlemiel to get promoted as quickly as a male schlemiel."

I had just witnessed Palin's power and the potential scope of her influence, and I thought it was a serious error to underestimate it, let alone mock it quite so cavalierly. As *Jezebel*'s Carpentier had pointed out, cruelty only made righteous the claims of conserva-

tives that liberals did not respect them. On a June 2009 visit to Seneca Falls, New York, the birthplace of the suffrage movement, Palin
would read aloud from the Declaration of Sentiments engraved
on the monument, "We anticipate no small amount of ridicule."
According to *Politico,* she then commented, "Some things never
change."

My experience with Palin's supporters left me alert to the fact
that she was building an army of followers—not just scared and
angry xenophobes, as the press about anti-Obama voters would
have us believe, but women (and men) who felt that their support
for this candidate was about an expansion of opportunities for
women. Ultimately Palin, like Clinton and Obama, was a candidate
onto whom millions of voters, and millions of women, had projected their own hopes and dreams and identifications. The fever
for Obama had demonstrated the emotional pull of history making. Now I felt a wave coming from the right, coming to wash over
feminism.

I was not wrong. Nearly a year to the day that Hillary Rodham
Clinton conceded the nomination for the presidency, an organization called the New Agenda would rally its troops in an art gallery
in Manhattan for an event called "One for the Herstory Books."
The organization's founder, forty-three-year-old former Wall Street
trader Amy Siskind, had gained some notoriety in 2008 as one of
the vocal Hillary dead-enders angrily pushing to count unofficial
primary votes in Michigan and Florida. Though she never officially
called herself a PUMA, in the months during which most Democrats had been rallying around Barack Obama in the general election she had worked to organize them, building a media presence
for the New Agenda, which she called "a sisterhood of support." Siskind's sisterhood differed from the feminist organizations that had
preceded it by not taking a position on abortion. As she explained
on the group's website, "For women in this country to have power,
we would need to focus on the issues that unite us, and put aside
the issues that divide us. . . . When we come to the New Agenda we
ask that you put that issue aside and work together on the 80% of
issues that impact all women."

Siskind's Wall Street savvy helped to land her a platform. Within
weeks of the official formation of the New Agenda she was speaking

as "a feminist" on Fox and later on CNN and PBS; she was quoted in the *Boston Globe*, the *Los Angeles Times*, the *New Republic*, the *Wall Street* journal, and the *Washington Post*, and wrote columns for the *Daily Beast* and the *Huffington Post*. In these venues Siskind hammered home some fundamental feminist points about the continued wage gap and the toll it takes on both women and men. She assured readers, "The next wave is here. The players are different. The words are different." Perplexingly, she wrote, "Gone is 'equal rights.' . . . This wave is about reaching down beneath the surface to eradicate the roots of sexism that lie deeply buried in darkness, ignorance and bias. . . . Gone is 'feminism.' The word, hijacked by a few into an exclusive clique with liberal, pro-choice rites of entry, is being put to rest."

Siskind's feminism had been loosed from ideology, from policy investments that would otherwise tie it to the nominally more progressive party; it was antipathetic to a commitment to reproductive rights. It was supportive not just of Hillary Clinton and Sarah Palin, but of the burgeoning population of conservative female politicians—from Meg Whitman and Carly Fiorina (respectively running for governor and senator in California) to Minnesota Congresswoman Michele Bachmann—who did not support economic or social policies that helped women. And it would have an impact on institutional feminism and especially on those feminists whom Siskind believed had worked against either Clinton or Palin, like NOW's Kim Gandy. Siskind would claim that Gandy had secretly backed Obama in the primary. (Gandy campaigned for Hillary.) She would assert that Gandy had not defended Palin. (Gandy issued a statement condemning the "onslaught of double-standards and condescension" heaped on the Alaska governor.) At the annual NOW convention in the summer of 2009 some NOW members who had broken with the organization to support Palin campaigned against Latifa Lyles—the candidate whom Gandy had endorsed to succeed her as NOW president. Lyles lost the election by eight votes out of four hundred cast. Gandy told me, "I've probably been to thirty-four national conferences and . . . this was nasty and vicious and mean in a way I've never seen. I think it's going to be hard healing."

This was the energy I had first felt at the Palin rally in Pennsylvania. Something had been stirred up, not simply in the Republican

Party, but within feminism. It seemed to me that it was a mistake to ignore it. Palin's candidacy had empowered Republican women eager to claim their share of the feminist legacy and transform its institutions by making them more amenable to their anti-abortion positions and conservative policy positions. In light of the women's movement's history of losing battles over language and self-presentation, I feared that Elaine Lafferty might have been on to something beyond the candidate she was referring to when, in the days before the election knocked Palin off a presidential ticket but not out of the American consciousness, she wrote in the *Daily Beast,* "Will Palin's time come next week? I don't know. But her time *will* come."

12 THE AFTERMATH

IN HIS REMARKABLE victory speech on Election Night, Barack Obama addressed all those who had been driven apart by the election—not just right from left, but left from left, progressive from progressive, when he cited our sixteenth president: "As Lincoln said to a nation far more divided than ours: We are not enemies but friends.... Though passion may have strained, it must not break our bonds of affection." My colleagues and I watched with tears streaming down our faces.

On television it was the face of Jesse Jackson that provided the widest and most transparent window into the emotions of the night, the year, the new century, and the new America. In those first moments Jackson, who throughout the campaign had failed to hide his dissatisfactions with Obama, looked hardened, paralyzed by disbelief or regret or sadness or surprise or something that was certainly not yet fully realized joy. It was easy to project onto his closed face a million emotions, to imagine that his momentary reticence was born of the resentments built up during what had been, on generational and social and personal levels, for so many people a harrowing race for the American presidency.

In two years the eloquence and persuasive power of Barack Obama had steamrolled everything in its path, from racial bias to notions about how presidencies were won, to a Bradley tank of a primary opponent, to a long-held feminist fantasy, to the delicate reverence with which Jackson's generation of civil rights activism had been treated. But it was also true that Obama's win would likely not have been possible without the new and often uncomfortable dialogue about race, without the fire forging of the primary competition with Hillary Clinton, and certainly without the work and sacrifices of veteran activists, men and women who did not appear onstage with the president-elect, but who had sat in and marched and protested so that Americans like Obama might be treated as Americans. On Election Night Jackson was standing in for so many of his compatriots, a mere witness to the momentous history he'd devoted his life to making possible.

Twenty minutes after the news of Obama's victory had come the cameras again panned to Jackson, and this time his cheeks were wet with tears, his hand at his mouth. Now, among other things, he looked anxious, as if, like so many of the people wandering around him saucer-eyed and silent, he were still wound tight with fear: Is this happening? Is it real? But Obama's victory was real. In Brooklyn there were fireworks and people cheering as they ran along the sidewalk; from the roof of my building I could see that across the East River the Empire State Building had been lit up blue. On television, even Stephen Colbert was tearful. This was happening. America had cracked open.

Obama did not mention Jackson or Shirley Chisholm or Hillary Clinton in his Election Night speech. Instead he talked about someone whose name most of us had never heard before: Ann Nixon Cooper, a 106-year-old black woman who had voted for him and who would pass away almost exactly a year later. Obama told her story, a story that encompassed more than a century of American history and included in its sight line all the history makers who had preceded him. As Ta-Nehisi Coates later wrote, "He presented her not just as someone who'd been born a generation after slavery and had seen segregation, but as a woman who'd seen the women's-suffrage movement, the dawn of aviation and the automobile, the Depression and the Dust Bowl, and Pearl Harbor. He presented Nixon Cooper as an African American who was not doubly conscious, just conscious."

The America that Obama addressed on November 4 was one with shared rather than competing histories. And if everyone woke up on the morning of November 5 and headed once more into battles of perspectives and priorities, then fair enough. For a few minutes at least we had a spectacular view of the great American mash-up, in which mixed people of mixed experience and mixed ideologies were for an instant united in their difference, bound not by commonalities but by their participation in struggles that were often at cross-purposes but were ultimately in service of further perfecting our union.

What had revealed itself in Jesse Jackson's face was the rocky march to progress and its attendant trade-offs. When radical ideas about justice are presented to a society built on fundamental inequalities but masquerading as a harmonious union, the clash has the force necessary to break down brick walls, as Jackson's generation of civil rights and women's leaders had. But when those radical ideas take hold they become less radical, and get handed down to the next generation as assumptions. The fortunes of that generation rise and the purity of their convictions becomes diluted. They accept some things, both good and bad, from their forebears; they leave other things behind. Often we cannot predict what will remain and get passed on and what will get tossed overboard, which slights will reinflame resistance and which will pass. For a long period during my adolescence and early adulthood it seemed that I would not live to hear the word *feminist* uttered in earnest by anyone my age or younger. Just a decade into the new century it was back, embraced in a manner that broadened its reach, relaxed the rules about how it might be deployed, extended it so far outward that, yes, it became imperiled again. But its return also meant that someday feminism's legacy would bear fruit with regard to the presidency, even if it's not as sweet as many of us might have hoped.

In Arizona, where John McCain was conceding the election, Sarah Palin was hoping to give a speech of her own. She would not be allowed to do so, but her remarks would later be published.

Whether she won or lost, Palin planned to tell the nation and the world, "I will remember all the young girls who came up to me at our rallies . . . just to see only the second woman ever nominated by a major party in a national election. They know that in America there should be no ceilings on achievement, glass or otherwise."

In 2009 Palin quit partway through her term as governor of Alaska but remained a sensation. Her memoir, *Going Rogue,* was a best-seller, and John Coale, who had urged McCain to pick a woman and who later helped Palin with business dealings, told me in 2010, "I went to one of the book signings in Fairfax, Virginia. There was wet snow, but still, four thousand people lined up in the parking lot in this snow to wait to buy the book and have it signed. It's a phenomenon that I have never seen."

After the election Palin's politics moved increasingly rightward. "You go where it's warm," Elaine Lafferty told me in 2009. "Sadly, and I think mistakenly . . . Palin [is] more right wing today than she was. . . . I don't know how she feels about feminism these days, but I will always believe that she was the kind of woman who should have been on our side on a number of issues, and might have been."

In the spring of 2010 Palin returned to the work of co-opting and redefining "feminism" for the right. In a speech in May to the anti-abortion organization the Susan B. Anthony List, Palin deployed the f-word several times while arguing that antiabortion women hewed closer to first-wave feminist ideology than their pro-choice counterparts. She also began to speak often of a "Mama Grizzly" model of female Republican candidate, claiming that there was an "emerging feminist coalition" of conservative women on the rise.

And indeed, the consequences of Palin's appearance on the political stage became increasingly evident: the excitement she had generated on the right raised the profiles of other right-wing women, like Carly Fiorina, Meg Whitman and Michele Bachmann, who in a fundraising letter begged her supporters, "Don't let them Palinize me!" About Fiorina and Whitman, along with increasingly visible Republican offspring Meghan McCain and Liz Cheney, conservative columnist Kathleen Parker wrote, "This doesn't sound like your daddy's Republican Party, but it could be your daughter's."

* * *

Choosing presidential candidates is a funny business. Ideally, loyalty might be born of careful consideration of each contender's policy stances and voting records. But in a political system that rewards those politicians willing to dull their colors until they meld into one dingy, centrist gray it's rare to find anyone who mirrors our most heartfelt beliefs. If the liberal Democrats who split so passionately over Clinton and Obama had initially supported the candidate who, like many of them, believed that universal single-payer health care was the humane and practical course, that the Patriot Act eroded the basic civil liberties on which the nation was built, that gay people should have the same rights as straight people, that America should rejoin the Kyoto Protocol, that we should invest in alternative fuel sources, that the government should cut the money it spends on war and invest instead in education, that going to war in Iraq was a tragic mistake, then the Democratic nominee for president would have been Dennis Kucinich, a man who perhaps not coincidentally admitted during one presidential debate that he once saw a UFO at Shirley MacLaine's house.

In reality our presidential choices are based on factors less lofty than candidates' positions on emissions standards. We're looking for the pols who make practical mates, who can best provide for us in terms of fund raising and charisma, whom we like enough to give money to, to whose fortunes our moods, to say nothing of the well-being of our party and our nation, will be tied, someone we will be able to defend (at least to the point of indefensibility), someone who, in those final fretting weeks, will be the last person we think of before we go to sleep at night and the first person we think of when we get up in the morning. If we've chosen wisely, and often even if we've chosen poorly, we develop an intense bond with this famous stranger. His or her successes become our triumphs; his or her failures bring us low.

I originally chose to support John Edwards, who turned out to be a bad and stupid man. Elaine Lafferty, experiencing some post-election buyer's remorse of her own for having worked for Palin, teased during one of our interviews, "Compared to John Edwards, Sarah Palin was [Liberian president] Ellen Johnson Sirleaf!"

In the postgame analysis of Edwards's venal flame-out, an enormous amount of blame would be heaped at the feet of his wife, Elizabeth, for having been less saintly than her fans might have hoped, for having been nasty to and demanding of her husband's campaign staff, for having made disparaging remarks about John's intellect, for having been ambitious, short-tempered, and suspicious of John's aides. The unpleasant characterizations of Elizabeth made me sad. I believed them. But I was not sure that they actually contradicted my longtime beliefs about her: that she was aggressive, smarter than her husband, and usually right about stuff. I had never considered her saintly; I had thought her steely and formidable. I was not surprised that she was paranoid, controlling, and grumpy; it seemed to me that this kind of behavior might well have been exacerbated by the fact that, at the time she was exhibiting it, she was terminally ill with cancer, her husband was having sex with his videographer, and his staff was covering it up for him.

What was altered was my vision of Elizabeth as sensible, forthright, and honest. It turned out that she had enabled her husband's deception, that she had supported his decision to stay in the race and perhaps encouraged it even though she knew that he had had an affair that would make him unelectable if ever it were exposed. She had not let him take the obvious excuse—the return of her cancer—to bow out. And she had thus taken an enormous risk with the well-being of the nation she claimed to want to help through better health care and economic policy. She may not have believed that a marital transgression of the sort committed by so many politicians before him should bar her husband from highest office; I could even reach back far enough into my idealized view of her priorities and imagine that perhaps she believed so firmly in the work she could do for the country that she stormed forward, believing that that work superseded the dopey choices of her dopey husband. I had always believed that it was Elizabeth who truly wanted to be the president. Unlike Hillary, she would never even get close.

* * *

For the wife who was actually living in the White House, life was happily less tawdry, but under just as much scrutiny. Michelle Obama, whose image had been scrupulously reshaped in the final months of the campaign to emphasize her roles as mother, wife and fashion plate, was a sensation. In the period between the election and her husband's inauguration, the press went bananas for Michelle, while her team broadcast as loudly as possible that there would be nothing Hillaryish about her stay on Pennsylvania Avenue: she wanted naught to do with policymaking, she said again and again. Michelle dubbed herself "mom-in-chief," a sobriquet comforting enough to have been conjured by the editors of *Good Housekeeping* in 1956. In her first year in the White House she dedicated herself most publicly to advocacy of healthier eating, planting a vegetable garden on the White House lawn; she worked on behalf of military families and visited bases regularly; she invited local schoolchildren into the White House, reminding everyone that it was "the people's house"; and she spent time in her new city, at soup kitchens and homeless shelters, doing what she had been committed to in Chicago: working to weave together disparate communities in shared neighborhoods.

All of her tasks were authentically Michelle: from fitness to community relations, from Jimmy Choo to J. Crew, there had been traces of all her identifying first-lady characteristics back when I met her in Iowa in 2007. But it did seem that her public presentation was a bit muffled. Michelle was undeniably appealing in her first year in the White House. She was also a little bit Stepfordized, missing some of the cool self-assurance, the fiercely held and candid views on American history and economic injustice, the biting humor, and the dauntless energy that had motored her through her high-powered career and juiced her introduction to America as an outspoken independent thinker.

On some level, to be sure, my dismay was rooted in my white-lady perspective, which perhaps did not account for the ways in which adoration of Michelle as a maternal, sartorial, and physical ideal were themselves progressive in a culture that mostly still saw black women as caretakers of other people's children and that rarely celebrated nonwhite female bodies. Melissa Harris-Lacewell wrote that Michelle was crucial to broadening and correcting the distorted caricatures of black women "as crack mothers, welfare queens, and matriarchs." The *Nation*'s Patricia Williams argued that we had long been missing a discussion of black women as "loving mothers, beloved wives, valued partners, cherished daughters," and that "Michelle Obama represents a more comprehensive identity for all women, but particularly for black women."

It was all true. But it didn't take away from the fact that the popular vision of Michelle as beautiful, well-dressed mother and wife seemed to include no room for the other aspects of her personality and life, from personal ambitions to independent identity outside her family. Michelle Obama had been described by her first boss as the most ambitious associate he'd ever seen. In *The Audacity of Hope* her husband had written of first meeting his wife, "Michelle was . . . full of plans . . . on the fast track, with no time, she told me, for distractions—especially men." Michelle had gone on to enjoy a career to which she had been committed, her own substantial paycheck, and a rich, independent life in a city in which she was entrenched. Now all of that was temporarily, or perhaps permanently, on hold.

In its postelection piece about the adjustments faced by the Obama family, the *New York Times* did not mention the presumed end of Michelle's job at the University of Chicago Medical Center. It did suggest that, once she had settled her children into the White House, she would have to figure out "exactly what sort of first lady she wants to be." The *Times* noted, "Although she dresses with unusual care . . . friends say she has only a certain amount of patience for the domestic arts. She is a get-it-done efficiently Rachael Ray type, they say, not given to elaborate Martha Stewart–like efforts." In *New York* magazine David Samuels wrote admiringly, "She went to excellent schools, got decent grades, stayed away from too much intellectual heavy lifting, and held a series of practical, modestly salaried jobs while accommodating her husband's wilder dreams and raising two lovely daughters. In this, she is a more practical role model for young women than Hillary Clinton, blending her calculations about family and career with an expectation of normal personal happiness."

There was very little media recognition of the fact that Michelle was a woman whose lifetime of personal success had had nothing to do with Rachael Ray, Martha Stewart or the crafts they plied. Instead most of the coverage affirmed the satisfaction America had taken in successfully recasting this complicated, outspoken, querulous and ambitious woman as a more digestible sort. Erased was the woman whose robust energies and domestic disclosures laid bare her dissatisfactions and disappointments with having to accommodate "her husband's wilder dreams"; in her place was one who could comfortably serve as inspiration to the next generation of women who apparently should not yearn to exceed expectations, but instead satisfy themselves with middling success and a more successful spouse, the more attainable form of female happiness.

Toward the end of Obama's first year in office there were some in the media, admirers of the more complicated vision of Michelle, who were getting itchy. Noting the impossibly high expectations that greeted the first lady when she entered the White House, *Newsweek*'s Allison Samuels wrote that she was now hoping for more from her. The first lady's solid approval ratings gave her "an opportunity to plug both the president's agenda . . . and her own. . . . Imagine turning her healthy-eating quest into a full-blown anti-obesity campaign that takes on the junk-food lobby. Or making AIDS prevention and condom use a part of the national healthcare debate." Samuels acknowledged that taking a stand would mean that Michelle would "risk controversy and maybe even failure. But if she doesn't use this chance to take on the issues that really matter, that's just a failure of another kind."

Michelle Obama remained, as she had been from the start, in an uncomfortable bind.

☆ ☆ ☆

In January 2009 Hillary Clinton was sworn in as Barack Obama's secretary of state. Zipping around the world, keeping her head down and her nose to the State Department grindstone, she worked so quietly in her first year on the job that some pundits assumed that she had had her wings clipped. After all, the notion of Hillary as unmanned by her new boss and former adversary was gratifying; it kept alive the rivalry that had so titillated us; it perpetuated the vision of Hillary as villain, as irritant and player. As it turned out, even those who didn't much like Hillary didn't want her to disappear. Describing what was missing from New York City in the fall of 2009, journalist Peter Kaplan wrote wistfully in *New York* magazine, "The one-woman ambition generator named Hillary R. Clinton is exporting her Lucy Van Pelt–like certitude to other nations."

Clinton had settled into one of the stages that always seemed to surprise people, no matter how regularly she entered them: she was wonking out, delegating work to competent colleagues, and strengthening her own position within the company, in this case Barack Obama's administration. It seemed to be going very well, actually. Hillary Clinton had managed a phoenix flight out of the ruins of her presidential campaign and out of the opprobrium in which she had been held by Democrats and Republicans, in varying degrees, for so long.

In 2009 her favorability ratings rose above Obama's, both among Democrats, 91 percent of whom believed she was doing a good job at the State Department, and among Republicans, who in October told pollsters that they approved of her over Obama by a margin of 16 percent. An annual Gallup poll at the end of 2009 found Hillary the most admired woman in America; it was the fourteenth time since 1993 that she had secured the top spot (though in 2009 Sarah Palin was behind her by just one percentage point).

At a March 2010 Women of Courage Awards presentation, Michelle Obama thanked her "dear friend" Hillary, accidentally referring to her as "Senator" instead of "Secretary." Obama recovered by joking, very warmly, "I almost said *President* Clinton."

On Clinton's first day at Foggy Bottom, State Department employees gathered to greet and applaud her like trilling munchkins after Dorothy dropped a house on the Wicked Witch of the East. In a profile in *Vogue* Jonathan Van Meter described her joint interview, alongside Secretary of Defense Bob Gates, in front of students at George Washington University: "She is a rock star. Students camped out in line for hours to get tickets to the event, which sold out in minutes. When she first appeared onstage the audience leaped to their feet, and the applause was deafening. . . . And despite the gravity of the occasion, a young woman bellowed at the top of her lungs, '*I love you, Hillllary!!!!*,' as if she were at a Lady Gaga concert." Van Meter went on to describe how capably Clinton played the crowd, cracking jokes about herself and earning big laughs, and in a later letter to *Vogue,* a young man would write to kvell about Clinton and take credit for having been the bellower.

The funniest thing had happened, after all the ugly, all the crazy, all the compromise and slippery politics and game playing and backbiting: Hillary Rodham had returned, at least briefly. And this time she was popular, cool, beloved, competent, maternal, warm, and even funny. More remarkable was that she was unafraid to be the woman who had gone to Beijing in 1995 and made a resounding feminist statement, the woman whose nuanced pro-woman politics had been muffled, if not squelched, during her campaign for political currency and on the road to the Oval Office. "Of particular concern to me is the plight of women and girls, who comprise the majority of the world's unhealthy, unschooled, unfed, and unpaid," said Clinton in her statement to the Senate Foreign Relations Committee on January 13, 2009. "If half of the world's population remains vulnerable to economic, political, legal and social marginalization, our hope of advancing democracy and prosperity is in serious jeopardy. The United States must be an unequivocal and unwavering voice in support of women's rights in every country on every continent." When questioned about her commitment to women's issues by committeewoman Barbara Boxer, Clinton replied, "I want to pledge to you that as secretary of state I view these issues as central to our foreign policy, not as adjunct or auxiliary or in any way lesser than all of the other issues that we have to confront."

In April 2009, when Afghanistan made moves to allow the government to legislate the frequency of sexual congress within marriage, Clinton stepped in and challenged President Hamid Karzai, who agreed to review the law. At a press conference, alongside Karzai and President Asif Ali Zardari of Pakistan, Clinton spoke about the necessity of women's rights under their oppressive regimes: "I will also reinforce, as I have on many occasions that this is not just me speaking, but this is the American government speaking. That we do not believe either Afghanistan or Pakistan can achieve lasting progress without the full participation of all of your citizens, including women and girls." During a House Foreign Relations Committee hearing, Clinton tussled with Chris Smith, a pro-life representative from New Jersey, who asked her whether the Obama administration included abortion in its definition of reproductive health, and if there were plans to undermine anti-abortion legislation in Africa or Latin America. Clinton unblinkingly responded, "When I think about the suffering I have seen, of women around the world—I've been in hospitals in Brazil, where half the women were enthusiastically and joyfully greeting new babies, and the other half were fighting for their lives against botched abortions. I've been in African countries where twelve- and thirteen-year-old girls are bearing children. I have been in Asian countries where the denial of family planning consigns women to lives of oppression and hardship. . . . We happen to think that family planning is an important part of women's health, and reproductive health includes access to abortion." Michelle Goldberg would later write of Clinton's remark, "[It] stands as the strongest defense of reproductive rights worldwide ever to issue from the lips of a senior government official."

Gloria Feldt speculated to me in 2009 that Clinton's dedication to women's issues had been reawakened by her presidential odyssey. "I think she's more authentic and that her inner feminist has come out much more," she said. "She's always had a strong sense of justice about feminism, about women, but I think the campaign forced her to just go ahead and be it." Latoya Peterson agreed: "[She] was able to say that one of the key state strategies is women and the economic security of women around the globe, and that it's a key component of our diplomatic strategy. That's huge! We would never have been able to do that before." The fact that Clinton was emphasizing the importance of women in society, and that international success depends in part on the economic stability and education of women around the world, said Peterson, was "an amazing, revolutionary thing to say. . . . And it would not have happened if things didn't shake out the way they did. . . . All the backlash against gender has opened up a very unique position for the Obama administration to actually verbalize a lot of things that I think would not have been acceptable beforehand."

In trips to South Korea and Turkey Clinton was treated like royalty, swamped by crowds in much the way her husband was received abroad. In fact it was astounding that not two years after the Clinton campaign had relied on—and worried about—her husband's epically persuasive charms, Hillary, as *Double X*'s Dayo Olopade noted in her response to a profile of Bill in the *New York Times Magazine,* had wound up "with an ability to barn-burn and kiss babies and rile a political base of her own, bigger (or, in the Internet age, at least more quantifiable) than her husband's." It was impossible not to notice how unfettered she appeared—free, now, to be unflinching about the terms of her independent success. When, on a trip to Africa in the summer of 2009, she was asked by a Congolese student to relay her husband's opinion on an international economic issue, she shot back, "You want me to tell you what my husband thinks? My husband is not secretary of state. I am."

Michelle Goldberg had fought fiercely on behalf of Barack Obama and against the older women who called Clinton's campaign a feminist imperative. Marking the anniversary of Clinton's concession with a piece for the *Daily Beast,* she admitted that when she listened to the "rousing and gracious" speech now she couldn't "help but tear up." Still glad she supported Obama, Goldberg nonetheless wrote, "Hillary Clinton has been the feminist hero of this administration." Gore Vidal, who had switched his allegiance from Clinton to Obama during the primaries, said in a September interview that he regretted the choice: "Hillary knows more about the world and what to do with the generals. History has proven when the girls get involved, they're good at it."

As the Obama administration made its inevitable compromises, especially in the months before passage of health-care reform, there were occasional rumblings of retrospective reconsideration, what the writer Linda Hirshman and I took to calling WWHHDs ("What would Hillary have done?"). Of course many of Obama's fiercest supporters still took comfort, especially when they felt most dubious about whether or not he was doing a great job, in asserting that Hillary would have been much, much worse.

Me, I was glad that Hillary was not the president. Not because I didn't think she'd be good. I thought, as I'd always thought, that her presidency would have looked very much like Obama's. As someone who had never entertained many progressive fantasies about an Obama presidency, it was easier for me to be generally satisfied with his administration. I also knew that if she had made all of the same decisions that he had—sending more troops to Afghanistan, passing a too-small stimulus, bailing out the banks without any strings attached, not getting out of Iraq within the year, forsaking a public option in the health care bill—the loathing and censure of her, the projections of how much finer a leader Obama would have been, would have driven me mad. I thought frequently of Gloria

Steinem's answer to the question of what she felt when Clinton conceded: relief. Yes, there was relief. I was so relieved that I didn't have to defend her, and more than that, that now there seemed to be so many others who were cheering her.

But perhaps all the bonhomie surrounding Clinton reflected a depressing truth: that it was easier to embrace this woman in a state of diminished power, once she had lost the big prize, when she was no longer threatening the chances of the cool guy. In February 2009 Chris Matthews bestowed a "Hardball Award" on Clinton; it was the first he'd ever given to a woman. Though it was meant to reward "personal moxie, savvy, [and] basic street smarts," Matthews made clear what had earned Clinton her mention; showing clips of her Denver speech urging her voters to back Obama, he said, "[This award is] for a bit of timely humility, for . . . a willingness to serve our country over self. We salute you. I salute you."

Steinem saw the change in attitude toward Clinton as quite predictable. "It's always been okay for women to sing the blues," she told me. "Just not so good for us to win. We all know deep in our hearts if we want to be loved we have to lose." But when I told her that the directness of this equation, like so many of the ways in which people had behaved toward Clinton, startled me, she replied that that in itself was a hopeful sign: "I'm glad it surprised you because that means you have higher standards, as you should. I devoutly want you to be surprised."

It was in this same interview that Steinem first told me that she voted for Clinton because she did not believe she could win her party's nomination. Believing Steinem to have misspoken, I interrupted her. "Because you knew she *couldn't* win?" I prompted, waiting for the correction. "Right," she said gently. "I've always known she couldn't win."

Our conversation took place on the afternoon before Steinem's seventy-fifth birthday and six weeks before my thirty-fourth. Only forty-one years separated us, but her statement left me pole-axed. Whatever my doubts about Hillary, it had never crossed my mind that she couldn't win. I had always believed, with varying degrees of dismay and hope, that she *might* win. There were days that I believed that she *would* win. In truth, she almost did win. The difference between Steinem's and my perspective on possibility demonstrated the changes in four decades in America.

The standards would be even higher for the children who had watched this story unfold, like one girl George Packer described in New Hampshire, who had held aloft a placard that read, "Hillary 2008, Sophia 2040," or my friend Geraldine's seven-year-old niece Libby, whose mother had taken her to the polls on election day to vote for Barack Obama only to discover, as she joked to Geraldine, that Libby was a PUMA, still too indignant over Hillary's defeat to fully embrace Obama. My memory of voting for Geraldine Ferraro had stuck; I imagined that these girls would not easily forget their early political attachment to a female candidate.

Many convictions were shaken and strengthened in the tumult of 2008. But the important part, no matter how tempered by imperfection and regret, rebellion and rapprochement, fury and hurt feelings, was that the raising of American expectations would not end with Gloria Steinem or Jesse Jackson or Hillary Clinton or Barack Obama or Sarah Palin, any more than it had with Frederick Douglass or Elizabeth Cady Stanton. That was the often maddening path of progress: moving forward despite or in reaction to setbacks, sometimes in circles, sometimes in great leaps; occasionally—terrifyingly—falling backward. The road was circuitous and rough, but in 2008 we had inched further toward ensuring that the inequities of the present will surprise the inheritors of the future.

ACKNOWLEDGMENTS

I'D LIKE TO express deep gratitude to my exceptional agent, Linda Loewenthal, and terrific editor, Wylie O'Sullivan, as well as to everyone at Free Press, especially Martha Levin, Dominick Anfuso, Sydney Tanigawa, Jill Siegel and Christine Donnelly.

Thanks to the colleagues alongside whom I reported on women in politics and pop culture, especially Caitlin Shamberg, Alex Koppelman, Mike Madden, Kerry Lauerman, Walter Shapiro, Lynn Harris, Judy Berman, Tracy Clark-Flory, Kate Harding, Hillary Frey, Ruth Henrich and Katharine Mieszkowski. And also to the editors for whom I wrote the stories that eventually became this book, including Lori Leibovich, Mark Schone, Kevin Berger, Jeanne Carstensen, Joy Press and Sarah Hepola at *Salon,* Richard Kim at the *Nation* and Lisa Chase at *Elle*. Special gratitude to Lori and to Lisa, who have been editors and friends as long as I have been in journalism, and to Joy, whose wise early edits were fundamental to the shape of this book. Extra thanks also to my friend and boss Joan Walsh for sending me to cover the election and then giving me time to write a book about it.

Thank you to everyone who spoke with me on and off the record and to the friends and family members who permitted me to recount their experiences here, including Geraldine Sealey, Merideth Finn, Becca O'Brien and especially Barbara and Daniel Traister, who remain remarkably sanguine about my cannibalizing their life for my work.

To Anna Holmes, Jean Howard, Lynda Obst, Nora Ephron, Colin Robinson, Linda Hirshman, Caitlin Klevorick, Paul Starr, Alex Rossmiller and Katha Pollitt for ideas, advice and bracing disagreement. To Katherine Lanpher for the title, Joan Leibovich for a kick in the pants, Nancy Rathbun for swift transcription, Bradley Rife for aggressive fact-checking, Sara Culley for going to Africa with me, Laura Miller for the Scrivener tip, Bonnie Berger for more video clips than I could watch in a lifetime and Sarah Karnasiewicz for the photographs. Thanks to the late Mary Parvin, who thought I was a writer before I did.

I am grateful to the several people who read portions of the manuscript as I worked, including Katie Baker, Elisabeth Franck-Dumas, Heather McPherson and Aaron Traister. I simply could not have written this book without the editing, counsel and friendship of Zoë Heller.

Thanks to my family: Barbara and Daniel Traister, Aaron and Karel Traister, the Howard-Bakers, Howard-Twitchells, Traister-Nobles, Judy and Pheroze Wadia and the Wadia-Haackes.

My most profound thanks go to Darius Wadia, who doesn't really think that gender is that big a deal, and with whom I have more fun than I knew possible.

NOTE ON THE AUTHOR'S USE OF HER PREVIOUSLY PUBLISHED WORK

A NOTE ABOUT reporting: Throughout this book, I have drawn on my reporting, and in some instances my own writing, about women and politics and the 2008 elections. Though in most cases I have rewritten and reworked the material, there are some sentences, paragraphs and ideas that I have stolen from myself. I thank *Salon, Elle* and *The Nation* for the opportunities to report and publish the following pieces, to which I have returned in this volume.

FROM *SALON*

"Stand By Your Man '04," January 23, 2004

"Is America Ready for the Wild Kerry Family?," February 4, 2004

"Behind the Scenes at the March for Women's Lives," April 26, 2004

"Vote Your Vagina!" June 11, 2004

"W is for Women?," August 30, 2004

"Teresa, Full of Grace," July 28, 2004

"Morality Play," February 9, 2005

"Thelma for President!," September 29, 2005

"Obama on Tour," November 11, 2005

"Putting Out for Women," March 16, 2006

"Hillary Is Us," October 16, 2006

"The Ladies' Man," January 29, 2007

"Hillary's Chest War," July 30, 2007

"The 9/11 Backlash against Women," October 3, 2007

"Stop Lying to Yourself. You Love Dennis Kucinich," November 5, 2007

"America's Next Top Spouse," November 13, 2007

"Michelle Obama Gets Real," November 28, 2007

"Campaigning While Female," December 19, 2007

"The Witch Ain't Dead and Chris Matthews Is a Ding-Dong," January 9, 2008

"Undecided 08: Should I Vote for Clinton or Obama?," February 4, 2008

"Big Blue (State)," February 5, 2008

"Yentas for Obama!," February 5, 2008

"Clinton Gets Her Party Started," February 6, 2008

"Hey Obama Boys: Back Off Already!," April 14, 2008

"Attention, Pundits: It Ain't Over," April 22, 2008

"Hillary Clinton's Bionic Quest Continues," April 23, 2008

"Feminism Is the New Funny," April 25, 2008

"What's So Bad about Sweetie, Anyway?," May 16, 2008

"Hillary's Final Curtain," June 8, 2008

"Why Clinton Voters Say They Won't Support Obama," June 23, 2008

"Angry PUMAs on the Prowl in Denver," August 26, 2008

"Isn't She Lovely," August 26, 2008

"Palin, Pregnancy and the Presidency," September 1, 2008

"Zombie Feminists of the RNC," September 11, 2008

"McCain Skewered on 'The View,'" September 12, 2008

"The Sarah Palin Pity Party," September 30, 2008

"How the Election Ate Daytime Television," October 9, 2008.

"Ladies of the Nightly News," October 30, 2008

"Sarah Palin: 'The Time for Choosin's Comin' Real Soon,'" October 31, 2008

"A Scary Halloween with Sarah Palin," November 1, 2008

"America Has Cracked Open," November 5, 2008

"The Momification of Michelle Obama," November 12, 2008

FROM *ELLE*

"The Second Coming: Can the Most Alpha of Males Comfortably Morph into a First Lady?," December 2007

"Our Favorite Female Comedians: They've Made Feminism Funny," March 2009

"Katie Couric: Reports of Her Demise Were Greatly Exaggerated," April 2009

FROM *THE NATION*

"Rachel Maddow's Life and Career," July 30, 2008

SELECTED BIBLIOGRAPHY

SO MUCH RESEARCH for this book happened years before I knew it was research. In some ways I have been reading for the twenty years since I began high school about the events, and some of the characters, that shaped this story. The list below (organized by chapter, and in the order in which I used them as reference) is my attempt to catalogue the published sources on which I drew directly in the course of reporting and writing this book, but I'm afraid that it is probably incomplete.

I have not, for reasons having to do with time and resources, included in this bibliography the hundreds of television clips to which I make reference in the previous pages. But I'd like to extend my profound thanks to the many websites—most notably Media Matters, The Huffington Post and Jezebel—that kept their thousand eyes on what seemed like a thousand channels, and in doing so created a video record of a couple of crazy years in media.

INTRODUCTION

"Taking Sexism Seriously." Third Estate Sunday Review blog.

Seigel, Deborah. *Sisterhood Interrupted: From Radical Women to Girls Gone Wild.* New York: Palgrave Macmillan, 2007.

Hirshman, Linda. *Get to Work: A Manifesto for Women of the World.* New York: Viking Adult, 2006.

Bennetts, Leslie. *The Feminine Mistake: Are We Giving Up Too Much?* New York: Voice, 2008.

Levy, Ariel. *Female Chauvinist Pigs: Women and the Rise of Raunch Culture.* New York: Free Press, 2005.

CHAPTER 1

Bernstein, Carl. *A Woman in Charge: The Life of Hillary Rodham Clinton.* New York: Knopf, 2007.

Steinem, Gloria. "Right Candidates, Wrong Question." Op-ed. *New York Times,* February 7, 2007.

Douglas, Susan J. "Why Women Hate Hillary." *In These Times,* April 26, 2007.

Douglas, Ann. "The Extraordinary Hillary Clinton." *Vogue,* December 1998.

Lewis, Judith. "Do the Jane Fonda." *LA Weekly,* May 3, 2007.

Wilentz, Amy. "Yellow Pantsuit." In *Thirty Ways of Looking at Hillary: Reflections by Women Writers,* edited by Susan Morrison, 1–8. New York: HarperCollins, 2008.

Clinton, Hillary Rodham. *Living History.* New York: Simon & Schuster, 2003.

Balterman, Lee. "Class Leader Hillary Rodham of Wellesley College." *Life,* June 11, 1969.

Rodham, Hillary D. "1969 Student Commencement Speech." Wellesley College. May 31, 1969. Wellesley College website.

Mundy, Liza. "The Hillary Dilemma." *Washington Post Magazine,* March 21, 1999.

LiCari, Jonnel. "Molly Ivins: She Did Say That." *Wisconsin State Journal,* May 20, 1992.

Wills, Garry. "H. R. Clinton's Case." *New York Review of Books* 30, no. 5 (1992).

Ungles, Janet. "I'm Not a Romantic, I'm an Ironic." *Newsday,* June 24, 1993.

Ephron, Nora. "Remarks to Wellesley College Class of 1996." Wellesley College. 1996. Wellesley College website.

Packer, George. "The Choice." *The New Yorker,* January 28, 2008.

Starr, Paul. "The Hillarycare Mythology." *American Prospect,* September 14, 2007.

Clinton, Hillary Rodham. "Remarks by First Lady Hillary Rodham Clinton." United Nations Economic and Social Council. December 10, 1997.

Furchgott-Roth, Diana, and Christine Stolba. *The Feminist Dilemma: When Success Is Not Enough.* Washington, DC: AEI Press, 2001.

Green, Joshua. "Hillary's Choice." *The Atlantic,* November 2006.

Ivins, Molly. "I Will Not Support Hillary Clinton for President." *Columbus Free Press,* January 20, 2006.

Ephron, Nora. "But Who's the Candidate?," *Huffington Post,* April 18, 2006.

Chaudhry, Lakshmi. "What Women See When They See Hillary." *The Nation,* June 14, 2007.

Quindlen, Anna. "The Brand New and Same Old." *Newsweek,* May 28, 2007.

Hantschel, Allison. "I Won't Support Hillary Just Because She's a Woman." *Sirens Magazine,* October 19, 2006.

CHAPTER 2

Edwards, Elizabeth. *Saving Graces: Finding Solace and Strength from Friends and Strangers.* New York: Broadway, 2006.

Goldfarb, Zachary A. "Edwards Takes Heat over Quotations about Hillary." *Washington Post,* October 22, 2006.

Hirshman, Linda. "Homeward Bound." *American Prospect,* November 21, 2005.

Brooks, David. "The Year of Domesticity." *New York Times,* January 1, 2005.

Flanagan, Caitlin. *To Hell with All That: Loving and Loathing Our Inner Housewife.* Boston: Little, Brown, 2006.

Bennetts, Leslie. *The Feminine Mistake: Are We Giving Up Too Much?* New York: Voice, 2007.

Hawkes, Ellen. "Elizabeth Edwards, the Strategist." *Ms. Magazine,* spring 2004.

Koppelman, Alex, and Rebecca Traister. "Edwards Campaign Fires Bloggers." Salon, February 7, 2007.

Marcotte, Amanda. "Why I Had to Quit the John Edwards Campaign." *Salon,* February 16, 2007.

Broder, John M. "Edwards's Bloggers Cross the Line, Critic Says." *New York Times,* February 7, 2007.

Shark-Fu. "My People Call It Accurate." *Angry Black Bitch,* February 7, 2007.

Zuzu. "This Is Really Getting Out of Hand." *Feministe,* February 7, 2007.

Klein, Ezra. "Edwards, Marcotte, and McEwan." Tapped blog. *American Prospect,* February 7, 2007.

Schachner, Judith. *Skippyjon Jones.* New York: Dutton Juvenile, 2003.

Kantor, Jodi, and Jeff Zeleny. "Michelle Obama Adds New Role to Balancing Act." *New York Times,* May 18, 2007.

Lee, Tonya Lewis. "Your Next First Lady?" *Glamour,* September 3, 2007.

Dowd, Maureen. "She's Not Buttering Him Up." *New York Times,* April 25, 2007.

Collins, Lauren. "The Other Obama." *The New Yorker,* March 10, 2008.

Tkacik, Moe. "Maybe It's Just Us, but Michelle Obama Seems Pissed about Something Other Than Never Having to Work Again." *Jezebel,* May 21, 2007.

Glover, Mike. "Michelle Obama Goes Solo in Iowa." *Chicago Sun Times,* April 1, 2007.

Mundy, Liza. *Michelle: A Biography.* New York: Simon & Schuster, 2008.

Amusa, Malena. "Michelle Obama for President." *RaceWire,* May 22, 2007.

Giddings, Paula J. "The Woman beside Him." *Essence,* January 2009.

Dickerson, Debra. "Michelle Obama's Sacrifice." *Salon,* May 21, 2007.

CHAPTER 3

Sullivan, Ronald. "Dakotan Beats Humphrey by a Big Margin in Jersey." *New York Times,* June 7, 1972.

Santora, Marc. "Pointed Question Puts McCain in a Tight Spot." *New York Times,* November 14, 2007.

Green, Joshua. "The Front-Runner's Fall." *The Atlantic,* September 2008.

Green, Joshua. "The Hillary Clinton Memos." *The Atlantic,* September 2008.

Kornblut, Anne E. *Notes from the Cracked Ceiling: Hillary Clinton, Sarah Palin, and What It Will Take for a Woman to Win.* New York: Crown, 2009.

Lowy, Joan A. *Pat Schroeder: A Woman of the House.* Albuquerque: University of New Mexico Press, 2003.

Walsh, Joan. "Elizabeth Edwards Didn't Call Hillary Clinton a Man." *Salon,* July 17, 2007.

Scherer, Michael. "Hillary Is from Mars, Obama Is from Venus." *Salon,* July 12, 2007.

Abcarian, Robin. "Clinton Not an Easy Sell to All Women." *Los Angeles Times,* December 7, 2007.

Kissling, Frances. "Why I'm Still Not for Hillary." *Salon,* January 10, 2008.

Givhan, Robin. "Hillary Clinton's Tentative Dip into New Neckline Territory." *Washington Post,* July 20, 2007.

Chisholm '72: Unbought and Unbossed. Dir. Shola Lynch. 20th Century Fox, 2005.

Healy, Patrick. "For Clintons, Delicate Dance of Married and Public Lives." *New York Times*, May 23, 2006.

Simon, Roger. "Edwards Is Mad and Won't Take It Anymore." *Politico*, July 23, 2007.

Andrews, Helena. "Hillary and the Giant Peach." *Politico*, July 24, 2007.

"The Most Significant Photo of 2007 . . ." *Immodest Proposals*, December 17, 2007.

Althouse, Ann. "That Picture of Hillary on Drudge Right Now." *Althouse*, December 17, 2007.

Rich, Frank. "Is Hillary Clinton the New Old Al Gore?" *New York Times*, September 30, 2007.

Bumiller, Elisabeth. "Clinton and Obama Clash on 'Piling on' Remarks." *New York Times*, November 2, 2007.

CHAPTER 4

"Clinton Campaign Memo in Iowa." *New York Times*, May 23, 2007.

Klein, Ezra. "The Press Corps." *American Prospect*, January 6, 2008.

Packer, George. "The Choice." *The New Yorker*, January 28, 2008.

Alter, Jonathan. "How Tomorrow Became Yesterday." *Newsweek*, January 14, 2008.

Tapper, Jake. "Hillary's Debate Moment." Political Punch blog. ABC.com, January 5, 2008.

Steinem, Gloria. "Women Are Never Front-Runners." Op-ed. *New York Times*, January 8, 2008.

O'Rourke, Meghan. "Hillary's Moment, and the Problem of 'Seeming' Sexism." XX Factor blog. *Slate*, January 8, 2008.

Valenti, Jessica. "Hillary Tears Up on Campaign Trail, Edwards Attacks." *Feministing*, January 7, 2008.

Valenti, Jessica. "Hillary Sexism Watch: If a Woman Is President, Who Will Iron the Shirts?" *Feministing*, January 8, 2008.

Warner, Judith. "Emotion without Thought in New Hampshire." Opinionator blog. *New York Times*, January 10, 2008.

Tkacik, Moe. "So Basically, Women Voters Just Chose the 'Crying Will Get You What You Want' Candidate. Awesome." *Jezebel*, January 9, 2008.

Kornblut, Anne E. *Notes from the Cracked Ceiling: Hillary Clinton, Sarah Palin, and What It Will Take for a Woman to Win*. New York: Crown, 2009.

Grose, Jessica. "What Were New Hampshire Women Thinking When They Picked Hillary? Who Knows?" *Jezebel*, January 9, 2008.

Spaulding, Pam. "New Hampshire Primary Open Thread." *Pam's House Blend*, January 8, 2008.

Yglesias, Matt. "The Clinton Comeback." *The Atlantic*, January 9, 2008.

Healy, Patrick, and Michael Cooper. "Clinton Is Victor, Turning Back Obama; McCain Also Triumphs." *New York Times*, January 9, 2008.

CHAPTER 5

Steinem, Gloria. "Right Candidates, Wrong Question." Op-ed. *New York Times,* February 7, 2007.

Woolf, Virginia. *A Room of One's Own.* 1929. New York: Mariner, 2005.

Democracy Now! PBS, January 14, 2008.

Foner, Eric. *A Short History of Reconstruction.* New York: Harper Perennial, 1990.

Petty, Leslie. *Romancing the Vote: Feminist Activism in American Fiction, 1870–1920.* Athens: University of Georgia Press, 2006.

Douglass, Frederick. *Frederick Douglass on Women's Rights.* Edited by Philip S. Foner. Cambridge, MA: Da Capo, 1992.

Stanton, Elizabeth Cady, Susan B. Anthony, and Matilda Joslyn Gage, eds. *The History of Woman Suffrage.* Vol. 2, *1861–1876.* New York: Fowler and Wells, 1881.

Fang, Jennifer. "Gloria Steinem: Pitting Race against Gender." *Racialicious,* January 9, 2008.

Harris-Lacewell, Melissa. "Rally for Him Now: How Black America Can Revive Obama's Campaign." *Slate,* January 9, 2008.

The Education of Shelby Knox. Dir. Rose Rosenblatt and Maion Lipschutz. Incite Pictures, 2005.

Packer, George. "The Choice." *The New Yorker,* January 28, 2008.

"Unite, Not Divide, Really This Time." Editorial. *New York Times,* January 9, 2008.

Brown, Carrie Budoff. "Obama 'Unhappy' with Racial Memo." *Politico,* January 16, 2008.

Crenshaw, Kimberle, and Eve Ensler. "Feminist Ultimatums: Not in Our Name." *Huffington Post.* February 5, 2008.

Murray, Shailagh. "For Black Superdelegates, Pressure to Back Obama." *Washington Post.* March 3, 2008.

Seeley, Katharine Q. "Jackson: Not Upset by Clinton Remarks." *New York Times,* January 28, 2008.

Belton, Danielle. "Most Overhyped 'Obama' Fight: Poor Pitiful Politicians and the Black Blogger Revolt." *Black Snob,* April 9, 2008.

Jenkins, Carol. "The Invisible Majority." Women's Media Center. 2008.

Samuels, Allison. "The Legacy of My Grandmother." *Newsweek,* March 17, 2008.

Reed, Adolph, Jr. "Obama No." *The Progressive,* May 2008.

Smith, Ben. "A Ferraro Flashback." *Politico,* March 11, 2008.

"Morning in America: A Letter from Feminists on the Election." *The Nation,* February 27, 2008.

CHAPTER 6

Rush, George, and Joanna Molloy. "Obama Girl Has Hil Thrill." *New York Daily News,* August 23, 2007.

Kantor, Jodi. "Chelsea Clinton Talks Policy in Obama Territory." *New York Times,* February 16, 2008.

Wheaton, Sarah. "Obama's the Big Man on Campus." Opinionator blog. *New York Times,* February 2, 2007.

Steinem, Gloria. "Women Are Never Front-Runners." Op-ed. *New York Times,* January 8, 2008.

Morgan, Robin. "Good-bye to All That." Reprinted in *Dear Sisters: Dispatches from the Women's Liberation Movement,* edited by Rosalyn Baxendall and Linda Gordon. New York: Basic, 2001.

Morgan, Robin. "Good-bye to All That #2." *The Guardian,* February 14, 2008.

Levy, Ariel. "Goodbye Again." *The New Yorker,* April 21, 2008.

Friedman, Ann. "Goodbye Indeed." *Feministing,* February 5, 2008.

Goldberg, Michelle. "Hell Hath No Fury." *The Guardian,* March 13, 2008.

Dominus, Susan. "Feminists Find Unity Is Elusive." *New York Times,* February 1, 2008.

Collins, Gail. *When Everything Changed: The Amazing Journey of American Women from 1960 to the Present.* Boston: Little, Brown, 2009.

Bennetts, Leslie. "Go Away? Why Should She?" *Los Angeles Times,* March 9, 2008.

Hirshman, Linda. "Yo Mamma." *Slate,* April 18, 2008.

Martin, Courtney. "The Emotional Voter." Glamocracy blog. *Glamour,* April 3, 2008.

Hirshman, Linda. "The Trouble with Jezebel." *Double X,* May 12, 2009.

Dickerson, Debra J. "The Future of Abortion Providers." Mojo blog. *Mother Jones,* March 10, 2009.

Dickerson, Debra J. "Throwing Clinton under the Bus to Spite Mom." Mojo blog. *Mother Jones,* April 21, 2008.

Fortini, Amanda. "The Feminist Reawakening." *New York Magazine,* April 13, 2008.

Hirshman, Linda. "Looking to the Future, Feminism Has to Focus." *Washington Post,* June 8, 2008.

Powell, Kevin. "Time for New Black Leaders." *Huffington Post,* July 15, 2008.

Harris, Mark. "The Gay Generation Gap." *New York Magazine,* June 21, 2009.

Martin, Courtney E. "Generation Y Refuses Race-Gender Dichotomy." *Alternet,* June 18, 2008.

Valenti, Jessica. "The Sisterhood Split." *The Nation,* March 6, 2008.

Grose, Jessica. "*Ms.* Matriarch to Daughter: 'When Push Comes to Shove [Why] Can't You Vote for a Woman?" *Jezebel,* March 12, 2008.

Dickerson, Debra J. "Don't Trust Any Feminists under 30." Mojo blog. *Mother Jones,* March 16, 2009.

Martin, Courtney E.. "More Than a Mother-Daughter Debate." *American Prospect,* April 21, 2008.

CHAPTER 7

Pollitt, Katha. "Iron My Skirt." *The Nation*, June 5, 2008.

Wakeman, Jessica. "On Sexist Media Coverage of Hillary Clinton." *Huffington Post*, April 27, 2008.

Rosen, Ruth. *The World Split Open: How the Modern Women's Movement Changed America*. Revised edition. New York: Penguin, 2006.

Keetley, Dawn. *Public Women, Public Words: A Documentary History of American Feminism*. Madison, WI: Madison House Publishers, 2003.

DuPlessis, Rachel B., and Ann Snitow, eds. *The Feminist Memoir Project: Voices from Women's Liberation*. New Brunswick, NJ: Rutgers University Press, 2007.

Barber, David. *A Hard Rain Fell: SDS and Why It Failed*. Jackson: University of Mississippi Press, 2008.

Chafe, William H. *The Paradox of Change: American Women in the 20th Century*. New York: Oxford University Press, 1991.

Morgan, Robin. "Good-bye to All That." Reprinted in *Dear Sisters: Dispatches from the Women's Liberation Movement*, ed. Rosalyn Baxendall and Linda Gordon. New York: Basic, 2001.

Moulitsas, Markos. "Pie Fight Ad." *Daily Kos*, June 5, 2005.

Moulitsas, Markos. "The Curse of the Single Issue Groups." *Daily Kos*, May 23, 2005.

Harding, Kate. "Stupak: Two More Years?!?" *Salon*, January 14, 2010.

Harding, Kate. "Female 'Person of the Year.'" *Salon*, December 17, 2009.

Moulitsas, Markos. "Ditch the DCCC." *Daily Kos*, November 9, 2009.

Moulitsas, Markos. "Clinton's License to Do Harm." *Daily Kos*, April 17, 2008.

Packer, George. "The Choice." *The New Yorker*, January 28, 2008.

Hill, John. "Crash Course Looks to Super Tuesday." *Sacramento Bee*, January 21, 2008.

Geier, Kathleen. "Barack Obama Is Not Jesus." TPM Café blog. *Talking Points Memo*, February 5, 2008.

Hayden, Tom, Bill Fletcher Jr., Danny Glover and Barbara Ehrenreich. "Progressives for Obama." *The Nation*, March 24, 2008.

Fortini, Amanda. "The Feminist Reawakening." *New York Magazine*, April 13, 2008.

Kantor, Jodi. "The First Marriage." *New York Times Magazine*, November 1, 2009.

Alter, Jonathan. "Hillary Should Get Out Now." *Newsweek*, March 3, 2008.

Goldberg, Michelle. "Three A.M. for Feminism." *New Republic*, June 25, 2008.

Reed, Adolph, Jr. "Obama No." *The Progressive*, May 2008.

Spaulding, Pam. "Hillary Invokes RFK Assassination." *Pam's House Blend*, May 23, 2008.

Green, Joshua. "The Hillary Clinton Memos." *The Atlantic*, September 2008.

Shark-Fu. "A Toast from This Hard-Working American." *Angry Black Bitch*, May 8, 2008.

Krugman, Paul. "Sexism? Who Us?" *New York Times*, June 13, 2008.

Tannen, Deborah. "I'm Sorry, I Won't Apologize." *New York Times Magazine*, July 21, 1996.

Krugman, Paul. "Obama Does Harry and Louise, Again." The Conscience of a Liberal blog. *New York Times*, February 1, 2008.

Klein, Ezra. "Obama's 'Harry and Louise' Ad." Tapped blog. *American Prospect*, February 1, 2008.

Leibovich, Mark. "Man's World at the White House? No Harm, No Foul, Aides Say." *New York Times*, October 24, 2009.

Thurston, Baratunde. "This Primary Campaign Has Brought Out the Best and Worst in Me." *Huffington Post*, June 3, 2008.

Klein, Joe. "The Incredible Shrinking Democrats." *Time*, April 24, 2008.

"The Low Road to Victory." Editorial. *New York Times*, April 23, 2008.

Dowd, Maureen. "Wilting over Waffles." *New York Times*, April 23, 2008.

Sklar, Rachel. "Olbermann's Idea for Beating Hillary: Literally Beating Hillary." *Huffington Post*, May 2, 2008.

Boehlert, Eric. "So Now the Press Tells Candidates When to Quit?" *Media Matters*, April 30, 2008.

CHAPTER 8

Ephron, Nora. *Crazy Salad: Some Things about Women*. New York: Knopf, 1975.

Kantor, Jodi. "Clinton Bloc Becomes the Prize for Election Day." *New York Times*, June 7, 2008.

Boyer, Peter J. "One Angry Man." *The New Yorker*, June 23, 2008.

Horowitz, Jason. "Clinton Bundler on Obama's Doyle Pick: The Biggest 'Fuck You' Ever." *New York Observer*, June 16, 2008.

Heilemann, John, and Mark Halperin. *Game Change: Obama and the Clintons, McCain and Palin, and the Race of a Lifetime*. New York: HarperCollins, 2010.

Curtis, Mary C. "The Loud Silence of the Feminists." *Washington Post*, June 21, 2008.

Geraghty, Jim. "Contrasting John McCain and Michelle Obama." *National Review Online*, February 19, 2008.

Hitchens, Christopher. "Are We Getting Two for One?" *Slate*, May 5, 2008.

Coates, Ta-Nehisi. "Christopher Hitchens on Obama and Rev. Wright: When All Else Fails Blame Women." *The Atlantic*, May 6, 2008.

Koppelman, Alex. "Fox News Calls Michelle Obama 'Obama's Baby Mama.'" *Salon*, June 12, 2008.

Saul, Michael. "With the Help of Off-the-rack Dress, Michelle Obama Eases Harsh Image." *New York Daily News*, June 19, 2008.

CHAPTER 9

Heilemann, John, and Mark Halperin. *Game Change: Obama and the Clintons, McCain and Palin, and the Race of a Lifetime*. New York: HarperCollins, 2010.

Draper, Robert. "John McCain—The Making (and Remaking and Remaking) of the Candidate." *New York Times Magazine*, October 22, 2008.

Kornblut, Anne E. *Notes from the Cracked Ceiling: Hillary Clinton, Sarah Palin, and What It Will Take for a Woman to Win*. New York: Crown, 2009.

Vick, Karl. "'I'll Sell My Soul to the Devil'; Corruption Scandals Involve Alaska's Biggest Political Names." *Washington Post*, November 12, 2007.

Carpentier, Megan. "Any Excuse to Run a Picture of Sarah Palin." *Wonkette*, November 12, 2007.

Johnson, Rebecca. "Altered State." *Vogue*, February 2008.

Dittrich, Luke. "Todd Palin Is the Man for America Now." *Esquire*, May 2009.

Murphy, Jen. "Running Alaska: Sarah Palin." *Wall Street Journal Magazine*, September 2008.

Grose, Jessica. "Why Sarah Palin Incites Near-Violent Rage in Normally Reasonable Women." *Jezebel*, September 5, 2008.

Palin, Sarah. *Going Rogue*. New York: HarperCollins, 2009.

Sheppard, Kate. "McSexist." *In These Times*, July 21, 2008.

Seelye, Katharine Q. "Palin's 17-Year-Old Daughter Is Pregnant." The Caucus blog. *New York Times*, September 1, 2008.

Sullivan, Andrew. "Things That Make You Go Hmmm." The Daily Dish blog. *The Atlantic*, August 31, 2008.

Seelye, Katharine Q. "Palin's Teen Daughter Is Pregnant; New G.O.P. Tumult." *New York Times*, September 1, 2007.

Quinn, Sally. "Palin's Pregnancy Problem." On Faith blog. *Washington Post*, August 29, 2009.

Estrich, Susan. "Sarah Palin and the Double Standard." Fox News, September 3, 2008.

Lippert, Barbara. "Analysis: Feminism's Next Wave." *Adweek*, September 8, 2008.

CHAPTER 10

Palin, Sarah. *Going Rogue*. New York: HarperCollins, 2009.

Greenwald, Glenn. "Correction on Sarah Palin." *Salon*, September 25, 2009.

Warner, Judith. "Poor Sarah." Opinionator blog. *New York Times*, September 25, 2009.

Faludi, Susan. *The Terror Dream: Fear and Fantasy in Post 9/11 America*. New York: Metropolitan, 2007.

Carr, David. "A Ship Leaks, but She Wants to Anchor It." *New York Times*, March 13, 2006.

Carr, David. "The Media Equation: An Anchor Lets Down Her Hair." *New York Times,* September 14, 2008.

Steinberg, Jacques. "'The View' Has Its Eye on Politics This Year." *New York Times,* September 23, 2008.

Hall, Jane. "Q&A with Phil Donahue: Breaking a News 'Chokehold.'" *Los Angeles Times,* November 12, 1992.

Gold, Matea. "'The View' Gets Political: Viewers Love It (and So Does D.C.)." *Los Angeles Times,* February 8, 2010.

Hitchens, Christopher. "Why Women Aren't Funny." *Vanity Fair,* January 2007.

Stanley, Alessandra. "Who Says Women Aren't Funny?" *Vanity Fair,* April 2008.

Unterbrink, Mary. *Funny Women: American Comediennes, 1860–1985.* Jefferson, NC: McFarland, 1987.

Valenti, Jessica. "Sense and Humour." *The Guardian,* November 19, 2008.

Dowd, Maureen. "What Tina Fey Wants." *Vanity Fair,* January 2009.

Heffernan, Virginia. "Annals of Entertainment: Anchor Woman." *The New Yorker,* November 11, 2003.

CHAPTER 11

Smith, Ben. "Palin Allies Report Rising Camp Tension." *Politico,* October 25, 2008.

Kristol, William. "The Wright Stuff." *New York Times,* October 5, 2008.

Bosmon, Julie. "Palin Speaking Up for Herself." *New York Times,* October 21, 2008.

Parker, Kathleen. "Palin Problem." *National Review,* September 26, 2008.

Levine, Suzanne Braun. "Having It All." *Huffington Post,* October 1, 2008.

Harris, John F., and Beth Frerking. "Clinton Aides: Palin Treatment Sexist." *Politico,* September 3, 2008.

Wilson, Cintra. "Pissed about Palin." *Salon,* September 10, 2008.

Young, Cathy. "Why Feminists Hate Sarah Palin." *Wall Street Journal,* September 15, 2008.

Carpentier, Megan. "Please, People: Stop Making Me Defend Sarah Palin—Girl on Girl Crime." *Jezebel,* September 10, 2008.

Kolhatkar, Sheelah. "Les Ms.-erables Bust Cover." *New York Observer,* April 3, 2005.

Goodman, Ellen. "Sarah Palin Could Be a 'Bridge to Nowhere' for Women." *Boston Globe,* September 3, 2008.

Collins, Gail. *When Everything Changed: The Amazing Journey of American Women from 1960 to the Present.* Boston: Little, Brown, 2009.

Lafferty, Elaine. "Sarah Palin's a Brainiac." *Daily Beast,* October 27, 2008.

Smith, Ben. "Sarah Palin Takes Low-Key Return to the Road." *Politico,* June 6, 2009.

Siskind, Amy. "Letterman Quietly Ushers In the Next Wave of Feminism." *Huffington Post,* June 15, 2009.

CHAPTER 12

Coates, Ta-Nehisi. "American Girl." *The Atlantic,* January 2009.

Walshe, Shushannah. "Sarah Palin's Lost Speeches." *Daily Beast,* November 3, 2009.

Thrush, Glenn. "Bachmann: 'Don't Let Them Palinize Me!'" *Politico,* August 13, 2009.

Parker, Kathleen. "Republican Women: Hear Them Roar." *Washington Post,* October 15, 2009.

Heilemann, John, and Mark Halperin. *Game Change: Obama and the Clintons, McCain and Palin, and the Race of a Lifetime.* New York: HarperCollins, 2010.

Harris-Lacewell, Melissa. "Michelle Obama: Mom in Chief." *The Nation,* May 5, 2009.

Williams, Patricia. "Mrs. Obama Meets Mrs. Windsor." *The Nation,* April 8, 2009.

Obama, Barack. *The Audacity of Hope.* New York: Crown, 2006.

Kantor, Jodi. "Striking a Balance While Becoming a First Family." *New York Times,* November 6, 2008.

Samuels, David. "Regarding Michelle Obama: Normalizing the President." *New York Magazine,* March 15, 2009.

Samuels, Allison. "What Michelle Obama Must Do Now." *Newsweek,* October 24, 2009.

Kaplan, Peter W. "Couch Warfare." *New York Magazine,* September 6, 2009.

Landler, Mark. "Secretary of State Clinton Arrives at Foggy Bottom." The Caucus blog. *New York Times,* January 22, 2009.

Carpentier, Megan. "Hillary Clinton Taled the (Girl) Talk at Senate Confirmation." *Jezebel,* January 14, 2009.

Van Meter, Jonathan. "Her Brilliant Career." *Vogue,* December 2009.

Goldberg, Michelle. "Hillary's New Crusade." *Daily Beast,* June 7, 2009.

Olopade, Dayo. "Bill Clinton Has Finally Figured Out First Dudeship." *Double X,* May 27, 2009.

Teeman, Tim. "Gore Vidal: 'We'll Have a Dictatorship Soon in the U.S.'" *The Times (London),* September 30, 2009.

INDEX